BRITISH AND CANADIAN PUBLIC LAW
IN COMPARATIVE PERSPECTIVE

This book explores current human rights controversies arising in UK law, in the light of the way such matters have been dealt with in Canada.

Canada's Charter of Rights predates the United Kingdom's Human Rights Act by some 20 years, and in the 40 years of the Charter's existence Canada's Supreme Court has produced an increasingly sophisticated body of public law jurisprudence.

In its judgments, it has addressed broad questions of constitutional principle relating to such matters as the meaning of proportionality, the 'horizontal' impact of human rights norms, and the proper role of judicial 'deference' to legislative decision-making.

The court has also considered, more narrowly, specific issues of political controversy such as assisted dying, voting rights for prisoners, the wearing of religious symbols, parental control of their children's upbringing, labour relations and collective bargaining, the meaning of obscenity in the context of pornography, and the law regulating libel actions brought by politicians.

All of these issues are discussed in the book.

The contributions to this volume provide detailed analyses of such broad and narrow matters in a comparative perspective, and suggest that the United Kingdom's public law jurisprudence and scholarship might benefit substantially from a closer engagement with their Canadian counterparts.

British and Canadian Public Law in Comparative Perspective

Edited by
Ian Loveland

•HART•
OXFORD • LONDON • NEW YORK • NEW DELHI • SYDNEY

HART PUBLISHING

Bloomsbury Publishing Plc

Kemp House, Chawley Park, Cumnor Hill, Oxford, OX2 9PH, UK

1385 Broadway, New York, NY 10018, USA

29 Earlsfort Terrace, Dublin 2, Ireland

HART PUBLISHING, the Hart/Stag logo, BLOOMSBURY and the Diana logo are
trademarks of Bloomsbury Publishing Plc

First published in Great Britain 2021

A catalogue record for this book is available from the British Library.

Library of Congress Cataloging-in-Publication data

Names: Loveland, Ian, editor.

Title: British and Canadian public law in comparative perspective / edited by Ian Loveland.

Description: Oxford, UK ; New York, NY : Hart Publishing, an imprint of Bloomsbury Publishing, 2021. |
"The final written versions of the papers in this collection emerged from a conference held at City [City
Law School, London, England] in the summer of 2018" | Includes bibliographical references and index.

Identifiers: LCCN 2021000174 (print) | LCCN 2021000175 (ebook) |
ISBN 9781509931095 (hardback) | ISBN 9781509947348 (paperback) |
ISBN 9781509931118 (pdf) | ISBN 9781509931101 (Epub)

Subjects: LCSH: Human rights—Canada—Congresses. | Human rights—Great Britain—Congresses.

Classification: LCC K3239.8 .B75 2021 (print) | LCC K3239.8 (ebook) | DDC 342.41—dc23

LC record available at https://lccn.loc.gov/2021000174

LC ebook record available at https://lccn.loc.gov/2021000175

ISBN: HB: 978-1-50993-109-5
       ePDF: 978-1-50993-111-8
       ePub: 978-1-50993-110-1

Typeset by Compuscript Ltd, Shannon

To find out more about our authors and books visit www.hartpublishing.co.uk.
Here you will find extracts, author information, details of forthcoming events
and the option to sign up for our newsletters.

PREFACE

This book has been a rather long time in gestation. For some years now I have been teaching an elective LLB module at City, University of London on Canadian constitutional law. That has been a consistently stimulating experience both because of the intrinsic interest of the material we explore in the class and because of the enthusiasm and ability of many of the students (mostly graduate students and almost all – unsurprisingly – Canadian).

I teach that class alongside a class in the Constitutional law of the USA, a subject about which I have also been writing for some years. This project follows the style and method of two conferences and subsequent edited collections of essays exploring the inter-relationship of British and American public law published in the 1990s, respectively *A special relationship* and *Importing the First Amendment*. Both of those projects rested on the premise that the US offered a much richer jurisprudential tradition in relation to questions of civil liberties and human rights protection than we could find in the case law of British courts and the ECtHR, and on the consequential assumption that our understanding of our domestic law on such issues might benefit from a more extensive and systematic appreciation of the way in which US courts had treated such issues.

Ian Loveland
London
Autumn 2020

PREFACE

ACKNOWLEDGEMENTS

The final written versions of the papers in this collection emerged from a conference held at City in the summer of 2018, where many of the contributors offered their formative thoughts on their respective topics. I owe all the participants a vote of thanks for making that conference an enjoyable and instructive event. I am also grateful for the financial support provided for the conference by the Canada/UK Foundation, and to the expert editorial and production assistance offered by the staff at Hart in putting the book into its final form.

TABLE OF CONTENTS

CONTRIBUTORS

Nicholas Bamforth is a Fellow in Law and University Lecturer in Law at Queens College, University of Oxford, where he teaches undergraduate and graduate classes in the fields of public law and comparative human rights. He is the author of *Sexuality, morals and justice* (1997, Cassell); *Patriarchal religion, sexuality and gender: a critique of new natural law* (2008, Cambridge University Press); and *Discrimination law: theory and context (2008, Sweet and Maxwell)*, and co-editor of inter alia *Public law in a multi-layered constitution* (2003, Hart) and *Accountability in the contemporary constitution (2013,* Oxford University Press*)*.

Tara Beattie is a PhD student (supervised by Gavin Phillipson) and tutor at Durham University's Law School. She teaches undergraduate classes in the fields of public and media law. Her PhD research, supported by an AHRC scholarship award, explores the legitimacy of the criminalisation of pornography in England and Wales. She has worked as a research assistant on Fenwick, Phillipson and Williams' *Text, cases and materials on public law and human rights* (4th edn, 2016, Routledge), and for an impact case study on image-based sexual abuse.

Carmen Draghici is Reader in Law at City, University of London where she teaches and writes in the areas of family law and human rights law. Her major publications include *The legitimacy of family rights in Strasbourg case law* (2017, Hart); (2014) 'The Human Rights Act in the shadow of the European Convention ...' *European Human Rights Law Review* 154; and (2015) 'The blanket ban on assisted suicide: between moral paternalism and utilitarian justice' *European Human Rights Law Review* 285.

Susan Easton is Professor of Law at Brunel University. She previously lectured at Sheffield University and Sussex University. She teaches classes in several areas of criminal justice policy. She is the author of, inter alia, *Prisoners' Rights: Principles and Practice* (2011, Routledge), *The Politics of the Prison and the Prisoner: Zoon Politikon* (2018, Routledge) and the joint author of *Sentencing and Punishment: the quest for justice* (2016, Oxford University Press). Professor Easton is also the founding editor of the *International Journal of Discrimination and the Law*.

Keith Ewing is Professor of Public Law at Kings' College, London. He teaches and writes in the fields of public and labour law. His major publications include *The Bonfire of the Liberties: New Labour, Human Rights and the Rule of Law* (Oxford University Press, 2010), and most recently (with Joan Mahoney and Andrew Moretta) *MI5, the Cold War and the Rule of Law* (Oxford University Press, 2020).

Keith is also the co-author (with Anthony Bradley and Christopher Knight) of several editions of *Constitutional and Administrative Law* (Pearson, 2018) and is currently the editor of the revamped *Kings Law Journal*.

Nick Hatzis is a Senior Lecturer in Law at City, University of London. He was previously a research fellow at Lady Margaret Hall, Oxford University. Nick teaches and writes in the areas of media law and comparative human rights. His publications include the *Research Handbook on EU Law and Human Rights* (co-editor with Sionaidh Douglas-Scott) (2017, Edward Elgar); (2011) 'Personal religious beliefs in the workplace: how not to define indirect discrimination' *Modern Law Review* 287; and (2013) 'Detention of irregular migrants and the European public order' *European Law Review* 259.

Ian Loveland is Professor of Law at City, University of London, where he teaches classes in Canadian, American and British public law. He previously held academic posts at Brunel, Queen Mary and Oxford Universities. Ian is the author of successive editions of *Constitutional law, administrative law and human rights* (2018, Oxford University Press), now in its eighth edition, and *Political libels* (1999, Hart) and (as editor) *Importing the First Amendment* (1999, Hart) and *A special relationship* (1995, Oxford University Press).

Gavin Phillipson is Professor of Law at Bristol University. He teaches and writes in the fields of public law, human rights, media law and comparative free speech law in both the British and international contexts. Professor Phillipson has published frequently on those subjects in leading academic journals in the UK and Canada. He is the co-author of *Text, cases and materials on public law and human rights* (4th edn, 2016, Routledge) and *Media freedom under the UK Human Rights Act* (2006, Oxford University Press) and his work has been cited in the UK by the Supreme Court and Court of Appeal and by the New Zealand Court of Appeal. He is co-writing a monograph for Hart, *Debating hate speech*, with Professor Eric Heinze.

Rachel Taylor is a Fellow and Lecturer in Law at Exeter College, Oxford University. Her research and teaching specialisations lie in the areas of family law and human rights law. Her recent publications include (2015) 'Responsibility for the soul of the child: the role of the state and parents in determining religious upbringing and education' *International Journal of Law, Policy and the Family* 15 and (2013) 'Secular values and sacred rights' *Child and Family Law Quarterly* 336.

1

Introduction

IAN LOVELAND

For British public lawyers with only rudimentary knowledge of Canada's constitutional history, a first acquaintance with Canada's foundational constitutional document – the British North America Act 1867 (BNA)[1] – invariably prompts at the least a scholastic equivalent of a raised eyebrow. The preamble to the BNA announces that Canada is to have a constitution 'similar in principle to that of the UK' but the subsequent text reveals quite clearly that Canada was to be a federal polity, within which both the 'national' and provincial legislatures were lawmakers of limited jurisdiction, and where the courts would – though this was a matter of necessary inference rather than explicit textual provision[2] – exercise a power to invalidate 'Acts' from either legislative sphere if they considered that those limits had been transgressed.

The 'similar in principle' descriptor had prompted Professor Dicey, in the first (1885) edition[3] of his (subsequently) celebrated *Introduction to the study of the law of the constitution*, to suggest that the Act preamble was an exercise in 'official mendacity'.[4] Dicey's primary objection was of course that Canada had been constituted as a federal state, in which the national and provincial spheres of government had defined and judicially enforced limits on their respective legislative competences, characteristics which clearly did not feature at all in the (1867) British constitution. By the time the fifth edition was published in 1915, Dicey had moderated the tone, if not the substance, of his initial indignation, dropping the 'mendacity' comment while retaining the passage reproduced below:

> If preambles were intended to express anything like the whole truth, for the word 'Kingdom' ought to have been substituted the words 'States': since it is clear that the Constitution of the Dominion is in its essential features modelled on that of the Union.[5]

---

[1] The BNA 1867 – as amended – has been titled the Constitution Act 1982 since the completion of the Pierre Trudeau-led reforms of the early 1980s. In this book, the measure is referred to as the BNA 1867 in relation to pre-1982 events and as the Constitution Act 1982 for later periods.

[2] See the judgment of the New Brunswick Supreme Court in *R v Chandler* (1869) Carswell NB 43, (1869) 12 NBR 556.

[3] Which is available free online at https://ia800908.us.archive.org/31/items/lecturesintrodu03dice-goog/lecturesintrodu03dicegoog.pdf.

[4] At p 152–53.

[5] At p 93; p 153 in the first edition.

Dicey's first reaction and his second thoughts were perhaps rather overstated, particularly if one construes them as suggesting that judicial construction of the BNA was consciously seeking to fashion a political society with a constitution similar in principle to that of the US. The initial flirtation that Canadian courts conducted with the case law of their US counterparts in construing the BNA was rapidly and firmly disapproved by the Privy Council, both explicitly[6] and by the implicit device of simply not bothering to engage at all with American authorities which had been painstakingly examined by Canadian judges.[7]

The existence of a federal polity and consequently judicial review of legislation in Canada were manifestly matters of dissimilarity between the UK and Canadian constitutions.[8] The similarities were nonetheless appreciable, albeit that they existed – particularly in the UK – as much in the realm of convention as that of law. Both constitutions hosted a bicameral national legislature with only one elected house with assent to bills given by the Queen or her appointee. Both countries formed national ministries on the basis of a government responsible to the lower house and thence to the electorate. And until very recently, neither jurisdiction – nor the legislatures, governments and courts within them – had been much troubled by the challenge of reconciling legislative preferences with moral principles relating to human rights protection articulated in nationally applicable statutory or supra-statutory legal instruments.

The Canadian law reports certainly contain examples of what we now regard as human rights norms being indirectly protected by judicial decisions which invalidated provincial legislation on the basis that the relevant statute interfered unacceptably with a matter within the jurisdiction of the Dominion Parliament.[9] And in the 1950s the Supreme Court produced a sprinkling of decisions in which that dominion-provincial allocation of powers issue was framed in terms of the 'rights' of particular individuals.[10] However, Prime Minister Diefenbaker's Bill of

---

[6] See for example the Supreme Court's judgment in *City of Fredericton v R* (1880) 3 SCR 505, in which several judges engaged with an extensive analysis of US decisions. In *Bank of Toronto v Lambe* the Quebec courts were divided on the question of whether the BNA 1867 contained an equivalent of the US doctrine of the implied immunities of instrumentalities fashioned by Marshall CJ in *McCulloch v Maryland* (1819) 17 US 316. In the subsequent appeal to the Privy Council, Lord Hobhouse cursorily observed that it was 'impossible' to argue by analogy from US jurisprudence when construing the BNA 1867; [1887] AC 575 at 587.

[7] When the issue which had so vexed the Canadian courts in *Fredericton* reached the Privy Council – as *Russell v R* (1882) 7 AC 829 – the Court disposed of the matter without reference at all to American case law.

[8] Quite when Canada became a 'country' rather than a colony is open to dispute. As a matter of law, the relevant date is presumably 1931 following the enactment of the Statute of Westminster, but de facto Canada had been operating autonomously on the international stage since the early 20th century.

[9] For example, *Union Colliery of BC v Bryden* [1899] AC 580; (race discrimination in employment) *A-G for Ontario v Hamilton Street Railway Co* [1903] AC 524; (Sunday trading laws) *Reference Re Alberta Legislation* (freedom of the press and political speech). See generally Weiler (1973) 'The Supreme Court and the law of Canadian federalism' 23 *U of Toronto LJ* 307 at pp 342–52; Scott (1949) 'Dominion jurisdiction over human rights …' *CBR* 497.

[10] Most notably the Quebec Jehovah's Witnesses case; eg *Boucher v R* [1951] SCR 265: *Saumur v City of Quebec* [1953] 2 SCR 299; *Chaput v Romain* [1955] SCR 834. See also *Switzman v Elbling*

Rights, enacted in 1960, had little substantive impact, in part because its reach was limited to the actions of the national legislature and government and in part because of distinct timidity within the Supreme Court in the construction and application of the Act's terms.[11] And of course the dominant orthodoxy in the UK was that even if the refashioning of the constitution in that manner should ever be thought politically desirable by a parliamentary majority, itself a most unlikely proposition, our adherence to a Blackstonian and Diceyan understanding of the sovereignty of Parliament meant that any legislative attempt to do so would be legally futile.[12]

By the mid-1970s, in the UK context, directly effective European Community law provided a possible source of supra-statutory protection for those aspects of human rights law which could be brought within the initially limited reach of community law matters,[13] particularly following the House of Lords' (1991) conclusion in *Factortame (No 2)* that directly effective community law was not subject to the orthodox doctrine of implied repeal by subsequently enacted statutory provisions.[14] Whether that judgment should properly be seen as an evolution or revolution in the UK's constitutional order has become a somewhat moot point given our departure from the European Union,[15] but for a (in constitutional terms) brief period of some 30 years the significance of community law as supra-legislative source of human rights protections in the UK grew appreciably as the scope of community (and then Union) law increased.[16] In the same era, we also

---

[1957] SCR 285 (freedom of political speech and association): *Winner v SMT* [1951] SCR 887 (freedom of economic activity).

[11] See especially the judgments in *Lavell v AG of Canada* [1974] SCR 1349 – and particularly Bora Laskin's dissent from the majority opinion; 38 DLR (3d) 481; and the bizarre conclusion reached in *Bliss v AG of Canada* [1979] 1 SCR 183. For a general overview, see Tarnopalowsky (1975) 'The Supreme Court and the Canadian Bill of Rights' *CBR* 649.

[12] The classic modern restatement of that position being Wade's seminal article; (1955) 'The basis of legal sovereignty' *Cambridge LJ* 172. For Canadian readers unfamiliar with the paper and critiques of it, the most helpful source is perhaps Gordon (2009) 'The conceptual foundations of parliamentary sovereignty: reconsidering Jennings and Wade' *Public Law* 519.

[13] The impact was initially oblique. The landmark case of *Van Duyn v The Home Office* [1974] ECR 1337 was of course argued as a matter concerning economic rights of free movement, but its obvious subtext was a concern with freedom of religious action and expression; Ms Van Duyn being a scientologist, a movement of which successive British governments had strongly disapproved. On the scientologists' more recent 'constitutional' engagements in Canada see ch 5 herein at pp 157–64.

[14] The Charter does provide for the possibility of (temporary) legislative override of some of its provisions through the s 33 mechanism but, save for its blanket invocation by Quebec in the early 1980s, s 33 has been a very little used feature of Canada's constitutional law; see Cameron (2004) 'The Charter's legislative override: feat or figment of the constitutional imagination' *Supreme Court LR* (2d) 135; Dodek (2016) 'The Canadian override: constitutional model or bete noire of constitutional politics?' *Israel LR* 45.

[15] On the 'revolution' thesis see Wade (1996) 'Sovereignty – revolution or evolution' *LQR* 568. On the evolution perspective see Craig (1991)'Sovereignty of the United Kingdom Parliament after Factortame' *Yearbook of European Law* 221.

[16] See for example *P v S and Cornwall County Council* (Case C-13/94) [1986] ECR I-2143 in which community law provided a trans person with protection against employment discrimination that could not then be found either in domestic law or in the ECHR.

saw a gradual emergence and hardening of a notion of 'legal certainty' or 'common law constitutionalism', which was sporadically invoked by the judiciary as a justification to construe statutory provisions which courts regarded as interfering with fundamental constitutional principles in ways which accommodated rather than conflicted with those principles.[17]

But neither jurisdiction faced the challenge long familiar to courts in the US of subjecting all spheres of legislative and executive governance to review against a clearly articulated coda of supra-legislative human rights norms. Some 20 years ago the UK took a tentative step in that direction when its Parliament enacted the Human Rights Act 1998 (HRA 1998). The HRA 1998 can properly be seen as a significant step in the evolution of the UK's constitution, alongside the near contemporaneous moves made to establish devolved systems of government in Scotland, Wales and Northern Ireland. Those changes obviously pale in significance when compared to the peaceful revolution brought about in Canada's constitutional arrangements in 1982, which removed many of the 'similarities' between the two countries' constitutions by identifying aspects of Canada's legal order as 'fundamental' in a legal rather than simply conventional sense, and subjecting their alteration to a variety of lawmaking mechanisms that required a much higher level of political consent than simply bare majoritarian support in a national legislature.

Whether those reforms – which lent Canada's constitutional arrangements a distinctly American hue – have left it with a governmental system which is notably 'better' than that retained in the UK – is a question which does not permit of any easy answer. And that is not a task which this book even attempts to address. Much more modestly, this collection of essays seeks to explore some of the insights that British public lawyers might gain from the head start that Canadian courts and politicians have had over their British counterparts in respect of some major public law matters because of the relative longevity of the Charter in comparison with the HRA 1998. The Charter is now almost 40 years old, and has spawned a remarkably extensive and sophisticated body of judicial decisions, dealing both with a panoply of specific human rights issues and with systemic concerns relating to the proper delineation of lawmaking responsibility between courts, legislatures and the sentiments of 'the people' as expressed in a constitutional text. We (by which I mean academic and practitioner lawyers in Britain) perhaps do not know

---

[17] For an overview of the trend see especially Poole (2003) 'Back to the future? Unearthing the theory of common law constitutionalism' *OJLS* 435; Jowell (2006) 'Parliamentary sovereignty under the new constitutional hypothesis' *Public Law* 562; Steyn (2006) 'Democracy, the rule of law and the role of the judges' *EHRLR* 243; Young (2020) 'Fundamental common law rights and legislation' in Elliot and Hughes (eds) (2020) *Common law constitutional rights*. The leading judgments on the issue are perhaps: *R v Lord Chancellor, ex parte Witham* [1998] QB 575; *R v Secretary of State for the Home Department, ex parte Pierson* [1998] AC 539; *R v Home Secretary, ex parte Simms* [2000] 2 AC 115. The 'common law constitutionalism' moniker has also been applied – a point overlooked by many British commentators – to the aforementioned initiatives taken by the Canadian Supreme Court in the 1950s, and particularly in the judgments of Ivan Rand; see especially ch 4 ('The framework of freedom') in Kaplan (2009) *Canadian maverick: the life and times of Ivan C Rand.*

as much as we should about Charter jurisprudence, nor indeed about other facets of Canadian public law and history. Acquiring a broader and deeper understanding of the ways in which Canadian courts and politicians have addressed issues of common concern to each of our respective countries is of course no guarantee that we will produce 'better' solutions to the issues we confront, but insofar as the legitimacy of our laws rests in part on the intellectual rigour with which they have been produced, applied and evaluated, cross-jurisdictional analysis of the sort undertaken here offers at least a small contribution to achieving that objective.

I. The Chapters in this Volume

In chapter two, Carmen Draghici analyses the UK and Canadian approaches to the legalisation of assisted suicide. Draghici examines the different outcome of constitutional challenges to the previous blanket prohibition of such actions in both jurisdictions, most notably the 2015 landmark cases of *Nicklinson*[18] (UK) and *Carter*[19] (Canada), and the legislative change prompted by successful litigation in Canada (the amendment of the criminal code so as to allow medical assistance in dying).

The arguments in the two Supreme Courts are assessed in light of the wider public debate over end-of-life decision-making in the two jurisdictions. The chapter identifies several commonalities in the bioethical discourses underlying both courts' rulings: the emphasis on protecting the vulnerable rather than on the sanctity of life as an absolute principle; the recognition of a right to decide the timing and manner of one's death as part of self-determination rights; the prevalence of individual autonomy over a collective belief in the value of life; the refusal to read a right to a certain quality of life or a right to die into the right to life; the acceptance of the moral equivalency of physician-assisted suicide and refusal of life-prolonging medical treatment; deference to the legislative branch as regards the detailed regulation of this area; and references to the lack of prosecution in most cases of assistance in practice.

Draghici also evaluates these courts' different understandings of their role in facilitating legislative change in morally divisive areas, through a declaration of incompatibility with the HRA 1998 in the UK or a declaration of unconstitutionality in Canada, and, ironically, the British Court's reluctance to exercise its control function despite the more limited reach of the remedial relief it can offer under the HRA compared to the powers exercised by Canada's Supreme Court under the Charter. Whilst drawing attention to the distinct conceptualisation of the rights engaged by assisted suicide claims under the HRA 1998 (self-determination) and the Canadian Charter of Rights and Freedoms (liberty and security, life,

---

[18] *R (Nicklinson) v Ministry of Justice* [2014] UKSC 38, [2015] AC 657.
[19] *Carter v Canada* (Attorney-General) [2015] 1 SCR 331.

non-discrimination), the author concludes that the different outcome of legal challenges revolves around the interpretation of the requirement of proportionality of government action restricting individual rights and the feasibility of careful regulation, capable of establishing effective safeguards against error and abuse. She also notes the additional arguments in the Canadian debate (in part stemming from the different factual circumstances, ie terminally ill applicants still capable of taking their own life), in particular the alleged right not to be forced to commit suicide prematurely for fear that no assistance will be available when the person is no longer able to act independently; analogous arguments have recently been rejected by UK courts in the *Conway* case.[20]

The chapter further discusses the greater reception in the Canadian Supreme Court of arguments based on a change in social attitudes and evidence of successful implementation of safeguards against abuse in other jurisdictions that have decriminalised assistance in dying. The author criticises the British judges' refusal to find an inconsistency with the HRA 1998 in the absence of a bill offering absolute certainties and their questionable interpretation of parliamentary supremacy. She suggests that a more appropriate judicial response would have been to issue a declaration of incompatibility and leave Parliament the task of crafting a legislative scheme that reconciles the interests of vulnerable individuals with the rights of competent adults wishing to terminate their life in a non-traumatic way and without exposing family members to the risk of prosecution.

Draghici's chapter discusses an issue in which government(s) and legislature(s) stand clearly in the role of what the Canadian courts have referred to as a 'singular antagonist'[21] towards individuals affected by the relevant law, rather than occupying a position which seeks to reconcile the competing interests of various different groups. That 'singular antagonist' positioning is equally evident in respect of the matter addressed by Susan Easton in chapter three; that of voting rights for prisoners. The rationale for including or excluding prisoners from the democratic process has come under scrutiny in Canada and the UK. The landmark case of *Sauvé v Canada (No 2)*[22] in 2002 saw felon disenfranchisement as an arbitrary and additional punishment, which was not linked to blameworthiness of the offender and provisions denying the vote to prisoners in conflict with s 3 of the Charter. Echoing Draghici's analysis of the assisted dying issue, Easton suggests that the Canadian constitution's treatment of this matter compares well in terms of rigour and rationality with the approach taken in the UK, where successive national governments' support for a blanket ban on sentenced prisoners' voting persisted, despite criticism from the Strasbourg Court and the domestic courts.

The chapter also discusses the ways in which judges and legislators have characterised the political purposes that felon disenfranchisement has been assumed to serve in both jurisdictions. The issue of prisoners' voting rights

---

[20] [2017] EWHC 2447 (Admin), [2018] 2 WLR 322, [2018] EWCA Civ 1431, [2020] QB 1.
[21] See further below at pp 14–16.
[22] [2002] 3 SCR 519.

raises questions regarding parliamentary sovereignty, theories of punishment, democratic deficits, the commitment to human rights, the links between 'voting' and 'virtue', and whether the presence of prisoners in the electorate undermines or strengthens the integrity of the electoral process.

In chapter four, Nicholas Bamforth explores a more thematic doctrinal question: that of the 'horizontal effect' of the HRA 1998 and the Charter; that is to say, their applicability in litigation between private parties which did not turn on the meaning of legislative provisions. This is – ostensibly peculiarly – an issue that has exercised the minds of judges and academic lawyers to a much greater extent in the UK than in Canada. As Bamforth, suggests, the issue has spawned a very substantial amount of analytical literature in the UK, and continues – most recently in the field of housing law – to pose challenging questions both for domestic courts and for the European Court of Human Rights (ECtHR).

In Canada the horizontality question arose shortly after the Charter came into force in *Retail, Wholesale and Department Store Union v Dolphin Delivery Ltd*[23] (hereafter *Dolphin Delivery*). As Bamforth observes, the Canadian Supreme Court had little difficulty in concluding that the Charter did not have a direct horizontal effect, and that conclusion has not been much criticised or challenged since. The Court did however also indicate that the Charter could have an indirect effect in such litigation, insofar as what the Court termed 'Charter values' – in contradistinction to 'Charter Rights' – could properly inform the development of common law rules and principles in areas where the national or provincial legislatures had yet to tread.

Bamforth identifies several factors which may explain the varying degrees of difficulty which appear to attend judicial application and academic analyses of horizontality in each jurisdiction. The first relate to the 'nature' of the contested rights, both in a general sense and a case-specific context. The second turns on the textual drafting of the relevant provisions of the Charter and the HRA 1998, both in terms of the clarity (or lack thereof) of their identification of potential litigants in legal proceedings. The third, closely related, issue turns on the remedial regimes which each country's courts are empowered or obliged to apply in Charter or HRA proceedings. That third issue is intimately linked to a fourth question: to what extent is it possible in each jurisdiction for a court to protect the substance of a claimed right in a horizontal action by providing a remedy that lies within the ambit of pre-existing causes of action or remedies. (In cases involving the application of statutes in 'horizontal' situations, this question tends to be swallowed up in discussion of the permitted limits of reinterpretation of the statute concerned given its drafting.) The final, more holistic, consideration relates to the normative aims (as judicially interpreted) of the measure. As a matter of logic, a perceived commitment to give 'maximum' protection to relevant rights may encourage a court – within the limits associated with the other factors set out above – to give

---

[23] [1986] 2 SCR 573.

those rights the widest possible application. A narrower view of the measure's aims may encourage a stronger view of the strength of relevant limitations.

Analysed in combination, these factors offer a credible explanation of what might initially seem an anomalous disjuncture between the way in which Canadian and UK human rights law have addressed the horizontality question.

Ian Loveland lends a narrower substantive focus to the issue of horizontality in chapter five, which evaluates the significant changes which have latterly occurred in both jurisdictions in relation to political libels. Until very recently, the Canadian and British constitutions were similar both in principle and practice in their treatment of political libels, in the sense that neither country drew any meaningful distinction in relation to the law regulating libels dealing with political matters and those raising purely private questions. The first part of the chapter explores the unwillingness of either legislatures or courts in both jurisdictions to follow the lead given by courts in the US, both at state level and nationally,[24] in recognising that traditional English-derived approaches to libel law could operate as a substantial impediment to freedom of political discussion and, by extension, to the capacity of voters to make informed choices about which politicians to entrust with the exercise of political power on their behalf.

Loveland then analyses the Canadian Supreme Court's ostensibly very surprising decision in *Hill v Church of Scientology*[25] that the notion of 'Charter values' which the Court had identified in *Dolphin Delivery* made no difference at all to the content of the common law on the question of political libels. The chapter continues by examining the impact made on UK law by a series of ECtHR judgments in the 1990s, culminating in the radical innovation made by the House of Lords in *Reynolds v Times Newspapers*[26] in 2001, and considers the evident inability or unwillingness of the lower courts to apply *Reynolds* in the liberal fashion that the House of Lords had apparently intended. The penultimate section of the chapter assesses the Canadian Supreme Court's de facto if not de jure reversal of *Hill* in *Grant v Torstar Corporation*[27] and identifies strengths and weakness both in the Court's reasoning and the result that it reached. The chapter concludes by considering the 'dialogue' of a sort between the UK's judiciary and legislature which led to the eventual enactment of the Defamation Act 1913, a measure which promises to effect a significant liberalisation of libel laws not just in relation to 'political' matters, but to other categorises of speech as well.

The concern with freedom of expression is continued in chapter six, in which Tara Beattie and Gavin Phillipson examine recent initiatives relating to the criminalisation of pornography. Beattie and Phillipson suggest that the project of comparing porn laws in the UK and Canada is of particular interest because in both countries significant recent reform has been driven, at least in part, by

---

[24] In particular the US Supreme Court judgment in *New York Times v Sullivan* (1964) 376 US 255.
[25] [1995] 2 SCR 1130.
[26] [2001] 2 AC 127.
[27] [2009] SCR 64.

feminist arguments that certain kinds of pornography amount to a form of hate speech damaging to women. However, the *means* by which reform has occurred in each country is very different.

In the UK, traditional obscenity law has been left in place but supplemented by new legislation (the 2008 'Extreme Pornography' provisions) targeted at the *consumers* of 'extreme' porn. Unlike obscenity law, which relies on a vague definition of material likely to 'deprave and corrupt', the new legislation instead identifies various categories of sexual activity – that depicting violence, rape, bestiality and necrophilia – which are very specifically defined; the possession of such images is made an imprisonable offence, subject to certain narrow defences. This reform was driven largely by feminist academics and campaigners, most prominently, in the UK, McGlynn and Rackley[28] – although the new law has also been criticised by them as having compromised its focus on harm to women by mixing it with more traditional concerns around moral disgust. The offence is also open to the wider criticism that it rests upon vague and un-evidenced claims about the alleged broader 'cultural harm' of extreme pornography and the claimed beneficial *effects* of criminalising users of pornography.

In Canada, the impetus for reform also clearly came from feminist critiques of pornography, but in this case the *means* was not legislative change, but judicial *reinterpretation*. The Canadian Supreme Court in *R v Butler*[29] recast existing obscenity law so that it has the aim, not of 'impos[ing] a certain standard of public and sexual morality', but instead of combating material that 'effectively reduces the human or equality or other Charter rights of individuals'. This shifted the target of the law from a certain level of explicitness to material that seeks to 'make degradation, humiliation, victimization, and violence in human relationships appear normal and acceptable'. But this shift has also been considered problematic. The judges claim that in making judgments about what material falls into the forbidden categories, the arbiter is the values of 'the community as a whole'. But this has been criticised as simply dressing up judicial 'value judgments' in: 'the objective garb of community standards'.[30] Is the Canadian position simply 'moral censorship in new dress'?[31]

This chapter therefore uses these two case studies of feminist-driven law reform to draw out the similarities and contrasts between the different routes to reform of the porn laws that each country took. What is the significance of the fact that one was brought about legislatively and the other judicially for the *legitimacy* of each reform – and the extent to which each was driven by credible evidence? Which may be seen as answering most purely to feminist concerns? Were they driven by

---

[28] (2007) 'Striking a balance: arguments for the criminal regulation of extreme pornography' *Criminal LR* 1; (2009) 'Criminalising extreme pornography: a lost opportunity' *Criminal LR* 245.
[29] [1992] 1 SCR 452.
[30] Moon (1993) '*R v Butler*: the limits of the Supreme Court's feminist re-interpretation of section 163' *Ottawa LR* 361.
[31] Fenwick and Phillipson (2006) *Media freedom under the Human Rights Act* p 458.

essentially the same feminist arguments? Which is most in tension with liberal – and feminist – concerns for privacy, respect for minority sexual identities and the importance of free expression around sexual identity, fantasy and desire? Do both simply amount to a new instance of the enforcement of morals under the fig leaf of harm-prevention?

In chapter seven, Keith Ewing revisits an analysis of the Canadian Supreme Court's treatment of aspects of the country's labour laws that he co-authored in 1988.[32] In this new paper, Ewing analyses two ground-breaking decisions handed down by the Supreme Court at the beginning of 2015. The decisions in question – *Mounted Police Association of Ontario v Canada*[33] (hereafter *Mounted Police*) and *Saskatchewan Federation of Labour v Saskatchewan*[34] (hereafter *SFL*) respectively – were the final stages of a development in which the Supreme Court had since 2002 began to repudiate the conservative decisions of the 1980s on labour rights in the so-called 'labour trilogy' judgments.

The chapter argues that the recent decisions are of great significance internationally and teach important lessons with cross-jurisdictional implications. The first concerns the enduring power of dissenting decisions; the second relates to the nature and significance of litigation strategies and the role of co-ordinated legal teams in developing appropriate strategies; the third highlights emerging willingness of the courts throughout the world to be guided by international law in contemporary constitutional adjudication.

The decisions – and especially the *SFL* judgment – have been rightly celebrated, and deployed internationally in response to a concerted employer campaign globally against the right to strike as a protected human right, raising questions about the significance of national constitutional law in the development of international law, as well as the significance of the latter on the former. The Saskatchewan decision had been greatly feared by representative organisations of employers, but paradoxically was relied upon by the US Government in particular at the International Labour Organization (ILO) in 2015 to resist attempts to weaken international protection of labour rights. The politics of the decision beyond Canada were thus immense, the Supreme Court following a similar journey on the same issue undertaken contemporaneously by the ECtHR.

Ewing's chapter assesses the legal significance of the recent Supreme Court decisions for labour relations in Canada, but also examines their implications more widely. Although there is much to celebrate in the initiatives taken by the Canadian Supreme Court, there is nevertheless reason to be cautious, and to read carefully the small print that tends to be obscured in moments of triumph and celebration. Is this really a victorious moment for labour?

---

[32] Christian and Ewing (1988) 'Labouring under the Canadian Constitution' *Industrial LJ* 73. The chapter also develops points raised in Ewing (2015) '"The Lady doth protest too much methinks" – the right to strike, international standards and the Supreme Court of Canada' 18 *Canadian Labour and Employment Law Journal* 517.

[33] (2015) SCC 1, [2015] 1 SCR 3.

[34] (2015) SCC 4, [2015] 1 SCR 245.

Nick Hatzis' concern in chapter eight is with the way in which the Canadian and UK legal systems have protected people's entitlement to manifest their religious beliefs through the wearing of particular forms of dress or symbols. In recent years, the constitutional status of the right to wear religious symbols in public has become one of the most litigated issues in the area of freedom of religion. It also plays a central role in the wider political controversy about the proper place of religion in public space and the legitimacy of granting exemptions from neutral laws to religious claimants. Hatzis explores the Canadian and British approaches under the Charter and the HRA 1998 respectively by looking at cases such as *Multani v Commission Scholaire*,[35] *Grant v Canada*,[36] *Eweida v British Airways*,[37] *R (SB) v Governors of Denbigh High School*[38] and *Williamson v Secretary of State for Education and Employment*.[39] The chapter focuses on three questions: first, what kind of religious beliefs may support a claim for exemptions from prohibitions on wearing religious symbols; second, the reasons invoked by governments for imposing the prohibitions; and third, the way courts have conducted the balancing exercise between religious freedom and governmental interests. Discussion of those issues helps to bring into focus the normative assumptions underlying judicial rulings in Canada and Britain and the way those rulings reflect broader societal attitudes to religion.

The analysis of 'broader societal attitudes to religion' is continued in the final chapter, in which Rachel Taylor considers the way in which UK and Canadian law have accommodated the wishes of parents to raise their children in accordance with unorthodox religious or cultural beliefs. Canada and the UK have faced similar dilemmas as to how to accommodate diverse religious and cultural beliefs within a multicultural society. A particularly acute problem is posed by those who profess unorthodox or extreme beliefs that reject the values that underpin liberal democratic society and which might be considered constitutional. In both countries, the upbringing of children has been an important site for these conflicts and each has developed a broadly similar framework for the resolution of those disputes. Both jurisdictions have advanced from the common law position, which gave broad protection to paternal rights to determine the child's religious upbringing, to one which emphasises the responsibility of both parents to decide that upbringing. In both jurisdictions disputes between parents are resolved according to the internationally recognised principle of the best interests of the child. Further, both jurisdictions recognise that protection for parents' rights to religious freedom does not extend to decisions that may harm the child or infringe his or her own rights. Despite the broad similarities between the jurisdictions, terms such as 'best interests' and 'harm' do not have fixed meanings, instead reflecting

---

[35] [2006] 1 SCR 256.
[36] [1994] FCJ no.1001.
[37] [2010] EWCA Civ 80, [2010] ICR 890.
[38] [2006] UKHL 15, [2007] 1 AC 100.
[39] [2005] UKHL 15, [2005] 2 AC 246.

the values and norms of the society in which they are determined. For this reason, the subject provides a particularly illuminating comparative study as to how similar legal tests are given meaning within each jurisdiction.

As both Canada and the UK have adopted ever more secular values, the position of parents who hold religious beliefs that reject those values has become increasingly fraught. Fundamentally, each jurisdiction has had to address the question of whether welfare and harm should be determined according to the values of the religious community in which the child lives, or according to the standards prevalent in wider society. The developing law increasingly favours the latter: the growing use of supposedly neutral values in welfare decisions and in education imposes increasingly firm outer boundaries on parental religious choice. This paper considers the derivation of those values and their application across a range of areas that have arisen in both jurisdictions. First, attention is given to the way in which matters of sexuality and gender identity are treated in determining the welfare of children within religious communities. Second, the paper considers the extent to which certain forms of religious extremism are themselves considered to be harmful to children, particularly within the context of radicalisation. Finally, the paper addresses the question of how far the state can insist that children are educated according to standards that may conflict with the religious and cultural beliefs or parents and children, for example, in relation to equality, religious tolerance and scientific orthodoxy. In addressing each of these areas the paper also contrasts the extent to which children have themselves been viewed as holders of constitutional rights within each jurisdiction.

II. Thematic Concerns

The contributions to this volume address diverse substantive issues, but are linked by several pervasive doctrinal themes. The most significant of these – which are flagged in this introductory chapter to avoid the need for constant repetition in the chapters which follow – are, respectively, the notion of proportionality, the horizontality (or lack thereof) of particular legal norms, and the phenomenon of 'dialogue' between different governmental actors.

A. Proportionality – And Deference

Shortly after the HRA 1998 came into force I had a conversation with a colleague in chambers who was – to put the point mildly – very much agitated by the curiosity shown by a circuit judge in the Shoreditch County Court about the judgment of Canada's Supreme Court in *R v Oakes*.[40] My colleague was acting for a

---

[40] [1986] 1 SCR 103.

local authority in a housing possession case, the defendant being a person with no demonstrable legal right to occupy the property, and relying for her defence solely upon the provisions of HRA 1998, Sch 1, Art 8. There being at that point no domestic authority on the meaning of the proportionality requirement within Art 8 in the context of housing possession actions,[41] the defendant's counsel had imaginatively suggested to the (receptive) judge that she might usefully take a lead from the formulation of that principle in *Oakes*.

The scheme of the Charter is that breaches of the various rights identified in its text may be justified in accordance with the provisions of s 1:

> 1. The *Canadian Charter of Rights and Freedoms* guarantees the rights and freedoms set out in it subject only to such reasonable limits prescribed by law as can be demonstrably justified in a free and democratic society.[42]

After a brief flurry of early cases in which neither the parties nor the Supreme Court seemed quite to know what to make of or do with s 1,[43] *Oakes*[44] offered a lengthy explanation of the purpose s 1 was to serve and the way in which it was to be applied:

> 69. To establish that a limit is reasonable and demonstrably justified in a free and democratic society, two central criteria must be satisfied. First, the objective, which the measures responsible for a limit on a *Charter* right or freedom are designed to serve, must be 'of sufficient importance to warrant overriding a constitutionally protected right or freedom': *R. v. Big M Drug Mart Ltd., supra*, at p. 352. The standard must be high in order to ensure that objectives which are trivial or discordant with the principles integral to a free and democratic society do not gain s. 1 protection. It is necessary, at a minimum, that an objective relate to concerns which are pressing and substantial in a free and democratic society before it can be characterized as sufficiently important.
>
> 70. Second, once a sufficiently significant objective is recognized, then the party invoking s. 1 must show that the means chosen are reasonable and demonstrably justified. This involves 'a form of proportionality test': *R. v. Big M Drug Mart Ltd.*, supra, at p. 352. Although the nature of the proportionality test will vary depending on the circumstances, in each case courts will be required to balance the interests of society with those of individuals and groups. There are, in my view, three important components of a proportionality test. First, the measures adopted must be carefully designed to achieve the objective in question. They must not be arbitrary, unfair or based on irrational considerations. In short, they must be rationally connected to the objective.

---

[41] There is now a great deal. For an overview see Loveland (2017) 'Nearly twenty years later: assessing the significance of the Human Rights Act 1998 to residential possession proceedings' *The Conveyancer and Property Lawyer* 169.

[42] That scheme is conceptually distinct from the arrangement in the ECHR and HRA 1998, in which 'justification' for interference with a protected right is taken to mean that the relevant right has not been breached at all.

[43] See particularly *Law Society of Upper Canada v Skapinker* [1984] 1 SCR 357; *Hunter v Southam* [1984] 2 SCR 145; *R v Big M Drug Mart* [1985] 1 SCR 295.

[44] The case concerned the constitutionality of a reverse onus burden of proof in relation to a narcotics offence. A similar reverse onus provision in the context of drunk driving had been found consistent with the Bill of Rights in *R v Appleby* [1972] SCR 303.

Second, the means, even if rationally connected to the objective in this first sense, should impair 'as little as possible' the right or freedom in question: *R. v. Big M Drug Mart Ltd.*, supra, at p. 352. Third, there must be a proportionality between the effects of the measures which are responsible for limiting the Charter right or freedom, and the objective which has been identified as of 'sufficient importance'.

Section 1 is of course applicable to the actions of government bodies, and would likely have been a significant innovation even if its scope had been limited to the administrative law arena. But it is unsurprisingly its use as a device to calibrate the legal defensibility of legislative provisions that has prompted most attention both in Canada and elsewhere.

Canada's Supreme Court settled quickly and apparently with little doctrinal anxiety on the principle that the formula articulated in *Oakes* was a very elastic construct in both a process and outcome sense; the rigour with which statutory provisions would be interrogated by the judiciary and thence the substantive boundaries confining the relevant legislature's lawmaking powers could quite properly vary – and significantly so – from case to case. The context-specific nature of the s 1 test was announced in *Oakes* itself.[45] Context-driven legal principles obviously raise questions as to legal certainty (at least until such time as there are multiple contextual decisions to provide a credible basis for predicting what legal response will be forthcoming in a *strictu sensu* novel situation). The Supreme Court was manifestly alert to this tension, and a dichotomous organising principle was articulated and applied in a pair of free expression cases decided the following year. *Ford v Quebec*[46] addressed the constitutionality of Quebec's French language laws – enacted in 1974 – which, inter alia, essentially sought to criminalise the use of language other than French in many commercial contexts.[47] *Irwin Toy v Quebec*[48] was concerned with Quebec legislation which placed strict controls on television advertising promoting products aimed at children.

In *Ford* and *Irwin* the Supreme Court indicated that the rigor of the justificatory burden which s 1 imposed on the government body defending either its own actions or the legislation it was seeking to implement would likely very significantly depend on whether the law positioned a government body as a 'singular antagonist' (as in *Ford*) to the persons or organisations who claimed a Charter right had been infringed, or whether the government/legislature's role was better characterised (as in *Irwin*) as mediating between or balancing the interests of differently situated groups or individuals:

> When striking a balance between the claims of competing groups, the choice of means, like the choice of ends, frequently will require an assessment of conflicting scientific evidence and differing justified demands on scarce resources. Democratic institutions

---

[45] [1986] 1 SCR 103 at [70].
[46] [1988] 2 SCR 712.
[47] *La charte de la langue française; 'popularly' known as (loi 101).*
[48] [1989] 1 SCR 927.

are meant to let us all share in the responsibility for these difficult choices. Thus, as courts review the results of the legislature's deliberations, particularly with respect to the protection of vulnerable groups, they must be mindful of the legislature's representative function. ...

In other cases, however, rather than mediating between different groups, the government is best characterized as the singular antagonist of the individual whose right has been infringed. For example, in justifying an infringement of legal rights enshrined in ss. 7 to 14 of the Charter, the state, on behalf of the whole community, typically will assert its responsibility for prosecuting crime whereas the individual will assert the paramountcy of principles of fundamental justice. There might not be any further competing claims among different groups.[49]

The inference that might arise from the language used in the second sentence of the quotation from *Irwin Toy* above – that government and legislatures but not courts are 'democratic institutions' and that consequently the Charter itself is somehow an affront to 'democracy' – has fuelled a substantial body of anti-Charter literature in Canada,[50] and is redolent of the infantile simplicity which has long afflicted debate in the UK as to the desirability of seeking constitutional reform which curbs Parliament's capacity to legislate on all issues by simple majority bicameral vote. The near-modern roots of that discourse in the UK perhaps lie in the influence wielded by successive editions of John Griffith's *Politics of the judiciary*, but it is something of a never-ending story: in recent years both Labour and Conservative governments in the UK have raised the banner of 'judicial supremacism' in attempts to delegitimise specific judgments – and public law doctrines in the round – when met by decisions which they find politically unpalatable or inconvenient.[51]

---

[49] ibid at [994].

[50] For an introduction to the controversy see the sources cited in Constitutional Law Group (2017; 5th edn) *Canadian constitutional law* ch 16; and especially Russell (1983) 'The political purposes of the Canadian Charter of Rights and freedoms' *CBR* 30: Bogart (1994) *Courts and country*; Petter (1987) 'Immaculate deception: the Charter's hidden agenda' *Advocate* 857.

[51] See the episodes discussed in Loveland (2018; 8th edn) *Constitutional law, administrative law and human rights* pp 507–15, 583–86, 648–49. Canada's Supreme Court had sounded an early alarm against criticism from the political left that the Charter would have a *Lochner*-esque effect on economic and socially progressive legislation. In *R v Edwards Books and Art Ltd* – a case considering Ontario's Sunday closing laws – Dickson CJ expressed a concern that the Charter might be misused from the political right as a source of reactionary values, especially in the sphere of economic policy: 'In interpreting and applying the *Charter* I believe that the courts must be cautious to ensure that it does not simply become an instrument of better situated individuals to roll back legislation which has as its object the improvement of the condition of less advantaged persons': [1986] 2 SCR 713 at 779. *Lochner v New York* ((1905) 198 US 45) is the infamous decision in which the Supreme Court invoked the liberty clause of the 14th amendment to invalidate state legislation which placed a maximum-hours limit on the working week of employed bakers. The criticism from the left rather overlooks the facts that *Lochner* itself was a fiercely contested five-to-four decision on the Court, had (even at the time it was decided) limited substantive scope (inapplicable to 'dangerous' occupations (*Holden v Hardy* (1898) 169 US 366) and women and children (*Muller v Oregon* (1908) 208 US 412), and had partially been reversed by 1917 (*Bunting v Oregon* (1917) 243 US 426 and was fully overturned by 1937 (*West Coast Hotel v Parrish* (1937) 300 US 379.

From that perspective, the force of the s 1 analysis offered by Beverley McLachlin's judgment in *RJR-MacDonald Inc v Canada (Attorney-General)*[52] might seem particularly problematic. The relevant passages perhaps merit extensive quotation here, as their visibility in UK public law circles seems rather low:

> 127 … First, to be saved under s. 1 the party defending the law (here the Attorney General of Canada) must show that the law which violates the right or freedom guaranteed by the Charter is 'reasonable'. In other words, the infringing measure must be justifiable by the processes of reason and rationality. The question is not whether the measure is popular or accords with the current public opinion polls. The question is rather whether it can be justified by application of the processes of reason. In the legal context, reason imports the notion of inference from evidence or established truths. This is not to deny intuition its role, or to require proof to the standards required by science in every case, but it is to insist on a rational, reasoned defensibility.
>
> 128 Second, to meet its burden under s. 1 of the Charter, the state must show that the violative law is 'demonstrably justified'. The choice of the word 'demonstrably' is critical. The process is not one of mere intuition, nor is it one of deference to Parliament's choice. It is a process of demonstration. This reinforces the notion inherent in the word 'reasonable' of rational inference from evidence or established truths.
>
> 129 The bottom line is this. While remaining sensitive to the social and political context of the impugned law and allowing for difficulties of proof inherent in that context, the courts must nevertheless insist that before the state can override constitutional rights, there be a reasoned demonstration of the good which the law may achieve in relation to the seriousness of the infringement. It is the task of the courts to maintain this bottom line if the rights conferred by our constitution are to have force and meaning. The task is not easily discharged, and may require the courts to confront the tide of popular public opinion. But that has always been the price of maintaining constitutional rights. No matter how important Parliament's goal may seem, if the state has not demonstrated that the means by which it seeks to achieve its goal are reasonable and proportionate to the infringement of rights, then the law must perforce fail.

McLachlin J's conclusion was likely driven in part by the fact that the national Government had refused to disclose evidence it had gathered as to the impact of advertising on tobacco consumption; a refusal which raises the obvious inference that the evidence concerned provided no support for the substantive objectives which the legislation was said – by the national Government – to promote. Nonetheless, the might credibly be seen as a high-water mark of judicial disinclination to defer to politicians' evaluations of the constitutional defensibility of their actions (whether in creating or implementing legislation), or – to offer an alternative characterisation – as among the most forceful applications of the *Oakes* principle.[53]

---

[52] [1995] 3 SCR 199. *RJR* addressed the constitutionality of proposed national laws which would significantly restrict and control the content of tobacco advertising in the Canadian media.

[53] That it was asserted in *RJR* is perhaps surprising, given the case's factual matrix might credibly be classified as one involving the law as a balancing force between competing interests groups (as in *Irwin Toy*) rather than as a singular antagonist of the 'victim'.

It is not however difficult to find examples of Charter decisions in which the Supreme Court has shown a marked reluctance – even in what might seem clearly to be singular antagonist scenarios – to put legislation and executive action to such an exacting test, or indeed to any real evidential test at all. Beattie and Phillipson address that point in the context of obscenity legislation in chapter six, although the point is most clearly conveyed by the very lax evidential regimes approved by the Court on the leading hate speech cases of *R v Keegstra*[54] and *Ross v New Brunswick School District*.[55]

The varying nature of the proportionality test in Canada is brought out in some detail both within and between the various chapters in this book. UK courts have reached much the same substantive end point – albeit with rather more agonising along the way and without adopting a variant of the singular antagonist/balancing dichotomy – in respect of the meaning of proportionality review under the HRA 1998.

Oakes has acquired an increasingly high profile within UK courts' proportionality jurisprudence,[56] a process initiated by the approval afforded to it by the Privy Council in *de Freitas v Permanent Secretary of Ministry of Agriculture, Fisheries, Lands and Housing*[57] and given perhaps its most fulsome expression by Lord Reed in *Bank Mellat v HM Treasury (No 2)*:[58]

> 74. The judgment of Dickson CJ in Oakes provides the clearest and most influential judicial analysis of proportionality within the common law tradition of legal reasoning. Its attraction as a heuristic tool is that, by breaking down an assessment of proportionality into distinct elements, it can clarify different aspects of such an assessment, and make value judgments more explicit.

The textual basis of the proportionality test required by the Charter is prima facie more rigorous than its HRA counterpart. McLachlin's fierce exposition of the principle in *RJR* was hung very firmly on s 1's 'demonstrably justified' peg. UK courts have rather less text to work from in respect of the HRA's 'necessary in a democratic society' proviso, but that is perhaps an invitation – and certainly seems to have been construed as such by UK courts – to lend the proportionality concept a meaning which is as variegated and contextually specific as that afforded to s 1 of the Charter by the Canadian courts.

That issue is explored in the chapters of this volume, and those analyses need not be foreshadowed here. For Canadian readers unfamiliar with the development of HRA jurisprudence, it might simply be noted here that the UK Supreme Court has perhaps come closest to embracing the scepticism exhibited by McLachlin J in *RJR* as to the bona fides and competence of governmental decision-making

---

[54] [1990] 3 SCR 697.
[55] [1996] 1 SCR 825.
[56] A westlaw search for 'R v Oakes' in September 2020 records 160 cases citing *Oakes*.
[57] [1999] 1 AC 69 at [80].
[58] [2014] AC 700. The [74] reference is to [74] in the substantive appeal at ibid at p 790.

in *R (Aguilar Quila) v Secretary of State for the Home Department.*[59] In *Quila* the Court conjured up 10 questions to the Cameron/Clegg coalition Government (and specifically to the Home Office then led by Theresa May) to which it would require appropriate answers before accepting that the government's policy was lawful. *Quila* may be an outlier within HRA 1998 proportionality jurisprudence in terms of the rigour of the analysis it imposes. A more mainstream division has solidified, however, between a formally structured approach typified by the judgment in *Huang v Secretary of State for the Home Department* and a very relaxed test offered in *Manchester CC v Pinnock.*[60]

B. The Horizontality of Legal Norms

Neither the Charter nor the HRA 1998 offer an explicit textual answer in either a positive or negative sense to the question of whether their respective provisions[61] apply in litigation which does not involve a government actor. In both countries, that issue seems to have been resolved unproblematically when the outcome of the case turned on the construction of statutory provisions.[62] Canada also seems to have uncovered – 'created' may be a more apposite term – much the same complexity in its Charter case law concerning the meaning of 'government' within s 32[63] as the UK courts have found in the meaning of 'public authority' and 'function of a public nature' within HRA 1998, s 6.[64] That is perhaps surprising given the measures' respective texts:[65] 'government' being plausibly a narrower concept than public authority, and the Charter making no reference to 'functions of a governmental nature'.

That textual difference might be taken to explain the Canadian Supreme Court's early conclusions that public universities' and public hospitals' employment policies were not regarded as raising a s 32 issue in *McKinney v University of Guelph and Harrison v University of British Columbia*[66] and *Stoffman v Vancouver General*

---

[59] [2011] UKSC 45.

[60] [2007] UKHL 11, [2007] 2 AC 167: [2001] UKSC 6, [2010] 3 WLR 1441.

[61] These being primarily HRA, s 6 and s 32 of the Charter.

[62] Compare *Wilson v First County Bank* [2001] EWCA Civ 663, [2002] QB 74, [2003] UKHL 40, [2004] 1 AC 816 and *Ghaidan v Medoza* [2002] EWCA Civ 1533, [2003] Ch 380, [2004] UKHL 30, [2004] 2 AC 557 with *RWDSU v Dolphin Delivery* [1986] 2 SCR 573. Keith Ewing's, Nick Hatzis' and Rachel Taylor's chapters herein suggest that this conclusion is not as obviously unproblematic as one might think.

[63] '**Application of Charter** 32. (1) This Charter applies (*a*) to the Parliament and government of Canada in respect of all matters within the authority of Parliament including all matters relating to the Yukon Territory and Northwest Territories; and (*b*) to the legislatures and governments of each province in respect of all matters within the authority of the legislature of each province.'

[64] See in particular the divergent approaches taken by the Court of Appeal in *Aston Cantlow and Wilmcote with Bilesley Parochial Church Council v Wallbank* [2001] EWCA Civ 713, [2002] Ch 51, [2004] UKHL 37, [2004] 1 AC 546. More generally see the survey by Sumkin (2004) 'Pushing forward the frontiers of human rights protection: the meaning of public authority under the Human Rights Act' *Public Law* 643.

[65] See further Bamforth's chapter herein at pp 106–07.

[66] [1990] 3 SCR 451.

Hospital respectively,[67] a conclusion which would seem unsustainable if applied to HRA 1998, s 6. Similarly, UK public lawyers might find quite it remarkable that the question of whether a local authority created under provincial law fell within s 32, but the matter was seriously contested in *Godbout v Longeuil (City)*[68] in 1997.

Nonetheless, parallels between the construction of s 32 and s 6 can be seen in subsequent Canadian case law, which explored the circumstances in which de jure private sector actors might be drawn within s 32. Despite the lack of a 'function of a governmental nature' proviso in s 32, the Supreme Court has after the *McKinney, Harris* and *Stoffman* decisions produced a series of judgments in which an analogous concept has been read into the text and which bear obvious and close comparison with the core and hybrid public authority concepts developed in the UK in respect of s 6.[69] The Canadian position is perhaps best captured by the comment of Deschamps J in *Greater Vancouver Transportation Authority v Canadian Federation of Students*:[70]

> [16] … If the entity is found to be 'government' either because of its very nature or because the government exercises significant control over it, all of its activities will be subject to the Charter. If the entity is not itself a government entity but nevertheless performs governmental activities, only those activities which can be said to be governmental in nature will be subject to the Charter.

Indeed, notwithstanding the ostensibly less helpful (than s 6) textual ground that s 32 offers to advocates of horizontal effect,[71] it seems unlikely, for example, that the factual matrix presented to the House of Lords in *YL v Birmingham CC and Others*[72] (that a care home provider to which local authorities had contracted out their responsibility to provide to accommodate and provide care to vulnerable people under the National Assistance Act 1948, s 21) would have led the Canadian Supreme Court to find that the care provider was not a s 32 entity.

The Canadian and UK courts have also found common ground in accepting that the outcome of 'horizontal' litigation which turns on the meaning of common law principles – or which exposes a complete vacuum in the content of the law – cannot be controlled directly by the provisions of the Charter and HRA 1998 respectively. Both countries have, however, accepted that the 'values' inherent in those measures can be properly invoked by the courts to mould the development

---

[67] [1990] 3 SCR 229 and [1990] 3 SCR 483.

[68] [1997] 3 SCR.

[69] *See for example Eldridge v British Colmbia* [1997] 3 SCR 624; *Blencoe v British Columbia (Human Rights Commission* [2000] 2 SCR 307; *Greater Vancouver Transportation Authority v Canadian Federation of Students* [2009] 2 SCR 295.

[70] [2009] 2 SCR 295.

[71] Curiously, as observed above, the converse is that case in respect of the respective instruments' proportionality provisions.

[72] [2007] UKHL 27, [2008] 1 AC 95. Canada obviously lacks the easy remedy for 'wrong' Charter decisions that was available in the UK in response to *YL*; namely prompt legislative reversal. See Loveland (2018) op cit pp 564–65.

of common law principles, particularly in areas relating to privacy and freedom of expression where legislatures have shown some reluctance to tread.[73]

Several of the chapters in this volume point to the blurry edges of the horizontal/vertical divide in both jurisdictions. The issue is pursued most systematically in Nicholas Bamforth's chapter; while Hatzis, Taylor and Ewing all identify complications which can arise from the simple assumption that the presence of a statutory provision on which the Charter or HRA 1998 can bite necessarily resolves all the difficult substantive arguments which the horizontal effect can raise; and Ian Loveland explores the distinctly variegated impact that human rights 'values' have been accorded in both jurisdictions in a very short time period on the development of the common law in the field of defamation.

C. 'Dialogue(s)'

The very broad discretion afforded to the Canadian courts by s 24 of the Charter[74] to respond to unjustified breaches of Charter rights – to grant such remedy 'as the court considers just and appropriate' – in conjunction with the identification in s 52 of (inter alia) the Constitution Act 1982 as normatively superior to national and provincial legislation[75] places Canada's courts in a quite different constitutional position from that occupied by UK courts under the terms of the HRA 1998.[76] Imaginative use of HRA 1998, s 3 by UK courts may have the indirect effect of lending statutory provisions meanings so unexpected that governments are prompted to promote legislative amendments, and thus far successive UK governments have generally responded to s 4 declarations of incompatibility by introducing legislative reform.[77] Nonetheless, the 'simple' judicial invalidation of legislative provisions provided for by the Constitution Act 1982 remains a very distant prospect in the UK's constitutional setting.

The notion of 'simple' is used archly here because the Canadian Supreme Court has frequently presented its judgment finding breaches of Charter provisions more as an invitation to the national or provincial legislatures to reflect upon and modify

---

[73] UK observers frustrated by legislative inactivity might refer to the fascinating judgment in *Vriend v Alberta* [1998] 1 SCR 493, in which the Court's response to a refusal by the Alberta legislature to include sexual orientation as a protected category in the Province's human rights law was simply to write the category into the relevant legislation.

[74] **'Enforcement of guaranteed rights and freedoms** 24. (1) Anyone whose rights or freedoms, as guaranteed by this Charter, have been infringed or denied may apply to a court of competent jurisdiction to obtain such remedy as the court considers appropriate and just in the circumstances.'

[75] **'Primacy of Constitution of Canada 52.** (1) The Constitution of Canada is the supreme law of Canada, and any law that is inconsistent with the provisions of the Constitution is, to the extent of the inconsistency, of no force or effect.'

[76] UK courts arguably occupied a comparable role in respect of directly effective EU law while the UK remained in the Union.

[77] Chandrachud (2014) 'Reconfiguring the discourse on political responses to declarations of incompatibility' *Public Law* 624.

the impugned law than a denunciation of legislative excess. The analyses of this process by Peter Hogg and his colleagues[78] have brought the notion of judicial-legislative 'dialogue' firmly into the lexicon of Canadian constitutional discourse. Dialogue in the Canadian context is perhaps much assisted by the longstanding provision – originally enacted as s 52 of the Supreme Court Act 1875[79] – which permits the national Government to refer draft legislation to the Supreme Court for an assessment of its constitutionality; a mechanism within which a government 'defeat' has no immediate practical consequences.

The dialogue process had manifestly had some ameliorative impact on the force of the 'anti-democratic' critiques targeted at the Charter. What it has perhaps also done is lend a more informed and exacting character to legislative consideration of how laws should be tailored to meet the Charter's requirements. That phenomenon is brought out very strongly in Draghici's chapter, which paints a notably positive picture of the way in which the national Parliament responded with new legislation to a Supreme Court judgment on the assisted dying issue.[80] In contrast, lest dialogue be thought a panacea for all such disagreement, Easton's chapter highlights the notably feeble efforts of legislators to address the Court's invalidation of prisoner disenfranchisement legislation and the Court's subsequent caustic dismissal – authored by McLachlin J in terms substantively and stylistically reminiscent of her 'demonstrable justification' analysis in *RJR* – of the ensuing remedial statute.[81]

In the UK context, 'dialogue' on HRA issues has perhaps been viewed more as entailing a conversation between the House of Lords/Supreme Court and the ECtHR than between the judiciary and the legislature. That process has been seen at its most protracted in the areas of criminal procedure and residential possession proceedings. It took a perhaps surprisingly long time for the House of Lords/Supreme Court to underline the rather obvious statutory point (in HRA 1998, s 2) that Convention Rights under the HRA 1998 and Convention Articles under the European Convention on Human Rights (ECHR) were quite distinct juridic creatures. That issue was eventually clarified in *R v Horncastle*,[82] in which the Supreme Court rejected as ill-informed the ECtHR's judgment in *Al-Khawaja and Tahery v United Kingdom*[83] that various provisions of domestic law concerning the admissibility of hearsay evidence breached Art 6 ECHR. The inter-court dialogue on the possession proceedings question was conducted over a decade and more than a

---

[78] Hogg and Bushell (1997) 'The Charter dialogue between courts and legislatures (or perhaps the Charter isn't such a bad thing after all' *Osgoode Hall LJ* 75: Hogg, Thornton and Wright (2007) 'Charter dialogue revisited: or much ado about metaphors' *Osgoode Hall LJ* 1.

[79] '52. It shall be lawful for the Governor in Council to refer to the Supreme Court for hearing or consideration, any matters whatsoever as he may think fit ...'.

[80] pp 35–38 below.

[81] pp 78–81 below.

[82] [2009] UKSC 14, [2010] 2 AC 373.

[83] (2009) 49 EHRR 1. The slow route to this conclusion is discussed in Metcalfe (2010) 'Free to lead as well as to be led: section 2 of the Human Rights Act and the relationship between the UK courts and Strasbourg' *Justice Journal* 7.

dozen cases before apparently settling on the basis of concessions from both sides as to Art 8's (ECHR and HRA) requirements.[84]

Such inter-judicial dialogue between the Supreme Court and the EtCHR, marked more by a conversational than (as in the criminal procedure and possession contexts) confrontational ethos, also features heavily in the chapters by Draghici, Easton and Loveland. Canada's Supreme Court has been spared that inter-jurisdictional difficulty in respect of the Charter. As some contributors to this volume note, Charter 'dialogue' has sometimes been conducted between lower Canadian courts and the Supreme Court when lower courts have pushed very firmly at the boundaries of Supreme Court judgments;[85] a phenomenon which appeared only very briefly in the UK and was firmly disapproved of by the House of Lords.[86]

Legislature–court dialogue has been a rather more contentious issue in the UK.[87] That may be in part because – unlike the position in Canada – the 'last' word lies with Parliament rather than the Supreme Court.[88] Susan Easton's chapter on prisoner voting rights addresses the most stark example in the UK context of politicians being unwilling even to engage in any serious sense with judicial analyses – be they UK or ECHR in origin – of the defensibility of blanket prisoner disenfranchisement. As Draghici suggests in chapter two, the UK Parliament's response to ECtHR and domestic judgments in relation to assisted dying offers a less dispiriting example of legislative inertia. But it might be suggested that both episodes illuminate a crucial difference between the Canadian and UK human rights regimes: if the substance of statutory provisions remains unaltered by judicial condemnation, there is no compelling incentive for politicians to take a reformist initiative.[89]

III. Conclusion

An allusion to 'dialogue' between differently situated constitutional actors within particular jurisdictions is perhaps a good place to end this introductory chapter.

---

[84] Reviewed in Loveland (2017) op cit. The concessions were certainly not one-way from the Supreme Court to the ECtHR: see the discussion of the horizontality issue in this context in Bamforth's chapter at pp 118–24 herein.

[85] See especially pp 69–70, 167–74 and 240–42 herein.

[86] See *D v East Berkshire Community NHS Trust* [2005] UKHL 23, [2005] 2 AC 373.

[87] The most incisive critiques are perhaps Young (2010) 'Deference, dialogue and the search for legitimacy' *OJLS* 815; (2011) 'Is dialogue working under the Human Rights Act?' *PL* 773.

[88] As yet, constitutional amendment has not shown itself to be a practicable route to 'remedying' Supreme Court judgments of which politicians disapprove. The Charter's entrenchment is not quite as deep as that provided in the constitution of the US, but the Constitution Act 1982, s 38 requires bare majority support in the Commons and Senate and then approval by at least two-thirds (ie seven) of the Provinces, which represent at least 50% of the national population.

[89] Although of course one of the more remarkable features of Canada's constitutional law is that the invalidation of national abortion legislation in 1988 in *R v Morgentaler* [1988] 1 SCR 30 has left a void in Canadian law into which no new legislation has yet to be introduced.

The dialogue envisaged here is intended for the rather more modest setting of academic journals and classrooms. While there is no doubt a great deal about which modern day public law scholars would find themselves in disagreement with Professor Dicey, it can sometimes be forgotten that his seminal textbook was rooted very firmly in the methodological presumption that a sophisticated under-standing of UK constitutional law and practice required readers to be provided with rather more than a rudimentary insight into other constitutional orders. We hope this book offers a minor contribution to that project.

2

Assisted Dying

CARMEN DRAGHICI

For decades, terminally ill patients and sufferers of locked-in syndrome have attempted to persuade lawmakers that their fundamental rights are infringed by laws which criminalise the assistance given to mentally competent adults seeking a peaceful and dignified death. In this debate, the UK and Canada have positioned themselves at opposite ends of the spectrum. In the UK, human rights challenges to the blanket prohibition on assisted suicide have been consistently unsuccessful (notably the *Nicklinson*[1] and *Conway*[2] cases), as have parliamentary reform initiatives.[3] Conversely, Canada's Supreme Court ruled a similar ban unconstitutional in its landmark *Carter* decision,[4] and the national legislature amended the Criminal Code to allow medical assistance in dying (MAiD) in some circumstances.[5] This chapter examines the legal and ethical issues underlying these contrasting developments, and suggests – in common with the conclusion reached by other contributors to this volume – that Canada's response has been more rigorous in evaluating and reconciling competing claims.

I. The Resilience of the British Blanket Ban on Assisted Dying

In England and Wales, 'encouraging and assisting' another to commit suicide is criminalised under the Suicide Act 1961, s 2(1) (SA 1961)[6] and punishable with up to 14 years' imprisonment;[7] the statute contemplates no exceptions. Parliamentary

---

[1] *R (Nicklinson) v Ministry of Justice* [2014] UKSC 38, [2015] AC 657.
[2] *R (Conway) v Secretary of State for Justice* [2018] EWCA Civ 1431.
[3] See sections I and VI.
[4] *Carter v Canada (Attorney General)* [2015] 1 SCR 331.
[5] An Act to amend the Criminal Code (medical assistance in dying), SC 2016, c 3 (Bill C-14). See new ss 241.1–241.3 Criminal Code, RSC 1985, c C-46.
[6] As amended by the Coroners and Justice Act 2009, s 59(2). See Wicks (2016) *The State and the body: Legal regulation of bodily autonomy* pp 71–85.
[7] Under Scottish law, the potential consequence is life imprisonment. See Stark (2014) 'Necessity and policy in R (Nicklinson and others) v Ministry of Justice' *Edinburgh LR* 104 at p 107.

debates leading to its adoption reveal mainly practical objections to the continued criminalisation of attempted suicide.[8] They indicate that, while decriminalisation was not intended to encourage or condone what was viewed as a mortal sin, it was thought that persons having attempted suicide did not benefit from prison treatment and that the law ought to focus on society's responsibility to assist them. Concerns were expressed that, without recourse to penal machinery, the police would no longer have compulsory powers to look after such persons and mental health treatment might be refused. There was, conversely, no discussion about the possible exemption of assisters from criminal liability. Several legal challenges to s 2(1) were brought by individuals suffering from irreversible medical conditions and wishing to end their lives, but who either were physically unable to do so without assistance from a family member or healthcare professional or wanted to avoid a traumatic and premature self-inflicted death.

A. The *Pretty* Litigation

The first case was *Pretty v Director of Public Prosecutions*.[9] The complainant suffered from motor neurone disease, was paralysed from the neck down, tube-fed and nearly incapable of speaking, with a life expectancy of a few months, and wished to be assisted to die before the painful and humiliating final stages of her illness. She challenged the refusal of the Director of Public Prosecutions (DPP) to issue an undertaking not to prosecute her husband if he helped her travel to Switzerland, where the Dignitas service lawfully provides MAiD.

The House of Lords found that her fundamental rights were not engaged by the DPP's decision. The right-to-life guarantee in Art 2 ECHR did not encompass a right to die.[10] Nor did the denial of proleptic immunity from prosecution constitute inhuman treatment contrary to Art 3 ECHR, insofar as Mrs Pretty's suffering stemmed from her disease, not the impugned decision.[11] The court also rejected the contention that personal autonomy, as protected under Art 8 ECHR, included a right to decide when or how one wished to die.[12] Even if Art 8 was engaged, the Law Lords reasoned, the interference was justified by the need to protect a broader class of vulnerable persons who would otherwise be induced to commit suicide.[13] The court equally dismissed the claim under Art 9 ECHR: freedom of conscience did not include the right to act upon a belief held, and, if the provision

---

[8] See *HLD* 2 March 1961 cc 247–76; *HLD* 9 March 1961 cc 535–61; *HLD* 16 March 1961 cc 975–90; *HCD* 14 July 1961 cc 834–45; *HCD* 19 July 1961 cc 1408–26; *HCD* 28 July 1961 cc 823–25.

[9] *R (Pretty) v DPP* [2001] UKHL 61. See Pedain (2003) 'The human rights dimension of the Diane Pretty case' *Cambridge LJ* 181.

[10] [2001] UKHL 61 at [59], [62], [87].

[11] ibid at [92]–[97].

[12] ibid at [61].

[13] ibid at [26], [30], [99]–[102].

was engaged, the restriction aimed to protect the vulnerable and was permissible.[14] Having found no substantive ECHR right engaged, the court further dismissed the claim that the applicant had suffered discrimination contrary to Art 14 on the ground of disability.[15]

When *Pretty* was examined by the ECtHR, the key distinction from the House of Lords' analysis was the unequivocal recognition that Art 8 applies to right-to-die claims. According to the Strasbourg court, the notion of 'private life' covers 'the physical and psychological integrity of a person' and 'personal autonomy'.[16] This extends to conduct threatening one's own life:

> [62] [T]he ability to conduct one's life in a manner of one's own choosing may also include the opportunity to pursue activities perceived to be of a physically or morally harmful or dangerous nature for the individual concerned.

The court drew a parallel with patients' right to refuse life-prolonging medical treatment, grounded in the same principle of (potentially self-harming) autonomy.[17] Consequently, criminalising assisted suicide interfered with Art 8 rights and required justification. Despite this favourable premise, the ECtHR accepted that the measure was within the UK's margin of appreciation and proportionate to the aim pursued, ie the protection of the life of vulnerable persons unable to make informed decisions.[18] After *Pretty v UK*, unsuccessful attempts between 2003 and 2006 to pass an Assisted Dying for the Terminally Ill Bill left the law unchanged.[19]

B. The *Purdy* Litigation

In *R (Purdy) v DPP*,[20] the House of Lords followed *Pretty v UK* and recognised the applicability of Art 8 to right-to-die cases. The claimant's position was similar to Mrs Pretty's: she suffered from primary progressive multiple sclerosis, an incurable disease causing gradual deterioration, and needed her husband's assistance to travel to Switzerland to end her life before her condition became intolerable.[21] Her legal claim was, however, different. It neither attacked SA 1961, s 2(1) nor

---

[14] ibid at [63].
[15] ibid at [105].
[16] *Pretty v UK* (2002) 35 EHRR 1 at [61]. Arts 3 and 9 claims were dismissed; ibid at [53]–[56], [82]–[83]. See Merkouris (2011) 'Assisted suicide in the jurisprudence of the European Court of Human Rights: A matter of life and death' p 107 in Negri (ed) *Self-determination, dignity and end-of-life care. Regulating advance directives in international and comparative perspective.*
[17] (2002) 35 EHRR 1 at [63].
[18] ibid at [74]–[78].
[19] See Keown (2012) *The law and ethics and medicine. Essays on the inviolability of human life* pp 235–74.
[20] *R (Purdy) v DPP* [2009] UKHL 45.
[21] ibid at [17].

challenged the unavailability of proleptic guarantee of non-prosecution for carers providing assistance. Rather, she questioned the insufficient clarity of s 4 of the Act as regards the DPP's exercise of discretion to allow prosecution, which made it impossible to reach an informed decision on whether to request assistance.[22]

The court cited Lord Hope's acknowledgement of self-determination rights in *Pretty*, endorsed by the ECtHR:[23] 'The way she chooses to pass the closing moments of her life is part of the act of living, and she has a right to ask that this too must be respected.'[24] According to the judgment, the Code for Crown Prosecutors did not ensure predictability as regards the consequences of aiding a person who is terminally ill or severely and incurably disabled and wishes to travel to a country where assisted suicide is lawful, having decisional capacity and fully understanding the implications;[25] therefore, it did not protect the right to exercise a genuinely autonomous choice.[26] The court concluded that the interference with private life was not 'in accordance with the law' as required under Art 8(2) ECHR, as the law did not satisfy the criteria of accessibility and foreseeability; the absence of a crime-specific policy regulating the DPP's consent to prosecution did not allow the public to anticipate how prosecutorial discretion would be exercised in assisted suicide cases.[27]

The judgment led the DPP to adopt new policy guidance in 2010.[28] Whilst the document did not introduce exemptions from SA 1961, s 2, it established that prosecution 'is less likely to be required' if:

[45] 1. the victim had reached a voluntary, clear, settled and informed decision to commit suicide; 2. the suspect was wholly motivated by compassion; 3. the actions of the suspect, although sufficient to come within the definition of the offence, were of only minor encouragement or assistance; 4. the suspect had sought to dissuade the victim from taking the course of action which resulted in his or her suicide; 5. the actions of the suspect may be characterised as reluctant encouragement or assistance in the face of a determined wish on the part of the victim to commit suicide; 6. the suspect reported the victim's suicide to the police and fully assisted them in their enquiries into the circumstances of the suicide or the attempt and his or her part in providing encouragement or assistance.

The policy guidance further states that the list of public interest factors tending against prosecution is not exhaustive; each case must be considered on its own merits.[29]

---

[22] ibid at [30]–[31], [42].
[23] (2002) 35 EHRR 1 at [64].
[24] [2002] 1 AC 800 at [100].
[25] [2009] UKHL 45 at [54].
[26] ibid at [65].
[27] [2009] UKHL 45 at [40]–[41], [46]–[56].
[28] DPP (2010) *Suicide: Policy for prosecutors in respect of cases of encouraging or assisting suicide* (updated 2014), available at www.cps.gov.UK/legal-guidance/suicide-policy-prosecutors-respect-cases-encouraging-or-assisting-suicide.
[29] ibid at [47].

C. The *Nicklinson* Litigation

In 2014, *Nicklinson* belied the prediction that, having grounded a right to die in personal autonomy, *Purdy* heralded the legalisation of assisted suicide.[30] The litigants (Mr Nicklinson, Mr Lamb and Martin) were afflicted by catastrophic disabilities as a result of a stroke or automobile accident, almost completely paralysed and unable to communicate, and described their lives as 'miserable', 'demeaning', 'distressing', 'intolerable', 'undignified'.[31] They had reached a settled decision to end their lives and wished to have a doctor or carer assist them in administering lethal drugs or travelling to Dignitas.

They required the Supreme Court to either interpret SA 1961, s 2 as permitting the assistance sought, so as to reconcile that provision with ECHR rights per the Human Rights Act 1998, s 3 (HRA 1998), or to issue a s 4 declaration of incompatibility. The DPP appealed the lower court's decision that the prosecutorial policy was still insufficiently detailed; Martin's cross-appeal claimed that the decision had not gone far enough.

The Supreme Court majority continued to uphold the blanket prohibition.[32] First, protecting the vulnerable was a legitimate aim under Art 8(2) ECHR:

> [171] The main justification advanced for an absolute prohibition on assisting suicide ...
> is the perceived risk to the lives of other, vulnerable individuals who might feel them-
> selves a burden to their family, friends or society and might, if assisted suicide were
> permitted, be persuaded or convince themselves that they should undertake it, when
> they would not otherwise do so.

The interference with Art 8 was also found proportionate, insofar as no lesser measure, such as a permissive scheme accompanied by safeguards against error and abuse, could secure that aim. For Lord Neuberger: 'it is impossible ... to say with confidence in advance that any such scheme could satisfactorily and appropriately be fashioned.'[33]

Conversely, Lady Hale reasoned, dissenting, that a system identifying well-informed requests for assistance in dying was achievable;[34] the law therefore exceeded the minimum interference necessary:

> [317] To the extent that the current universal prohibition prevents those who would
> qualify under such a procedure from securing the help they need, I consider that it is a
> disproportionate interference with their right to choose the time and manner of their
> deaths. ... It fails to strike a fair balance between the rights of those who have freely
> chosen to commit suicide but are unable to do so without some assistance and the inter-
> ests of the community as a whole.

---

[30] See Cleary (2010) 'From "personal autonomy" to "death-on-demand": Will Purdy v. DPP legalize assisted suicide in the UK?' *Boston College International and Comparative LR* 289 at p 304.

[31] [2015] AC 657 at [3], [8], [9].

[32] [2015] AC 657.

[33] ibid at [186], [188].

[34] ibid at [314].

The majority's analysis was further influenced by the role accorded to the legislature in weighing conflicting interests in controversial policy areas and the presence of an assisted dying Bill before Parliament; irrespective of the proportionality of the ban, they viewed a s 4 declaration institutionally or constitutionally inappropriate.[35]

For the ECtHR, the Supreme Court's refusal to pronounce on the law's ECHR-compatibility did not breach applicants' Art 8 procedural rights, insofar as the substance of the claim had been heard, it was open to courts to find that sensitive matters were better left to Parliament, and the great weight attached by judges to Parliament's views: 'does not mean that they failed to carry out any balancing exercise'.[36]

A reform proposal was introduced in June 2016 in the Lords but made no progress. The scheme of the Assisted Dying Bill 2016–2017 was predicated on High Court authorisation of assistance for terminally ill adults 'reasonably expected to die within six months', who have decisional capacity and express a 'voluntary, clear, settled and informed wish' to die, in a declaration countersigned by two medical practitioners verifying those circumstances and that the person has been informed of palliative care options.[37]

The matter soon returned before the courts; post-*Nicklinson* case law contradicted the expectation that the intervening *Carter* judgment in Canada would prove influential in other common law jurisdictions.[38]

D. The *Conway* Litigation

The 2017 challenge to SA 1961, s 2(1) in *Conway* differed from *Nicklinson* in four respects: it regarded terminally ill patients with a six-month prognosis rather than individuals facing acute suffering indefinitely; the applicant was still physically capable of the final act required to end his life; a legislative scheme was offered as an alternative to the blanket ban; and no Bill was before Parliament on the matter.[39]

The High Court rejected the claim, citing precedent, Parliament's repeated reaffirmations of its position, and 'slippery slope' concerns.[40] The Court of Appeal agreed that Parliament was better placed to assess highly contested policy issues and conflicted evidence and that it had shown readiness to consider reform.[41] The appellate judgment also supported the finding that Mr Conway's scheme did

---

[35] See section VI.
[36] See *Nicklinson v UK* (2015) 61 EHHR SE7 at [84]–[85].
[37] HL Bill 42 Arts 1–3. See also the End of Life Assistance (Scotland) Bill 2010, discussed in Mason (2010) 'Assistance in dying or euthanasia? Comments on the End of Life Assistance (Scotland) Bill 2010' *Edinburgh LR* 493.
[38] See Attaran (2015) 'Unanimity on death and dignity – legalising physician-assisted dying in Canada' *New England Journal of Medicine* 2080 at p 2082.
[39] *R (Conway) v Secretary of State for Justice* [2017] EWHC 2447 (Admin).
[40] ibid at [115], [127].
[41] [2018] EWCA Civ 1431 at [186]–[189], [200], [205]–[206].

not adequately protect the vulnerable, failed to give proper weight to the sanctity of life, and could undermine trust between doctor and patient.[42]

In 2018, the Supreme Court dismissed Mr Conway's application for permission to appeal, adducing that his claim had insufficient prospects of success.[43] It did not engage in any substantive analysis, merely noting that judges' opinions differed as to whether the absolute ban is a justified interference with Convention rights, and, if so, whether it is appropriate to make a declaration to that effect. Considering the four-year timespan lapsed since, in *Nicklinson*, the court had expressed confidence in Parliament's reconsideration of the law, and the different factual and legal matrix in *Conway*, it may have been in the public interest to allow the debate to continue, informed by the insights of the highest judicial authority.

E. The Latest Challenges: *T* and *Newby*

R (T) v Secretary of State for Justice[44] and *Newby*[45] further tested the resilience of the British ban. Unlike Mr Conway, Mr T suffered from multiple system atrophy and his death was not foreseeable in the immediate future; he wished to be able to die safely, painlessly and with dignity. In deciding on a preliminary issue regarding evidence, the High Court indicated that it was bound by the intervening *Conway* decision in the Court of Appeal and that Mr T's position was not sufficiently different.[46] Permission to lodge a 'leapfrog' appeal to the Supreme Court was denied as premature.[47] As the post-script to the judgment notes, after its circulation to the parties the claimant travelled to Switzerland with assistance to end his life.

In 2019, the *Newby* case cemented the judiciary's reluctance to take a stand on assisted dying. Citing *Conway* and *Nicklinson*, the High Court held that: 'the courts lack legitimacy and expertise on moral (as opposed to legal) questions'.[48] Not only was Parliament seen as the appropriate forum for controversial ethical questions,[49] but the ruling marked a further retreat on the issue of justiciability:

> [42] [T]here are some questions which, plainly and simply, cannot be 'resolved' by a court as no objective, single, correct answer can be said to exist. ... The private views of judges on such moral and political questions are irrelevant, and spring from no identifiable legal principle.

The *Newby* case included a novel submission: the law prompted the applicant to take his life prematurely before reaching the stage where unassisted suicide

---

[42] ibid at [204].
[43] *R (Conway) v Secretary of State for Justice* [2018] UNSC B1 at [7]–[8].
[44] *R (T) v Secretary of State for Justice* [2018] EWHC 2615 (Admin).
[45] *R (Newby) v Secretary of State for Justice* [2019] EWHC 3118 (Admin).
[46] [2018] EWHC 2615 (Admin) at [22].
[47] ibid at [25]–[26].
[48] [2019] EWHC 3118 (Admin) at [40].
[49] ibid at [38], [43], [50].

became impossible. For the High Court, the considerations on which Art 8 claims failed under *Conway* also applied to Art 2.[50]

Although *Nicklinson* appeared to be 'a final warning for Parliament to act,'[51] the focus on procedural objections to adjudicating assisted dying claims in subsequent case law suggests that a reappraisal of the matter by the judiciary is unlikely in the near future. The open-ended approach in *Nicklinson* was replaced by the view that assisted dying policy is not governed by legal principles and it would be inappropriate for courts to decide instead of Parliament.

II. The Canadian Assisted Dying Reform: Striking a Fair(er) Balance?

Before June 2016, Canada's approach to assisted dying mirrored the UK's SA 1961. Whilst suicide was decriminalised in 1972,[52] assisters incurred criminal liability as a result of the combined operation of two Criminal Code provisions: s 241(b) made it an offence to aid or abet a person in committing suicide and s 14 established that no person could consent to death being inflicted on them. Legislative reform was triggered, however, by legal challenges under the Canadian Charter of Rights and Freedoms ('the Charter').

A. The *Rodriguez* Litigation

A first constitutional challenge was brought in 1993 in *Rodriguez v British Colombia*,[53] and the Canadian Supreme Court upheld the absolute ban on assisted dying for reasons similar to those underpinning UK rulings. The appellant, afflicted by amyotrophic lateral sclerosis with a prognosis of 2–14 months, expected to rapidly lose her ability to swallow, speak and move unassisted, and thereafter become unable to breathe or eat without medical equipment. She wished that, when she could no longer enjoy life, a physician be permitted to provide the technical means enabling her to die when she chose. She unsuccessfully sought a declaration that s 241(b) of the Criminal Code breached her Charter rights under s 7 (life, liberty and security of the person), s 12 (protection against cruel treatment) and s 15(1) (non-discrimination).[54]

---

[50] ibid at [49].

[51] Davis and Finlay (2015) 'Would judicial consent for assisted dying protect vulnerable people?' *British Medical Journal* h4437 p 2.

[52] The provision criminalising attempted suicide (s 238 Criminal Code 1892, SC 1892, c 29) was repealed by the Criminal Law Amendment Act 1972, SC 1972, c 13.

[53] *Rodriguez v British Columbia (AG)* [1993] 3 SCR 519. See Freedman (1994) 'The Rodriguez case: sticky questions and slippery answers' *McGill LJ* 644.

[54] [1993] 3 SCR 519 at pp 530–31.

Unlike the first British assisted dying ruling, *Rodriguez* recognised the ban's interference with fundamental rights; personal security in s 7 was found to encompass: 'personal autonomy, at least … the right to make choices concerning one's own body, control over one's physical and psychological integrity, and basic human dignity'.[55] The court conceded that, by depriving the appellant of autonomy over her person, s 241(b) caused her physical pain and psychological stress which impinged on the security of her person.[56] Nonetheless, in a markedly split decision, the court found that the interference was not contrary to the principles of fundamental justice, which require a fair balance between state and individual interests. The prohibition aimed to protect vulnerable persons who might be induced to commit suicide and reflected the state's policy in upholding the value of human life, grounded in society's fundamental belief in the sanctity of life.[57] Additionally, a similar prohibition was the norm in most Western democracies.[58] As regards the alleged s 12 violation, 'treatment' required more active state process, rather than a mere prohibition on certain conduct.[59] Finally, the court deemed it preferable not to pronounce on the scope of s 15, but to assume that it was infringed, as any infringement was justified under s 1: the prohibition was rationally connected to the objective of protecting, and maintaining respect for, human life, and no halfway measure could achieve it; there was no assurance that an exception could limit assisted death to patients who genuinely desired it.[60] The majority also accepted that, in this contentious morals-laden area, Parliament had to be afforded flexibility; as long as the Government had reasonable grounds to believe that the blanket ban was minimally impairing, it was not the courts' role to speculate whether an alternative was preferable.[61]

For the dissenters, however, the legislative scheme infringed s 7 by placing an arbitrary limit on the autonomy of individuals physically unable to end their lives;[62] nor was that infringement justified under s 1, as the objective of eliminating abuse was already addressed by criminal law and could be supplemented by the condition of court authorisation.[63] Moreover, s 241(b) discriminated against those physically disabled, limiting their capacity to make fundamental decisions about their lives based on an irrelevant personal characteristic; slippery slope concerns could not justify the over-reach of the ban, which went beyond the vulnerable and caught situations of free consent.[64]

---

[55] ibid at p 588 (per Sopinka J).
[56] ibid at p 589.
[57] ibid at p 595.
[58] ibid at p 605.
[59] ibid at pp 611–12.
[60] ibid at pp 612–14.
[61] ibid at pp 614–15.
[62] ibid at pp 620–21 (per McLachlin J).
[63] ibid at p 617.
[64] ibid at pp 549–69 (per Lamer CJ).

B. The *Carter* Litigation

In 2015, the momentous *Carter v Canada* ruling reversed the *Rodriguez* position and held that s 241(b) deprived competent adults who suffered intolerably, due to a grievous and irremediable medical condition, of their constitutional rights under s 7 of the Charter.[65] The right to life was found to be engaged whenever: 'the law or state action imposes death or an increased risk of death on a person, either directly or indirectly'.[66] The Supreme Court accepted that the blanket ban on MAiD amounted to indirect deprivation of life, insofar as: 'it ha[d] the effect of forcing some individuals to take their own lives prematurely, for fear that they would be incapable of doing so when they reached the point where suffering was intolerable'.[67] The rights to liberty and security of the person were also affected, as the prohibition raised concerns about autonomy and quality of life.[68] An individual's response to a grievous and irremediable medical condition was critical to their dignity and autonomy; the impugned prohibition denied them the right to make decisions concerning their bodily integrity and medical care, trenching on their liberty.[69] Moreover: 'by leaving them to endure intolerable suffering, it impinge[d] on their security of the person';[70] this finding echoes the unsuccessful submission in *Pretty* that the assisted dying ban amounted to inhuman and degrading treatment.

The court concluded that the prohibition infringed Charter rights in a manner inconsistent with the principles of fundamental justice. The ban achieved its objective, namely: 'to protect vulnerable persons from being induced to commit suicide at a time of weakness',[71] and thus it did not deprive individuals arbitrarily of their rights.[72] However, it caught people outside the class of intended protected persons and therefore was overbroad; the limitation placed on those individuals' rights was not connected to the objective.[73] Given this conclusion, the court found it unnecessary to decide whether the prohibition also violated the principle against gross disproportionality.[74] Having ascertained a breach of s 7, the court also found it unnecessary to consider whether the prohibition deprived physically disabled persons of their right to equal treatment under s 15.[75]

---

[65] [2015] 1 SCR 331.
[66] ibid at [62].
[67] ibid at [57].
[68] ibid at [62].
[69] ibid at [64], [66], [68].
[70] ibid at [66].
[71] ibid at [75]–[78].
[72] ibid at [84].
[73] ibid at [85]–[88].
[74] ibid at [89]–[90].
[75] ibid at [93].

The court further determined that the ban not was saved by s 1 of the Charter. Although it was prescribed by law, which had a: 'pressing and substantial objective',[76] the limiting measure was not proportionate to the objective:

> [109] The trial judge made no palpable and overriding error in concluding, on the basis of evidence from scientists, medical practitioners, and others who are familiar with end-of-life decision-making in Canada and abroad, that a permissive regime with properly designed and administered safeguards was capable of protecting vulnerable people from abuse and error.

The Supreme Court endorsed the trial judge's finding that: 'vulnerability can be assessed on an individual basis, using the procedures that physicians apply in their assessment of informed consent and decisional capacity in the context of medical decision-making more generally'.[77] Consequently, the absolute prohibition was not minimally impairing.[78] Having reached that conclusion, the court found it unnecessary to weigh the impact of the restriction on Charter rights against its beneficial effects for the greater public good.[79]

Without purporting to legislate, the Supreme Court provided several parameters for reform in wording the remedy afforded to the applicants:

> [127] The appropriate remedy is therefore a declaration that s. 241(b) and s. 14 of the Criminal Code are void insofar as they prohibit physician-assisted death for *a competent adult person* who (1) *clearly consents to the termination of life*; and (2) has a *grievous and irremediable medical condition* (including an illness, disease or disability) that *causes enduring suffering that is intolerable to the individual* in the circumstances of his or her condition.[80] 'Irremediable', it should be added, does not require the patient to undertake treatments that are not acceptable to the individual.

The court recognised the systemic nature of the offending law by issuing a declaration of invalidity, suspended for 12 months,[81] rather than a free-standing constitutional exemption.

In January 2016, the federal Government obtained a four-month extension of the suspension of invalidity to compensate for the interruption of legislative work between August and December 2015 caused by federal elections.[82] In *Carter v Canada (No 2)*, the Supreme Court, while acknowledging the delay, made the order reluctantly:

> [2] To suspend a declaration of the constitutional invalidity of a law is an extraordinary step, since its effect is to maintain an unconstitutional law in breach of the constitutional

---

[76] ibid at [96].
[77] ibid at [116]–[117].
[78] ibid at [121].
[79] ibid at [122].
[80] Emphasis added.
[81] ibid at [126]–[128].
[82] *Carter v Canada (AG) (No 2)* [2016] 1 SCR 13.

rights of members of Canadian society. To extend such a suspension is even more problematic. The appellants point to the severe harm caused to individuals by an extension.

The decision further granted Quebec's request to be exempted from the suspension, having already adopted an Act Respecting End-of-Life Care under its
concurrent health jurisdiction. The court saw no need: 'to unfairly prolong the
suffering of those who meet the clear [*Carter*] criteria', and Quebec's exemption:
'[rose] concerns of fairness and equality across the country'; consequently, it
permitted those who wished to seek MAiD during the extension period to apply
to the superior court of their jurisdiction for relief.[83]

C. Parliament's Response

The suspension gave Parliament an opportunity to amend the law to cure the
incompatibility. The new s 241.2(1) of the Criminal Code allows MAiD if several
conditions are cumulatively met: the patient is an adult entitled to health care
services in Canada, he or she has a grievous and irremediable medical condition,
made a voluntary request without external pressure, and gave informed consent to
receiving MAiD after being advised of options to relieve suffering, including palliative care. The 'grievous and irremediable medical condition' criterion is satisfied
if the four factors in s 241.2(2) are present: (a) the patient has a serious and incurable illness, disease or disability; (b) he or she is in an advanced state of irreversible
decline in capability; (c) that illness, disease, disability or state of decline causes
enduring physical or psychological suffering that is intolerable to the patient and
cannot be relieved under conditions the patient considers acceptable; and (d) the
patient's natural death has become reasonably foreseeable, taking into account all
his or her medical circumstances, without a specific prognosis on how long they
have left to live. Legal safeguards include two witnesses attesting to the patient's
written request, two medical opinions, a 10-day waiting period, and reiteration of
consent immediately prior to receiving assistance.

By limiting eligibility to patients whose death is already foreseeable, Bill C-14
narrowed the categories granted access to MAiD when compared to *Carter*.
A person such as the *Re H.S.* claimant, who refused to live her life sedated and
semi-conscious to escape pain,[84] qualified under the *Carter* criteria, but may be
ineligible under s 241.2(2). Stewart aptly queried the constitutionality of s 241.2(2):
by condemning persons who meet all criteria except 'foreseeable death' to suffer
indefinitely, the restriction is out of sync with the object of the law (allowing
individuals to end permanent suffering) and hence grossly disproportionate.[85]

---

[83] ibid at [6].
[84] See *Re H.S.* [2016] ABQB 121 at [116]: 'It is not acceptable to me to live sedated to the point of
unconsciousness until I choke on my own bodily fluids'.
[85] See Stewart (2018) 'Constitutional aspects of Canada's new medically-assisted dying law' in Ross
(ed), *Assisted death: Legal, social and ethical issues after Carter* 435 at pp 453–55.

Interestingly, two lower-court rulings finding that 'grievous and irremediable' in *Carter* did not mean 'terminal'[86] intervened as Bill C-14 was progressing through Parliament, casting doubt on its constitutionality before it became law.[87] Nonetheless, Rahimi predicted that challenges to Bill C-14 would fail, relying on the finding in *R v O'Connor*[88] and *R v Mills*[89] that Parliament can alter common-law standards established in declarations of invalidity as long as its approach remains constitutional; Bill C-14's reconciliation of s 7 rights with the protection of the vulnerable, albeit not identical to that in *Carter*, could be seen as a permissible balancing act.[90]

Unsurprisingly, constitutional challenges to the new MAiD regulation, in particular *Lamb* and *Truchon*, have already targeted s 241.2(2)(d).[91] In *Lamb*, expert evidence before the British Colombia Court showed the expansive interpretation given by doctors to the 'reasonably foreseeable' requirement, encompassing cases of refusal of life-prolonging care, and the applicant, who seemingly qualified, requested that the case be adjourned.[92] However, in *Truchon*, the Quebec Superior Court ruled s 241.2(2)(d) invalid.[93] It suspended the invalidity for six months to allow provincial and federal legislators to amend the law, while affording the applicants constitutional exemptions. The Supreme Court will not have an opportunity to express its views, as the federal and Quebec Governments decided not to appeal,[94] a choice criticised as allowing one judge excessive power to undo what Parliament deemed best for society.[95] The Quebec Superior Court agreed

[86] *Canada (AG) v E.F.* [2016] ABCA 155 (Court of Appeal of Alberta) and *I.J. v Canada (AG)* [2016] ONSC 3380 (Ontario Superior Court of Justice).

[87] See Nicolaides and Hennigar (2018) 'Carter conflicts: The Supreme Court of Canada's impact on medical assistance in dying policy' p 320 in Macfarlane (ed) *Policy change, courts and the Canadian Constitution*.

[88] [1995] 4 SCT 411.

[89] [1999] 3 SCR 668.

[90] Rahimi (2017) 'Assisted death in Canada: An exploration of the constitutionality of Bill C-14' *Saskatchewan LR* 457 at p 480. Justifying the cautious federal response to *Carter*, see Lemmens et al (2017) 'Why Canada's medical assistance in dying legislation should be C(h)arter compliant and what it may help to avoid' *McGill JL & Health* S61.

[91] *Lamb v Canada (AG)* 2017 BCSC 1802; *Truchon c Procureur général du Canada* 2019 QCCS 3792. See McMorrow (2018) 'MAID in Canada? Debating the constitutionality of Canada's new medical assistance in dying law' *Queen's LJ* 69 at pp 81–87.

[92] See https://bccla.org/news/2019/09/release-b-c-supreme-court-adjourns-b-c-civil-liberties-associations-assisted-dying-case; Downie (2019) 'Two major legal developments in the space of a week on Canada's medical assistance in dying laws could help more Canadians end their suffering' *Policy Options*, available at https://policyoptions.irpp.org/magazines/september-2019/a-watershed-month-for-medical-assistance-in-dying.

[93] 2019 QCCS 3792 at [741].

[94] See www.ahbl.ca/truchon-v-procureur-general-du-canada-superior-court-of-quebec-finds-limiting-access-to-medical-assistance-in-dying-maid-to-end-of-life-unconstitutional/?utm_source=Mondaq&utm_medium=syndication&utm_campaign=LinkedIn-integration.

[95] See Lemmens and Jacobs, 'The latest medical assistance in dying decision needs to be appealed: Here's why', *The Conversation* (24 October 2019), available at https://theconversation.com/the-latest-medical-assistance-in-dying-decision-needs-to-be-appealed-heres-why-124955.

to extend the deadline to 11 July 2020.[96] A further five-month extension of the suspension was requested by the federal Government in June 2020, due to the Covid-19 pandemic's disruption of parliamentary proceedings.[97]

An amendment of federal legislation, as opposed to the inapplicability of s 241.2(2)(d) in Quebec, would achieve legal certainty and a uniform MAiD regime in all provinces. The repeal of s 241.2(2)(d) would bring Canada's law closer to more liberal MAiD statutes, such as the Belgian and Dutch ones,[98] which include those suffering intolerably from long-term, but not fatal, conditions; that category might arguably benefit the most from choosing the time of their death. O'Reilly and Hogeboom highlight further controversial restrictions in Canadian law when compared to other jurisdictions: the absence of provision for advance directives for individuals likely to lose their ability to consent in the near future,[99] the ineligibility of mature minors[100] and persons complaining of acute mental rather than physical suffering.[101] von Tigerstrom argued that the failure to provide for advance consent to MAiD (by contrast with the option of advance directives to withdraw/withhold life-saving treatment) might be overbroad, since it condemns some individuals to intolerable suffering without justification, and might violate the right to life, as individuals who risk losing competence or capacity to communicate are pressurised into premature suicide.[102] Intrinsically inconsistent end-of-life legislation (permitting advance directives in respect of life-support withdrawal, but not MAiD) may affect fundamental rights disproportionately.[103] Some of these objections emerged before the enactment of Bill C-14, in the course of proceedings under *Carter (No 2)*, putting parliamentarians on notice.

---

[96] See https://globalnews.ca/news/6618538/quebec-ottawa-four-months-assisted-dying-law.

[97] See www.cbc.ca/news/politics/maid-assisted-dying-lametti-1.5607681.

[98] See Luzon (2019) 'The practice of euthanasia and assisted suicide meets the concept of legalization' *Criminal Law and Philosophy* 329 at pp 329–31; Jackson (2012) 'In favour of the legalisation of assisted dying' pp 62–66 in Jackson and Keown (eds) *Debating euthanasia*; Mishara and Weisstub (2013) 'Premises and evidence in the rhetoric of assisted suicide and euthanasia' *International JL & Psychiatry* 427; Hillyard and Dombrink (2001) *Dying right: The death with dignity movement* pp 211–34; Cormack (2000) 'Euthanasia and assisted suicide in the post-Rodriguez era: Lessons from foreign jurisdictions' *Osgoode Hall LJ* 591.

[99] On advance directives, see du Bois-Pedain (2007) 'Is there a human right to die' pp 78–81 in Brooks-Gordon et al (eds) *Death rites and rights*. The main objection is that incompetent patients having made decisions based on value judgments might enjoy unanticipated experiences (ibid at p 80).

[100] See MacIntosh (2016) 'Carter, medical aid in dying, and mature minors' *McGill JL & Health* S1, arguing that the exclusion of mature minors from the MAiD regime violates the Charter.

[101] O'Reilly and Hogeboom (2017) 'The framing and implementation of law: Assisted death in Canada' *Journal of Parliamentary and Political Law* 699 at pp 711–14.

[102] von Tigerstrom (2015) 'Consenting to physician-assisted death: Issues arising from Carter v. Canada (Attorney General)' *Saskatchewan LR* 233.

[103] See *mutatis mutandis Costa and Pavan v Italy* (54270/10, 28 August 2012); legislation prohibiting embryo pre-implantation diagnosis for sufferers of cystic fibrosis, whilst permitting abortion if the foetus had that condition, violated Art 8 ECHR.

D. Applying the *Carter* Criteria to Requests for Individual Constitutional Exemption

During the period of extension of the suspension of invalidity following *Carter (No 2)*, Canadian courts have addressed questions of capacity to consent, vulnerability and indirect coercion in several cases.

In *H.S. v Canada*, the Alberta Court of Queen's Bench extracted five criteria from para 127 of *Carter*, also endorsed by the Superior Court of Ontario's 2016 decision in *A.B. v Canada*: (1) the person seeking authorisation is a competent adult; (2) he or she has a grievous and irremediable medical condition; (3) the condition is causing intolerable suffering; (4) the suffering cannot be alleviated by any treatment he or she finds acceptable; and (5) he or she clearly consents to the termination of life.[104] The Superior Court of Ontario further defined 'grievous medical condition' as a condition that greatly interferes with that person's quality of life.[105] Importantly, in *E.F.*, the Alberta Court of Appeal clarified that the constitutional exemption granted in *Carter (No 2)* does not require the person's medical condition to be terminal.[106]

The *O.P. v Canada* ruling rejected the argument that, after the expiration of the suspension of invalidity, physician-assisted dying had become permissible without court order even if Parliament had failed to legislate; the rule of law and the protection of the vulnerable required judicial oversight until a legislative response was available.[107]

E. Applying the Amended Criminal Code

Remarkably, the new law does not require judicial intervention. As noted by the Superior Court of Ontario in its 2017 *A.B.* decision:[108]

> [62] Bill C-14's legislative history (and its language) demonstrates Parliament's intention that the physicians and nurse practitioners who have been asked to provide medical

---

[104] *Re H.S.* [2016] ABQB 121 at [94]; *A.B. v Canada (AG)* [2016] ONSC 1912 at [22]. See further [2016] ONSC 1912 at [23]–[28], discussing these criteria.

[105] [2016] ONSC 1912 at [25]. See also *I.J. v Canada (AG)* [2016] ONSC 3380.

[106] *Canada (AG) v E.F.* [2016] ABCA 155. Before Bill C-14 was adopted, consensus that terminal illness should not be an access criterion was evidenced by reports of the Provincial-Territorial Expert Advisory Group on Physician Assisted Dying (www.health.gov.on.ca/en/news/bulletin/2015/docs/eagreport_20151214_en.pdf) and Special Joint Committee on Physician-Assisted Dying, a federal parliamentary body (www.documentdoud.org/documents/2721231-Report-of-the-Special-Joint-Committee). See Schuklenk (2016) 'Canada on course to introduce permissive assisted dying regime' *Journal of Medical Ethics* 490 at p 491.

[107] *O.P. v Canada (AG)* [2016] ONSC 3956.

[108] *A.B. v Canada (AG)* 2017 ONSC 3759. In the UK, the Supreme Court has shifted the decision-making process regarding the withdrawal of clinically assisted nutrition and hydration from patients in a persistent vegetative state from courts to medical professionals; see *NHS Trust v Y and Another* [2018] UKSC 46.

assistance in dying are exclusively responsible for deciding whether the *Code's* criteria are satisfied without any pre-authorization from the courts.

This solution followed the 2015 report of the Provincial-Territorial Expert Advisory Group on Physician-Assisted Dying.[109] Criticising its recommendations, Chan and Sommerville noted that judicial authorisation of MAiD was seen as an essential safeguard by Lord Neuberger in *Nicklinson* and McLachlin J in her dissent in *Rodriguez*, as well as by the *Carter (No 2)* interim regime of individual exemptions, and failing to generalise it in the permanent regulatory regime was unjustified.[110]

The *A.B.* ruling also clarified the meaning of 'reasonably foreseeable death' in s 241.2(2)(d), noting that an elderly person: 'in an advanced state of incurable, irreversible, worsening illness with excruciating pain and no quality of life' was eligible for assistance.[111] It also emphasised that the natural death referred to in the Criminal Code: 'need not be connected to a particular terminal disease or condition and rather is connected to all of a particular person's medical circumstances'.[112] In addition, it explained the role of the courts under the amended legislation: whilst they may neither decide for the doctors if a patient qualifies nor pre-determine criminal liability and interfere with prosecutorial discretion, they can nevertheless interpret civil law;[113] this interpretative role was particularly important given the novelty of, and public interest in, the assisted dying regime and the gravity of the issues at stake.[114]

III. Principled Concerns: Inviolability-of-Life vs Self-Determination

The starting point of judicial deliberations over legalising MAiD was, in both jurisdictions, whether the law should be subordinated to grand moral principles like sanctity of life or embrace moral neutrality, whilst protecting the vulnerable. Admittedly, the abrogation of the crime of suicide did not establish the law's preference for self-determination over sanctity of life. Finnis argued that, although some British judges saw decriminalisation of suicide as a shift towards autonomy, its objective, found in s 2(1)'s legislative history, lay elsewhere: the offence was not an effective deterrent, it cast unwarranted stigma on the deceased's family, and led to the prosecution of patients recovering from suicide attempts.[115]

---

[109] Cit fn 106.
[110] Chan and Sommerville (2016) 'Converting the "right to life" to the "right to physician-assisted suicide and euthanasia": An analysis of Carter v Canada (Attorney-General), Supreme Court of Canada' *Medical LR* 143 at pp 172–73, citing [2014] UKSC 38 at [108] and [1993] 3 SCR 519 at p 627.
[111] [2017] ONSC 3759 at [87].
[112] ibid at [81].
[113] ibid at [63]–[67].
[114] ibid at [73].
[115] See Finnis (2015) 'A British "Convention right" to Assistance in Suicide?' *LQR* 1 at p 5; *Pretty* [2001] UKHL 61 at [35].

Sopinka J, delivering the majority judgment in *Rodriguez*, similarly viewed decriminalisation of suicide in Canada as recognising the non-legal roots and solutions of suicide, rather than as evidence of consensus on the prevalence of autonomy.[116] However, medical law in both countries unquestionably indicates that society cannot impose the sanctity-of-life belief on individuals over their autonomy rights.

A. Autonomy and Compassion in Medical Law: Refusal of Life Support, Children's Medical Treatment and Involuntary Euthanasia for Incompetent Adults

English common law recognises, as vividly captured by Lord Goff in *Bland*, that: 'the principle of the sanctity of human life must yield to the principle of self-determination'.[117] Competent patients have an absolute right to refuse life-saving treatment. They can do so for irrational reasons or no reasons at all.[118] Continuing to provide life-sustaining treatment to patients against their wishes is also unlawful.[119] Additionally, incompetent patients are entitled to the respect of advance refusal of treatment expressed while they were competent.[120] Through the Mental Capacity Act 2005, Parliament: 'has afforded a framework wherein persons in situations far less dire than those of Mr Lamb and Mr Nicklinson can choose to end their lives'.[121] Attempts to justify SA 1961, s 2(1) by reference to the absolute inviolability of life would be incongruous.

Canadian case law has also established that patients have a right to refuse life-saving treatment.[122] Courts: 'have rejected a vitalist or "life-at-any-cost" philosophy, and have accepted the legal option of mentally competent free individuals to risk preventable death rather than be compelled to live under conditions they find objectionable'.[123] Medical law requires physicians to respect patients' decision to request removal of life support (eg feeding tube, respirator or dialysis) even where they do not deem it in the patients' best interests.[124] As summarised

---

[116] [1993] 3 SCR 519 at pp 597–98.

[117] *Airedale NHS Trust v Bland* [1993] AC 789 at p 864.

[118] *Re T (Adult: Refusal of Treatment)* [1993] Fam 95.

[119] *Re B (Adult: Refusal of Treatment)* [2002] EWHC 429 (Fam).

[120] See Michalowski (2005) 'Advance refusals of life-sustaining medical treatment: The relativity of an absolute right' *Modern LR* 958.

[121] Coggon (2017) 'Judgment 2 – *R (on the Application of Nicklinson and Another) v Ministry of Justice* [2014] UKSC 38' p 213 in Smith et al (eds) *Ethical judgments. Rewriting medical law*.

[122] See *British Columbia (AG) v Astaforoff* [1984] 6 WWR 385; *Malette v Schulman* [1990] 72 OR (2d) 417; *Nancy B v Hôtel-Dieu de Québec* [1992] RJQ 361.

[123] Dickens (1993) 'Medically assisted death: Nancy B v. Hôtel-Dieu de Québec' *McGill LJ* 1053 at p 1065.

[124] Schafer (2013) 'Physician assisted suicide: The great Canadian euthanasia debate' *International JL&Psychiatry* 522 at p 526.

in *Rodriguez*: 'To impose medical treatment on one who refuses it constitutes battery and our common law has recognized the right to demand that medical treatment which would extend life be withheld or withdrawn.'[125]

Using inviolability-of-life arguments to reject assisted dying claims is also inconsistent with the law's approach to withdrawal of life support from children with extreme medical conditions. In *Charlie Gard*[126] and *Alfie Evans*,[127] authorising hospitals to discontinue treatment against the parents' wishes, the UK's Supreme Court implicitly recognised that there is a minimum quality of life below which it is not in the child's best interests to continue living. In *Charlie Gard*, it also accepted that prolonging the child's suffering without realistic prospects of improvement exposed him to significant harm. *Alfie Evans* went further: 'it is not lawful for [doctors] to give treatment to [a child] which is not in his interests' even if continued treatment does not cause significant harm.[128] Strikingly, parents, doctors and courts can decide whether the life awaiting sick children is worth living; indeed, courts can authorise termination of treatment even if parents view life support in their child's best interests. If third parties can decide for minor patients when illness reduces their quality of life to unacceptable levels, it appears irrational to prevent competent adults from deciding where that threshold lies for themselves.

Re A (Conjoined Twins)[129] casts further doubt on the law's absolute belief in the inviolability of human life. The compromise here was even greater: the hastened death of the weaker twin as a result of surgical separation aimed to secure the best interests of her sister (whose death was avoidable), not her own. For Lewis, the uniqueness of the case did not make it an authority for a defence of necessity in euthanasia cases; the death was inevitable and the act hastening it achieved net saving of life by avoiding another person's death.[130] However, if hastening death is exceptionally accepted as 'the lesser evil', and without the patient's consent, surely the patient ought to be permitted a similar judgment call for their person.

The law's approach to involuntary euthanasia for incompetent adults also undermines the inviolability-of-life justification for the ban on MAiD. In *Bland*, a

---

[125] [1993] 3 SCR 519 at p 588. On the right to refuse life-sustaining treatment see du Bois-Pedain, op cit fn 99 at p 77.

[126] See www.supremecourt.uk/cases/docs/charlie-gard-190617.pdf, refusing permission to appeal *Great Ormond Street Hospital v Yates, Gard and Gard* [2017] EWCA Civ 410. The ECtHR endorsed the decision; see *Gard v UK* (2017) 65 EHRR SE9.

[127] See www.supremecourt.uk/cases/docs/alfie-evans-reasons-200318.pdf, refusing permission to appeal *Evans and James v Alder Hey Children's NHS Foundation Trust, Alfie Evans* [2018] EWCA 984 (Civ).

[128] ibid at [16].

[129] *Re A (Children) (Conjoined Twins: Medical Treatment)* [2001] Fam 147.

[130] Lewis (2013) 'The failure of the defence of necessity as a mechanism of legal change on assisted dying in the common law world' pp 284–85 in Baker and Horder, *The sanctity of life and the criminal law*.

case concerning an adult in permanent vegetative state (PVS), the court accepted that there is a threshold below which merely being alive procures individuals no participation in, or enjoyment of, life.[131] If the law allows compassionate termination of life at the request of third parties (family/doctors), a fortiori competent patients should be able to decide where they draw the line between a life worth living and one offering no gratification. As Lord Neuberger observed in *Nicklinson*, withdrawal of life support from another is: 'a more drastic interference in that person's life and a more extreme moral step' than authorising the assistance in dying sought by the patient.[132]

PVS patients' right to die is based on the assumption that they would refuse the indignities to which the deterioration of their bodies subjects them, albeit unconscious and unperturbed by them. Paradoxically, lucid individuals trapped in decaying bodies, capable of expressing their wish to die, are left – powerless – to endure those indignities. Equally ironic is another judicial inconsistency: given the intense 'anguish of awaiting execution', exposing convicts to the 'death-row phenomenon' was recognised as psychological ill-treatment;[133] forcing patients to live with the spectre of a painful and undignified death was not deemed such.

B. The Relative 'Absoluteness' of the Right to Life

A rights-based version of inviolability-of-life arguments invokes the absolute nature of the right to life under Art 2 ECHR. According to Finnis: 'Such absoluteness not only eliminates margin of appreciation but entails obligations to avoid creating any "real risk" of violation by *anyone*'.[134] This claim is unsupported by the text of Art 2 or its jurisprudential interpretation. By contrast with the unqualified prohibition of ill-treatment (Art 3) or slavery (Art 4(1)), Art 2(2) permits intentional deprivation of life and potentially lethal use of force (eg to defend innocents against third-party violence) as long as they are 'no more than necessary'. Torturing criminals in a 'ticking bomb' scenario is unlawful;[135] killing

---

[131] [1993] AC 789. See Price (2009) 'What shape to euthanasia after Bland? Historical, contemporary and futuristic paradigms' *LQR* 142; Beyleveld and Brownsword (2001) *Human dignity in bioethics and biolaw* pp 244–54.

[132] [2015] AC 657 at [94]. For a comparative survey of case-law on refusal of life-saving treatment, parents' right to refuse treatment for children and guardians' decision-making powers for comatose adults, see Gorsuch (2006) *The future of assisted suicide and euthanasia* pp 181–215. On the distinction between active/passive euthanasia, ie killing/letting the patient die (eg injecting lethal substances versus withholding life-saving treatment), see Luzon, op cit fn 98 at p 333.

[133] See *Soering v UK* [1989] 11 EHRR 439 at [111].

[134] Finnis, op cit fn 115 at p 6 (original emphasis).

[135] See *Gäfgen v Germany* (2011) 52 EHRR 1; Bjorge (2011) 'Torture and "ticking bomb" scenarios' *LQR* 196 at p 199.

terrorists as a last-resort law-enforcement measure is not.[136] Absolute rights do not permit interferences, and the right enshrined in Art 2 does. Outside the human-rights context, Battin noted that: 'the intrinsic-wrongness-of-killing argument falls to its counterexamples of war and self-defence without adequate rebuttal'.[137]

Moreover, an individual has the *right* to life, not the *obligation* to exercise it; nor are states expected to compel individuals to exercise this right, much like the right to vote (Protocol 1, Art 3) does not oblige citizens to vote and does not require states to prevent electoral absenteeism. Finnis's suggestion that states must protect life against violation by anyone, including oneself, only applies, according to Strasbourg case law, to the narrow situation of individuals afflicted by mental disorders that include suicidal behaviour, where a limited duty of care arises. *Keenan v UK* established a mere obligation of conduct, not of result, for prison authorities in respect of mentally ill inmates, ie to take reasonable precautions to prevent suicide.[138] Importantly, in such cases, as Wicks noted, the duty to treat suicide as a risk to prevent, rather than as a choice to respect, stems from the fact that mental disorder may preclude autonomous choices.[139] More clearly dispositive of the issue, *Lambert v France* found legislation permitting end-of-life decisions ECHR-compliant.[140] It is also a well-established principle that the ECHR: 'must be read as a whole, and interpreted in such a way as to promote internal consistency and harmony between its various provisions'.[141] Art 2 cannot be interpreted as requiring states to coerce patients into receiving life-saving treatment, as this would clash with Art 8 obligations to protect physical self-determination and Art 9 respect for freedom of conscience; for that same reason, it cannot be seen as requiring states to force individuals to stay alive.

Coggon argued that a 'high-sounding moral principle' like the sanctity of life cannot justify restrictions on individual rights, and their rationale may only lie in the 'rights of others'.[142] This is particularly true of bans affecting bodily self-determination. To ground SA 1961, s 2(1) in a collective philosophical belief is tantamount to saying that patients like Mrs Pretty are compelled to endure death by suffocation because society (*rectius*, the majority) sees it preferable to hastened pain-free death. As Dworkin wrote: 'Making someone die in a way that others approve, but he believes a horrifying contradiction of his life, is a devastating, odious form of tyranny'.[143]

[136] See *McCann and Others v UK* (1995) 21 EHRR 97.
[137] Battin (2005) *Ending life: Ethics and the way we die* p 39.
[138] See *Keenan v UK* (2001) 33 EHRR 903.
[139] Wicks, op cit fn 6 at p 78.
[140] *Lambert v France* (2016) 62 EHRR 2.
[141] *Stec v UK* 43 EHRR 1027 at [48]; *Saadi v UK* (2007) 44 EHRR 50 at [62]; *Hirsi Jamaaa v Italy* (2012) 55 EHRR 21 at [171]; *Demir and Baykara v Turkey* (2009) 48 EHRR 54 at [66].
[142] Coggon, op cit fn 121 at p 211. On the inviolability-of-life principle see Keown (2012) *The law and ethics of medicine: Essays on the inviolability of human life* pp 3–22.
[143] Dworkin (1993) *Life's dominion: An argument about abortion and euthanasia* p 217.

C. The Moral Neutrality of Assisted Dying Legislation

British and Canadian highest courts have accepted that self-determination encompasses a right not to believe in the prevalence of sanctity-of-life considerations over dignity in dying[144] and avoiding incurable suffering. In the UK, post-*Pretty* case law rejected the sanctity-of-life justification for the ban, seen in competition with the principles of individual autonomy and human dignity.[145] In *Rodriguez*, the Canadian Supreme Court conceded that sanctity of life (understood in the secular sense that human life has intrinsic value), albeit a deeply rooted belief in society, does not prevail over liberty and security of the person; rather, it is: 'one of the values engaged' in MAiD deliberations.[146] Nothing in the case law suggests that the legalisation of MAiD sanctions any particular view on the value of life; the debate largely revolved around the risks of accommodating private opinion on human intervention with the natural course of life and death.[147]

Nicklinson accepted the moral neutrality of assisted dying legislation and adduced practical concerns about shielding the vulnerable from abuse. Papadopoulou thus noted a change in judicial attitudes since the robust support for the prohibition in *Pretty*: 'judges are now dealing not with whether the law should change, but with how the law could change'.[148] However, *Conway* marked a conservative retreat from that stance. The High Court reopened the sanctity-of-life debate and found that this principle could justify interferences with private life, being subsumed under the 'protection of morals' permitted by Art 8(2) ECHR.[149] The court warned against downplaying the sanctity-of-life principle where a person has six months left to live (Mr Conway's proposed threshold criterion for assisted dying).[150] The Court of Appeal also placed sanctity of life on an equal footing with other legitimate justifications (protecting the vulnerable, promoting trust between patients and doctors),[151] even if the judgment, like *Nicklinson* and *Carter*, focused on pragmatic 'slippery slope' arguments. Ethical concerns were revived in *Newby*, according to which: 'the court is not an appropriate forum for the discussion of the sanctity of life'.[152]

---

[144] According to Velleman (2015) *Beyond Price: Essays on birth and death* p 33 the phrase 'dying with dignity' is misleading, as '[t]he operative concept is undignified life, not dignified death'. However, both might be at stake: life in distressing circumstances and the foreseeable manner of death.

[145] See [2015] AC 657 (fn 1) at [199], [209], [358].

[146] [1993] 3 SCR 519 at pp 585–86.

[147] See also Heywood (2010) 'R. (on the application of Purdy) v DPP: clarification on assisted suicide' *LQR* 5 at p 6: 'Individuals may attach greater importance to certain lifestyle characteristics than others and that is their choice, in the same way that those who value the sanctity of life above all else make a conscious decision to do so. It is impossible to say either belief is right or wrong for the very reason that they are matters of private opinion'.

[148] Papadopoulou (2017) 'From Pretty to Nicklinson: Changing judicial attitudes to assisted dying' *European Human Rights LR* 298 at p 307.

[149] [2018] EWCA Civ 1431 at [47].

[150] ibid at [33]–[34].

[151] ibid at [61], [204].

[152] [2019] EWHC 3118 (Admin) at [50].

The moral neutrality of MAiD legislation, whereby states merely defer to individual moral beliefs, remains highly contested. Foster labelled MAiD 'government-endorsed suicide'.[153] White noted that, while the *Carter* plaintiffs invoked human dignity to claim end-of-life choice, intervening disability-advocate groups also relied on dignity to suggest that removing the ban would send the message that life with significant impairment is not worth living.[154] Such submissions overlook the fact that MAiD initiatives proceeded from disabled individuals, not the state, and the change they pursued was not the state's evaluation of what makes a life worth living, but everyone's right to make that subjective judgment for their person.

Similarly, in *Conway*, the Court of Appeal suggested that, to decide on the ban's proportionality, advances in palliative care to manage distressful symptoms had to be considered,[155] which underrated patients' subjective assessment of what constitutes satisfactory treatment. More sensibly, the new Canadian law takes palliative care options into account when assessing MAiD eligibility, not as a justification for a blanket ban. Significantly, under s 241.2(2) of the Criminal Code, the care available must be acceptable to the patient. Whether or not the treatment offers relief without excessively diminishing the patient's quality of life cannot be objectively determined by doctors or courts.

D. Killing and Letting Die: The Elusive Distinction

Sanctity-of-life reasoning also underpins the alleged moral distinction between acts and omissions. Its supporters condemn acts causing death (complicity in suicide), but condone fatal omissions (discontinuing life-sustaining treatment).[156] This distinction is largely artificial; in both cases, motivation (compassionate, ie relieve suffering), intention (implement patients' decision) and foreseeable consequence (patients' death) are identical.[157] For Cohn and Lynn, withdrawal of support is different from assisted dying because doctors' intent is to respect patients' wishes not to receive undesired treatment;[158] however, physicians providing MAiD are

---

[153] Foster (2018) 'The fatal flaws of assisted suicide' *The Human Life Review* 51 at p 58.

[154] White (2019) 'A role for human dignity under the Canadian Charter of Rights and Freedoms' p 320 in Albert – Daly – Macdonnell (eds) *The Canadian Constitution in transition.* According to Elliot (2018) 'Institutionalizing inequality: The physical criterion of assisted suicide' *Christian Bioethics* 7, laws making MAiD eligibility dependent on severe health deterioration degrade the very sick and dying, suggesting that their lives are not deemed worthwhile.

[155] See [2018] EWCA Civ 1431 at [177].

[156] See Huxtable (2007) *Euthanasia, ethics and the law: From conflict to compromise* p 12.

[157] See also Schafer, op cit fn 124 at p 526; Jackson, op cit fn 98 at pp 29–33; Meisel (2012) 'Physician-assisted suicide: A common law roadmap' pp 375–380 in Beauchamp et al (eds) *Contemporary issues in bioethics.* Unlike these authors, I do not consider the intention to be ending life.

[158] Cohn and Lynn (2002) 'Vulnerable people: Practical rejoinders to claims in favor of assisted suicide' p 247 in Foley and Hendin (eds) *The case against assisted suicide: For the right to end-of-life care.* Meisel similarly argued that the true justification for passively hastening death is: 'self-determination implemented through consent' (op cit fn 157 at p 380), but the same legitimises conduct actively hastening death.

equally animated by the intention to respect patients' wishes, not to bring about their death. Doctors/relatives offering assistance in dying have no autonomous intention to end life, they are instrumental to patients' decision, enabling them to exercise control over their body. In terms of moral responsibility for the death, the distinction between foresight (disconnecting ventilation with the knowledge that the patient will die) and intention (administering drugs that will cause the patient to die) is also tenuous.[159]

Even categorising conduct as (positive) act or (passive) omission is not straightforward. To differentiate between disconnecting the feeding tube and not supplying nutrients down the tube would be spurious.[160] Moreover, to classify the active removal of ventilatory support as *withholding* treatment (an omission) is semantically problematic, although admittedly it is possible to let die (of natural causes) through an act (terminating medical assistance).[161] In *Re A*, the Court of Appeal rejected the lower court's finding that surgical separation of conjoined twins, depriving the weaker one of vital sustenance, was akin to withdrawal of support, and hence an omission.[162] It is also worth noting that the law does not treat the rejection of life-sustaining treatment as suicide (otherwise doctors withdrawing life support would be guilty of assistance in suicide), but the distinction between refusal of treatment and self-starvation, which does constitute suicide, is feeble.[163]

Notwithstanding the flaws of the act/omission theory, respondent governments in right-to-die litigation have attempted to distinguish MAiD on this basis from withdrawal/non-provision of life-saving treatment. Both Supreme Courts received the argument with scepticism. They accepted that medical law prioritises self-determination over preservation of life as an absolute objective, and if a person cannot be coerced into treatment to save their life, the same autonomy should be recognised in relation to assisted dying. The two courts differed on whether curtailing self-determination rights was justified in order to protect the rights of others.

In *Conway*, however, the UK's Court of Appeal rationalised the law's permissive approach to withdrawal of treatment by distinguishing 'an act or omission which allows causes already present in the body to operate' from 'the introduction of an external agency of death'.[164] This dichotomy is equally unconvincing. Both allowing the disease to kill and introducing death-hasting substances result in the patient's death, and do so with foreknowledge, the moral authorship of the decision rests with the patient, and the motivation of those implementing it is

---

[159] See Smith (2012) *End-of-life decisions in medical care principles and policies for regulating the dying process* pp 78–84.
[160] See Huxtable, op cit fn 156 at p 6.
[161] See McGee (2015) 'Acting to let someone die' *Bioethics* 74.
[162] [2001] Fam 147 at pp 189, 215, 247–50.
[163] See Meisel (2004) *The right to die: The law of end-of-life decision-making* pp 12.14–12.24.
[164] [2018] EWCA Civ 1431 at [176]. For an analogous approach in Canada see [1993] 3 SCR 519 at pp 606–08 (per Sopinka J).

compassionate. Worryingly, the *Conway* justification gives credence to the ethics of 'allowing nature to follow its course'; suffice it to recall the infamous US cases involving 'faith healing' families, where parents refused to administer medication to their children for religious reasons, and children died from treatable illnesses.[165] They, too, allowed natural causes present in the body to follow their course; applying the *Conway* test, since parents introduced no external cause of death, their conduct was morally virtuous and legally acceptable. Kuhse and Singer highlighted the absurd consequences of the argument that letting die of natural causes is morally distinct from compassionate killing: if starving an infant to death or failing to treat a preventable infection merely allows nature to take its course, parents could ensure the death of unwanted children without being responsible for it.[166] They also criticised the oversimplification behind the conclusion that, when doctors refrain from treating patients, the latter's death is caused by nature: 'Both the illness and the omission are part of the "sum total of the conditions positive and negative taken together" which is the full causal account of the death'.[167]

E. Assisted Dying Bans: The Fundamental Rights Engaged

The same substantive debate led to a different conceptualisation of the rights engaged in Canada and the UK. Both countries recognise an individual entitlement to end-of-life convictions and decisions. However, autonomy, specifically bodily self-determination, is seen as a matter of privacy under Art 8 ECHR, whereas for the Canadian Charter it engages the right to liberty and personal security. There is, of course, no textually explicit 'privacy' right in the Charter; as in the US, effective recognition of a privacy right in Canadian law has been extracted from other textual sources.[168] The UK's acceptance of end-of-life decision-making as part of privacy rights was relatively recent and driven by the ECtHR. In Canada, the impetus for recognition of self-determination vis-à-vis the time and manner of one's death was purely domestic and dates back to *Rodriguez*, which preceded *Pretty v UK* by a decade.

Although euthanasia and assisted suicide are often used co-terminously, both *Nicklinson/Conway* and *Carter* drew an important agency-based distinction: assisted suicide does not involve deciding about a third-party's life; rather, it means

---

[165] See Lederman (1995) 'Understanding faith: When religious parents decline conventional medical treatment for their children' *Case Western Reserve LR* 891.

[166] Kuhse and Singer (2004) 'Killing and letting die' p 48 in Harris (ed) *Bioethics*. Omissions causing death can attract criminal liability (eg failure to provide children with food by those who owed them a duty of care); see *R v Gibbins and Proctor* (1918) 13 Crim App Rep 134, discussed in Biggs (2001) *Euthanasia, death with dignity and the law* p 51.

[167] ibid at p 50.

[168] See the discussions in the chapters by Beattie and Phillipson; Hatzis; and Taylor. On the various foundations of constitutional challenges to the criminalisation of MAiD in Canada, the UK and the US see Lewis (2007) *Assisted dying and legal change* pp 12–42.

empowering competent adults who, due to devastating disabilities, cannot implement their own decisions over their bodies.[169] Criticising *Carter*, Keown suggested that, if assistance to die benefits patients who suffer, the logical consequence is that it should be available to those who are mentally incompetent, because the duty of beneficence applies even where patients cannot consent.[170] This *reductio ad absurdum* seems based on a questionable interpretation of beneficence as an objective standard in situations of intractable suffering, whereas individual responses differ, and what makes compassionate assistance morally/legally permissible is the patient's own determination that assistance benefits *them*. Whether death is beneficial or harmful will depend on each patient's perception of their circumstances.[171] As recently recalled in a Court of Protection case, when deciding on life-sustaining treatment for incapacitous persons, their 'best interests' under the Mental Capacity Act 2005, s 4 depend on their ascertainable wishes, values and beliefs; the presumption in favour of prolongation of life is not absolute.[172] The judge's reflections on respect for personal autonomy in the face of severe illness, eroding quality of life, self-esteem and interpersonal relationships, could apply to MAiD requests as much as they did to advance directives on treatment:

> [47] He has made a practical, utilitarian calculation that life in these circumstances is not what he wants. ... this is not a case about choosing to die, it is about an adult's capacity to shape and control the end of his life. This is an important facet of personal autonomy ....

In addition to self-determination, the right to life featured prominently in *Carter* and was unsuccessfully invoked in *Conway*. Whilst the *Nicklinson* pleas came from individuals who could not end their lives unassisted, *Carter* regarded patients whose ability to end their lives was likely to be impaired in the near future and who felt pressurised into doing so prematurely. The Canadian Supreme Court agreed that this interfered with their right to life. Although Art 2 ECHR submissions were not before the *Nicklinson* court, that concern was expressed in Lord Neuberger's judgment: by forcing sufferers of degenerative diseases to die while they are still able to do so unassisted, the impugned prohibition 'indirectly cuts short their lives'.[173] Huxtable recalled cases where: 'this legal obstacle has prompted some patients to act alone, while they still could ..., one of whom made legal history after she suffocated herself with a plastic bag'.[174]

---

[169] Some distinguish between 'doctor-assisted suicide' (patient's self-administration of lethal drugs supplied by the doctor) and 'voluntary euthanasia' (drugs administered by the doctor at patient's request); see Otlowski (1997) *Voluntary euthanasia and the common law* pp 7–9. This chapter's reference to 'assisted dying' covers all assistance given to competent patients at their request to enable them to control the time and manner of their death (provision and/or administration of drugs, assistance to travel to clinics lawfully offering MAiD).

[170] See Keown (2018) '*Carter*: A stain on Canadian jurisprudence?' p 16 in Ross (ed), op cit fn 85.

[171] See also Smith, op cit fn 159 at p 127.

[172] *Barnsley Hospital NHS Foundation Trust v MSP* [2020] EWCOP 26 at [20]–[28], citing *Aintree University Hospital NHS Trust v James* [2013] UKSC 67 at [26], *Briggs v Briggs* [2017] 4 WLR 37 at [7].

[173] [2015] AC 657 at [96].

[174] Huxtable, op cit fn 156 at p 58.

Submissions based on the prohibition of inhuman and degrading treatment regrettably failed in English courts. As Mullock argued, the law should balance the protection of the vulnerable against the "'cruelty" of those unwillingly trapped in life to live on'.[175] Even in Canada, the law is yet to fully recognise, under the right to protection against cruel treatment, a moral imperative to end human suffering upon request. Albeit not requiring terminal illness or a specified prognosis, Bill C-14 reserved eligibility for assistance to cases of reasonably foreseeable death; further reform is, however, expected after *Truchon*. The latest British Assisted Dying Bill also excluded individuals who are not terminally ill but who suffer from constant pain, with no acceptable palliative care available, and are dependent on others in ways they consider undignified.[176] Such patients arguably have an even greater need to control the timing of their death; prompting this category to seek disturbing alternatives to MAiD appears irrational. Moreover, since patients can request withdrawal of treatment to passively hasten death without being terminally ill, no sound justification exists for making it a pre-condition for requests to actively hasten death.[177]

A related concern, underexplored in litigation but dramatically manifest after the defeat of autonomy claims in *Nicklinson*, is the type of death available in the absence of medical assistance. After losing his High Court battle, Mr Nicklinson embarked upon self-starvation, shortened by pneumonia; Martin engaged in an aborted attempt at self-starvation after the High Court judgment.[178] The blanket ban on MAiD forces competent adults having reached a settled decision to end their lives due to constant suffering to resort to agonising suicide methods (sometimes botched attempts, leaving them worse off) instead of a controlled medical procedure. Jackson argued that everyone is entitled to experience a 'good death', which may require assistance in dying, and that in a secular society, recognising different moral views, individuals should not be compelled to deaths they find intolerable.[179] Lord Goff also noted the law's hypocrisy in allowing doctors to disconnect life support and let the patient die slowly, while prohibiting assistance that would: 'put him out of his misery straight away, in a more humane manner, by a lethal injection, rather than let him linger on in pain until he dies'.[180] A right to 'the least painful death available' may be based on the prohibition of

---

[175] Mullock (2015) 'The Supreme Court decision in Nicklinson: Human rights, criminal wrong and the dilemma of death' *Professional Negligence* 18 at p 28, referring to Lady Hale's statement in *Nicklinson* ([2015] AC 657 at [313]) that the appellants 'experience the law's insistence that they stay alive for the sake of others as a form of cruelty'.

[176] HL Bill 42, Arts 1–2.

[177] See Meisel, op cit fn 163 at pp 12.109–12.110.

[178] [2015] AC 657 at [6], [12].

[179] Jackson, op cit fn 98 at pp 1–5. See also Kuhse and Singer, op cit fn 166 at p 60 on marginally-viable infants: 'killing an infant is not worse than letting the infant die. Often it will be better, because the swifter death will cause less suffering'.

[180] *Bland* [1993] AC 789 at p 865.

inhuman treatment,[181] engaged whenever the state: 'blocks avenues which people might otherwise opt for to secure a less distressing death'.[182]

Surprisingly, non-discrimination claims were not given adequate consideration in right-to-die rulings (even *Carter* declining to examine s 15 arguments),[183] although these were eminently equality cases. Since the law recognises patients' right to choose death by switching off the life-support machine or travelling abroad to receive MAiD services, they must be able to ask for assistance from relatives or doctors if, due to disability, they can only exercise that right through a willing other. As Spriggs noted, autonomy may encompass 'affirmative demands', ie require acts 'fostering autonomous decision making'.[184] For patients reliant on others to govern their bodies, medical assistance may be necessary to effectively respect decisional autonomy. To the extent that severely disabled individuals, who cannot act independently, are only left with the tragic option of a slow painful death through self-starvation and self-dehydration, the prohibition on MAiD affects them with particular force.

IV. Pragmatic Concerns: The 'Protection of the Vulnerable' Argument

The only arguable justification for curtailing the rights of patients seeking MAiD is the unintended effect of legalisation on vulnerable individuals pressurised into ending their lives. Dworkin noted that opponents of assisted suicide also invoke the principle of autonomy: 'they worry that if euthanasia were legal people would be killed who really wanted to stay alive'.[185] The argument that the assisted dying ban pursued the legitimate aim of protecting the vulnerable was readily accepted in the courts of both Canada and the UK.

However, there was surprisingly limited discussion of the notion of 'vulnerability'. Treating all mentally competent disabled persons as vulnerable and restricting their autonomy in the name of protecting them would be moral paternalism.[186] A narrow definition of vulnerability, based on mental health and personal circumstances, is arguably required. In *Pretty*, the ECtHR expressly rejected the

---

[181] See du Bois-Pedain, op cit fn 99 at p 87.

[182] ibid at p 90.

[183] On the trial judge's decision on s 15 and criticising the Supreme Court's refusal to endorse it see Deckha (2016) 'A missed opportunity: Affirming the section 15 equality argument against physician-assisted death' *McGill JL & Health* S69. Against the judge's finding of discrimination see Keown (2014) 'A right to voluntary euthanasia? Confusion in Canada in Carter' *Notre Dame JL Ethics and Public Policy* 1 at 17–20.

[184] Spriggs (2005) *Autonomy and patients' decisions* p 82.

[185] Dworkin, op cit fn 143 at p 190.

[186] See Draghici (2015) 'The blanket ban on assisted suicide: Between moral paternalism and utilitarian justice' *European Human Rights LR* 286 at p 296.

claim that severely disabled persons contemplating suicide were to be regarded as vulnerable.[187] It is worth noting that the applicants for individual exemptions under *Carter (No 2)* were well-educated and well-off, and their relatives had initially opposed the decision to seek MAiD.[188] Importantly, as Schafer observed, patients requesting withdrawal of life-sustaining treatment are not deemed vulnerable, even though their life is equally at stake, and they may also be unduly influenced by over-burdened families, emotional hardship or depression.[189] The Canadian Supreme Court judiciously accepted in *Carter* that no different vulnerability concerns arise with respect to assisted dying when compared to other end-of-life decisions:

> [115] [T]here is no reason to think that the injured, ill, and disabled who have the option to refuse or to request withdrawal of lifesaving or life-sustaining treatment … are less vulnerable or less susceptible to biased decision-making than those who might seek more active assistance in dying.

Beaudry argued that deliberative autonomy cannot be ascertained satisfactorily, because wilful decisions may be the product of social conditions, and so under the new Canadian MAiD regime: 'a desperate, marginalized citizen socially cornered into suicide may … be cast as an autonomous patient that has been treated respectfully'.[190] Why 'social autonomy' concerns arise in relation to MAiD, but not withdrawal of life-sustaining treatment, is left unanswered. A double standard, whereby patients requiring third-party assistance to end their lives are treated as vulnerable, while those who can do it unaided are not, is arbitrary and discriminatory.

Furthermore, if the vulnerable require protection against pressure to end their life, a blanket ban on assisted suicide is both overbroad and insufficient: it catches persons outside that class and fails to reach intended recipients. The ban cannot prevent vulnerable individuals from ending their life under pressure as long as this can be achieved by discontinuing treatment or they are physically able to commit suicide or travel to a jurisdiction permitting MAiD. As Mullock noted, this lack of effective protection for vulnerable patients calls into question the rational connection between the ban and its objective.[191] Critically, the ban impacts competent individuals of limited means or who lost command of their body; they are denied a right everyone else has to see their end-of-life decisions respected. Admittedly, this is a narrow category; however, the low number of individuals affected is not a valid justification for restrictions upon fundamental rights. That contention was

---

[187] (2002) 35 EHRR 1 at [73].

[188] See *Re A.B.* [2016] ONSC 2188; *Re H.H.* [2016] BCSC 971; *Re Tuckwell* [2016] ABQB 302; *Patient 0518 v RHA 0518* [2016] SKQB 176; *Re A.A.* [2016] BCSC 570; *C.D. v Canada (AG)* 2016 ONSC 2431; *E.F. v Canada (AG)* 2016 ONSC 2790; *M.N. v Canada (AG)* 2016 ONSC 3346.

[189] See Schafer, op cit fn 124 at p 526.

[190] Beaudry (2018) 'The way forward for medical aid in dying: Protecting deliberative autonomy is not enough' p 385 in Ross (ed), op cit fn 85.

[191] Mullock, op cit fn 175 at p 22.

rejected by Strasbourg authorities.[192] In *Bedford*, the Canadian Supreme Court also clarified that, even if a law has a grossly disproportionate effect on one individual only, it still violates the Charter.[193]

While both Supreme Courts accepted the vulnerability rationale, they differed on whether it had to be addressed through a blanket prohibition, as opposed to a mechanism ensuring that assistance is only provided in appropriate cases. In the unanimous judgment of the Canadian Supreme Court, it was possible to allow MAiD and establish a system of safeguards. Conversely, the majority in the UK Supreme Court felt unable to decide in the absence of a specific legislative scheme, and supported a policy excluding risks of error and abuse. The Court of Appeal in *Conway* concluded that the scheme before it was not foolproof and similarly preferred a precautionary approach. Nevertheless, the avoidance of potential risks generates the absolute certainty of curbing some individuals' basic rights on speculative grounds.[194] This in turn speaks to questions of proportionality.

V. Necessity and Proportionality

The meanings ascribed to the notions of necessity and proportionality in both jurisdictions provide a constant theme for analysis in the chapters in this volume. In the assisted dying context, three facets of proportionality have particular prominence: the onus of establishing a preferable alternative scheme; 'slippery slope' concerns; and the toleration of assistance in the prosecutorial practice.

A. Apportioning the Burden of Proof: Must Claimants Devise Unassailable Alternatives?

The conceptualisation of justifications for interferences is marginally different between Canada and the UK. Under s 7 of the Canadian Charter, interferences must be in accordance with 'principles of fundamental justice', ie not arbitrary, overbroad or having consequences grossly disproportionate to the objectives.[195] Section 7 infringements can still be saved by s 1, if they pursued a pressing objective and observed proportionality, the latter being defined by: (1) rational connection; (2) minimal impairment; and (3) deleterious effects and salutary benefits.

---

[192] See *Dickson v UK* (2008) 44 EHRR 21 at [84]; *Hatton v UK* (2003) 37 EHRR 611, Joint dissenting opinion at [14].

[193] *Canada (AG) v Bedford* [2013] SCC 72 at [122].

[194] See [2015] AC 657 at [352] (per Lord Kerr): 'section 2(1) applies to many people who are not in need of its protection and who are prejudiced by its application to them. ... In the absence of evidence ... that this was required, it is impossible to conclude that the interference with the appellants' rights is proportionate'.

[195] See further [2015] 1 SCR 331 at [72].

Art 8(2) ECHR establishes a three-pronged test: the measure must be 'prescribed by law' (not arbitrary), pursue one of the 'legitimate aim(s)' listed, and be 'necessary in a democratic society'; the third criterion requires a proportionality test, ie demonstration of a pressing need and recourse to the minimum interference sufficient to achieve the aim.[196] The Charter and the ECHR frameworks legitimising restrictions are therefore similar, even if the algorithms for analysis follow slightly different paths.

In assisted dying case law, there are two striking features in the British courts' approach to justification: first, the acceptance without demonstration of great risks associated with regulation, as opposed to complete ban;[197] second, the focus on the exact substitute for the ban, and specifically the claimant's responsibility to devise it. Since it was acknowledged that the blanket ban curtails individual rights, one would expect the respondent to be required to provide cogent justification, absent which the measure breaches the HRA 1998. However, the Supreme Court majority in *Nicklinson* shifted the burden onto applicants to demonstrate that the interference was *not* justified, and nothing short of a fully perfected legislative scheme met that burden.[198] This influenced the claimant's submissions in *Conway*, which took the unusual form of a legislative proposal; in fact, much of the High Court's assessment revolved around the merits of that solution, instead of examining the status quo. The appellate decision also focused on Mr Conway's solution, concluding that it did not offer adequate protection to the vulnerable. The expectations placed by the Court of Appeal on individual litigants are astounding:[199]

> [174] It is not satisfactory to say ... that all of those practical and regulatory details could be worked out by Parliament ... Those considerations are relevant as to whether the court is in a position to hold section 2(1) to be incompatible in the first place.

By contrast, in *Carter*, the Canadian Supreme Court did not expect claimants to prove that liberty-limiting legislation was disproportionate; rather, it required the respondent to demonstrate the necessity of the restriction pursuant to the *Oakes* test.[200] Nor did it attempt to decide the exact alternative to the status quo. The Court invalidated the provisions banning all assistance in dying, but the task of revisiting the law was left to Parliament. The only legislative direction included in the judgment was the requirement that any new MAiD rights for patients be reconciled with doctors' rights not to be compelled to provide assistance.[201]

---

[196] See Draghici (2017) *The legitimacy of family rights in Strasbourg case law: 'Living instrument' or extinguished sovereignty?* pp 300–302.

[197] The absence of realistic examination of risks was already noted in relation to the *Pretty* case; see Morris (2003) 'Assisted suicide under the European Convention on Human Rights: A critique' *European Human Rights LR* 65 at p 90.

[198] See Martin (2018) 'Declaratory misgivings: Assisted suicide in a post-Nicklinson context' *Public Law* 209 at pp 214–15.

[199] [2018] EWCA Civ 1431.

[200] See pp 12–18 above for a discussion of the proportionality test established in the early Charter jurisprudence in *R v Oakes* [1986] 1 SCR 103.

[201] [2015] 1 SCR 331 at [132].

The minority in *Nicklinson* had taken the same approach. For Lord Kerr, the absence of a well-thought-out replacement scheme should not affect the evaluation of the present ban's proportionality:

> [354] It is entirely possible to assert that a particular provision would go beyond what it seeks to achieve without having to describe the details of a more tailored measure that would attain that aim. ... The measure must be intrinsically proportionate.

This view better reflects the HRA 1998, s 4 mechanism, which empowers courts to decide if a law breaches human rights, not how it should be amended; the exact remedy is left to the legislature. It follows that a substitute for the offending law should not be claimants' onus either.

The House of Lords in *Bellinger* refused to strain the interpretation of the Matrimonial Causes Act 1973, s 11(c) under HRA 1998, s 3[202] (preferring a s 4 declaration instead) precisely because the court was not the appropriate institution for shaping complex legislative schemes with systemic implications.[203] The *Bellinger* judgment found that the failure to recognise transsexual persons' acquired gender and capacity to marry according to it breached Arts 8 and 12 ECHR. That no clear criteria for gender reassignment were available did not preclude a s 4 declaration (nor had this been an obstacle for the ECtHR in *Goodwin v UK*).[204] Mrs Bellinger was not required to demonstrate how the law would resolve the difficulties regarding medical evidence of intention to live in the new gender permanently, the amount of time in the new social gender required for legal sex change, or the status of mother/father of children born before gender reassignment. Parliament made those decisions in the Gender Recognition Act 2004. Analogously, judicial assessment of the assisted dying ban can precede the elaboration of a new legislative scheme to address HRA-incompatibilities.

B. The 'Slippery Slope' Argument

The crux of the assisted dying controversy lies in the lack of scope for exceptional authorisation. Proportionality requires that interferences be no more than necessary to safeguard legitimate aims; consequently, blanket bans affecting human rights are rarely defensible, because they make no allowance for special circumstances and do not permit a remedy strictly commensurate with the problem.[205] Moreover, a fair balance presupposes a reasonable reconciliation between competing rights. A blanket ban fails to achieve a balance, as one party is required to sacrifice all. McLachlin J, dissenting, concluded in *Rodriguez*: 'Sue

---

[202] Under s 11(c), repealed by the Marriage (Same Sex Couples) Act 2013, a marriage was void if: 'the parties are not respectively male and female'.

[203] See *Bellinger v Bellinger* [2003] UKHL 21 at [37].

[204] (2002) 35 EHRR 18.

[205] On blanket bans in Strasbourg case law see Draghici, op cit fn 186 at pp 292–93.

Rodriguez is asked to bear the burden of the chance that other people in other situations may act criminally to kill others or improperly sway them to suicide. She is asked to serve as a scapegoat.[206] From a bioethical perspective, law presupposes a 'compromise' between contrasting interests in society: 'both sides getting a bit of what they want while neither side gets all of what it wants';[207] the blanket ban on MAiD fails to achieve a reasonable compromise, because it gives one side absolutely nothing.

This extreme position was rationalised in the literature by 'slippery slope' arguments, broadly reducible to two claims: (1) once MAiD is permitted, the practice cannot be contained within its anticipated boundaries, as further demands based on autonomy/mercy killing will follow; (2) whatever criteria are adopted, abuse cannot be excluded, and patients falling outside those criteria will be assisted to die ('empirical' slippery slope).[208] The second version of the slippery slope was prominent in assisted dying litigation in both jurisdictions, when courts inquired whether an absolute ban was necessary and proportionate.

For the Canadian Supreme Court, the ban unjustifiably infringed the rights of competent consenting adults suffering intolerably; a permissive regime with proper safeguards could protect vulnerable people from abuse and error. As Schafer explained: '*Oakes* requires that there must be strong evidence (rather than mere a priori speculation) that coercive restrictions are both necessary and sufficient to promote the values in question.'[209] The minority in *Nicklinson* also challenged the proportionality of an absolute prohibition. For Lady Hale, the ban violates Art 8 ECHR insofar as: 'it does not provide for any exception for people who have made a capacitous, free and fully informed decision to commit suicide but require help to do so'.[210]

Conversely, the *Nicklinson* majority accepted speculative scenarios of vulnerable people pressurised into choosing death and noted the absence of an alternative before the court, concluding that the ban struck a fair balance. For the Court of Appeal in *Conway*, where a specific scheme was available, proportionality was satisfied by the theoretic impossibility of removing all risks: 'an element of risk will inevitably remain in assessing whether an applicant has met the criteria'.[211] The court invoked 'the potential for indirect coercion or undue influence'; in particular, it adduced that: 'A sense of being a burden may be projected subconsciously and then expressed ... as a genuinely felt belief'.[212] Since risks remained

---

[206] [1993] 3 SCR 519 at p 621.
[207] Smith (2017) 'Ethical commentary – Nicklinson and the ethics of the legal system' p 223 in Smith et al (eds), op cit fn 121.
[208] See Arras (1997) 'Physician-assisted suicide: A tragic view' *Journal of Contemporary Health Law and Policy* 361 at pp 368–73. On 'slippery slope' arguments see also Lewis, op cit fn 168 at pp 159–87.
[209] Schafer, op cit fn 124 at p 525.
[210] [2015] AC 657 at [321].
[211] [2018] EWCA Civ 1431 at [171].
[212] ibid at [160].

a factor in examining proportionality, the court deferred the entire assessment to the legislator:

> [171] [T]he weight to be given to that risk, in deciding whether or not the blanket ban on assisted suicide is both necessary and proportionate, involves an evaluative judgement and a policy decision, which … Parliament is … better placed than the court to make.

There was no discussion of the consistency of the law, and how the ban protects terminally ill or severely disabled patients who, ridden with subconscious guilt or subjected to undue influence, retain the capacity to disconnect a breathing tube or travel to Dignitas. The court further voiced concerns over medical complications potentially arising from assisted dying,[213] without considering premature or botched suicide attempts prompted by the lack of professional assistance, causing injury or a more painful death.

The Court of Appeal also over-emphasised the six-months eligibility criterion and the impossibility of accurate predictions.[214] This focus on a precise diagnosis stands in contrast with the fluid language of s 241.2(2)(d) of the Canadian Criminal Code, requiring that the patient's 'natural death has become reasonably foreseeable'. Addressing a difference of medical opinion on a patient's eligibility in *A.B. v Canada*, the Ontario Court stressed that, according to its legislative history, s 241.2(2)(d) was deliberately flexible, to indicate that its purpose was not to require terminal illness, but rather: 'to ensure that people who are on a trajectory toward death in a wide range of circumstances can choose a peaceful death instead of having to endure a long or painful one'.[215]

The UK and Canadian courts' position varied radically on whether court authorisation is a reliable safeguard against mistake and abuse. *Conway* expressed strong doubts about the costs and effectiveness of judicial supervision.[216] It is worth noting that the Crown Prosecution Service reported only 138 assisted suicide cases between 1 April 2009 and 31 January 2018.[217] The trifling average number each year (even considering a possible increase if MAiD becomes available) does not support the objection that courts lack resources to assess MAiD requests.[218] Moreover, the lack of confidence in courts' expertise cannot be reconciled with their existing role in medical cases; as Pedain observed: 'doctors – and sometimes judges – already have to assess the capacity of individuals to make life-and-death choices in the related context of a patient's wish to refuse treatment necessary to keep her or him alive'.[219]

---

[213] ibid at [173].
[214] ibid at [142].
[215] [2017] ONSC 3759 at [43], citing the Attorney General's speech in the House of Commons.
[216] [2018] EWCA Civ 1431 at [174], [183].
[217] See www.cps.gov.UK/publication/assisted-suicide.
[218] State funding is already required to appoint guardians ad litem for children or to represent incapacitated persons. The resources required to secure the rights of the narrow category of persons seeking MAiD should not hinder reform.
[219] Pedain (2002) 'Assisted suicide and personal autonomy' *Cambridge LJ* 511 at p 513.

By contrast, in *Carter (No 2)* the Canadian Supreme Court characterised the regime of judicial authorisation of individual exemptions during the extended suspension of invalidity as 'an effective safeguard against potential risks to vulnerable people'.[220] The cases decided under *Carter (No 2)* confirmed courts' ability to assess consent. In *Re H.S.*, the first of such cases, the Court of Queen's Bench of Alberta reviewed testimony that the applicant had been inquiring into assisted dying options for two years, had shown resolve to end her life peacefully in multiple discussions with medical professionals, family and friends, had received counselling regarding palliative care, and had been informed of the risks associated with physician-assisted death.[221] Examining further petitions for permission to proceed with MAiD, provincial courts conducted similar inquiries and were satisfied without hesitation that the applicants met the *Carter* criteria.[222]

Significantly, when assessing proportionality in *Pretty*, the ECtHR accepted that the general prohibition on assisted suicide was mitigated by the 'flexibility … provided for in individual cases by the fact that consent is needed from the DPP to bring a prosecution' and by 'a system of enforcement and adjudication which allows due regard to be given in each particular case to the public interest in bringing a prosecution'.[223] What the ECtHR had not considered, and became manifest in *Purdy*, was that the unpredictable exercise of DPP discretion deterred patients from requesting assistance and physicians/carers from providing it. It also meant that assistance will usually involve relatives' help to travel abroad, which is costly and unavailable to patients without willing relatives, like Martin in *Nicklinson*. The fact that few cases are prosecuted[224] is distinct from an anticipatory exemption, especially given the stakes: deprivation of liberty, criminal record and social stigma attached to committing a criminal offence. Lord Rees highlighted the impact on relatives offering assistance during parliamentary debates on the Assisted Dying Bill 2016–17: 'Those acts may not result in prosecution, but a shadow of criminality hangs over them and adds to the grief of those whose motive is compassion'.[225] While the ECtHR was satisfied that, overall, the regime was within the boundaries of the UK's margin of appreciation, domestic courts can take a stricter approach to Parliament's balancing act.

C. Proleptic Immunity for Assisters vs Ex Post Facto Prosecutorial Assessment

Rather alarmingly, the combination of legislative ban and prosecutorial toleration disadvantages the class of vulnerable individuals whom the ban should protect.

---

[220] [2016] SCC4 at [6].

[221] *Re H.S.* [2016] ABQB at [103]–[108].

[222] See fn 188 for references.

[223] [2002] 35 EHRR 1 at [76].

[224] The DPP prosecuted two out of 124 cases referred between 1 April 2009 and 25 April 2016 (one involving a vulnerable adult with mental health issues and no compassionate circumstances); see Adenitire (2016) 'A conscience-based human right to be "doctor death"' *Public Law* 613 at p 627.

[225] *HLD* 6 March 2017 c 1183.

The evidence before English courts showed that compassionate assistance in dying is rarely prosecuted, despite its criminalisation. As Lord Neuberger suggested in *Nicklinson*, the practice comes close to tolerating assisted dying.[226] In Canada, a similar trend was noted before the 2016 reform, resulting from prosecutorial and judicial discretion.[227]

This practice casts doubt on the proportionality of the interference with fundamental rights. As Adenitire argued, the expectation to immunity from prosecution, generated by the DPP's guidelines and consistent non-prosecution policy, shows that the blanket ban is not truly necessary.[228] There is also a troubling discrepancy between the law (criminalising all assistance) and the state's/society's recognition that exceptional assistance is morally appropriate. In *Bland*, Hoffmann LJ held that euthanasia: 'is not an area in which any difference can be allowed to exist between what is legal and what is morally right'.[229] The same stands true of assisted dying. The law should not collide with, but accommodate, the treatment of individual cases. Lord Sumption controversially suggested that: 'the law should continue to criminalise assisted suicide, and ... be broken from time to time';[230] this approach avoids finding a legal solution and perpetuates the separation between law and morality.

On a practical level, non-prosecution instead of anticipatory authorisation of assistance undermines the protection of the vulnerable. Lord Mance noted in *Nicklinson* that individuals are currently assisted despite the prohibition and without prior review.[231] The DPP's retrospective assessment of circumstances cannot adequately protect the vulnerable.[232] The scrutiny of planned assistance, under a regime of exceptional authorisations, would better serve the aim of the law: more evidence would be available, consent and undue influence could be more accurately ascertained, and improper assistance could be prevented. Moreover, for patients' and assisters' peace of mind, the *certainty* of prior authorisation is fundamentally different from the *likelihood* of subsequent condonation.

From an institutional perspective, Parliament is abdicating its mandate if, in difficult areas, it relegates to prosecutors the task of adjusting the inequities of the law. In *R (Kenward) v DPP*, rejecting the claim that the DPP's amended policy for prosecutors placed vulnerable individuals at risk, the High Court struggled to establish that the policy: 'does not remove bright lines ... and no assistance or encouragement is rendered lawful', while admitting that the decision whether to prosecute: 'will always involve a very detailed consideration of all the facts and,

---

[226] [2014] UKSC 38 at [111].
[227] Schafer, op cit fn 124 at p 523.
[228] See Adenitire, op cit fn 224 at pp 625–29.
[229] [1993] AC 789 at p 825.
[230] Bowcott (2019) 'Ex-supreme court justice defends those who break assisted dying law' *The Guardian* (17 April 2019), available at www.theguardian.com/society/2019/apr/17/ex-supreme-court-jonathan-sumption-defends-break-assisted-dying-law, citing Lord Sumption's BBC Reith Lectures speech.
[231] [2015] AC 657 at [186].
[232] See Reidy (2012) 'English law on assisted suicide: A dangerous position' *Medico-Legal Journal of Ireland* 68 at p 74.

ultimately, a balanced judgement'.[233] A bright-line rule and a composite judgment are mutually exclusive, and the statute should be amended to reflect the latter approach.

Moreover, since Parliament has set a blanket ban and compassionate assistance in dying is in practice decriminalised, a conflict emerges between primary legislation and prosecutorial policy, buttressed by the courts' ambivalence. Lewis has criticised the: 'opaque process of informal legal change by prosecutors'.[234] However, as Stark observed: 'If the DPP's prosecution policy becomes too specific it may constitute a (presumably illegitimate) usurpation of this clear legislative statement by carving out an area of assisted suicide that is, *de facto*, decriminalised'.[235] From a constitutional standpoint, it is undesirable for courts to endorse a *contra legem* administrative policy as a corrective tool, instead of prompting Parliament to devise statutory exceptions, also more attuned with the certainty-of-law principle.

VI. The Constitutional Role of the Judiciary in Highly Divisive Ethical Debates

British and Canadian assisted dying rulings revealed similar concerns over how the legal system is structured to decide sensitive ethical matters: whether they are the exclusive realm of Parliament or the role falls on Parliament assisted by the courts. The different answers to this question might be explained in part by British courts' limited prerogatives under the HRA 1998 when compared to the constitutionally entrenched strike-down power of Canadian courts under the Constitution Act 1982.[236] However, courts' function under HRA 1998, s 4 is not merely an advisory one; they are called upon to authoritatively assess the law's respect for human rights. Rather, the outcome of applications appears explained by judges' personal views of their mission and of the justiciability of the dispute. An interpretation of the margin of appreciation left to states under the ECHR as parliamentary discretion acts as an additional break on judicial review. This is compounded by the UK's strict adherence to precedent, by contrast with lower courts' ability to revisit the validity of laws according to Canadian jurisprudence.

A. Democratic Law-Making and Judicial Self-Restraint

British and Canadian courts view the role of the judiciary very differently in ethically divisive policy areas. In *Carter*, the Canadian Supreme Court showed no

---

[233] *R (Kenward) v DPP* [2015] EWHC 3508 (Admin) at [53].

[234] Lewis (2011) 'The limits of autonomy: Law at the end of life in England and Wales' in Negri (ed), op cit fn 16 at p 247.

[235] See Stark, op cit fn 7 at p 108.

[236] See Martin (2017) 'A human rights perspective of assisted suicide: Accounting for disparate jurisprudence' *Medical LR* 98 at p 106.

institutional self-doubt in assessing Charter-compatibility regardless of the subject matter of the dispute. Conversely, many British judges deemed certain policy areas non-justiciable or considered that judicial intervention should be limited in deference to parliamentary sovereignty. Lord Bingham in *Pretty* suggested that the court was unable to make ethical and moral decisions, insofar as it was not a legislative body.[237] In *Nicklinson*, the court was extremely divided as regards its proper role. For several justices, the issue engaged an important determination on social policy and a moral judgment on the balance between competing rights, and the legislative process was best placed to resolve controversial and complex questions.[238] However, Lord Neuberger noted courts' historical engagement with moral choices:

> [98] [T]he mere fact that there are moral issues involved plainly does not mean that the courts have to keep out. Even before the 1998 Act came into force, the courts were prepared to make decisions which developed the law and involved making moral choices of this type.

The idea that courts adjudicating HRA claims are not competent to entertain disputes involving questions of morality is unconvincing. Most cases occasioning s 4 declarations concerned morally sensitive issues: recognition of transsexuals' acquired gender; sham marriage and immigration control; posthumous fatherhood; detention without trial of foreign terrorist suspects; and decriminalisation of certain consensual sexual behaviour.[239] Indeed, proceedings leading to s 4 declarations are unlikely to concern straightforward matters, which Parliament could have easily regulated without affecting human rights. Stark insisted that: 'resolving such value conflicts is not the courts' constitutional role'.[240] However, rights cannot be dissociated from values. The scope of a right depends on the boundaries between the competing values engaged, and courts are tasked to interpret rights. Insofar as this is a mandate given by Parliament, it does not contravene parliamentary sovereignty. Admittedly, morals-laden disputes can attract greater deference to Parliament when courts assess balancing acts, but the justiciability of the claim should not be questioned. As Coggon argued: 'For a functioning, democratic system to operate, the last thing the courts must do is shirk their responsibilities simply because of moral controversy and ethical disagreement'.[241]

However, British assisted dying decisions disclose institutional unease with upholding challenges to legislative measures. Concerns were expressed in *Nicklinson* over institutional remits: 'the legislative function is committed to Parliament and courts must not usurp it'.[242] Although for five judges the court had the constitutional authority to declare the ban incompatible with Art 8, only

---

[237] [2002] 1 AC 800 at [2] (per Lord Bingham).
[238] [2015] AC 657 at [228]–[232].
[239] See Draghici, op cit fn 186 at p 295.
[240] Stark, op cit fn 7 at p 106.
[241] Coggon, op cit fn 121 at p 210.
[242] [2015] AC 657 at [259].

two (Lady Hale and Lord Kerr) were prepared to do so; they reasoned that, when issuing a s 4 declaration, courts do precisely what the HRA 1998 empowered them to do, ie remit an issue to Parliament for a political decision.[243] While the limited reach of declarations of incompatibility might be expected to stimulate greater scrutiny of legislative action, the High Court in *T* justified self-restraint precisely by contrast with Canadian courts' powers:[244]

> [19] The provisions of the [Charter] give the Canadian courts a central role, as, in effect, a constitutional court, interpreting a written constitution, with no question of any inhibition derived from the role of the Canadian legislature.

This analysis may unduly diminish the pivotal role of judicial protection of human rights under the UK's unwritten constitution and downplay the HRA mandate for British courts. In a country lacking a formal constitution, statutes 'of constitutional importance' within the meaning of *Thoburn v Sunderland City Council*,[245] such as the HRA 1998, should carry particular weight. The different legal effect of a finding of incompatibility as opposed to a judgment of invalidation already absorbs any distinction between the UK Supreme Court and a constitutional court; a further self-imposed restriction *ratione materiae* on judicial oversight would constitute a double ceiling on courts' democratic control.

Given the history of consistent parliamentary accommodation of declarations of incompatibility,[246] some judges might view s 4 as more powerful in practice than under the statute,[247] almost tantamount to legislative decisions made by an institution lacking democratic credentials. This position, however, would entail that, when enacting the HRA 1998, Parliament intended for courts to use s 4 powers only for uncontroversial issues, requiring marginal changes. By removing the most critical issues from the scope of judicial supervision and diminishing human-rights protection, such an interpretation would go against the purpose of the statute. Nor is there any unwritten constitutional rule that all s 4 declarations must be followed, as shown by the failure to address prisoners' right to vote following *Smith v Scott*[248] (admittedly, not a Supreme Court decision and one lacking popular support).[249]

---

[243] ibid at [325], [343]–[344]. Under HRA 1998, s 4(6)(a), a declaration 'does not affect the validity, continuing operation or enforcement of the provision'.

[244] [2018] EWHC 2615 (Admin).

[245] *Thoburn v Sunderland City Council* [2002] EWHC 195 (Admin).

[246] See *Responding to human rights judgments*. Report to the Joint Committee on Human Rights on the Government's response to human rights judgments 2018–2019 (October 2019), available at https://assets.publishing.service.gov.uk/government/uploads/system/uploads/attachment_data/file/842553/responding-human-rights-judgments-2019.pdf; see Stark (2017) 'Facing facts: Judicial approaches to section 4 of the Human Rights Act 1998' *LQR* 631 at p 649, noting that all but one breaches signalled by s 4 declarations were remedied.

[247] See King (2015) 'Parliament's role following declarations of incompatibility under the Human Rights Act' pp 165–92 in Hooper et al (eds) *Parliaments and human rights: Redressing the democratic deficit*, suggesting that other government branches apparently feel obligated to act upon s 4 declarations.

[248] *Smith v Scott* [2007] SC 345.

[249] See Crawford (2013) 'Dialogue and declarations of incompatibility under section 4 of the Human Rights Act 1998' *The Denning LJ* 43 at pp 76–77.

Another qualification on the use of s 4 added by the case law is that courts should refrain from issuing a declaration on matters before Parliament. In *Nicklinson*, three justices found that SA 1961 might breach HRA provisions, but it would be inappropriate for the court to assess compliance before giving Parliament an opportunity to reconsider its position.[250] *Conway* confirmed this *a contrario*; the High Court held that, since Parliament was not actively considering the law at the time of the proceedings, nothing precluded it from revisiting the matter.[251] Not only does s 4 not require courts to abstain from issuing a declaration on matters pending in Parliament, but that seems, conversely, an auspicious time for courts to contribute their legally trained views. One purpose of s 4 is, in fact, to invite the legislature to re-examine a statute with the benefit of the highest courts' professional opinion.

The refusal in *Nicklinson* to issue a s 4 declaration due to the contemporaneous parliamentary debate was an unfortunate departure from *Bellinger*,[252] where the court took the opposite view on the dialogue between courts and Parliament on HRA-incompatibility issues:

> [55] [W]hen proceedings are already before the House, it is desirable that in a case of such sensitivity this House, as the court of final appeal in this country, should formally record that the present state of statute law is incompatible with the Convention.

Crawford noted that, in several cases in which s 4 declarations were issued: 'the process of amending the impugned legislation was well underway, or indeed completed, by the time the court made the declaration of incompatibility'.[253]

An equally questionable requirement read into HRA 1998, s 4 by the *Nicklinson* majority is that courts must have a viable legislative alternative in order to issue a declaration of incompatibility. This requirement is nowhere in the statute, and for courts to choose the 'correct' alternative would actually be out of step with the separation-of-powers principle.[254] The dissenters in *Nicklinson*, who saw their remit as deciding if the law breached fundamental rights and demanded rethinking, criticised the majority's demand for a ready-made replacement. Regrettably, the Supreme Court majority's approach in *Nicklinson* was magnified by the Court of Appeal, for whom the court's role in *Conway* was to assess the litigant's legislative proposal rather than the impugned law: 'the court is restricted to considering the suitability of the precise scheme proposed by Mr Conway'.[255] *Conway* thus consolidated the view that, under the HRA 1998, courts must decide not only if

---

[250] [2015] AC 657 at [116].
[251] [2018] EWCA Civ 1431 at [9].
[252] [2003] 2 AC 467.
[253] Crawford, op cit fn 249, citing *Re an Application for Judicial Review by McR* [2002] NIQB 58, *Blood and Tarbuck v Secretary of State for Health* (High Court, 28 February 2003, unreported), *Bellinger v Bellinger* [2003] UKHL 21, *R (M) v Secretary of State for Health* [2003] EWHC 1094 (Admin), *R (Wilkinson) v Inland Revenue Commissioners* [2005] UKHL 30, *R (Wright) v Secretary of State for Health* [2009] UKHL 3.
[254] See Martin, op cit fn 198 at p 217.
[255] [2018] EWCA Civ 1431 at [187].

the status quo breaches any rights, but also – as a prerequisite for that conclusion – how the breach should be remedied.

The Court of Appeal also justified self-restraint by stressing courts' limited ability to gauge social support for reform: 'Unlike Parliament, ... the court cannot conduct consultations with the public ... and cannot engage experts and advisers on its own account'.[256] Since the s 4 declaration would remit the issue for consideration to Parliament, the latter can launch public consultations before any legal change is effected. Additionally, nothing precludes courts from considering the evidence of societal support for reform publicly available. Indeed, various surveys indicate substantial popular support for MAiD in the UK.[257]

Importantly, s 4 declarations are agenda-setting. So far, most attempts at reform have failed due to lack of parliamentary time, Bills failing to progress after the formality of the first-reading stage, which does not involve debate.[258] A s 4 declaration would place the issue firmly on the British Parliament's agenda. It would be erroneous to infer from the lack of success of parliamentary attempts to date[259] that the matter has been adequately considered and the prevailing view is that the blanket ban is preferable to a nuanced solution. In the Canadian Parliament, 16 legislative attempts at changing assisted dying policy took place before *Carter*, none of which were Government-sponsored Bills.[260] It was the Supreme Court's ruling that finally galvanised legislative efforts.

Addressing claims that judicial review under the Canadian Charter is undemocratic, Hogg and Bushell argued that a Charter decision: 'causes a public debate in which *Charter* values play a more prominent role';[261] it forces Parliament to examine a topic, but this 'dialogue' between institutions: 'culminates in a democratic decision'.[262] Their sequel article clarified: 'since the last word can nearly always be (and usually is) that of the legislature, the anti-majoritarian objection to judicial

---

[256] ibid at [189]. This appears inconsistent with the finding in [204]: 'it is impossible to say that the Divisional Court did not have material on which properly to come to their conclusions on the inadequacy of the proposed scheme to protect the weak and the vulnerable ...'.

[257] See Bowcott (2019) 'Legalise assisted dying for terminally ill, say 90% of people in UK' *The Guardian* (3 March 2019), citing a National Centre for Social Research survey, available at www.theguardian.com/society/2019/mar/03/legalise-assisted-dying-for-terminally-ill-say-90-per-cent-of-people-in-uk; Davis and Finlay, op cit fn 51, citing Populus' Dignity in Dying poll (March 2015), available at www.populus.co.uk/wp-content/uploads/Dignity-in-Dying-Poll-March-2015-WEBSITE-DATATABLES.pdf; Dyer (2013) 'Assisted suicide for the dying would reduce suffering, says Falconer' *British Medical Journal* 5.

[258] Parliament was prorogued after the first reading of Assisted Dying Bills [HL] 2013–14, 2015–16 and 2016–17, and after the committee stage in the case of the 2014–15 Bill. The Assisted Dying (No 2) Bill 2015–16 did not pass the second reading.

[259] On post-*Nicklinson* Bills see Martin, op cit fn 236 at p 101.

[260] See Snow and Puddister (2018) 'Closing a door but opening a policy window: Legislating assisted dying in Canada' pp 44–45 in Macfarlane (ed), op cit fn 87. On attempts to pass legislation decriminalising MAiD see also O'Reilly and Hogeboom, op cit fn 101 at p 701.

[261] Hogg and Bushell (1997) 'The Charter dialogue between courts and legislatures (or Perhaps the Charter of Rights isn't such a bad thing after all)' *Osgoode Hall LJ* 75 at p 79.

[262] ibid at p 80.

review is not particularly strong'.[263] The same holds true (even more so) of the relationship between courts and legislature under the HRA scheme.

Some hesitation as to courts' proper role was also seen in the earlier right-to-die Canadian case law. In *Rodriguez*, while the majority did not feel precluded from examining Charter-compatibility by the moral complexities of the case, it was overly deferential in its examination of proportionality.[264] That position was abandoned in *Carter*, which adopted a more stringent standard of review. Many saw the ruling as a legitimate exercise of a function conferred by the Constitution. In fact: 'the *Charter* enables Supreme Court justices to push forward policy through rights-based litigation'.[265] Others viewed *Carter* as an expression of judicial activism, with reference, in particular, to the detailed remedy provided. Newman lamented the court's 'over-specificity in itself crafting a regime within its declaration that … constrains parliamentary choices'.[266] It is difficult to see, however, how the judgment could have defined the scope of the breach without identifying those unlawfully caught by the ban: competent adults suffering from a grievous medical condition with no acceptable treatment available and having reached an informed decision to end their lives.

Opinions also differed on the practicality of the remedy in *Carter*. For Surtees, the court: 'wisely provided Canadians with a default regulator in the event that our elected representatives choose not to act'.[267] Conversely, Ettel criticised *Carter* for the unclear remedy, should Parliament not respond to the declaration.[268] The limited usefulness of declarations of incompatibility for individual applicants might be an inevitable consequence of the court's strike-down, as opposed to legislative, powers and the system's reliance on inter-institutional cooperation. Even so, *Carter (No 2)*, by offering interim constitutional exemptions, better reconciled the separation of powers with practical remedies to applicants (and others in their position). This solution was, however, not exempted from criticism. Rahimi described it as: 'a vivid example of the judiciary usurping the legislative role of Parliament by implementing a de facto regulatory system overseeing [MAiD]'.[269]

The *Lamb* case presented the Supreme Court with an opportunity to relax its control over the MAiD regime by upholding Parliament's scheme notwithstanding its contrast with the more liberal *Carter* criteria. According to Rahimi: 'Endorsing

---

[263] Hogg et al (2007) 'Charter dialogue revisited – or "much ado about metaphors"' *Osgoode Hall LJ* 1 at p 54.

[264] [1993] 3 SCR 519 at pp 614–15.

[265] Ma (2016) 'A critical assessment of Supreme Court judicial reasoning: The constitutionality of health care policies in Canada' *Journal of Parliamentary and Political Law* 397 at p 408.

[266] Newman (2015) 'Judicial method and three gaps in the Supreme Court of Canada's assisted suicide judgment in Carter' *Saskatchewan LR* 217 at p 223.

[267] Surtees (2015) 'The authorizing of physician-assisted death in Carter v. Canada (Attorney General)' *Saskatchewan LR 225* at p 231.

[268] See Ettel (2018) '"To the extent of the inconsistency": Charter remedies and the constitutional dialogue' *National Journal of Constitutional Law* 279.

[269] Rahimi, op cit fn 90 at p 484.

Bill C-14 as constitutional would allow the courts to reverse the prescriptive judgment in *Carter*, which was arguably an overreach by the SCC'.[270] With the *Lamb* case adjourned, and the finding of invalidity in *Truchon* unchallenged, the Supreme Court no longer has to choose between full rights protection and democratic concessions to Parliament.

Canada's recent experience – courts' willingness to tackle sensitive policy choices and Parliament's response to findings of invalidity – suggests that a dynamic legislative process relies on inter-institutional prompts and checks. Meanwhile, British courts seem to be moving towards a complete referral to Parliament on assisted dying regulation, rather than co-shaping this area of law.

B. Charter 'Dialogue' and the Suspension of Declarations of Invalidity

The suspension of the declaration of invalidity in *Carter* was met with doctrinal criticism, given the historical rationale for suspensions as emergency tools,[271] and practical objections, since it imposed an additional year of suffering on individuals whose rights *Carter* found violated and who meanwhile could lose capacity to consent.[272] Burningham noted that, unlike the power to strike down legislation, grounded in the Constitution Act 1982, s 52, the suspension of declarations of invalidity is a judicial creation, designed to prevent intolerable situations,[273] whereas ordering the immediate invalidity of s 241(b) would not have generated either legal chaos or danger to the public (as per *Schachter v Canada*).[274] The text of s 52 indeed suggests that a finding of unconstitutionality attracts the immediate nullity of the offending law,[275] the declaration merely acknowledging that it was void *ab initio*. However, it is not far-fetched to argue that danger to the public existed: without careful regulation, vulnerable individuals could have resorted to MAiD in unwarranted cases. For that very reason, *Carter (No 2)* temporarily replaced regulation with judicial scrutiny in provincial courts.

Hogg et al have defended the practice of suspensions of declarations of invalidity based on a different rationale in Charter jurisprudence after *Schachter*: inter-institutional dialogue, a theory recognising that Parliament is better placed to design corrective laws and select from several alternatives.[276] However, given the

---

[270] ibid.

[271] See Burningham (2015) 'A comment on the Court's decision to suspend the declaration of invalidity in Carter v. Canada' *Saskatchewan LR* 201 at pp 201–04.

[272] ibid at p 206.

[273] *Re Manitoba Language Rights* [1985] 1 SCR 721.

[274] *Schachter v Canada* [1992] 2 SCR 679. See Burningham, op cit fn 271 at p 205.

[275] See Constitution Act 1982, s 52: '[A]ny law that is inconsistent with the provisions of the Constitution is, to the extent of the inconsistency, of no force or effect'.

[276] Hogg et al, op cit fn 263, at pp 14–18.

urgency for those deprived of constitutional rights and the potentially irreversible damage, a better compromise, halfway between exceptionalism and dialogue, might have been a suspension of invalidity accompanied by individual constitutional exemptions, similar to the regime introduced after the original 12-month suspension. Ultimately, the decision in *Carter (No 2)* to suspend the invalidity and grant individual exemptions as an interim emergency measure also shows adherence to the 'dialogue' doctrine, observing the different remits of Parliament and courts.[277]

C. 'Margin of Appreciation' under the ECHR and HRA 1998, s 4 Declarations

In *Pretty*, the ECtHR found the British assisted dying regime consistent with Art 8(2), and subsequent judgments did not alter ECHR standards. According to *Haas v Switzerland*, the minimum common denominator in Europe on the scope of privacy did not encompass a right to receive assistance in dying, and a wide margin of appreciation continued to apply to end-of-life issues; European states: 'are far from having reached a consensus with regard to an individual's right to decide how and when his or her life should end'.[278] A wide margin was confirmed in *Koch v Germany*.[279] As evidenced by *Lambert v France*, authorising withdrawal of artificial life-sustaining treatment is a legitimate exercise of state discretion.[280]

Simplistically, it might be thought that, if the right to assisted dying under the ECHR has been declined in Strasbourg proceedings, a different conclusion by UK courts is unwarranted. This would overlook, however, the margin left to states to reassess the boundaries of Art 8 in *non liquet* cases, where the court does not take a stand, accepting both the impugned law and its opposite as ECHR-compatible.[281] The ECHR is the minimum European common standard, and domestic authorities can afford greater protection.[282] British courts have accepted that 'Convention rights' under the HRA 1998 may go beyond the level required for international compliance with the ECHR. In *Fitzpatrick*, the House of Lords recognised that committed same-sex partners constituted 'family life' under Art 8[283] before

---

[277] See Burningham, op cit fn 271 at p 203.

[278] *Haas v Switzerland* (2011) 53 EHRR 33 at [55]. *Pretty v UK* (and subsequent case law) reflected the ECtHR's cautiousness not to alienate states by restricting discretion in areas where domestic policies vary; see Merkouris, op cit fn 16 at p 125.

[279] *Koch v Germany* (2013) 56 EHRR 6 at [70].

[280] (2016) 62 EHRR 2.

[281] See eg *Evans v UK* [2007] 1 FLR 1990 (destruction of embryos created with gametes from a partner withdrawing consent to implantation), *S.H. v Austria* [2012] 2 FCR 291 (heterologous fertilisation); both rulings found the respondents' legislative solution within their margin of appreciation, but also deemed the applicants' proposed solutions consistent with the Convention.

[282] See Draghici (2014) 'The Human Rights Act in the shadow of the European Convention: are copyist's errors allowed?' *European Human Rights LR* 154 pp 167–68.

[283] See *Fitzpatrick v Sterling Housing Association Ltd* [2001] 1 AC 27 at [80].

the ECtHR did so in *Schalk and Kopf v Austria*.[284] The finding in *Ghaidan v Godin-Mendoza* that HRA 1998, s 3 required housing legislation to be read as assimilating same-sex cohabitants to couples living as spouses for the purposes of succession to tenancies[285] did not imply that all ECHR parties had that obligation.

The House of Lords confirmed the possibility of a distinct claim of HRA-incompatibility even where there is no ECHR breach in *Re G (Adoption: Unmarried Couple)*.[286] The dual scope of ECHR rights in international and domestic perspective was upheld by the ECtHR in *Oliari v Italy*: legal recognition for same-sex couples in Italy was a constitutional entitlement enforceable in ECHR proceedings, even if no such pan-European right existed.[287] In *Conway*, the High Court recalled that: 'the interpretation of the domestic version of the Convention rights in the HRA does not simply mirror the Convention rights in the ECHR'.[288] Consequently, a declaration of incompatibility does not always signal a breach of international obligations; it may regard an inconsistency with a Convention right as understood domestically. The s 4 declaration in *Z (A Child) (No 2)*, concerning single persons' ineligibility for parental orders following surrogacy arrangements,[289] was not based on ECHR regulatory standards, surrogacy remaining an area of wide state discretion.[290]

Moreover, a s 4 declaration based on Art 8 taken in conjunction with Art 14 (and many claimants in right-to-die cases invoked their right to non-discrimination) can also be granted in respect of purely domestic rights linked with ECHR rights.[291] The Supreme Court accepted this in *Steinfeld*, issuing a s 4 declaration in relation to the bar in the Civil Partnership Act 2004, s 3, which excluded heterosexual couples, although there was no ECHR right to form such partnerships.[292]

The potential HRA-incompatibility of SA 1961, s 2(1), notwithstanding the finding in *Pretty v UK* that it did not breach ECHR obligations, was recognised in *Nicklinson* and emphasised by the High Court in *T*. The latter judgment expressly indicated that the case was adjudicated only under the HRA 1998, insofar as Strasbourg authorities allowed for a wide margin of appreciation in end-of-life matters.[293] Nonetheless, judicial views varied on whether all government branches

[284] *Schalk and Kopf v Austria* 29 BHRC 396.
[285] *Ghaidan v Godin-Mendoza* [2004] UKHL 30.
[286] *Re G (Adoption: Unmarried Couple)* [2008] 3 WLR 76.
[287] *Oliari v Italy* [2015] ECHR 716. See Draghici (2017) 'The Strasbourg court between European and local consensus: Anti-democratic or guardian of democratic process?' *Public Law* 11.
[288] [2017] EWHC 2447 (Admin) at [45].
[289] *Z (A Child) (No 2)* [2016] EWHC 1191 (Fam).
[290] See Draghici, op cit fn 196 at pp 146–49.
[291] See Draghici (2017) 'Equal marriage, unequal civil partnership: A bizarre case of discrimination in Europe' *Child and Family LQ* 313 at pp 313–19.
[292] See *R (Steinfeld & Another) v Secretary of State for International Development* [2018] UKSC 32.
[293] [2018] EWHC 2615 (Admin) at [3].

contribute to the domestic balancing act within that margin. According to Lord Mance in *Nicklinson*, this is a shared responsibility:

[163] Where a 'considerable' margin of appreciation exists at the international level, both the legislature and the judiciary have a potential role in assessing whether the law is at the domestic level compatible with such rights.

By contrast, for Lord Hughes, the discretion left by the ECtHR must be exercised by Parliament as a matter of constitutional law:

[267] It is true that Strasbourg thus regards the question as one to be resolved by individual States within their margin of appreciation. But in this country, with our constitutional division of responsibility between Parliament and the courts, this is very clearly a decision which falls to be made by Parliament.

Newby suggested even more bluntly that courts should not reverse parliamentary decisions: 'courts are not the venue for arguments which have failed to convince Parliament'.[294] This counter-majoritarian remark instils concerns as to when HRA challenges to primary legislation could ever succeed.

D. Precedence and Legal Change in Lower Courts

Assisted dying claims, challenging established norms, raised the question of whether the impetus for reform can start in the lower courts, given the *stare decisis* principle presumptively applicable in both Canada and the UK. As Loveland notes in his chapter, Canada's lower courts 'played fast and loose'[295] with this principle in respect of Canadian libel law. Provincial courts produced judgments prima facie irreconcilable with supposedly binding Supreme Court authority. The effect was not to trigger a normative crisis in the Constitution's judicial hierarchy but to prompt the Supreme Court significantly to alter its own views.[296]

   A similar trend is evident in assisted dying cases. In *Carter*, the Supreme Court restored the trial judge's decision that the prohibition against MAiD infringed s 7 rights of competent adults suffering intolerably due to a grievous and irremediable medical condition and was not justified under s 1 of the Charter. That decision had been reversed on appeal, on the ground that the trial judge was bound by the Supreme Court's *Rodriguez* judgment, upholding the blanket ban.[297] The Supreme Court accepted that trial courts can reconsider settled rulings of higher courts where a new legal issue is raised or where there is a 'change in the circumstances or the evidence' that 'fundamentally shifts the parameters of the debate'; it found that

---

[294] [2019] EWHC 3118 (Admin) at [40].
[295] pp 169–172 below.
[296] See especially pp 172–175 below.
[297] [1993] 3 SCR 519.

both conditions were met in *Carter*: the legal conception of s 7 had advanced since *Rodriguez* (the law on overbreadth and gross disproportionality) and the legislative and social facts differed from the evidence before that court.[298]

The language of *Carter* on the rule of precedence is broad. It suggests that lower courts have significant discretion in ascertaining fundamental changes in legal culture, social opinion or medical evidence and disregarding precedent. This flexible view of precedence means that legal progress is not reined in by judicial hierarchy, and a case need not reach the Supreme Court if substantial changes in circumstances require a change in the law. However, this approach has not been universally welcomed. According to Newman, this departure from the rule against anticipatory overruling is unexplained and shows a 'striking disdain for precedent'.[299] One could argue that, in respect of new rights claimed under the Charter, a relaxation of *stare decisis* is desirable given the parties' inequality of arms; the respondent public authority will always have the resources to take the case to the final stage, whereas the financial burden on individual litigants means that the Supreme Court may never hear the case and have an opportunity to revisit its position.

In contrast with these developments in Canada, British courts have consistently supported a strict view of precedence. In *Conway*, the High Court found that it was not bound by *Nicklinson* only because of its peculiar context: an assisted dying Bill was before Parliament, which prompted the majority to defer the assessment of HRA-compatibility.[300] The Court of Appeal drew two further distinctions: *Nicklinson* regarded patients in long-term suffering rather than terminally ill patients within six months of death, and the appellant had put forward a specific legislative model that could replace the blanket prohibition.[301] The High Court in *Newby* found itself bound by the Court of Appeal decision in *Conway* even in the presence of a new claim under Art 2 ECHR.[302] Absent special circumstances, lower courts appear unwilling to provide a fresh reappraisal of arguments based on new evidence, intervening experience in other jurisdictions, or changes in social opinion.

E. Parliaments' Ambivalent View of Courts as Constitutional Interpreters

Mullock suggested that, despite the dismissal of the *Nicklinson* appeal, the judgment 'has almost had as much impact as a verdict in favour of Nicklinson,

---

[298] [2015] 1 SCR 331 at [44]–[47].
[299] Newman, op cit fn 266 at p 218. For further criticism of the impact of *Carter* on precedence see Bateman – LeBlanc (2018) 'Dialogue on death: Parliament and the courts on medically-assisted dying' p 387 in Ross (ed), op cit fn 85.
[300] [2017] EWHC 2447 (Admin) at [84].
[301] [2018] EWCA Civ 1431 at [134].
[302] [2019] EWHC 3118 (Admin) at [48]–[49].

Lamb and Martin',[303] and that the warning that a s 4 declaration might be issued in the future had the same influence as an actual declaration.[304] This proved to be over-optimistic. Ironically, the refusal of British judges to issue a s 4 declaration was a hindrance to parliamentary debates. Martin noted the confusion that *Nicklinson* generated as to what is expected of Parliament during the House of Commons' consideration of the 2015 Bill; this included the interpretation by MPs that the law did not need changing, insofar as only two judges found it incompatible with the ECHR, or that Parliament acted within the margin of appreciation.[305] Given courts' s 4 power to alert Parliament to legislative solutions falling short of HRA standards, any obiter comments on the desirability of reviewing the law, without a formal finding of incompatibility, are likely to remain inconsequential. Declarations of incompatibility have been consistently followed by compliant legislative responses and the continuation of the ban cannot be seen as parliamentary defiance of the courts. Rather, courts have chosen not to place any constraints on Parliament as regards assisted-death legislation, notwithstanding their constitutional mandate under the HRA 1998.

The unhelpfully ambiguous position of the UK Supreme Court in its dialogue with Parliament and Parliament's marginal focus on assisted dying proposals contrast with the clear message sent by the Canadian judiciary in *Carter* and its legislative aftermath. As Stewart noted, while s 241.2 was a departure from *Carter*, overall the legislative response followed the judgment.[306] Bill C-14 confirmed the validity of the 'dialogue' thesis, showing that Parliament preserves its place in fine-tuning the law after the entrenchment of the Charter. Conversely, for Macfarlane, despite the significant policy change effected, the new law was a surprising departure from the tendency of legislatures to follow courts' guidance on constitutionally permissible action.[307] Given the restriction to terminally ill patients, Nicolaides and Hennigar went so far as to conclude that Parliament's response denied judicial supremacy over constitutional interpretation;[308] it 'directly reject[ed] the Court's interpretation of what the rights set out in section 7 require regarding MAID eligibility'.[309] These authors view the new law as an expression of 'coordinate construction', a theory according to which neither branch of government holds the monopoly on constitutional interpretation and legislative responses to judgments can redefine the scope of rights.[310] There seems to be, however, scholarly

---

[303] Mullock, op cit fn 175 at p 18.

[304] ibid at p 24.

[305] Martin, op cit fn 198 at pp 216–17.

[306] Stewart, op cit fn 85 at pp 457–58.

[307] Macfarlane (2018) 'Conclusion: Policy influence and its limits – Assessing the power of courts and the Constitution' p 397 in Macfarlane (ed), op cit fn 87. See also Macfarlane (2013) 'Dialogue or compliance? Measuring legislatures' policy responses to court rulings on rights' *International PolScR* 39.

[308] Nicolaides and Hennigar, op cit fn 87 at p 326.

[309] ibid at p 327.

[310] ibid at p 313. See also pp 314–17 on theories about the relationship between Parliament and the judiciary in respect of Charter interpretation.

disagreement on whether 'dialogue' includes legislative attempts to modify a judi-cial invalidation or solely responses consistent with the judgments.[311]

The explanation for the departure of Bill C-14 from a unanimous judgment apparently lies in political considerations. According to Snow and Puddister, the adoption of a narrow eligibility scheme was the result of mixed responses from polls gauging MAiD support; consequently, 'the popular Trudeau government seemed averse to spending political capital on this controversial area.'[312] *Truchon* was an important test case for the framework of constitutional interpretation in Canada.[313] Since the executive did not appeal the Quebec judge's decision that 'reasonably foreseeable death' is an unlawful requirement, the Supreme Court's interpretation of s 7 rights will be restored. The federal Government's choice to amend legislation following *Truchon* without waiting for a 'second look' case in the Supreme Court treats the latter as the final arbiter in matters of Charter interpretation.

VII. Conclusion

This chapter has argued that the exceptional availability of physician-assisted dying in Canada after the intervention of the Supreme Court strikes a fairer balance between different interests than the absolute British ban. A number of commonalities have been nonetheless identified in these jurisdictions. Having established that the prohibition on assistance interferes with fundamental rights, and that subjective sanctity-of-life ideologies are unsatisfactory justifications, both countries' Supreme Courts have accepted that protecting the vulnerable consti-tutes a legitimate aim. Their conclusions mainly differed as regards the need for a blanket ban and the confidence in a scheme authorising assistance in limited circumstances. In the British debate, 'slippery slope' arguments drawing on fear of abusive or erroneous application of the law have so far prevailed. Conversely, the Canadian legal reform has permitted autonomous responses to catastrophic illness, subject to case-by-case medical assessment. It has been suggested here that a permissive MAiD regime including safeguards against abuse avoids the injustice of a bright-line rule that chooses between, as opposed to reconciling, competing rights.

In the UK, the encroachment upon self-determination rights in the name of speculative threats to others remains a disproportionate response to vulner-ability issues, despite the DPP's policy of non-prosecution of compassionate assistance. Rather, the incongruence between legislative bar and administrative

---

[311] See Macfarlane (2017–18) 'Dialogue, remedies, and positive rights: *Carter v Canada* as a micro-cosm for past and future issues under the Charter of Rights and Freedoms' *Ottawa LR* 107 at p 127.

[312] Snow and Puddister, op cit fn 260 at p 53.

[313] See section II.

toleration compromises the moral justification for the restriction and raises rule-of-law concerns. Nor could the blanket ban be successfully mitigated, as Huxtable suggested, by greater clarity on the factors used in prosecution or a specific statutory defence.[314] The DPP guidelines cannot be so prescriptive as to contradict the statute by reading an exemption into it; as Coggon noted, it would be improper for the DPP to legislate.[315] Parliament's intervention is essential to ensure a legitimate assisted dying regime, and a statutory exception based on *ex ante* judicial dispensation or medical authorisation is preferable to a legal defence.

In fact, any *ex post facto* assessment of criminal liability offers less protection to the vulnerable than an exception allowing prior examination of the case, as less evidence is available to verify consent and medical circumstances. The prospect of criminal proceedings also deters patients and potential assisters, especially medical professionals, unlikely to risk prosecution for patients unrelated to them. Reliance on family members typically limits assisted dying options to travelling abroad to permissive jurisdictions, and the high cost of travel and other arrangements raises equality issues.[316] In cases of extreme disability, for those unwilling or unable to summon assistance, the choice is between indefinite suffering and self-starvation as sole independent recourse. The law also prompts those approaching a stage where they would lose their independence to take their lives prematurely, often through a violent method. Several rights are compromised as a result: privacy, protection against inhuman treatment, right to life, non-discrimination.

A regulatory framework for assistance in dying would remove the inconsistencies within medical law, which subordinates provision of life-saving treatment to patients' consent and refers disputes on withdrawal of life support for children and incompetent adults to courts, guided by medical opinion. If sanctity-of-life and vulnerability considerations do not require the protection of competent adults against irrational refusal of life-preserving treatment or investigating whether such refusal was the product of undue influence, they should not be invoked to deny patients the choice to end intractable suffering and avoid a distressing death. The current ban affects severely disabled and/or impecunious patients who are not vulnerable, and hence not the intended target of the measure, whilst it fails to protect vulnerable individuals capable of travelling to Dignitas or ending their lives unaided, by disconnecting a life-support machine or otherwise. The interference with fundamental rights is therefore both ill-suited to meet its objective and overbroad.

Admittedly, removing the blanket ban presents difficulties over the justification of conditions and exclusions. Newman cautioned: 'once one moves away from

---

[314] Huxtable (2017) 'Judgment 1 – R (on the Application of Nicklinson and Another) v Ministry of Justice [2014] UKSC 38' p 206 in Smith at al (eds), op cit fn 121.
[315] Coggon, op cit fn 121 at p 213.
[316] See Mondal and Bhowmik (2018) 'Physician assisted suicide tourism – A future global business phenomenon' *The Business and Management Review* 35; Richards (2017) 'Assisted suicide as a remedy for suffering? The end-of-life preferences of British "suicide tourists"' *Medical Anthropology* 348.

a bright-line rule, a law on assisted suicide becomes subject to continual questioning concerning the boundary temporarily established'.[317] However, an unjust ban cannot be maintained solely to avoid addressing access issues and potential future challenges. The progressive fine-tuning of the law is inherent in the democratic process through which courts and Parliament update legislation, guided by social opinion and taking stock of experience.

It has also been submitted here that the Canadian Supreme Court's position in *Carter* better reflects the constitutional role of the judiciary in bringing about reform in sensitive policy areas. Democratic law-making relies on courts to place the cause of niche sections of the population on the legislative agenda and to advance human-rights protection in controversial, slow-changing aspects of the law. The comparative examination of assisted dying laws in Canada and the UK reveals a profound problem of democracy when courts fail to act as a corrective to majoritarian deliberation or inertia-ridden legislatures.

[317] Newman, op cit fn 266 at p 220.

3

Voting Rights for Prisoners

SUSAN EASTON

This chapter analyses the respective approaches taken by the national legislatures, governments and courts[1] of the UK and Canada to the controversial issue of voting rights for prisoners. This is a matter which is not complicated by some of the doctrinal questions arising in respect of other issues examined in this book – most notably those pertaining to the horizontal effect of human rights norms[2] and the need to balance the competing rights of discrete sections of society. The grant or removal of voting rights by legislation is manifestly a 'vertical' question, and in both countries the legislature stands vis-à-vis prisoners very much as a 'singular antagonist' rather than as a mediator between different social groups.[3]

I. Background Issues – History and Policy

At the time the Charter came into force, Canada's federal election law (the relevant provision being the Canada Elections Act 1985, s 51(e)) denied voting rights to 'every person undergoing punishment as an inmate in any penal institution for the commission of any offence'. Section 51(e) presented an obvious question of its compatibility with the Charter, s 3 of which provides that:

Democratic rights.

3. Every citizen of Canada has the right to vote in an election of members of the House of Commons or of a legislative assembly and to be qualified for membership therein.

The s 51(e) ban on prisoner voting in Canada appears to have origins in pre-federation Imperial law, the Constitutional Act 1791,[4] s 23 of which excluded from the franchise – inter alia – anyone 'who shall have been attainted for Treason

---

[1] Treating the ECtHR as a UK court for these purposes.
[2] Notably in the chapters by Bamforth, Hatzis and Loveland.
[3] See pp 14–17 above.
[4] 31 Geo III, c 31 (UK). The franchise was then obviously limited in scope, embracing (per s 20) only men who owned significant amounts of property. This exclusion was consistently applied in British colonial constitutional law throughout the eighteenth and nineteenth centuries.

or Felony in any Court of Law within any of his Majesty's Dominions'. Those provisions were retained in the voting rights sections of the British North America Act 1867.[5] The 1985 law was notably more restrictive than the 1789 version in that it reached to 'every person' serving a custodial sentence.

While felons in eighteenth-century Britain were denied voting rights, this situation arose indirectly rather than as a result of an explicit statutory ban. Persons convicted of felony or treason were subject at common law to attainder, one element of which was the loss of the right to hold property. Since (almost all) routes to franchise qualification then required property ownership, conviction brought with it disenfranchisement (although obviously few convicts would then have satisfied the property requirement in any event).[6] People convicted of misdemeanours were not automatically disenfranchised. As the 1832 and 1867 Reform Acts increased the size of the voting population by lowering the qualifying property threshold, so the misdemeanour convicts who were not expressly denied the right to vote also grew. In practical terms such convicts could not vote because they could not attend a polling station on election days.

The statutory denial of voting rights to prisoners originated shortly after the 1867 Reform Act in the Forfeiture Act 1870. The Act abolished the attainder of a felon's property, but s 2 of the Act prevented any felon sentenced for more than 12 months from voting, or standing for election. Those serving under 12 months were not prohibited from voting, but still were unable to vote, because they could not visit a polling station. Postal ballots were available only to those in the armed forces, until the 1948 Representation of the People Act, which extended postal voting to ordinary citizens. Some prisoners did vote using postal votes in the February 1950 election.[7]

The distinction between felonies and misdemeanours was subsequently abolished by the Criminal Law Act 1967, s 1. From 1967 to 1969, there was no statutory limit on the right to vote for prisoners. But as the qualifying address for postal votes was the offender's home address, and as the electoral register was published annually, prisoners could vote only until the new electoral register was published. In effect they had a maximum of one year to vote, as by the time of the next register they would not be at their home address.

The Representation of the People Act 1969 explicitly prohibited prisoners from voting. Section 4 provided that:

4. – Disfranchisement of offenders in prison, etc.

(1) A convicted person during the time that he is detained in a penal institution in pursuance of his sentence shall be legally incapable of voting at any parliamentary or local government election.

---

[5] Section 41.
[6] Joint Committee on the Draft Voting Eligibility (Prisoners) Bill (2013–2014) *Draft Voting Eligibility (Prisoners) Bill* at paras 9–13.
[7] Reported in *The Times* 24 February 1950.

Section 4 enacted a recommendation made in a wide-ranging review of electoral law conducted under the auspices of the Speaker of the House of Commons and published in 1968.[8] The prohibition in the 1969 Act was subsequently retained verbatim in s 1 of the Representation of the People Act 1983.

Exceptions were made for those incarcerated for contempt of court and non-payment of fines (s 3(2)(a),(c)). While remand prisoners were allowed to vote, in practice it was difficult for them to do so, because of the problems of designating their place of residence. However, the Representation of the People Act 2000, s 7A allowed remand prisoners to be regarded as resident at the place where they are detained for the purposes of being entered onto the electoral register.

As the UK's incarceration rate is the highest in Western Europe,[9] the impact of a blanket ban has had considerable impact, just as it has in the US, where mass incarceration has increased the impact of felon disenfranchisement.[10] In 2005, it was estimated that 48,000 sentenced prisoners were disenfranchised by the Representation of the People Act 2000.[11] The numbers would be even higher now, given the substantial rise in the prison population since then.[12]

Prisoner enfranchisement clearly raises constitutional matters, including the role of the judiciary in challenging rights violations. But the issue also raises penological questions relating both to sentencing policies and to prisoners' rights in a more general sense. Although the landmark case of *Sauvé v Canada (No 2)* (hereafter *Sauvé No 2*)[13] addresses the specific area of prisoners' voting rights, it also raised wider questions of elected representatives choosing to deprive a group of its fundamental rights and whether it is acceptable for unelected judges to have the power to override the will of the legislature and how to resolve this without undermining the role of either the legislature or the judiciary. This constitutional problem is highlighted by the situation of prisoners who are generally an unpopular group attracting little public sympathy or support. Felon disenfranchisement also raises questions regarding the purposes of punishment, the social exclusion of prisoners and the meaning of citizenship, as well as the role of public opinion in penal policy and the disparate impact of such a policy on specific groups.

The decision of the Canadian Supreme Court in *Sauvé No 2* is valuable for proponents of prisoners' voting rights because it has exposed the fundamental weaknesses of the justifications for felon disenfranchisement, challenged the arguments advanced by the legislature and reaffirmed the status of prisoners as citizens, whose rights follow them through the prison door. In contrast, the UK courts have been much weaker in defending prisoners' voting rights and the UK Government

---

[8] (1968) *Final Report of Mr. Speaker's Conference on Electoral Law* (Cmnd 3717).

[9] www.prisonstudies.org/world-prison-brief-data.

[10] Uggen, Larsen and Shannon (2016) *Six million lost voters: state level estimates of felony disenfranchisement.*

[11] Department of Constitutional Affairs (2006) 'Consultation Paper, Voting rights of convicted prisoners detained in the UK' p 15.

[12] See Sturge (2019) *UK Prison Population Statistics.*

[13] *Sauvé v Canada (No 2)* [2002] 3 SCR 519.

has consistently resisted granting sentenced prisoners those rights. However, *Sauvé* was cited approvingly in *Hirst v UK*[14] (hereafter *Hirst*) by the ECtHR, where the Strasbourg Court took a robust approach in criticising the 'civil death'[15] of prisoners which underpinned the UK's blanket ban. But since *Hirst* the ECtHR has modified its position, in terms of accepting the legitimacy of disenfranchisement for more serious offenders and its refusal to award costs or compensation to prisoners whose rights are infringed, or to give judges the power to decide on disenfranchisement.

II. The Canadian Approach – Issues Highlighted in *Sauvé v Canada No 2*

By 1992, s 51(e) had been subjected to Charter challenges in various lower courts, which had in turn produced judgments upholding and invalidating the ban.[16] Those challenges had been rooted primarily[17] in s 3 of the Charter. The highest profile – and most persistent – litigant was Richard Sauvé. His initial suit in the Ontario courts claiming that s 51(e) breached both s 3 and s 15 of the Charter had failed at trial,[18] but Sauvé succeeded before the Ontario Court of Appeal. Contemporaneously, the federal Court of Appeal reached the same conclusion in *Belczowski v Canada*.[19]

The parties in *Sauvé* had agreed that s 51(e) breached s 3; argument centred on whether the breach was justified per s 1. Taking the view that disenfranchisement laws presented a paradigmatic 'singular antagonist' scenario, the Ontario Court of Appeal considered that the *Oakes* test had to be rigorously applied. In a brief judgment, the Court rejected all three of the justifications (singly and in aggregate) that the Government advanced; those being (a) to affirm and maintain the sanctity of the franchise in our democracy; (b) to preserve the integrity of the voting process; and (c) to sanction offenders.[20]

---

[14] *Hirst v UK (No 2)* App No 74025/01 (6 October 2005), (2004) 38 EHRR 40. The Grand Chamber judgment is at (2006) 42 EHRR 41.

[15] A phrase used to convey the notion that imprisonment carries with it – in addition to loss of liberty – deprivation of other civil rights as well. On the history of the idea in the Anglo-American constitutional tradition see especially Chin (2012) 'The new civil death: rethinking punishment in the era of mass conviction' *University of Pennsylvania LR* 1789; Saunders (1970) 'Civil death: a new look at an ancient doctrine' *William and Mary LR* 988.

[16] Upheld in *Badger v Canada (AG)* [1989] 1 WWR 216 and in *ReJolivet and Barker and The Queen* (1983) 1 DLR (4th) 604 (BCSC).

[17] The equality or anti-discrimination provisions of s 15 have also been invoked on a secondary basis: '*Equality before and under the law and equal protection and benefit of law* 15(1). Every individual is equal before and under the law and has the right to the equal protection and equal benefit of the law without discrimination and, in particular, without discrimination based on race, national or ethnic origin, colour, religion, sex, age or mental or physical disability.'

[18] (1988) 66 OR (2d) 234, 53 DLR (4th) 595.

[19] (1992) 90 DLR (4th) 330.

[20] (1992) 90 DLR (4th) 330.

A. In the Supreme Court – *Sauvé (No 1)*

Both appellate court decisions were subsequently upheld in the Supreme Court. The Court's judgment *Sauvé v Canada* (Attorney-General) *(No 1)*[21] (hereafter *Sauvé No 1*) was extraordinarily succinct, comprising just six sentences in four paragraphs:

1   We are all of the view that these appeals should be dismissed.
2   The Attorney General of Canada has properly conceded that s. 51(*e*) of the *Canada Elections Act*, R.S.C., 1985, c. E-2, contravenes s. 3 of the *Canadian Charter of Rights and Freedoms* but submits that s.51(*e*) is saved under s. 1 of the *Charter*. We do not agree. In our view, s. 51(*e*) is drawn too broadly and fails to meet the proportionality test, particularly the minimal impairment component of the test, as expressed in the s.1 jurisprudence of the Court.
3   Accordingly, the first constitutional question is answered in the affirmative and the second constitutional question is answered in the negative.
4   Consequently, both appeals are dismissed with costs.

In one of the more obvious examples of the notion of dialogue between the judiciary and the legislature as to the proper extent of Charter Rights,[22] the national Parliament then enacted a new law. The amended s 51(e) provided that voting rights would be denied to inter alia: '(e) Every person who is imprisoned in a correctional institution serving a sentence of two years or more'. The constitutionality of this amendment was then challenged in *Sauvé No 2*. In a five-to-four split decision, the Supreme Court held the law invalid.

B. The Majority Judgment in *Sauvé No 2*

The majority ruled that the amended s 51(e) infringed s 3 and that it could not be justified under s 1. The majority therefore did not deem it necessary to consider the alternative argument that s 51(e) infringed the equality guarantee. The Court said that construing prisoners as lacking the moral virtue needed to vote undermines the constitutional commitment to recognise the worth and dignity of all citizens which is essential to the legitimacy of the democratic process.[23] The judgment noted that the ban in s 51(e) originated in what were in effect civil death statute provisions in the 1791 Constitutional Act, which prohibited prisoners serving over two years from voting. Its retention was considered by the majority to be unconstitutional because it was a regressive law inappropriate to a modern democratic society. Nor could s 51(e) be justified as a punitive measure, as it was arbitrary and

---

[21] [1993] 2 SCR 438.
[22] See generally the comments in the introductory chapter to this volume. For a more specific illustration see Draghici's chapter herein.
[23] [2002] 3 SCR 519 at [35].

disproportionate and not linked to the blameworthiness of the offender, or to the harm which the offender's crime had caused.

The approach in *Sauvé No 2* is valuable because the Court rightly stresses that the link between voting and virtue is difficult to reconcile with the universal nature of rights, which should not and do not depend on the characteristics of those who hold them. The majority also made clear that it could not allow elected representatives to deprive a section of the population of its voting rights. The Court highlighted the positive value of felon enfranchisement and challenged the notion of imprisonment as civil death. It rejected the Government's argument that denying the right to vote to prisoners requires deference to the legislature because it is a matter of social and political philosophy. While this might be appropriate to decisions involving competing social and political policies, it is not appropriate to decisions involving a limitation of fundamental rights.

McLachlin CJ held that the right to vote was fundamental to Canadian democracy and the rule of law and cannot be set aside, which was why the framers of the Charter exempted it from being overridden by the legislature; s 3 is not one of the Charter Rights that falls within the notwithstanding proviso in s 33 of the Charter.[24] The Government had failed in its s 1 submissions adequately to identify the particular problems that required denial of right of vote. The objectives it cited – enhancing civic responsibility and respect for the rule of law and to provide additional punishment – were vague and symbolic. Enhancing civic responsibility could be said to be the purpose of any criminal law and it was not clear why prisoners serving over two years required an additional punishment. The court also ruled that s 51(e) did not meet the proportionality test. Section 51(e) was likely to undermine respect for the law rather than enhance it. The court made clear that:

> The legitimacy of the law and the obligation to obey the law flow directly from the right of every citizen to vote. To deny prisoners the right to vote is to lose an important means of teaching them democratic values and social responsibility.[25]

If democracy is based on equal participation, this is incompatible with elected representatives deciding who should vote. The fact that other states may do so is not instructive on what is appropriate for Canadian democracy. The Charter makes clear that prisoners are protected through constitutional limits on punishment.

Felon disenfranchisement, in the Court's opinion, does not comply with the requirements for legitimate punishment, namely that it should not be arbitrary and should serve a valid criminal law purpose. There is no supporting evidence to suggest that it either deters offenders or rehabilitates them. It also does not meet the demands of retributive punishment as it applies to all, regardless of the severity or type of crime. Any benefits which might result from the loss of the vote – which are tenuous – are outweighed by its negative effects. For example, it

---

[24] Which permits legislatures to breach certain Charter rights (for a five-year renewable period) so long as the legislation so doing states in express terms that will be its effect.
[25] [2002] 3 SCR 519 at [38].

has a disproportionate impact on Canada's already disadvantaged First Nations peoples,who constitute a disproportionate number of prisoners, relative to their size in the population as a whole[26] and who did not get the full right to vote until 1960.[27] It also undermines respect for the law and democratic life.

The majority was not impressed by the national Government's justification arguments under s 1. While the majority was willing to accept that the Government's objectives of promoting civil responsibility and respect for law and imposing appropriate punishment although vague, were capable in principle of limiting Charter rights, but in this case the Government had failed to establish proportionality, because of the lack of connection between denying the vote to prisoners and its stated goals. It could not show that losing the vote encouraged prisoners to respect the law, or that it was a legitimate punishment. Rather, the Court stressed that the obligation to obey the law stems from the fact that the law is made by and on behalf of citizens and its legitimacy stems from the right of every citizen to vote. So disenfranchisement undermines this democratic legitimacy: '[D]enying citizens the right to vote runs counter to our constitutional commitment to the inherent worth and dignity of every individual'.[28]

The majority judgment in *Sauvé No 2* bluntly confronts the legitimacy of the notion of the social or civil death of prisoners: 'The idea that certain classes of people are not morally fit or morally worthy to vote and to participate in the law-making process is ancient and obsolete'.[29] The majority rejected the argument that only those who respect the law should participate in the political process: 'Denial of the right to vote on the basis of attributed moral unworthiness is inconsistent with the respect for the dignity of every person that lies at the heart of Canadian democracy and the Charter'.[30] If the Canadian Government is suggesting that some people are morally unworthy to vote, this decision is not theirs to make.

The majority also rejected the claim that prisoners by breaking the law had lost their right to participate in democratic life:

> The social compact requires the citizen to obey the laws created by the democratic process. But it does not follow that failure to do so nullifies the citizen's continued membership in the self-governing polity.[31]

It was clear that s 51(e) bore little relation to offenders' particular crimes as it did not differentiate between them. A blanket restriction – even one restricted by

---

[26] *Statistics Canada* 'Table 35-10-0016-01 Adult custody admissions to correctional services by aboriginal identity', available at https://doi.org/10.25318/3510001601-eng.

[27] By repeal of s 14(2) of the Canada Elections Act which had linked indigenous people's voting rights to relinquishing treaty status.

[28] [2002] 3 SCR 519 at [35]. The conclusion on this point echoed the argument of the South African Constitutional Court in *August and Another v Electoral Commission and Others* [1999] SALR 1 at [17]: 'the vote of each and every citizen is a badge of dignity and of personhood. Quite literally, it says that everybody counts'.

[29] *Sauvé v Canada (No 2)* [2002] 3 SCR 519 at [43].

[30] ibid at [44].

[31] ibid at [47].

the amended s 51(e) only to prisoners serving more than a two-year sentence – does not meet the requirements of denunciatory retributive punishment. Disenfranchisement undermines the legitimacy of government and the rule of law and the message that all are equal under the law. So it is more likely to erode respect for the law than to enhance it. It was also clear that prisoners could vote in other jurisdictions without problems.

C. The Dissenting Judgments

Gonthier J accepted that s 51(e) breached s 3 of the Charter, but he also accepted that the breach could be justified under s 1. He argued that s 51(e) met the proportionality test, as the law was not arbitrary, but rationally connected to its objectives, and the state's role is to promote civic responsibility. The provision recognised prisoners' dignity and applied only to those offenders who had committed more serious crimes and reflected the fact of incarceration and the length of sentence. Impairment of the Charter right is minimal and a less intrusive measure would not be as effective. Gonthier J stressed that it was only a temporary suspension, and based on serious criminal activity, unlike irrelevant personal characteristics such as class or gender. Most prisoners were deprived of the opportunity to vote in just one election, as 75 per cent of prisoners in federal prisons were serving sentences of five years or less. The amended s 51(e) also recognised the dignity of offenders because it treated them as autonomous individuals making choices and taking responsibility for the consequences of those choices.

Moreover, deference to Parliament was appropriate because the provision raises questions of penal philosophy and policy. Given that there are competing theoretical arguments on the issue, the practices of other liberal democracies and the reasoned view of its own democratically elected Parliament, it argued, should also be considered. There may be a range of approaches; other states have limited prisoners' voting rights and the appropriate threshold is a matter for Parliament rather than the courts. Gonthier J defended according such deference to the legislature in circumstances where – as had happened after *Sauvé No 1* – an amended law had been enacted after evaluation in the legislature and against the background of legislative and public concern about crime.

Gonthier J was also sceptical regarding the s 15 claim. The denial of the vote was a consequence of incarceration, which in turn arose from the commission of a crime by the individual prisoner and not from the personal attribution of ethnic origin, or social condition, or because of stereotypical assumptions regarding a group characteristic.[32] Nor was the measure targeted at a specific ethnic group: rather, it is the prisoner status which is significant. While Gonthier J was obviously

---

[32] These being the accepted triggers for a presumption that differential treatment imposed by legislation might be discriminatory per s 15; see particularly *Law v Canada* [1999] 1 SCR 497; *R v Kapp* [2008] 2 SCR 483.

correct in concluding that there was no such direct discriminatory objective in s 51, his analysis fails to take account of the fact while the measure was not specifically targeted at First Nations peoples, it does have a significant disparate impact on them in the context of the disproportionate numbers of First Nations people who are incarcerated.[33] Exclusion from the democratic process can reinforce inequality if certain groups are disproportionately imprisoned.[34]

III. The UK's Position on Prisoner Disenfranchisement

The interaction between the court and the legislature in Canada on the voting rights issue has been notably short and sharp: *Sauvé No 1*; a subsequent legislative amendment; and then *Sauvé No 2*. Until such time as either the Supreme Court is persuaded to reverse *Sauvé No 2* or a sufficient political majority emerges to modify the judgment's effect through a formal constitutional amendment,[35] the controversy has run its course. Draghici's chapter in this volume shows a similarly brief process at work over the question of the legal status of assisted dying in Canada. Draghici also records that the issue has been much more procedurally complex in the UK: despite multiple instances of litigation and attempts to introduce new legislation, the question remains unresolved. That complexity is also evident in relation to the prisoners' votes issue.

A. *Hirst v United Kingdom*

The current debate on restoring the right was triggered by the ECtHR's judgment in *Hirst v United Kingdom*[36] in 2005, which found the UK's blanket ban incompatible with Art 3 of Protocol No 1 to the Convention. Article 3 provides that states are obliged to hold free elections under conditions 'which will ensure the free expression of the opinion of the people in the choice of the legislature'. Although Art 3

[33] The '2016–2017 Annual Report: Office of the Correctional Investigator' indicates that while indigenous people constitute 5% of the Canadian population, 'they comprise 26.4% of the total federal inmate population. 37.6% of the federal women inmate population is Indigenous' (at p 48). They are also disproportionately over-represented in segregation placements and at maximum security institutions. While the federal prison population increased by less than 5% between 2007 and 2016: 'the Indigenous prison population increased by 37%' (at p 48). 'Indigenous' here refers to First Nations, Inuit and Métis peoples.

[34] Similar issues arise in relation to black Americans in the US; see Chung (2019) *Felony disenfranchisement: a primer*; and to indigenous groups in Australia, as highlighted in *Roach v Electoral Commissioner* [2007] HCA 43, (2007) 233 CLR 162.

[35] Which would per s 38 of the Constitution Act 1982 require a bare majority resolution in the Commons and Senate, and bare majority resolution in at least two-thirds of the Provinces, which Provinces in aggregate would have to contain at least 50% of the national population.

[36] [2006] 42 EHRR 41.

does not explicitly refer to the right to vote, it is clear from Convention jurisprudence that the right to vote and the right to stand for election are protected by it.

The voting ban was initially – and unsuccessfully – challenged by John Hirst and two other prisoners in the High Court in 2001.[37] Hirst's suit was one of the first to be brought on an HRA 1998 ground after the Act came into force. Art 3 of Protocol No 1 is one of the provisions of the Convention which is given Convention Right status by Sch 1 of the Act. The High Court was not persuaded that the ban beached Art 3. The Court thought that the UK's position lay in the middle of the spectrum of approaches in democratic societies and that its position on that spectrum was a matter for Parliament rather than the courts to determine.

Hirst then took his case to Strasbourg, and in *Hirst v United Kingdom* the ECtHR found the blanket ban infringed Art 3. The ban was not proportionate as there was no discernible link 'between the sanction and the conduct and circumstances of the individual concerned'.[38] The Court also said that any restriction should be limited to those who had committed major crimes.

The ECtHR acknowledged that Art 3 was not an absolute entitlement. It contains scope for implied limitations, and that states must be allowed a margin of appreciation, as there are different ways of organising elections. The UK Government, like the Canadian Government in *Sauvé*, had defended the legislative ban on the ground that it was intended to prevent crime, to enhance civic responsibility and respect for the rule of law, and to impose an additional punishment.

However, while the Court accepted that these were legitimate aims, they were not rationally linked to the loss of the vote because they applied to all regardless of the offence. The means by which these aims were pursued in the UK – an automatic restriction on all sentenced prisoners – fell outside the margin of appreciation. The UK measure did not meet its purported aims and there was no link between the denial of the vote and the prevention of crime, or respect for the rule of law. The ban was also disproportionate because it was not linked to the seriousness of the offence or the length of the sentence, but rather based on a desire to avoid offending the public. It was also an arbitrary punishment, as whether the punishment took effect in a particular case depended on the timing of the election. The exclusion of prisoners from the democratic process made it harder for them to have any influence on penal policy or other matters. The Court was also critical of the failure to consider the ban fully in Parliament. A dissenting judge did note that the Speaker's Conference on Electoral Law had considered the matter and that the UK did allow some prisoners, namely remand prisoners, to vote, and that ultimately the matter was one Parliament should decide. The Strasbourg Court's reference to *Sauvé No 2* also illustrates the increasing cosmopolitanism of legal reasoning as constitutional principles migrate between courts in different jurisdictions.[39]

---

[37] *Hirst v Attorney-General, Pearson and Martinez v Secretary of State for the Home Department* (2001) EWHC Admin 239, [2001] HRLR 39.

[38] *Hirst v United Kingdom (No 2)* App No 74025/01 (6 October 2005), (2006) 42 EHRR 41.

[39] See further pp 172–73, 219–20 and 242–43.

B. Political Reaction to *Hirst*

The (third) Blair Government and the subsequent Gordon Brown-led Labour administration showed no immediate inclination to promote legislation to address the judgment handed down in *Hirst*. A Consultation Paper[40] in December 2006 invited views on the issue as a matter of principle and on a range of possibilities, namely linking the ban to sentence length, or giving discretion to sentencers, or simply removing the vote for those convicted of electoral offences, approaches used in some other jurisdictions. A second Consultation Paper,[41] published in 2009, asked for views on where to set the threshold for voting. The options put forward were allowing prisoners to vote automatically if serving less than one year, less than two years, less than four years, or allowing prisoners serving between two and four years to apply for the right to vote subject to judicial permission. If the vote had been restored to prisoners serving under four years in 2009, it was calculated that 28,800 prisoners would have been able to vote.[42]

The matter remained unresolved when the Conservative–Liberal collation administration took power after the 2010 general election. Indeed, the coalition and Conservative administrations led by David Cameron indicated that they would rather withdraw the UK from the Convention than comply with the judgment. Shortly after becoming Prime Minister Cameron famously said that it made him '[P]hysically ill even to contemplate having to give the vote to anyone who is in prison. Frankly, when people commit a crime and go to prison, they should lose their rights, including the right to vote'.[43]

The position received explicit parliamentary support in the Commons. In a debate on the issue in 2011, the House of Commons had strongly supported a motion endorsing the status quo and made clear that decisions on such matters should be a matter for Parliament, for democratically elected lawmakers.[44] A year later, Prime Minister Cameron again made it clear that prisoners would not be given the vote under his government.[45] But effectively this is saying that it is a matter for the electorate to decide who should be permitted to vote, which is wrong in principle when a fundamental right is in issue, and contrasts sharply with the approach in *Sauvé No 2*.[46]

---

[40] Department of Constitutional Affairs (2006) 'Consultation Paper, Voting rights of convicted prisoners detained in the UK'.

[41] Ministry of Justice (2009) 'Voting rights of convicted prisoners detained within the UK, second stage Consultation'.

[42] ibid at [27].

[43] HCD 3 November 2010 c 921.

[44] HCD 10 February 2011 c 586. The vote was 234 in favour and 22 against.

[45] HCD 24 October 2012 c 923.

[46] Hirst had also argued that denial of the vote was 'tantamount to the elected choosing the electorate', [2006] 42 EHRR 41 at [46].

i. *The Joint Committee Report and Draft Bill*

The issue was nonetheless subsequently considered further by a Parliamentary Joint Committee in 2012. The Committee published a Draft Bill on 23 November 2012, which included three options: to disenfranchise sentenced prisoners serving over six months; to disqualify those sentenced to over four years; and to retain the status quo, with a ban on all convicted prisoners. The Committee had taken oral and written evidence from a wide range of interested parties, including prison reform groups, constitutional experts and penologists, and visited two prisons to ascertain prisoners' own views. In its Report[47] on the Draft Prisoner Voting Bill published in 2013,the Joint Committee emphasised that the majority of members endorsed some limited change, allowing those serving 12 months or less to retain their right to vote, with only three members dissenting.[48] This one-year threshold is relatively low and would have had minimal impact, allowing only 7,000 prisoners to vote, but was at least a step in the right direction, and if it operated without adverse effects would strengthen the case for extending it further.

The Joint Committee thought that restoring the vote to those convicted of more serious crimes would not be accepted by Parliament or the public. Its Report stressed the importance of the UK's compliance with its obligations under international law, and of respecting the rule of law and the desirability of remaining part of the Convention system. Using sentence length as a threshold would link the punishment to the seriousness of the crime. Its proposal would take the UK back to the situation when the Convention was signed, when 12 months was the threshold, and reinstate the pre-1967 position.[49] It also corresponds with the existing right of certain offenders to sit in the House of Commons or to stand for election.[50] It would mean that offenders convicted in the magistrates' court would not lose the vote, but those sentenced in the Crown Court would be unable to do so. The Committee did not rule out the possibility that prisoners serving longer sentences could regain their vote towards the end of their sentence. Prisoners would be allowed to apply six months before their scheduled release date to be registered to vote in the constituency into which they are due to be released.[51] It might also be possible for prisoners to earn back the right to vote, through good conduct, or by completing a citizenship course, or other educational programme.[52] But the Committee did not think it was feasible to leave the decision to a judge to determine on an individual basis.

While acknowledging the issue of parliamentary sovereignty, the Committee thought this rested in the power to withdraw from the Convention, rather than

---

[47] Joint Committee (2013) 'Report on the Draft Voting Eligibility (Prisoners) Bill'.
[48] ibid at [236].
[49] Twelve months would reflect the law in the Forfeiture Act 1870 where there was a loss of the vote for prisoners convicted for a felony, that is, attracting a sentence of more than 12 months.
[50] Representation of the People Act 1981, s 1.
[51] Joint Committee op cit, fn 47 above at [239].
[52] ibid at [219].

choosing which obligations to follow, or which decisions to implement.[53] It argued that the UK should comply with the decision in *Hirst* or renounce the Convention. But the Committee thought it would not be worth doing so for a relatively minor issue.

The Committee also found that the Government had failed to advance a plausible case in terms of penal policy. For example, it had not established the deterrent effect of disenfranchisement on offending. It also questioned whether the ban was a proportionate means to achieve the legitimate aim of enhancing civic responsibility. It recommended that the Government introduce a Bill with two options for consideration, variously representing compliance and non-compliance with the Strasbourg Court's judgment. Under the compliance option, which the majority of the Committee favoured, prisoners serving 12 months or less would be entitled to vote in all UK parliamentary, local and European elections, in the constituency where they were registered before sentencing. It was intended that prisoners would vote by post or by proxy, but not in person. If there is no identified prior residence, prisoners should register by means of a declaration of local connection, to address the potential problem of bloc voting. But despite the recommendations of the Committee and the pressure from Strasbourg, the blanket ban remained in place for the 2015 and 2017 general elections.[54]

C. Post-*Hirst* Judgments Before the ECtHR

While the ECtHR has – subsequent to its decision in *Hirst* – upheld prisoner disenfranchisement in some circumstances in other jurisdictions, it has not accepted a blanket ban.[55]

In *Frodl v Austria*[56] the Court was critical of the fact that a ban had been imposed without judicial consideration. However, in the later case of *Scoppola v Italy*[57] (hereafter *Scoppola*), the ECtHR rejected the requirement that the decision on who should retain the vote should be made by a judge in the context of an individual sentencing decision. In *Scoppola* the Court upheld a prohibition on voting for a five-year period by prisoners serving sentences of three to five years, and a lifetime ban for those serving five years or more. However, those who were permanently deprived of the right to vote were allowed to apply for restoration

---

[53] The failure to change the law in response to *Hirst* was also criticised by the Human Rights Joint Committee (2015) 'Seventh report, human rights judgments' at [3.22].

[54] Chris Grayling, the then Lord Chancellor, announced publication of the Draft Bill in November 2012. When he introduced the Bill, he said he recognised the importance of upholding the rule of law, but also recognised that Parliament was sovereign. He acknowledged the Report in a letter to the Chair of the Committee in February 2014, but no detailed response was given.

[55] See, for example, *Scoppola v Italy (No 3)* App No 126/05 (22 May 2012), (2013) 56 EHRR 19, in contrast to *Anchugovand Gladkov v Russia* App Nos 11157104 and 15162/05 (4 July 2013).

[56] *Frodl v Austria* App No 20201/04 (8 April 2010).

[57] *Scoppola* (2013) 56 EHRR 19.

three years after the end of their sentence, which the Court thought showed that the Italian system was not excessively rigid.[58] In Italy, the ban was not automatic or indiscriminate, because the legislation took into account the gravity of the offence and the conduct of the offender, in contrast to the UK's position.

The Court has also limited the remedies for breaches of Art 3 in *Greens v United Kingdom*[59] in 2010 and subsequently in *Firth v United Kingdom*[60] in 2016, declaring that a declaration of incompatibility is just satisfaction for non-pecuniary harm suffered by prisoners and that damages would not be awarded. Moreover, in *McHugh and others v UK*[61] in 2015, a case involving over 1,000 prisoners, they also declined to award costs unless they have been reasonably and necessarily incurred, which was not deemed to be the case here.[62] So, as this financial threat receded, the UK Government's incentive to change was undermined. Earlier in 2010, the coalition Government[63] had indicated that the vote might be restored to prisoners serving shorter sentences (of less than four years) in order to meet its international human rights obligations and also because of fears that there might be financial costs in paying compensation to the large numbers of prisoners affected, but no change was introduced.

The Strasbourg Court noted in *Firth* the steps the UK had taken to address the situation, with the publication of the Draft Bill and the parliamentary Joint Committee's report,[64] which took evidence from a range of parties, but as the law remained unchanged, the UK was still in breach of Art 3. The ECtHR also indicated in *Greens* that it would stop hearing repetitive applications, while awaiting compliance by the UK with the *Hirst* judgment.

Some cases on voting rights have been deemed inadmissible by the Strasbourg Court. For example, the application in *McLean and Cole v United Kingdom*[65] was ruled inadmissible because it was filed too late in relation to past elections and too prematurely for forthcoming elections. It also included local government elections and the Alternative Vote Referendum, which were not covered by the Convention. The Court stressed that local authorities have administrative rather than legislative

---

[58] ibid at [109].

[59] *Greens and MT v United Kingdom* App Nos 60041/08 and 60054/08 (23 November 2010), (2011) 53 EHRR 21. In *Greens* the Court used a pilot judgment procedure as they had received over 2,000 applications on the same issue. Under this procedure the Court will reach a decision on a leading case and the remaining cases are expected to be sent back to the domestic courts to deal with, in light of the pilot judgment.

[60] *Firth and Others v United Kingdom* App Nos 47784/09 and 47806/09 (12 August 2014), (2016) 63 EHRR 25.

[61] *McHugh and others v United Kingdom* App No 51979/08 and 1,014 others (10 February 2015), [2015] 2 WLUK 310, The Times (12 February 2015).

[62] See also *Tovey v Ministry of Justice* (2011) EWHC 271 (QB), [2011] HRLR 17 for further discussion of this issue in the domestic courts.

[63] HCD 20 December 2010 c 151.

[64] publications.parliament.uk/pa/jt201314/jtselect/jtdraftvoting/103/10302.htm.

[65] *McLean and Cole v United Kingdom* App Nos 12626/13 and 2522/13 (11 June 2013), [2013] 57 EHRR SE8.

powers. In *Dunn and Others v UK*,[66] the application was held inadmissible because it concerned forthcoming elections and it was unclear whether the 131 applicants would be detained at the time of the election.[67]

D. ... and Before the Court of Justice of the European Union

The issue was also considered in relation to EU law by the CJEU in the *Delvigne*[68] case, where the court ruled that the disenfranchisement for an indefinite period of a French prisoner, serving a 12-year sentence for murder, met the requirement for proportionality.[69] Delvigne argued that the ban was incompatible with his rights under Art 39 of the (EU) Charter of Fundamental Rights and Freedoms. The Court thought the ban reflected the nature and gravity of the offence and the duration of the penalty. It was also possible under French law to apply for the reinstatement of this right. The Court made it clear that the Charter did not rule out disenfranchisement for those convicted of serious crimes. It said that Art 39 does not preclude national legislation such as that at issue in the case in the main proceedings, provided always that it does not prescribe general, indefinite and automatic deprivation of the right to vote, without a sufficiently accessible possibility of review, which is a matter for the national court to establish.[70]

In *Delvigne*, the CJEU construed Art 39(2) as including the right to vote in elections to the European Parliament, in contrast to the UK Supreme Court's view in *Chester and McGeoch*[71] that EU law and the Charter did not create a right to vote for individuals, but only obligations on the part of the state. The Supreme Court in *Chester* dismissed a further challenge to the ban and also declined to issue a further declaration of incompatibility or award damages.[72] The Court argued that EU law did not incorporate a right to vote parallel to that recognised by the Strasbourg Court, but even if it did, Chester and McGeoch were unlikely to regain the vote under the options being considered by the Joint Parliamentary Committee, because they were serving life sentences for murder. The Court acknowledged the

---

[66] *Dunn and Others v United Kingdom* App Nos 566/10 (30 May 2014).

[67] The issue of voting in European parliamentary elections has also been considered. In *Millbank and Others v United Kingdom* (App Nos 44473/14 et al (30 June 2016), [2016] 7 WLUK 215, *The Times* (20 September 2016)) the ECtHR found a breach of Art 3 because the applicants were unable to vote in the European elections in 2014 and the Westminster elections in 2015.

[68] *Thierry Delvigne v Commune de Lesparre-Médoc and Préfet de la Gironde* Case C-6501/13 (2015), [2016] 1 WLR 1223 (herafter *Delvigne*).

[69] The French Criminal Code was amended in 1994 to limit the ban to 10 years but Delvigne had been convicted under the previous code.

[70] *Delvigne* [2016] 1 WLR 1223; opinion of Advocate General Cruz Villalon at [124].

[71] *R (on the application of Chester) v Secretary of State for Justice; McGeoch v The Lord President of the Council and another* [2013] UKSC 63, [2014] AC 271 (hereafter *Chester*).

[72] The domestic courts had also in some earlier cases refused to make further declarations of incompatibility, for example, *Smith v Scott, ex p Toner and Walsh* and *Chester v Secretary of State for Justice and another* (2009) EWHC 293 (Admin) and (2010) EWCA Civ 1439, [2011] 1 WLR 1436.

principles set out in *Hirst*, but said that there was no point in making a further declaration of incompatibility, and noted that prisoner disenfranchisement was being considered by the Joint Committee. While critical of Strasbourg for its inconsistencies in dealing with the issue, the Supreme Court affirmed the need for the UK to comply with Convention.[73] The Supreme Court noted that Strasbourg had modified its position on the court's role in deciding whether to strip a prisoner of his vote and had given the legislature much more room for manoeuvre in *Scoppola* than previously given in *Hirst*, but it said that the UK's blanket ban would still be unacceptable.[74]

The Supreme Court stressed that it was a matter for Parliament to complete its consideration of the position regarding the UK prohibition and that there was no further role for the domestic courts to play: 'In the domestic constitutional scheme, any scheme conferring partial eligibility to vote on some convicted prisoners is quintessentially a matter for the UK Parliament to consider, determine and arrange'.[75] So its deference to Parliament lies in sharp contrast to the position of the Canadian Court in *Sauvé*. It noted the value of a dialogue between the domestic courts and Strasbourg in recent years on other issues.[76] It also found the Government's goals underpinning the ban were legitimate.

E. Resolving the Legal Issue – The May Government's Response

Despite the evident disinclination of successive UK governments to accommodate the *Hirst* judgment, the line of post-*Hirst* authority from the ECtHR offered obvious scope for very modest changes to the law to satisfy the requirements of the Convention. The most that the May Government was prepared to concede was to allow prisoners released on temporary licence to vote. In November 2017 the then Secretary of State for Justice, David Liddington, announced to Parliament that it would make administrative changes to give the vote to offenders who are released on temporary licence, for example, to attend employment; and temporary release, of course, is subject to a risk assessment.[77] They would vote outside the prison. Relatively few offenders would to benefit from this, but prisoners not released on temporary licence would continue to be denied the vote.[78] Because the measure is

---

[73] *Chester* [2014] AC 271 63 at [86].
[74] ibid at [34].
[75] ibid at [74].
[76] ibid at [27]. An example would be hearsay evidence discussed in *R v Horncastle and another; R v Marquis and another; R v Carter* [2009] EWCA Crim 964, [2009] 4 All ER 183; *R v Horncastle and Others* [2009] UKSC 14, [2012] 2 AC 373; and *Al-Khawaja and Tahery v UK* App Nos 26766//05 and 22228/06 (15 December 2011), (2009) 49 EHRR 1, (2012) 54 EHRR 23 (Grand Chamber).
[77] HCD 2 November 2017 c 1007.
[78] Although the Government has indicated that it intends to expand the use of release on temporary licence in the future to encourage more prisoners into work; see Ministry of Justice (2018) 'Education and Employment Strategy' (Cm 9621).

deemed purely administrative, no change in the law would be required; the change could be effected simply by altering the Prison Service guidance.[79] In addition it was proposed that judges would make clear to offenders when sentencing that they will lose the right to vote. This concession was intended to meet the Strasbourg Court's objection to a blanket ban and comply with the UK's international legal obligations.

The Committee of Ministers in December 2017 expressed its satisfaction with this proposal, encouraged the May Government to implement it as soon as possible and requested to be updated on its implementation.[80] These changes were brought into effect in the summer of 2018. Guidance on the change has been sent to prison governors and a leaflet sent to prisoners.[81] The Committee of Ministers of the Council of Europe has confirmed that it has now closed the *Hirst* group of cases as it is satisfied that the UK has complied.[82]

But this clearly constitutes a minimal change, well short of the Committee's proposals, and is a disappointing outcome to a lengthy period of review, debate and litigation. In presenting the proposed change, the Justice Secretary stressed that other Council of Europe states prevent prisoners voting and that the Court's rulings since *Hirst* have acknowledged the legitimacy of denying the vote to prisoners convicted of serious crimes. The change also contrasts with the recommendations of the recent report of the Welsh National Assembly's Equality, Local Government and Communities Committee that the vote should be restored to prisoners in Wales serving sentences of less than four years.[83] That recommendation is now being considered by the Welsh Government and Assembly members and the National Assembly for Wales Commission. The Scottish Parliament has conducted a Consultation on Prisoner Voting which invited comments on a range of options.[84] The Scottish Government has indicated that it does not favour full re-enfranchisement, but it recognises that the law should change to achieve Convention compliance and that the criterion should be based on length of sentence. The prisoner would be registered to vote in the home constituency (using a postal vote) rather than the prison. The Scottish Elections (Franchise and Representation) Act 2020 has extended voting rights in relation to local and Scottish parliamentary elections to prisoners serving less than 12 months.

The UK position on voting rights contrasts with the worldwide trend towards re-enfranchisement. Since the late 1990s, many states have restored the vote, or at least narrowed the exclusions from voting for serving prisoners, including Nigeria,

[79] PS1 13/2015 'Release on temporary licence' would need to be amended.

[80] See Ministry of Justice (2017) 'Responding to the Joint Committee on Human Rights on the Government's response to human rights judgments 2016–17' (Cm 9535) at p 28.

[81] This was confirmed in an answer to a Parliamentary Question, PQ 157787, 4 July 2018.

[82] Cm/ResDH (2018) 467.

[83] National Assembly for Wales, Equality, Local Government and Communities Committee (2019) 'Voting Rights for prisoners'.

[84] Scottish Government, 'Consultation on Prisoner Voting' (14 December 2018). A temporary order was made allowing prisoners serving less than 12 months to vote in the Shetland by-election in August 2019.

Kenya and South Africa.[85] The Republic of Ireland and Cyprus also amended their laws after *Hirst*.[86] Across Europe many states allow some, if not all, prisoners to vote. In Spain and Sweden all prisoners can vote, while in France and Germany, those serving shorter sentences can vote.[87] The UK is one of the very few Council of Europe states that have such an extensive ban.[88] The shift towards felon re-enfranchisement in these countries reflects the increasing recognition of prisoners as citizens and the developing jurisprudence on prisoners' rights.

IV. On Dialogue and Deference

The UK's failure to grant more expansive voting rights to prisoners had been heavily criticised by the Strasbourg Court and the Committee of Ministers, which had expressed, on several occasions, its disappointment that the UK authorities failed to implement change to give effect to the Joint Committee's recommendation.[89] The voting rights issue has been caught up in the continuing clashes between successive UK governments and the Strasbourg Court on a range of criminal justice issues and in the debate on parliamentary sovereignty.[90] The domestic courts have also been more willing to challenge the Strasbourg Court and have argued that many of the problems addressed by Strasbourg are better dealt with in the context of domestic law.[91] For example, in *Kennedy v the Charity Commission*[92] the Supreme Court stressed that per HRA 1998, s 2 the domestic courts were not bound by Strasbourg's decisions, but rather those decisions were simply to be taken into account in determining the meaning of Convention Rights. However, the ECtHR has also modified its position in response to the concerns of the domestic courts on issues such as whether the admission of a hearsay statement, as the sole or

[85] See respectively *Victor Emenuwe and others v Independent National Electoral Commission and Controller-General of Nigeria's Prison Service*, High Court, Benin (18 December 2014); *Priscilla Nyokabi Kanyua v Attorney General and Another*, Interim Constitutional Dispute Resolution Court (23 June 2010) and *Ministry of Home Affairs v NICRO and Others* CCT 03/04 [2004] ZACC 10.

[86] See Electoral (Amendment) Act 2006 (Republic of Ireland) and 2006 amendment to the Civil Registry Law (Cyprus).

[87] See White (2012) *Prisoners' Voting Rights* pp 42–52.

[88] The others include Armenia, Bulgaria and Estonia. The blanket ban in Russia was modified in 2017 to comply with the Convention; available at: www.coe.int/en/web/execution/-/russia-abolished-blanket-ban-on-prisoners-voting.

[89] For example, Committee of Ministers, Meeting 25 September 2014 and Decision of the Committee of Ministers 24 September 2015.

[90] See, for example, Conservative Party (2014) 'Protecting human rights in the UK: The Conservatives' proposals on changing Britain's human rights laws'.

[91] See for example, *R v Horncastle and another, R v Marquis and another, R v Carter* [2009] EWCA Crim 964; [2009] 4 All ER 183: *R v Horncastle and Others* [2009] UKSC 14; [2010] 2 AC 273: and Lord Hoffmann (2009) *The universality of human rights* (Judicial Studies Board Annual Lecture 19 March 2009), where he criticised the way the court had sought to extend its jurisdiction by seeking to impose uniform rules on Member States. The lecture is online at; https://www.judiciary.uk/announcements/speech-by-lord-hoffmann-the-universality-of-human-rights/.

[92] *Kennedy v the Charity Commission* [2014] UKSC 20; [2015] AC 455.

decisive evidence against the accused, will automatically breach Art 6(1) of the Convention.[93]

In the 2015 election, the Conservative Party manifesto listed the continued denial of prisoners' voting rights as one of its key achievements.[94] It has also criticised the Strasbourg Court in its curiously titled paper, 'Protecting human rights in the UK',[95] for encroaching into the area of domestic policy, and noted its intention to seek to confine the court's role to an advisory one and to limit its intervention to the most serious rights breaches. It also said that if the powers of the Court could not be limited, it would consider withdrawing altogether from the Convention. Pressure to restore prisoners' voting rights is seen as a prime example of the Court over-reaching its original role.

While prisoners themselves have become more aware of their Convention rights and have challenged their conditions and continued detention through rights claims, the court's interventionism has been overstated by critics. The number of declarations of incompatibility in the Supreme Court has declined since 2010.[96] While the Court is more willing to challenge limits on prisoners' rights and poor conditions, which governments seek to justify in terms of cost[97] or expediency, or appeals to public opinion, its position on the voting rights issue, as we have noted, has weakened.

The relationship between the courts and lawmakers in Charter jurisprudence has been construed variously as one in which the courts have too much scope to overrule the legislature, while others see the relationship between the two as a dialogue. This dialogic[98] approach sees the decision-making process as collaborative, where the legislature may introduce safeguards and revise the law in response to the courts' judgments, while keeping the same legislative purpose. This seeks to avoid the contentious issue of parliamentary sovereignty versus judicial supremacy. But it means the courts may need to compromise rather than have the final word.

However, the validity of the dialogic approach has been questioned by Manfredi[99] in relation to *Sauvé*. The reference to reasonable limits in s 1 and the legislature's power to override in s 33 of the Charter,[100] it is argued, ensures that

---

[93] *Al-Khawaja and Tahery v UK* App. Nos. 26766//05 and 22228/06 (15 December 2011); (2009) 49 EHRR 1; (2012) 54 EHRR 23 (Grand Chamber).

[94] Conservative Party (2015) 'The Conservative Party Manifesto 2015: Strong leadership, a clear economic plan, a brighter, more secure future' at para 60.

[95] Conservative Party (2014) 'Protecting human rights in the UK: The Conservatives' proposals on changing Britain's human rights laws'.

[96] See Gearty (2014) *On fantasy island: Britain, Europe and human rights* p 97.

[97] For example, *Gusev v Russia* App No 67542/01 (15 May 2008); and *Elefteriadis v Romania* App No 38427/05 (25 January 2011).

[98] This approach originated in Hogg and Bushell (1997) 'The Charter Dialogue between courts and legislatures: (or perhaps the Charter of Rights isn't such a bad thing after all)' *Osgoode Hall LJ* 75.

[99] Manfredi (2007) 'The day the dialogue died: a comment on *Sauvé v Canada*' *Osgoode Hall LJ* 45.

[100] Section 33: (1) Parliament or the legislature of a province may expressly declare in an Act of Parliament or of the legislature, as the case may be, that the Act or a provision thereof shall operate notwithstanding a provision included in section 2 or sections 7 to 15 of this Charter.

the legislature has the final word in some policy issues (s 33 has limited scope, being applicable only to s 2 and ss 7–15 of the Charter). But the approach in *Sauvé*, argues Manfredi, is a clear move away from judicial deference and McLachlin's CJ's judgment allows no legislative response given that s 3 is not one of the Charter rights subject to the s 33 override. The only means to reverse or amend the judgment would be by constitutional amendment, a lawmaking process not in the gift of the national legislature. In practical terms, the Court clearly had the last word.

Fredman[101] also offers an alternative to the dialogic approach from a different standpoint. She argues that we need to move beyond a rigid dichotomy between the court and the legislature towards more collaborative approaches. She advocates a deliberative model which focuses on quality of the deliberation, which means the courts enhance rather than undermine democratic participation. Fredman argues that court's role is to ensure that human rights decisions are taken: 'deliberatively within the constraints set by the human rights themselves'.[102] Parties justify their decisions by an appeal to reasons and principles and the legislature and parliamentary committees can conduct rights-based debates in a deliberative manner. The court itself functions as a deliberative forum: 'Courts should enhance the democratic accountability of decision-makers by insisting on a deliberative justification for the interpretation or limitation of rights'.[103] They should take account of prior deliberative consensus on human rights and the state must persuade the court that it has met its human rights obligations.

Examples given by Fredman of the deliberative approach include the *NICRO*[104] case in the South African Constitutional Court in 2004, which reflected the approach in *Sauvé*, and the Strasbourg Court's decision in *Hirst*, although the Court has now retreated from that position in *Scoppola*.[105] In *NICRO*, a challenge by the South African Government to the *August* decision failed. The Court was sceptical regarding the Government's claim that allowing prisoners to vote would suggest to the public that it was too soft on crime, but even if the Government was concerned over the public's misunderstanding of this issue, this was an insufficient ground to deprive prisoners of a fundamental right. In *August* the Constitutional Court had insisted that state provide evidential or principled support before limiting a right. The Court drew on the values underpinning the republic, namely universal adult suffrage and the common law principle that prisoners retain rights not taken away by imprisonment. The Court made clear that any limits on rights must be informed by foundational values listed in s 1 of the Constitution. It noted the lack of evidence to support the Government's claims, for example, that the financial costs of voting diverted resources from other areas or that it sent a message to the public that it was soft on crime.

---

[101] Fredman (2013) 'From dialogue to deliberation: human rights adjudication and prisoners' right to vote' *Public Law* 292.

[102] ibid at 293.

[103] ibid at 297.

[104] *Minister of Home Affairs and Others v NICRO and Others* CCT 03/04 [2004] ZACC 10.

[105] *Scoppola v Italy (No 3)* App No 126/05 (22 May 2012).

There were also elements of the deliberative approach in the Strasbourg Court's jurisprudence on felon disenfranchisement. In *Hirst*, for example, it was stressed that proportionality required a link between the sanction and the conduct of the individual.[106] The Strasbourg Court was also critical of the fact that there had been no discussion in Parliament.[107] In *Frodl*[108] the court required the decision to remove the vote to be taken and explained by a judge. But the Court has now moved away from a deliberative approach, for example, in the case of *Scoppola*[109] where a lifetime ban was accepted by the Court and a judicial decision was no longer required. Moreover, in the UK parliamentary debate on felon enfranchisement in 2011,[110] as Fredman notes, there was no reasoned or evidential proof, but just assertions and an emotive debate. Since then, of course, we have had a major review and a report on this issue, but no further substantial progress has been made. Hodgson and Roach[111] are also critical of the lukewarm approach to prisoner voting of the Strasbourg Court in recent cases, for failing to engage fully with arguments of principle on the issue and a willingness to defer to state legislatures' defences of prisoner disenfranchisement, which they compare unfavourably to the robust approach of the Canadian court.

This difference may of course be attributable to the fact that the judiciary in Canada has a stronger role than in challenging legislation which violates Charter rights than UK courts have in respect of breaches of Convention Rights. The remedial provision in s 24 of the Charter and the Charter's status per s 52 of the Constitution Act 1982 as part of the supreme law of Canada itself gives judges powers to strike down laws which infringe Charter rights[112] in contrast to the HRA 1998, which gives judges powers only to interpret a statute in a way compatible with rights under s 3, or to issue a declaration of incompatibility under s 4 and refer the matter back to Parliament to consider. But while there may be procedural differences, the matters of principle which are raised by felon disenfranchisement arise in both jurisdictions.

V. Is Felon Disenfranchisement Justifiable?

The hostility of successive UK governments – and the matter has engaged the attention of six administrations since the ECtHR's *Hirst* judgment in 2005 – to

---

[106] (2006) 42 EHRR 41 at [77].

[107] ibid at [79].

[108] *Frodl v Austria* App No 20201/04 (8 April 2010), (2011) 52 EHRR 5.

[109] *Scoppola v Italy (No 3)* App No 126/05 (22 May 2012), (2013) 56 EHRR 13.

[110] *HCD* 10 February 2011 c 586; Fredman op cit n 101 above.

[111] Hodgson and Roach (2017) 'Disenfranchising as punishment: European Court of Human Rights, UK and Canadian responses to prisoner voting' *Public Law* 450.

[112] Section 52(1): The Constitution of Canada is the supreme law of Canada, and any law that is inconsistent with the provisions of the Constitution is, to the extent of the inconsistency, of no force or effect.

felon enfranchisement is based partly on political expediency. All of those governments have been mindful of the public's lack of support for change.[113] But it also reflects a more pervasive view that prisoners have lost the right to participate in the democratic process because of their crimes, and the ban is seen as proportionate, as for a custodial sentence to be imposed, the offence must meet a threshold of seriousness and the ban is also defended as an additional element of punishment. These are all problematic arguments which, as we have seen, were challenged and rejected by the majority of Canadian Supreme Court in *Sauvé No 2* when addressing similar claims made by the Canadian Government.

A. Voting and Virtue or Prisoner as Citizens

Rights do not depend on virtue and if they are universal then, by definition, they apply to all regardless of the unworthiness of the rights-holder. Denying suffrage on grounds of loss of virtue is also an internally inconsistent position for legislatures to adopt: many offenders do not receive a custodial sentence, but they are permitted to vote despite their crimes. There is also the dark figure of unrecorded crime which suggests the lack of virtue is more widespread than suggested by the formal badge of a criminal conviction. Studies of self-reported crime indicate a range of criminal behaviours across a wide range of groups which may not attract the attention of the police and therefore do not result in disenfranchisement.

Furthermore, the denial of a key citizenship right is inconsistent with the expectations that prisoners perform citizenship duties while in prison, for example, those with sufficient wealth or earnings will be subject to obligations to pay tax and to make further national insurance contributions. Prisoners also engage in active citizenship in a number of contexts in prison, including peer mentoring, support for listener and buddy schemes, and participation in prisoner and student councils.[114]

Disenfranchisement is often defended because the social contract has been breached by prisoners' wrongdoing, but even if a term of the contract has been breached, the offender is neither completely negating the contract nor denying its significance. The penalty of imprisonment is the means to address that breach and a further loss of the right to vote is superfluous. Otherwise prisoners are being punished simply because they have already been punished.

---

[113] A *Manchester Evening News* poll on 1 October 2005 found only 25% of respondents favoured giving prisoners the vote, with 75% opposed. In a YouGov/*Sunday Times* survey conducted in November 2012, 63% of respondents opposed prisoners voting, 8% thought all prisoners should be allowed to vote and 16% thought those serving less than six months should be able to vote, 9% thought prisoners serving less than four years should be able to vote and 5% were undecided. See http://d25d2506sfb94s. cloudfront.net/cumulus_uploads/document/lmlmhdqllh/YG-Archives-Pol-ST-results%20-%20 23-251112.pdf.

[114] See Easton (2018) *The Politics of the prison and the prisoner: zoon politikon* p 63.

Moreover, restoring the vote may be beneficial rather than harmful. Participation in the life of the community, performing public duties, may itself promote virtue, because the citizen looks to the community's interest rather than his or her own private interest. This view is advanced in Aristotle's *Politics* and his notion of a *zoon politikon*. For Aristotle a lack of virtue per se does not preclude citizenship, but performing the duties of citizenship may promote virtue. A similar argument is found in Mill's discussion of representative government, where he argues that taking part in political life promotes civic responsibility.[115]

B. An Appropriate Punishment?

A key justification of felon disenfranchisement for recent UK governments[116] is that it is an additional punishment for prisoners, which enhances civic responsibility and promotes respect for the law. Those governments have also stressed that it is not an excessive measure, as the right is restored as soon as the offender leaves custody, in contrast to some US states.[117] Both these claims are open to obvious criticism. The loss of liberty is the punishment and no further punishment is justifiable. There is sufficient censure in the sentence of imprisonment without an additional element being necessary. But even if we did accept disenfranchisement as a legitimate punishment, it is hard to see how depriving prisoners (or categories of them) en bloc of voting rights can be justified on established principles of punishment, as it applies to all offenders regardless of the degree of culpability, the seriousness of the offence and the harm caused. If disenfranchisement were linked to the offence in a coherent way, for example, to electoral offences or to crimes committed in public office, then that might be more justifiable.

Furthermore, the sanction is arbitrary because the impact of the punishment will depend on the timing of the election, which is unrelated to the original crime. It is also a degrading punishment in reducing the offender to a state of civil death. It clearly cannot be justified on retributivist grounds. But it is also problematic from the standpoint of utilitarian justifications of punishment. The deterrent effect of the loss of the vote, compared to the risk of a prison sentence, is questionable. The risk of losing the vote may carry far less weight than the loss of liberty or the threat of penal austerity, and it is also hard to see how a deterrent effect can be tested in this case, especially as many prisoners may be unaware of the relevant law. It also does not meet the rehabilitative justification of punishment as it embodies the social death of offenders and affirms their exclusion from society. Conversely, voting reminds voters of the obligations and responsibilities of

---

[115] Mill (1861) *Considerations on representative government* p 3.

[116] See *Hirst* [2006] 42 EHRR 41; and in *Scoppola v Italy (No 3)* App No 126/05 (22 May 2012), where the UK acted as a third-party intervener.

[117] See www.sentencingproject.org/publications/felony-disenfranchisement-a-primer.

citizenship, and involves prisoners in the life of the community, arguably assisting their reintegration.

As the Canadian Supreme Court stressed in *Sauvé No 2*, there is a connection between having a voice in making the law and the obligation to obey the law. The legitimacy of the law ultimately rests on the fact that all citizens have a stake in the law through the ballot box. Disenfranchisement has no rational link to the aim of promoting civic responsibility. Defending the ban in terms of public protection is also problematic as it is difficult to identify or establish harms to others which might result from permitting the vote. If voters used proxy or postal votes, then no public protection issues would arise from the presence of prisoners in the voting centres. So from the standpoint of the major justifications of punishment it is difficult to defend felon disenfranchisement.[118]

C. The Integrity of the Electoral Process

It has also been argued by advocates of felon disenfranchisement that the ban is necessary to maintain the integrity of the electoral process.[119] There have been concerns in the UK over the integrity of postal voting and the risk of personation, so the anxiety over reintroducing prisoners into the electorate might be understandable. But the integrity of postal voting has now been strengthened with new requirements to establish the identity of voters.[120] In any case, personation is harder to achieve in prison, where there are constant roll calls and identity checks, and fewer opportunities to arrange 'additional' votes at the voter's place of residence. Remand prisoners already vote without incident.[121] A 2009 report by the UK's Electoral Commission[122] has said that it would be feasible to allow prisoners to vote by proxy or postal votes, so prisoners do not need to leave the confines of the prison to exercise their democratic rights.

The other issue is bloc voting: that is, whether the presence of prisoners voting together in a numerically small constituency, or in a marginal seat would taint the electoral process; for example, if there were a large prison, or an amalgamation of smaller prisons, in a small constituency. This potentially could influence the outcome of an election. Prisoners might also sully the process by swaying the vote in favour of unsuitable candidates. There is a perception that offenders swayed by

---

[118] For further discussion see Easton (2006) 'Electing the electorate: the problem of prisoner disenfranchisement' *MLR* 443.

[119] See *Washington v State* 75 Ala 582 (1884); and *Shepherd v Trevino* 575 F.2d.110. See also 'Notes' (1989) 'The disenfranchisement of ex-felons: citizenship, criminality and "The purity of the ballot box"' *Harvard LR* 1300.

[120] Electoral Administration Act 2006, ss 14, 15 and 40.

[121] The current procedures are set out in Prison Service Order 4650, 'Prisoners' voting rights'.

[122] Electoral Commission (2009) 'Electoral Commission response to the Ministry of Justice consultation voting rights of convicted prisoners detained within the UK, second stage'.

self-interest and impulsivity will make 'bad' electoral choices, an issue raised in *Hirst* by the Latvian Government, in its submission as a third-party intervener.[123]

The Parliamentary Joint Committee's proposal of using the prisoner's former address, or a declaration of local connection, would address these concerns, as the offender would need to show that there was a genuine connection with the area. As prisoners are often housed far from home, their only connection with the locale of the prison will be their allocation to that particular establishment. The Committee said that it is hard to imagine that prisoners' votes – even if the vote were given to all prisoners – could significantly affect the outcome of an election.[124] In any case it would be wrong, as a matter of principle, to exclude voters on the grounds of whom they might elect, or where they live.

One might argue that individuals convicted of electoral fraud or interference with the democratic process have already demonstrated that they are a risk to the integrity of the process and may continue to pose a threat if allowed to vote. The Strasbourg Court has upheld voting bans with a limited scope in such cases in *Glimmerveen and Hagenbeek v the Netherlands*[125] and *MDU v Italy*.[126] The ECtHR also held in *Hirst* that a voting ban would be justified where the individual had undermined the democratic foundations of society by gross abuse of a public position.[127] But the UK ban is obviously much broader than this in extending the ban to all convicted offenders regardless of the offence.

It has also been argued by Ramsay[128] that permitting prisoners to vote is 'faking democracy', because incarcerated prisoners cannot be part of the democratic process of collective self-determination. But this argument overlooks the fact that there is *some* potential for prisoners to participate more actively in democratic life within the confines of the prison, by organising discussion of current political issues, through canvassing and distribution of materials. There is already rudimentary political activity in the election of members of prison councils. Moreover, encouraging participation in voting and the democratic process while in prison, may lead to prisoners becoming more engaged in political and civic life on release. Conversely, the exclusion of groups from the process undermines democracy.

A further question raised by critics of prisoner enfranchisement is whether prisoners would actually use the vote if it were restored. But this misses the key point that the right should be available as a matter of principle. There may be several reasons, apart from apathy, why electors may refrain from voting: for

---

[123] (2006) 42 EHRR 41 at [55].

[124] Joint Committee (2013) 'Joint Committee – Report on the draft Voting Eligibility (Prisoners') Bill' at [188].

[125] App Nos 8348/78, 84-06/78 (11 October 1979), (1982) 4 EHRR 260.

[126] *MDU v Italy* App No 58400/00 (23 January 2003).

[127] In Canada the courts have also accepted a ban on holding office in *Harvey v New Brunswick (Attorney General)* [1996] 2 SCR 876 and this was not rejected in *Sauvé*.

[128] Ramsay (2013) 'Faking democracy with prisoners' voting rights' *Law, Society and Economic Working Paper Series 7/2013* (LSE).

example, a dismal range of candidates, or as a protest over a particular issue. But the abstinence of *some* voters does not undermine the democratic case for re-enfranchisement. Most of the prisoners interviewed by the Joint Committee favoured prisoner enfranchisement and intended to vote.[129] The high number of prisoners involved in voting litigation in the UK also suggests that the campaign is widely supported.

IV. Conclusion

As has been argued, it is difficult to justify disenfranchisement as a punitive measure. In any case, loss of liberty is the punishment and prisoners should not be subjected to further punishment once in custody. Conversely, restoring the vote may offer benefits in protecting the public by promoting rehabilitation and strengthening prisoners' status as citizens. As the Canadian Supreme Court said in *Sauvé No 2*, denial of the right to vote undermines the principle of equality, but acknowledging the right strengthens the commitment to equality essential to democracy. There may also be some practical advantages to voting in terms of rehabilitation and reintegration, as reflecting on the political process in the period leading up to an election would encourage prisoners to contemplate what is best for the community and on both the burdens and benefits of citizenship. So it is arguable that enfranchisement would help prisoners' reintegration into society and ultimately support their desistance. As we have seen, the approach of the Canadian Court offers a principled defence of prisoner suffrage and furthers the protection of prisoners' rights, while the Strasbourg Court has been too tolerant of the UK Government's failure to comply with the Court's rulings on the issue.

Obviously prisoners' rights are much broader than the right to vote and in many other areas there remains the problem of implementing prisoners' rights in practice. For example, if legal aid for prisoners' rights litigation is limited, or prisons lack sufficient funds to implement improvements, or the courts are too deferential to the prison administration, then rights may exist in name only. While the European Convention has functioned in many respects as a prisoners' rights Charter facilitating improvements to procedural and substantive rights in a number of areas, it has been argued by Parkes[130] that despite 25 years of the Canadian Charter, prisoners in Canada are still treated by courts and the legislature as temporary outcasts from rights protection and the Charter has had more impact on procedural than substantive rights.

---

[129] Joint Committee, op cit fn 124 above. Moreover, Behan and O'Donnell found that initially after the vote was restored in the Republic of Ireland, the actual number of prisoners who registered was low, but those who did register had a high turnout; (2008) 'Prisoners, politics and the polls' *British Journal of Criminology* 319.

[130] Parkes (2007) 'A Prisoners' Charter? Reflections on prisoner litigation under the Canadian Charter of Rights and Freedoms' *UBCLR* 629.

Section 7 – the right to life, liberty and security of the person – has been invoked by prisoners mostly to claim procedural rights, in relation to disciplinary hearings, segregation and involuntary transfers. This has led to the right to be represented by counsel at certain prison hearings, but in practice it is difficult to bring a case without legal aid provision, and access to legal aid remains poor. So the problem of enforcement of these rights persists. Section 7 has had little impact on substantive rights. Often cases are settled before trial, or the court finds the prison context reduces the expectation of rights protections, eg a diminished expectation of privacy. When cases do reach court, the courts have retained their hands-off pre-Charter approach to prison policies in a number of cases.[131] Section 12 of the Charter, the prohibition on cruel and unusual punishment, has also had very little impact on prison conditions, with cases on overcrowding dismissed. Treatment has to be so excessive it outrages standard of decency, which is hard for prisoners to establish, and the equality right has also met with little success. The public in Canada, as in the UK, seems to be oblivious or tolerant of poor conditions as prisoners generally lack visibility. There are also problems of proof and mootness if the offender is released by the time the case is heard, although in some cases[132] the courts have addressed the underlying issue.

While *Sauvé No 2* affirms that prisoners retain their rights except for those limited by the fact of incarceration,[133] Arbel[134] argues that *Sauvé No 2* has been rarely used in cases on improper conditions of confinement, although the *Bacon* case does show its potential and significance beyond voting rights. *Sauvé No 2* made clear that 'punishment should not be administered in an unmodulated manner to effectively treat inmates as "temporary outcasts" from Canadian rights protection'.[135] It also made clear that the case that corrections protocols should not be imposed which increase the marginalisation of First Nations prisoners.[136]

In *Bacon v Surrey Pretrial Services Centre (Warden)*[137] the court found a remand prisoner's administrative segregation violated her s 12 rights. While the court gave the prisoner individual relief, it did not consider the constitutionality of the provision allowing administrative segregation of a remand prisoner. The management protocol allowed an enhanced regime of solitary confinement when certain conditions were met. It also had a disparate impact on First Nations women because of their over-representation in prison.[138] So while *Sauvé No 2* is

---

[131] For example, accepting the Government's perception of the disciplinary process as a non-criminal procedure.

[132] For example *Allard v Nanaimo Correctional Centre*, 2000 BCSC 1159, [2000] BCJ No 1602 (SC); and *Trang v Alberta (Edmonton Remand Centre)* 2010 ABQB 6, [2010] 19 Alta LR (5th) 36.

[133] See for example *Trang v Alberta (Edmonton Remand Centre)* 2010 ABQB 6, [2010] 19 Alta LR (5th) 36.

[134] Arbel (2015) 'Contesting unmodulated deprivation: *Sauvé v Canada* and the normative limits of punishment' (2015) *Canadian Journal of Human Rights* 121.

[135] ibid at p 126.

[136] [2002] 3 SCR 519 at [48]–[60].

[137] 2010 BCSC 11 Admin LR (5th) 1.

[138] '2016–2017 Annual Report: Office of the Correctional Investigator' p 48.

a highly progressive prisoners rights' decision, there is a lack of compliance with the spirit of the judgment in daily prison life. Arbel also notes the deference of the courts to the decisions of the prison management, the limits on legal aid funding for prison litigation and the lack of accountability and oversight of prisons. Even if prisoners' rights are formally protected by the Charter, this does not necessarily mean they are respected in practice.[139]

Similar problems have been encountered in the UK where substantial weight is placed on the administration's needs for efficiency and security, and the demands to define disciplinary hearings as criminal proceedings was strongly resisted for quite some time because this would mean that full due process rights would follow, including the right to representation. The domestic courts recognised the judicial function of these hearings in *R v Board of Visitors of Hull Prison ex parte St. Germain (No 1)*[140] and the ECtHR affirmed that such hearings constituted criminal trials for the purposes of Art 6 in *Campbell and Fell v United Kingdom*,[141] so a denial of legal representation and refusal to allow the prisoners to consult a solicitor did breach Art 6(1). Prisoners have continued to campaign for the right to vote and most of the prisoners involved are longer-serving prisoners on whom the ban has the most detrimental effect and who will have the time and resources to become involved in litigation. But limits on legal aid for prisoners in the Legal Aid, Sentencing and Punishment of Offenders Act 2012 and the Criminal Legal Aid (General) Regulations 2013[142] have restricted the potential of the Convention as a prisoners' rights Charter. While a legal challenge by the Howard League succeeded in removing some of these limits,[143] restrictions on legal aid in relation to offending behaviour programmes and disciplinary proceedings leading to additional days of imprisonment remain. Furthermore the campaign for prisoner's votes in the UK has suffered greatly from being swept along in the wider attack on human rights and on the European Convention,[144] with the regrettable result that the fundamental issues of civil death and the social exclusion of prisoners have been sidelined. The experience of the UK campaign on prisoners' voting rights and the treatment of the issue by the courts indicates that the Canadian Supreme Court is more committed to the matters of moral and legal principle raised by felon enfranchisement.

---

[139] In fact, Parkes op cit fn 130 above argues that the Correctional and Conditional Release Act 1985, s 4(e) which stipulated that: 'prisoners retain the rights and privileges of all members of society, except for those which are necessarily removed as a consequence of sentence' has had more impact on prisoners' lives. The Act also identifies very specific rights to health care and grievance procedures which are more amenable to judicial review.

[140] [1979] QB 425.

[141] (1984) 7 EHRR 165.

[142] SI 2013 No 2790.

[143] For example, in relation to segregation, licence conditions and applications to Mother and Baby Units. *R (Howard League for Penal Reform and Prisoners' Advisory Service) v The Secretary of State for Justice and the Governor of HMP Send* [2017] EWCA Civ 244, [2017] 4 WLR 92.

[144] See Easton (2011) *Prisoners' rights: principles and practice* p 248; Easton (2006) op cit fn 118 above pp 118–19: McNulty, Watson and Philo (2014) 'Human rights and prisoners' rights: the British press and the shaping of public debate' *Howard Journal of Crime and Justice* pp 360–76.

4

Horizontal Effect of Human Rights in the UK and Canada

NICHOLAS BAMFORTH

The usefulness of comparative constitutional analysis relates not only to what it can tell us about the individual legal systems under consideration, but in what is revealed about the nature of particular features or concepts – including causes of action, rights and procedural mechanisms – seemingly shared by those systems (debate can encompass whether a definable nature or concept can properly be described as 'shared').[1]

When the feature under scrutiny is the horizontal effect of human rights – that is, the force between private parties of legally protected human rights – a full analysis may need to encompass matters falling under four headings: the constitutional structures of the legal systems under comparison (including the roles of the courts and legislature); the legal nature of human rights (or of particular human rights) as protected in the systems concerned; so far as this is distinct, the legal mechanisms whereby effect is given to human rights (for example, the drafting of the underpinning rights legislation or code); and the nature of the area or areas of law in which the rights are being applied or received.

In the UK, horizontal effect proved to be, in the words of Sedley LJ: 'a subject of sharp division and debate among both practising and academic lawyers'.[2] This was before the Human Rights Act 1998 (HRA 1998) entered into force and entailed what Mummery LJ called: 'a wide range of views'.[3] The case law reveals that matters from each of the four headings listed have subsequently been relevant. In Canada, the Supreme Court first set out a position based upon the Charter four years after the Charter's entry into force in 1982, in its judgment in *Retail, Wholesale and Department Store Union v Dolphin Delivery Ltd* (hereafter *Dolphin Delivery*).[4]

---

[1] For analysis of factors which ease and hinder comparative analysis, including between the UK and Canada, see Saunders (2016) 'Common law public law: some comparative reflections', in Bell, Elliott, Varuhas and Murray (eds), *Public law adjudication in common law systems: process and substance*.

[2] *Douglas v Hello! Ltd* [2001] QB 967 at [128].

[3] *X v Y* [2004] EWCA Civ 662, [2004] ICR 1634 at [44].

[4] [1986] 2 SCR 573. While the case was heard in December 1984, judgment was not delivered until December 1986.

This decision generated considerable comment, but the topic has since faded sufficiently into the background that it escaped substantive attention in the recent and comprehensive volume, *The Oxford Handbook of the Canadian Constitution*.[5] The issue of horizontal effect has nonetheless remained a live matter in regard to specific areas of law (and features in several contributions to the current volume), underlining the ongoing constitutional importance of understanding the role of human rights where one party is not the Government or state.[6]

This chapter considers horizontal effect in a more comparative and systematic fashion. Analysis of the two jurisdictions will be used to suggest that whilst their constitutional provisions, including the legal mechanisms for protecting human rights, frequently diverge, considerations drawn from each of the four headings mentioned play important roles – albeit sometimes in different ways and to different extents – in relation to each. Prior to discussing either jurisdiction, this requires us to examine horizontal effect and the four headings in general terms to provide some mechanisms for evaluating the law.

I. Measuring the Extent and Highlighting the Underpinning Considerations

When comparing different jurisdictions' treatment of horizontal effect, a key point of reference is the *extent* to which rights are permitted to reach between private parties – something closely tied, in both logic and practice, to the *mechanisms or routes* through which the reach concerned is achieved. In this regard, detailed assessment schemes focusing mainly on individual legal systems provide (notwithstanding the differences of detail between them) helpful indicia for identifying, characterising and in turn comparing key aspects.[7] As Stephen Gardbaum indicates, however, these dimensions alone do not to provide a full picture.[8] A full analysis, and in turn comparison, needs also to consider similarities and differences between various *underpinning considerations* which govern or influence the operation of horizontal effect, including the nature of the rights involved, the obligations imposed upon the state (including courts), the areas of

---

[5] Oliver, Macklem and Des Rosiers (eds) (2017) *The Oxford Handbook of the Canadian Constitution* within which – with essays by multiple contributors – *Dolphin Delivery* receives only two mentions.

[6] See especially the chapters by Loveland, Taylor, Ewing and Hatzis.

[7] See for example, Gardbaum (2003) 'The horizontal effect of constitutional rights' *Michigan LR* 387 and (2006) 'Where the (state) action is' *International Journal of Constitutional Law* 760; Leigh (1999) 'Horizontal rights, The Human Rights Act and privacy: lessons from the Commonwealth?' *ICLQ* 57; Raphael (2000) 'The problem of horizontal effect' *EHRLR* 493; Young (2011) 'Mapping horizontal effect' in Hoffman (ed), *The impact of the UK Human Rights Act on private law*.

[8] Gardbaum (2003) op cit fn 7 pp 778–79. The list of factors in the text here is not the same as Gardbaum's. A differentiation is also drawn by Young op cit fn 7 pp 29–33.

law in which rights must operate, and (sometimes) whether statute or common law is in play. These considerations reflect the different headings mentioned above.[9]

A. Direct and Indirect Horizontal Effect

While, at a very general level, horizontal effect has been identified as the imposition on a private individual of an obligation to respect the rights of another, a basic distinction is drawn between its *direct* and *indirect* varieties.[10] Alison Young relates this to:

> [T]he *means* by which human rights are pleaded before the court, rather than the *extent* to which a particular legal system accepts horizontal effect – so it does not follow that direct horizontality provides for a greater protection of rights than indirect horizontality.[11]

Using this categorisation, which builds on Gavin Phillipson's work, direct horizontal effect occurs: 'when *an individual pleads a breach of a … right in and of itself before the court*, obtaining redress against *another* individual'.[12] The court is 'required to act so as to respect the … [corresponding] rights of others'.[13] The indirect version occurs 'when *the applicant pleads other legal provisions, which are in turn interpreted so as to contain or reflect* the … right in question. It is the alternative legal provision itself that imposes the obligation'.[14]

Under this second formulation, the law (whether contained in statute or common law) is made subject to the rights, with individuals required to uphold them 'through a modification of the law required to ensure that it complies'.[15] This may in practice influence the strength of horizontal effect in play, notwithstanding Young's and Phillipson's analytical focus on means rather than extent; for, as Hugh Collins puts it, in indirect cases: 'Fundamental rights present more of a nudge to private law rather than a requirement for a fundamental reconstruction or revision'.[16] The reinterpretation of the existing cause of action prevents

---

[9] See also Phillipson (2007) 'Clarity postponed: horizontal effect after *Campbell*' in Fenwick, Phillipson and Masterman (eds), *Judicial reasoning under the UK Human Rights Act* pp 149–50.

[10] See for example Young op cit fn 7 pp 18–22, 29.

[11] ibid at p 35.

[12] ibid. Young develops Phillipson's approach articulated in (1999) 'The Human Rights Act, "horizontal effect" and the law: a bang or a whimper?' *MLR* 824.

[13] Young op cit fn 7 p 36.

[14] ibid at p 35; see also Phillipson op cit fn 12 pp 826–27. Compare Gardbaum (2003) op cit fn 7 pp 433–37; (2006) op cit fn 7 pp 764–68. See also Cheadle (2005) 'Third party effect in the South African Constitution' in Sajo and Uitz (eds), *The Constitution in private relations: expanding constitutionalism* pp 61–63, 65.

[15] Young op cit fn 7 p 36. Schemes categorising horizontal effect often also consider the imposition of positive obligations on public authorities: for example Leigh op cit fn 7 pp 71–75, 78–80; Gardbaum (2006) op cit fn 7 pp 767–69.

[16] (2017) 'The challenges presented by fundamental rights to private law' in Barker, Fairweather and Grantham (eds) *Private law in the twenty-first century* p 226.

the private body from directly infringing upon the recognised rights of another private party.[17]

The use of means as the analytical basis for differentiation has the consequence that a wider range of situations is characterised as involving indirect rather than direct horizontal effect than would be the case if the focus was simply on whether statute or common law produced the effect concerned.[18] The strength of indirect effect – as characterised by both Young and Phillipson[19] – can also vary. Young associates this with '*the degree of obligation imposed upon the court* to ensure that private law is modified or extended to take account of … [protected] … rights'.[20] She also ties the point to whether the common law should be modified to take account either of those rights or of the values underpinning or reflected within them. Both strong and weak indirect horizontal effect place an obligation on the court to develop the law, but the strong variety protects rights and its weak counterpart values.[21] Under the 'strong' heading, the force of the approach adopted depends on whether courts are required to develop new causes of action to protect rights, or whether only reinterpretation – a weaker technique – is permissible.[22] Under the 'weak' heading, the strength of the approach adopted depends on whether the common law is being developed according to values in or reflected by rights, whether the rights are viewed as fundamental or as ordinary principles, and whether strong overriding reasons or merely a balance of reasons favouring the protection of competing values will be sufficient to justify a restriction.[23]

B. Underpinning Considerations

The points discussed so far concern the extent to which rights have horizontal effect and the routes through which it occurs. As noted previously, the considerations which underpin such phenomena are also significant when making comparisons.

The drafting of national rights measures has been mentioned as one such consideration. In reality, this is likely to be an initial, and sometimes basic, issue. The texts of some measures giving effect to human rights – whether or not entrenched – may aim to provide conclusive answers concerning horizontal effect. However, neither the HRA 1998 nor the Charter does this, rendering judicial

---

[17] Young op cit fn 7, especially pp 25, 35–6.

[18] This is one possible reading of, eg, Leigh op cit fn 7 pp 75–77, 82–85. Morgan is also keen to distinguish 'direct' from 'indirect': (2002) 'Questioning the "true effect" of the Human Rights Act' *Legal Studies* 259; (2003) 'Privacy, confidence and horizontal effect: "Hello" trouble' *Cambridge LJ* 444 p 467.

[19] See Phillipson op cit fn 12 pp 831–33.

[20] Young op cit fn 7 p 39.

[21] ibid.

[22] ibid at pp 42–47. A further factor is the extent to which there is an obligation to depart from pre-HRA precedent: see also Hunt (1998) 'The "horizontal effect" of the Human Rights Act' *Public Law* 423 pp 441–42; Raphael op cit fn 7 pp 504–06.

[23] Young op cit fn 7 pp 40–42. It is worth noting that for Phillipson, under this approach: 'the key to horizontal effect under the Human Rights Act 1998 will … be indirect effect': op cit fn 12 p 829.

interpretation crucial and meaning that the other underpinning considerations help to shape the readings adopted.

Logically, one such consideration, working at a deep level, is the prevalent understanding of the nature of the rights themselves. Deryck Beyleveld and Shaun Pattinson distinguish a 'right being held conceptually against other individuals from an individual having the power to enforce that right against other individuals'.[24] The first ('held') aspect concerns the conceptual nature and applicability of the right, the second ('power') aspect its role as or within a cause of action between the individuals. As Young notes, applicability refers to our conception of a right and serves as a prerequisite to its effect, which is the means through which the applicability is achieved. More exactly, 'to give rise to horizontal effect … the nature of the … right *must be such* that it is capable of creating obligations for private parties to respect'.[25] In the UK, the early days of the HRA 1998 saw debate about the consequences of the nature of Convention rights. Beyleveld and Pattinson characterised them as fully horizontally applicable, so that they acquired full horizontal effect in the absence of contrary primary legislation.[26] By contrast, Sir Richard Buxton argued that they were:

> [E]xigible only against, and their content can only consist of rights against, public bodies … [I]f the HRA did purport to create such rights against private citizens, it would simply beat the air: because the content of those rights does not impose obligations on private citizens.[27]

Whatever one's view of these competing positions – both of which are contentious – they serve to emphasise the logically fundamental part played by the nature of the rights themselves.

The constitutional structure of a given legal system, in particular the respective powers of the courts and the legislature (whether addressed within the rights measure in play, or elsewhere 'constitutionally' at national level, or both), can be a further crucial consideration in shaping the effect of rights between private parties.[28] A conspicuous example is found in the 1996 South African Constitution (a rights measure and a broader articulation of constitutional norms), which specifies that provisions of the Bill of Rights bind natural or juristic persons in addition to the state, so far as they are: 'applicable, taking into account the nature of the right and the nature of any duty imposed by the right'.[29] In turn, a juristic person is 'entitled to the rights in the Bill of Rights to the extent required by the nature

---

[24] (2002) 'Horizontal applicability and horizontal effect' *LQR* 623 p 626.

[25] Young op cit fn 7 p 30; emphasis added. Note the qualification at p 31 that horizontal application may influence the extent to which rights gain legal effect but has little bearing on the means through which it is achieved – which is a product of constitutional, institutional and legal factors.

[26] Beyleveld and Pattinson op cit fn 24.

[27] (2000) 'The Human Rights Act and private law' *LQR* 48 p 56.

[28] Young op cit fn 7 p 31. See also Saunders (2005) 'Constitutional rights and the common law' in Sajo and Uitz op cit fn 14.

[29] The Constitution of the Republic of South Africa 1996, s 8(2).

of the rights and the nature of that juristic person'.[30] Such express statements are unusual,[31] but a system's key 'constitutional' properties sometimes have direct consequences: in a constitution without judicial review of legislation, for instance, horizontal effect will lack the fullest remit possible because there will be cases between private parties in which rights are unable to 'bite' in the face of incompatible legislation. Instead, such legislation continues to apply, while rights produce effects through interpretation in situations falling short of incompatibility.[32]

Turning to matters of constitutional principle, conceptions of separation of powers, with associated limits to how far courts should use rights to develop the law, including remedies, may apply in the horizontal context (these can be called 'institutional considerations'). In more specific terms, the degree of direction a system applies to courts (whether through rules or the more amorphous notion of 'legal culture') may affect the judicial capacity and willingness to admit new types of evidence, make new remedies available, and engage in adventurous interpretation in rights litigation in horizontal cases.

A further important underpinning consideration may be the area of law in play. Debates have long proceeded in private law about whether disciplines such as contract, tort or restitution (or areas thereof) possess a particular juristic essence, or instead constitute more or less pragmatic or flexible responses to policy considerations, or some combination of these characteristics. This is important for present purposes because the nature of the area of private law in play may affect the ability of horizontal effect to ensure a measure of consistency with protected rights.[33] A more contentious claim might be that the more definite or embedded an area's pre-existing character (or perceived character), the stronger are likely to be the obstacles confronting rights in bringing about change, including in horizontal situations – for the pre-existing contours of a whole discipline (or a significant part of it) may be affected. In contrast, more case-specific or policy-driven areas may perhaps allow greater room for flexibility.

---

[30] ibid, s 8(4).

[31] See also the analysis of explicit horizontality under the Irish Constitution in Nolan (2014) 'Holding non-state actors to account for constitutional economic and social rights violations: experiences and lessons from South Africa and Ireland' *International Journal of Constitutional Law* 61.

[32] In contrast, the existence of judicial review of legislation does not guarantee horizontal effect: a system may contain further constraints to confine relevant challenges to the vertical context. The seminal and likely best-known example is the decision of the United States Supreme Court in the *Civil Rights Cases* (1883) 109 US 3, limiting the reach of the 14th Amendment to 'state action'. The gradual erosion of that position over the next 90 years is a fascinating element of that Court's constitutional jurisprudence; see especially *Corrigan v Buckley* (1926) 271 US 323; *Shelley v Kraemer* (1948) 334 US 1; *Burton v Wilmington Parking Authority* (1961) 365 US 715; *Bell v Maryland* (1964) 378 US 226; *Reitman v Mulkey* (1967) 387 US 369; *Jones v Mayer* (1968) 392 US 409.

[33] Tushnet (2005) 'The relationship between judicial review of legislation and the interpretation of non-constitutional law, with reference to third party effect' p 167 in Sajo and Uitz op cit fn 14. For a more general argument concerning the interaction with rights, values and theories of private law, see Weinrib and Weinrib (2001) 'Constitutional values and private law in Canada', in Friedmann and Barak-Erez (eds), *Human rights in private law*.

The nature of the decision-maker in issue may sometimes join with that of the area in influencing the possibility of horizontal effect. Consequences sometimes result from judicial characterisation of decision-makers which possess a combination of attributes, some of which seem typical of public law and others more typical of private law or one of its branches (an example might be a members' organisation empowered through a contract with a statutory decision-maker to perform an otherwise public function, and contracts for that purpose with each individual recipient of the function).[34] In such situations, judicial characterisation of matters as appropriate for a vertical human rights challenge may reduce or eliminate the space within which horizontal effect seems necessary and/ or plausible.[35] Nonetheless, such a linkage will affect *only a subset* of the cases in which horizontal effect is *potentially* relevant, for it presupposes the presence of *room for argument* about the classification of the decision-maker and/or its activities. In contrast, such scope is not visible when debating (say) whether rights-based claims for violation of personal privacy should be possible against privately-owned news media.[36]

C. Conclusion – A Full Analytical Basis

In practical situations, a combination of the underpinning considerations outlined in this section is likely to determine the operation of horizontal effect. Gardbaum thus notes that: 'the actual impact of specific constitutional norms [protecting rights] on private actors is a function of both the position adopted on the vertical-horizontal spectrum and the substantive content and interpretation of particular individual rights'.[37] By analogy, Young notes that while horizontal applicability influences the extent to which rights may be given legal effect: 'Models of

---

[34] As an example from the UK, see *R (Weaver) v London and Quadrant Housing Association* [2009] EWCA Civ 587, [2010] 1 WLR 363. In Canada, compare: *Black v Law Society of Alberta* [1989] 1 SCR 591; *McKinney v University of Guelph* [1990] 3 SCR 229; *Royal College of Dental Surgeons of Ontario v Rocket* [1990] 2 SCR 232 (issue absent from argument); *University of British Columbia v Harrison* [1990] 3 SCR 451; *New Brunswick Broadcasting Co v Nova Scotia* [1993] 1 SCR 319; *Eldridge v Attorney General of British Columbia* [1997] 3 SCR 624 at [20]–[22], [35]–[44] (La Forest J); *Greater Vancouver Transportation Authority v Canadian Federation of Students* [2009] 2 SCR 295 at [14] [17] [21] [24]–[25] (Deschamps J). For discussion, see Marin (2015) 'Should the Charter apply to universities?' *National Journal of Constitutional Law* 29; Sharpe and Roach (2017, 6th edn) *The Charter of Rights and Freedoms* pp 106–07; Hogg (2017) *Constitutional Law of Canada 2017 Student Edition* paras 37.2(c), 37.2(e).

[35] For the purposes of this chapter I have omitted any prolonged discussion (although the matter is sometimes alluded to) of the definition of 'public authority' and 'public function' under HRA 1998, s 6. For argument concerning connections between the vertical and the horizontal, see further the comments in the introductory chapter to this volume at pp 18–20 above.

[36] Depending upon one's approach to the applicability underpinning consideration, discussed in this section, rights-based propositions may in addition be more or less easily translatable from the vertical to the horizontal context.

[37] (2003) op cit fn 7 pp 455, 459.

horizontal effect are influenced by institutional, legal and constitutional factors'.[38] These include the division of powers between the legislature and the judiciary, and the terms of the rights legislation in force. An additional factor – not mentioned so far – may be the perceived significance of identifiable normative philosophies or aims in explaining the legal system and its human rights legislation. Where a philosophy is identified as driving a system or rights measure generally, it may well be associated with the positions taken concerning horizontal effect, notwithstanding the presence or strength of other underpinning considerations.[39] If, by contrast, institutional and procedural details are seen as playing the key part in explaining when and how far horizontal effect is possible, a strong role for normative commitments seems more likely to be absent.[40]

The key message of this section has been that to establish a full basis for comparing horizontal effect in different jurisdictions, we need to employ the classifications enabling us to distinguish between its possible varieties, *and* to identify the considerations underpinning judicial analysis. In practice, a combination of those considerations will be relevant, and the relative priority a given legal system gives to each may be crucial to how we understand it and compare it with others. The classifications and underpinning considerations will be discussed in relation to both the UK and Canada in subsequent sections.

II. Horizontal Effect under the HRA 1998

In the UK, the horizontal effect of Convention rights is associated with the provisions of the HRA 1998 dealing respectively with statutory interpretation (under ss 3–4) and the obligations of courts (under s 6) – with s 12, concerning the award of remedies in cases involving freedom of expression,[41] playing a reinforcing role. In terms of Young's and Phillipson's classifications, these provisions have helped generate forms of indirect horizontal effect through the reinterpretation of statutes and common law. Young nonetheless notes that there have been 'contradictory judicial statements concerning the scope of horizontal effect, combined with an apparent reluctance on the part of the judiciary to discuss the specific model created by the HRA'.[42]

---

[38] Young op cit fn7 p 31.

[39] For discussion of the role of political philosophy, see ibid at pp 30–31.

[40] For competing positions in this debate, compare: Tushnet (2003), 'The issue of state action/ horizontal effect in comparative constitutional law' *International Journal of Constitutional Law* 79; especially pp 88–92; Kumm and Ferreres Comella (2005) 'What is so special about constitutional rights in private litigation? A comparative analysis of the function of state action requirements and indirect horizontal effect' in Sajo and Uitz op cit fn 14; Gardbaum, (2006) op cit fn 7 pp 769–73, 778.

[41] See for example *Douglas v Hello! Ltd* [2001] QB 967 at [54], [92]–[95] (Brooke LJ), [131]–[137] (Sedley LJ), [148]–[153] (Keene LJ): *PJS v News Group Newspapers Ltd* (hereafter *PJS*) [2016] UKSC 26, [2016] AC 1081 at [19]–[20], [26], [33]–[37] (Lord Mance), [52], [54] (Lord Neuberger), [72] (Baroness Hale), [81]–[84] (Lord Toulson, dissenting).

[42] Young op cit fn 7 p 17.

It is argued here that this is borne out by the case law, and that horizontal liability in some areas – most visibly, invasion of privacy – has proven much more amenable to development in the light of Convention rights than has been the case elsewhere, for example in relation to the taking of possession of property from occupants with no statutorily defined security of tenure, following non-repayment of a contractually agreed loan. Important consequences have also followed more broadly from whether a horizontal relationship is underpinned by statute or common law. As this implies, the provisions of the HRA 1998 are insufficient *on their own* to explain the operation of horizontal effect: in practice, other underpinning considerations set out in the previous section have played a central role. For explanatory purposes, though, it is useful to begin by discussing the provisions themselves.

A. HRA 1998, ss 3–4

The requirements in the HRA 1998, ss 3–4 that legislation be interpreted as far as possible in the light of Convention rights, or declared incompatible, have been applied by the Supreme Court (and, previously, by the Judicial Committee of the House of Lords) without any discussion of the possibility that the horizontal context of litigation (in the sense that both parties are private) made any difference.[43] Indeed, in *Wilson* – initially involving two private parties and argument about the interpretation of the Consumer Credit Act 1974 in the light of Convention rights, but in which a later appeal to the House of Lords was brought by the relevant minister – Lord Rodger seemingly took care to separate matters from 'The extent to which the [1998] Act also operates between private individuals – the so-called 'horizontal effect'.[44] The horizontal role of s 3 was explained in greater detail by the Court of Appeal in *X v Y*, in which Mummery LJ stated that the provision 'draws no distinction between legislation governing public authorities and legislation governing private individuals'.[45] In fact, given the statutory basis of the

---

[43] An example is *Ghaidan v Godin-Mendoza* [2004] UKHL 30, [2004] 2 AC 557 at [25]–[35] (Lord Nicholls), [38]–[51] (Lord Steyn), [56]–[76], [101] (Lord Millett, dissenting), [104]–[124], [129] (Lord Rodger) and [144]–[145] (Baroness Hale). In the Court of Appeal, Keene LJ had highlighted the connection between the court's status, by virtue of HRA 1998, s 6(3)(a), as a public authority obliged due to s 6(2) not to act incompatibly with a Convention right unless giving effect to or enforcing provisions of primary legislation which could not be read or given effect compatibly, and the obligation under s 3 to read and give effect to legislation compatibly so far as it was possible to do so ([2002] EWCA Civ 1533, [2003] Ch 380 at [37]–[38]). For analysis, see Leigh op cit fn 7 pp 75–76, Young op cit fn 7 p 37. For criticism relating to private law aspects, see Leigh and Masterman (2008) *Making rights real: The Human Rights Act in its first decade* pp 252–57. See also *Bull v Hall* [2013] UKSC 73 [2013] 1 WLR 3741 at [41]–[55] (Baroness Hale) and [93] (Lord Hughes); and *Lee v Ashers Baking Company Ltd* [2018] UKSC 49, [2018] 3 WLR 1294 at [40] and [56] (Baroness Hale), [66] (Lord Mance).

[44] *Wilson v Secretary of State for Trade and Industry* [2003] UKHL 40, [2004] 1 AC 816 at [174]. For the Court of Appeal's handling of the purely private stages, see *Wilson v First County Trust Ltd* [2001] QB 407 and *Wilson v First County Trust Ltd (No 2)* [2001] EWCA Civ 633, [2002] QB 74.

[45] *X v Y* [2004] EWCA Civ 662, [2004] ICR 1634 at [57]; see also Dyson LJ at [66].

key employment law causes of action, 'in the case of private employers section 3 is more relevant than section 6 of the HRA'.[46]

B. HRA 1998, s 6

The main focus of debate about horizontal effect has been s 6, which – by deeming it unlawful for courts to give judgment incompatibly with Convention rights – has been widely argued to involve an obligation to develop common law causes of action between private parties in line with those rights.[47] As noted by Baroness Hale in *Campbell v Mirror Group Newspapers Ltd* (hereafter *Campbell*) the HRA 1998 did not: 'create any new cause of action between private persons'.[48] Instead, 'if there is a relevant cause of action applicable, the court as a public authority must act compatibly with both parties' Convention rights'.[49] This encompassed the horizontal context.

Phillipson observes that 'it is generally acknowledged that it is in the development of breach of confidence into a species of privacy tort that common law horizontal effect has been at its clearest and strongest'.[50] In *Campbell*, the equitable wrong of breach of confidence – categorised as the relevant vehicle for reinterpretation by Baroness Hale[51] – was held by the Supreme Court to protect privacy in a situation involving no prior confidential relationship,[52] with the Court subsequently suggesting in *PJS v News Group Newspapers Ltd*[53] (hereafter *PJS*) and *Khuja v Times Newspapers Ltd*[54] (hereafter *Khuja*) that an identifiable tort of invasion of privacy now exists. Each of these cases involved a balance between respect for private and family life under Art 8 and freedom of expression under Art 10 in determining whether to grant an injunction to prevent publication of private information.

---

[46] ibid.

[47] See Leigh op cit fn 7 pp 82–83: Raphael op cit fn 7 pp 494–98; Young op cit fn 7 pp 24–26, 31–36, 39–44. It has been argued that in addition to common law interpretation, HRA 1998, s 6 imposes constraints on court procedure and judicial discretion, including in relation to remedies: see Leigh op cit fn 7 pp 80–82, Raphael op cit fn 7 p 495; Young op cit fn 7 pp 22, 31–33. Mummery LJ drew attention in *X v Y* [2004] EWCA Civ 662, [2004] ICR 1634 at [59(1)], to the point that s 3 imposes its own duty to interpret on courts.

[48] *Campbell v Mirror Group Newspapers Ltd* [2004] UKHL 22, [2004] 2 AC 457 at [132]–[133].

[49] ibid at [132]. See also para [133], and Sedley LJ's discussion of 'incremental change' in *Douglas v Hello! Ltd* [2001] QB 967 at [129]. In *Douglas* Brooke LJ (para [91]) and Sedley LJ (para [128]) specifically avoided defining what might be meant by a judicial obligation, but Sedley LJ (paras [111], [129], [130], [137] and [139]) and Keene LJ (para [166]) applied such an idea in practice.

[50] (2011) 'Privacy: the development of breach of confidence – the clearest case of horizontal effect?' in Hoffman op cit fn 7. The very title of Phillipson's piece captures the perception he reports.

[51] *Campbell* [2004] UKHL 22, [2004] 2 AC 457 at [133].

[52] ibid at [13]–[14] (Lord Nicholls), [47]–[48], [51]–[52] (Lord Hoffmann), [85] (Lord Hope), [132] (Baroness Hale). Note also *Douglas v Hello! Ltd* [2001] QB 967 at [124]–[126] (Sedley LJ), [165]–[166] (Keene LJ); *Mosley v News Group Newspapers Ltd* [2008] EWHC 1777 (QB) at [7] (per Eady J).

[53] *PJS v News Group Newspapers Ltd* [2016] UKSC 26, [2016] AC 1081.

[54] *Khuja v Times Newspapers Ltd* [2017] UKSC 49, [2019] AC 161.

In a formulation later approved in *Campbell*[55] and *Khuja*,[56] Lord Woolf CJ had noted in *A v B plc* that Arts 8 and 10 had:

[P]rovided new parameters within which the court will decide, in an action for breach of confidence, whether a person is entitled to have his privacy protected by the court or whether the restriction of freedom of expression which such protection involves cannot be justified.[57]

This had been achieved by absorbing the rights protected by Arts 8 and 10 into breach of confidence, 'giving a new strength and breadth to the action so that it accommodates the requirements of those [A]rticles'.[58] In a development anticipated before the HRA 1998 by Lord Goff in *Attorney-General v Guardian Newspapers Ltd (No 2)*,[59] *Campbell* emphasised that liability now turned on whether the claimant had a reasonable expectation of privacy in respect of the disclosed facts (according to Lord Nicholls)[60] or whether the party subject to the duty of confidence was in a situation in which he or she knew or ought to have known that the other person could reasonably expect their privacy to be protected (as Lord Hope stated).[61] The *Campbell* approach was later applied by the Supreme Court in *Khuja*,[62] in which it was emphasised that balancing between privacy and expression was to be 'fact-specific'.[63]

C. Privacy: Uncertainties, Underpinning Considerations, and a Distinct Tort?

In *Campbell*, the bulk of the Supreme Court's attention was directly concerned with balancing.[64] In logic, this would have been impossible *without* an assumption

---

[55] *Campbell* [2004] UKHL 22, [2004] 2 AC 457 at [17] (Lord Nicholls), [48] (Lord Hoffmann), [85]–[86] (Lord Hope), [132] (Baroness Hale).

[56] *Khuja* [2017] UKSC 49, [2019] AC 161.

[57] [2002] EWCA Civ 337, [2003] QB 195 at [4].

[58] ibid.

[59] [1990] 1 AC 109 at 281; cited in *Campbell* [2004] UKHL 22, [2004] 2 AC 457 at [14] (Lord Nicholls), [47]–[48] (Lord Hoffmann), [85] and [106] (Lord Hope).

[60] ibid at [21] (Lord Nicholls). See also [137] (Baroness Hale).

[61] ibid at [85] (Lord Hope). See also paras [92], [95]–[100] (Lord Hope), [134]–[137] (Baroness Hale) and [161] and [166] (Lord Carswell): *A v B plc* [2002] EWCA Civ 337, [2003] QB 195 at [11(ix) and (x)] (Lord Woolf CJ).

[62] *Khuja* [2017] UKSC 49, [2019] AC 161 at [21]. See further *McKennitt v Ash* [2005] EWHC 3003 (QB), [2006] EMLR 178 at [59]–[62], [80]; *Terry (LNS) v Persons Unknown* [2010] EWHC 119 (QB), [2010] EMLR 16 at [55]–[56]; *TSE, ELP v News Group Newspapers Ltd* [2011] EWHC 1308 (QB) at [17]–[20]; *CTB v News Group Newspapers Ltd* [2011] EWHC 1326 at [22]: *Goodwin v News Group Newspapers Ltd* [2011] EWHC 1437 (QB), [2011] EMLR 502 at [85]–[87]: *Rocknroll v News Group Newspapers Ltd* [2013] EWHC 24 (Ch) at [27] and [28].

[63] *Khuja* [2017] UKSC 49, [2019] AC 161 at [23]. See the similar categorisations in *In re Guardian News and Media Ltd* [2010] UKSC 1, [2010] 2 AC 697 at [51]: *Hutcheson (KGM) v News Group Newspapers Ltd* [2011] EWCA Civ 808, [2012] EMLR 2 at [26]. Lord Sumption invoked the descriptions of the balance articulated by Lord Hoffmann in *Campbell* [2004] UKHL 22, [2004] 2 AC 457 at [55], and by Lord Steyn in *In re S* [2004] UKHL 47, [2005] 1 AC 593 at [17].

[64] *Campbell* [2004] UKHL 22, [2004] 2 AC 457 at [28]–[35] (Lord Nicholls), [55]–[77] (Lord Hoffmann), [103]–[124] (Lord Hope), [137]–[159] (Baroness Hale) and [166]–[170] (Lord Carswell).

that relevant Convention rights could in some way apply horizontally – something which in turn involved a view concerning their nature and applicability, an underpinning consideration discussed earlier.

Several references were indeed made to the nature of the rights, sometimes mixed with comments about s 6. Lord Nicholls emphasised that 'the *values underlying* articles 8 and 10 are not confined to disputes between individuals and public authorities'.[65] Such values were 'as much applicable in disputes between individuals or between an individual and a non-governmental body ... as they are in disputes between individuals and a public authority'.[66] Meanwhile, Lord Hoffmann noted that Art 8 was 'not directly concerned with the protection of privacy against private persons or corporations. It is, by virtue of section 6 of the 1998 Act, a guarantee of privacy only against public authorities'.[67] However, Lord Hoffmann could see 'no logical ground for saying that a person should have less protection against a private individual than he would have against the state'.[68] Baroness Hale noted that national courts had to face the problem of balancing rights between private parties, in contrast with the Strasbourg Court's focus on restrictions by the state.[69]

Three uncertainties were visible in *Campbell*. The first concerned how to classify the form of horizontal effect in play. It was clearly indirect using the criteria favoured by Young and by Phillipson, but its strength was less obvious.[70] Lord Nicholls noted that 'the values enshrined in articles 8 and 10 are now part of the cause of action for breach of confidence'.[71] Courts would thus be 'giving effect to the values protected by article 8'.[72] These comments seemingly use terminology associated with weak indirect effect. Similarly, Lord Hoffmann noted that 'the right to privacy is in a general sense one of the values, and sometimes the most important value, which underlies a number of more specific causes of action'.[73] (Young notes that he omitted to specify whether privacy was to be treated as a fundamental or an ordinary value.[74]) By contrast, commentators have suggested that Baroness Hale may have been supporting a strong model of indirect horizontal effect when talking of a court being required to act compatibly with Convention *rights* where

---

[65] ibid at [18] (Lord Nicholls did not speculate about s 6).

[66] ibid at [17]; emphasis added.

[67] ibid at [49].

[68] ibid at [50].

[69] ibid at [140].

[70] Young op cit fn 7 pp35–36. See also Leigh and Masterman op cit fn 43 pp250–52. Phillipson op cit fn 9 pp 157–67.

[71] *Campbell* [2004] UKHL 22, [2004] 2 AC 457 at [17]; see also at [16].

[72] ibid at [19].

[73] ibid at [43]. See also para [50]. Interestingly, in *Mosley v News Group Newspapers Ltd* [2008] EWHC 1777 at [7], Eady J talks of values underpinning the HRA 1998 (rather than the Convention specifically), although Arts 8 and 10 as *rights* are associated with damages at [181].

[74] Young op cit fn 7 p 41.

a relevant cause of action was available, albeit without developing a new cause of action.[75]

The Supreme Court's later decision in *Khuja* reinforces this first uncertainty, given that Lord Sumption (supported by Lord Neuberger, Baroness Hale, Lord Clarke and Lord Reed) described *Campbell* as expanding 'the scope of the equitable action for breach of confidence by absorbing into it the values underlying articles 8 and 10'.[76] The reference to 'underlying values', coupled with the rather passive idea of 'absorption', of course implies a weak form of indirect horizontal effect.

The second *Campbell* uncertainty was that Lords Hoffmann and Hope disagreed about the HRA 1998's influence on the development of breach of confidence. For Lord Hoffmann, the common law and the effect given to Art 8 by the Act had operated in parallel,[77] producing an extension in the applicable duties from good faith associated with protecting confidentiality to the vindication of human autonomy and dignity more generally, and resulting in 'a shift in the centre of gravity of the action for breach of confidence … as a remedy for the unjustified publication of personal information'.[78] Lord Hope, however, doubted that there had been such a shift. The language had changed with the availability of Arts 8 and 10 and the guidance offered by Strasbourg case law, but essentially the same balancing exercise was still in play, albeit 'plainly now more carefully focused and more penetrating'.[79] Although the two Law Lords reached opposite conclusions on the facts, it is not obvious that their differing formulations directly affected this. Nonetheless, it is easy to imagine that an approach which focused on broad human values and a shifting centre of gravity might in a future case be read as involving wider implications for the horizontal reach of Convention rights than one based merely on revised language. In any event, Lords Hoffmann and Hope both seemed to emphasise the influence – that is, as underpinning considerations – of the terms of the HRA 1998 and its place in the broader constitutional structure (the role it played *relative to* the common law).

Producing a third uncertainty, the House of Lords confirmed that the balance between Arts 8 and 10 remained subject to its earlier rejection in *Wainwright v Home Office* of the notion that Art 8 triggered the recognition (in Lord Hoffmann's words) of a general common law 'principle of "invasion of privacy" … from which

---

[75] *Campbell* [2004] UKHL 22, [2004] 2 AC 457 at [132]. See the commentaries by Young op cit fn 7 p 43: Leigh and Masterman op cit fn 43 p 252: Phillipson op cit fn 9 pp 157–61 (Phillipson also suggests that while Lord Hope's judgment was ambiguous, it may have involved strong indirect horizontal effect).

[76] *Khuja* [2017] UKSC 49, [2019] AC 161 at [21].

[77] *Campbell* [2004] UKHL 22, [2004] 2 AC 457 at [46]–[50].

[78] ibid at [51]. This might be associated with Lord Hoffmann's invocation of values. See also Young op cit fn 7 p 42.

[79] *Campbell* [2004] UKHL 22, [2004] 2 AC 457 at [86].

the conditions of liability in the particular case can be deduced'.[80] Instead, at a more concrete or micro level, specific common law, statutory and equitable remedies – including the action for breach of confidence – protected privacy, which was 'one at least of the underlying values' beneath them.[81] As noted earlier, Convention rights were held to find their force through existing causes of action rather than serving as free agents.

Given the Supreme Court's later acknowledgement in *PJS* and *Khuja* of a distinct tort of invasion of privacy,[82] an interesting question is how far the three uncertainties and the degree of constraint articulated in *Campbell* – which still officially applies – remain meaningful. In *PJS*, Lord Neuberger (supported by Baroness Hale, Lord Mance and Lord Reed) emphasised that: 'claims based on respect for privacy and family life do not depend on confidentiality (or secrecy) alone'.[83] The two were separable, with privacy-related claims being associated with intrusion. In first-instance decisions since *Campbell*, there had emerged a 'clear, principled and consistent approach ... to balancing the media's freedom of expression and an individual's rights in respect of confidentiality and intrusion'.[84] Respect for private life had been found to offer protection against *both* breach of confidentiality *and* unwanted intrusion, with many cases relying upon intrusion to justify an injunction even though the claimant had lost confidentiality.[85] Lord Neuberger also referred in passing to invasion of privacy as 'tortious'.[86]

---

[80] [2003] UKHL 53, [2004] 2 AC 406 at [19]. See also the descriptions of the hypothetical 'general principle' in [18] (a 'high-level generalisation which can perform a useful function in enabling one to deduce the rule to be applied in a concrete case'); [23] (a 'general cause of action for invasion of privacy'); [26] (a 'high-level right to privacy'); and [30] ('a high-level principle of invasion of privacy'). See also [19], [34] and [35]. Note also [32] concerning ECtHR case law. *Wainwright* was cited in *Campbell* [2004] UKHL 22, [2004] 2 AC 457 at [11] (Lord Nicholls), [43] (Lord Hoffmann), and [133]–[134] (Baroness Hale).

[81] *Wainwright* [2003] UKHL 53, [2004] 2 AC 406 at [18], expanded upon by Lord Hoffmann in *Campbell* [2004] UKHL 22, [2004] 2 AC 457 at [43].

[82] The tension between *Wainwright* as endorsed in *Campbell* and the judicial duty to give effect to Art 8 and Art 10 and develop the ambit of breach of confidence, was highlighted by the Court of Appeal in *Douglas v Hello! Ltd (No 3)* [2005] EWCA Civ 595, [2006] QB 125, paras [50]–[53] (Lord Phillips MR); at House of Lords level the case was categorised as one of confidentiality and not privacy, thus avoiding the tension: [2007] UKHL 21, [2008] 1 AC 1, para [118] (Lord Hoffmann), [255]–[259] (Lord Nicholls), [292]–[300] (Lord Walker).

[83] *PJS* [2016] UKSC 26; [2016] AC 1081 at [58]. See also [57], [59], [61].

[84] ibid at [60]. Lord Mance described the 'approach taken' by the lower courts as 'sound in general principle'; ibid at [32].

[85] ibid at [58], [59] and [61], citing *Goodwin v News Group Newspapers Ltd* [2011] EWHC (QB) 1437, [2011] EMLR 502 at [85]; *CTB v News Group Newspapers Ltd* [2011] EWHC 1326 at [23] and [24] and *CTB v News Group Newspapers Ltd* [2011] EWHC 1334 (QB) at [1] and [3], and referring to *McKennitt* [2005] EWHC 3003 (QB), [2006] ELR 178 at [81]; *X v Persons Unknown* [2006] EWHC 2783 (QB), [2007] EMLR 10 at [64]; *JIH v News Group Newspapers Ltd* [2010] EWHC 2818 (QB), [2011] EMLR 177 at [58] and [59]; *TSE, ELP v News Group Newspapers Ltd* [2011] EWHC 1308 (QB). In *Terry (LNS) v Persons Unknown* [2010] EWHC 119, [2010] EMLR 16 at [53] and [54], Tugendhat J referred to misuse of private information as a separate cause of action from breach of confidence. Paras [57] and [68] in *PJS* [2016] UKSC 26, [2016] AC 1081 highlight that the separation of privacy and confidentiality assisted the claimant in the circumstances (by contrast, see the shift in Lord Toulson's dissenting judgment from confidentiality at [86] to intrusion on privacy at [88]).

[86] *Campbell* [2004] UKHL 22, [2004] 2 AC 457 at [33].

Meanwhile, Lord Mance (supported by Lord Neuberger, Baroness Hale and Lord Reed) spoke in greater detail of what was openly labelled a tort of invasion of privacy – a term that was employed by Lord Nicholls alone in *Campbell*[87] – which he suggested would prima facie be constituted by the 'disclosure or publication of purely private sexual encounters'.[88] In a legal sense, there existed no public interest in such revelations. While the success or otherwise of a *confidentiality* claim might turn on a quantitative assessment of what had already been disclosed as against what remained undisclosed, case law concerning the distinct idea of *disclosure of personal information* emphasised 'the invasiveness and distress involved, even in repetition of [previously revealed] private material'.[89] In similar vein, Lord Sumption noted for the majority in *Khuja* that the 'cause of action for invasion of a claimant's right to private and family life is relatively new to English law'.[90] Nonetheless, it now existed and originated in the bringing into national law of the Convention via the HRA 1998. The absorption referred to in *Campbell* had 'effectively recognis[ed] a qualified common law right of privacy'.[91] The pre-existing action for breach of confidence was thereby expanded.

The position following *PJS* and *Khuja* is not entirely clear. While the references to 'values' and 'absorption' may suggest a weak form of indirect horizontal effect, both decisions seemingly go beyond *Campbell* in acknowledging the emergence of a *distinct* head of tort liability between private parties covering invasion of privacy. The earlier requirement of a pre-existing relationship of confidentiality has gone, and protection of privacy may now involve a direct balancing of Convention rights in litigation between private parties – something which would not have been possible prior to the HRA 1998. Nonetheless, the contrasting positions of Lords Hoffmann and Hope in *Campbell* underline the uncertainty surrounding how radical we should see this development as being, and how far matters can ultimately develop under the influence of Arts 8 and 10. In short, debate is possible about the strength of the indirect horizontal effect in play, although it is greater than was initially the case.

Phillipson's emphasis on the context in which privacy liability has developed can help in assessing how much change the cases represent. Phillipson suggests that while the HRA 1998 continued a process of flexible development which had

---

[87] ibid at [14] and [15].

[88] *PJS* [2016] UKSC 26, [2016] AC 1081 at [32]. This observation extended to the repetition of such a disclosure or publication. See further *Goodwin v News Group Newspapers Ltd* [2011] EWHC 1437 (QB), [2011] EMLR 502 at [88]–[112].

[89] *PJS* [2016] UKSC 26, [2016] AC 1081 at [26]; see also paras [27]–[31], [35]. Relevant cases include *Green Corns Ltd v Claverley Group Ltd* [2005] EWHC 958 (QB), [2005] EMLR 31 at [76]–[81]; *McKennitt* [2005] EWHC 3003 (QB), [2006] EMLR 178 at [81]; *JIH v News Group Newspapers Ltd* [2010] EWHC 2818 (QB), [2011] EMLR 177, especially at [58]–[60]; *CTB v News Group Newspapers Ltd* [2011] EWHC 1326.

[90] *Khuja* [2017] UKSC 49, [2019] AC 161 at [22].

[91] ibid at [21].

already begun in relation to privacy, there was nonetheless a clear lacuna at the time the Act came into force. Indeed:

> [T]wo critical conditions were in place: first, long-standing and serious dissatisfaction with the absence of proper protection in the existing law; second, clear evidence that the government was most unlikely to bring forward legislation to provide the particular remedy required, so that common law development was the only realistic way of doing the job.[92]

While the first point might suggest the need for a relatively pragmatic assessment of the HRA 1998's impact, the second brings into play the underpinning constitutional consideration (discussed earlier) by focusing on the appropriate roles of the legislature and courts in developing liability. In this vein, Sedley LJ appeared sympathetic in *Douglas v Hello! Ltd* to the argument that shifting from confidentiality to privacy 'is precisely the kind of incremental change for which the [1998] Act is designed'.[93] Whatever the accuracy of this statement, it seemingly suggests that in the absence of legislative involvement, judicial reinterpretation of an existing cause of action was not seen as an unduly radical step.[94]

D. Horizontal Effect in Other Areas

Notwithstanding the identification of privacy as the primary example of indirect horizontal effect, commentators have observed that absorption of Convention rights has varied according to the branch or area of law in play, reflecting, if this is right, the influence of another underpinning consideration highlighted earlier. In contrast with privacy, it has been suggested that while the tort of nuisance and areas of the law of property are *potentially* open (given their subject matters) to the influence of Convention rights in cases between private parties, this has not really been seen in practice.[95] In cases involving contracts, a more visible role has been played by Convention rights in employment law, although this is a field long dominated by statute. However, in *McDonald v McDonald* (hereafter *McDonald*) the Supreme Court chose to stress, in relation to a repossession claim relating to privately rented property, that Convention rights controlled the behaviour of the state *rather than* private parties.[96] The remainder of this section will focus on *McDonald* and the contract of employment cases, examining the role of various underpinning considerations – particularly the area of law in play.

In *McDonald*, the Supreme Court unanimously held, through a joint judgment by Lord Neuberger and Baroness Hale, that the right to respect for the

---

[92] Phillipson op cit fn 50 pp 159–60; see also p 162.

[93] [2001] QB 967 at [129].

[94] For arguments about limits to the judicial role, compare Hunt op cit fn 22; Phillipson and Williams (2011) 'Horizontal effect and the constitutional constraint' *MLR* 878.

[95] See Nolan (2011) 'Nuisance': and Goymour (2011) 'Property and housing' in Hoffman op cit fn 7.

[96] *McDonald* [2016] UKSC 28, [2017] AC 273.

home protected under Art 8 did not require a court to assess the proportionality of evicting an assured shorthold tenant of a residential property when deciding whether to grant a possession order to the freehold private owner.[97] Given that the entitlements and remedies associated with such tenancies are regulated by statute (the Housing Acts 1980, 1988 and 1996),[98] it may initially seem surprising that the proportionality issue was decided in terms of the obligations of courts under HRA 1998, s 6, with consideration given only later (and *obiter*) to whether the Housing Act 1988 might be reinterpreted pursuant to HRA 1998, s 3 to give effect to the parties' competing Convention rights balanced using proportionality. The most plausible explanation is that the wording of the provision concerned (Housing Act 1988, s 21(4)) was viewed by the Supreme Court as far narrower than that of housing provisions into which it had previously proven possible to read a proportionality requirement: to do so here would thus have gone beyond the limits of permissible reinterpretation under s 3 articulated in *Ghaidan v Godin-Mendoza* (hereafter *Ghaidan*).[99] Unfortunately, *McDonald* is complicated by broader *obiter dicta* about the nature of Convention rights, and – in relation to s 6 – by a failure to explain the position adopted with sufficient clarity.

Previous cases had confirmed that when a public authority sought possession as landlord of a residential property it had let under applicable legislation, the court *might* consider the proportionality of granting a possession order and of its terms.[100] This reflected the interpretation placed upon Art 8 in the Strasbourg Court's decisions, and the HRA 1998's drafting in the form of the obligations of public authorities under s 6. The latter point prompted the question in *McDonald* whether courts – given their inclusion within s 6 – were *obliged* to consider proportionality, including when determining possession claims by *private owners*.[101]

Factors associated with three of the underpinning considerations seemingly played a crucial role in the Supreme Court's answer. While logically distinct, they were somewhat inter-mixed in the judgment. The first set concerned the nature and requirements (ie applicability) of Convention rights, generally and individually;

---

[97] The factual circumstances in the case were slightly more complex, involving default on a loan secured by a charge on the property: see *McDonald* [2016] UKSC 28, [2017] AC 273 at [2]–[5]. For a critique of the judgment in the housing law context see Nield and Laurie (2019) 'The private–public divide and horizontality in the English rental sector' *Public Law* 724.

[98] Relevant provisions are set out in ibid at [15]–[30].

[99] See ibid at [65], [68]–[70]. The cases concerned were *Manchester City Council v Pinnock* [2010] UKSC 45, [2011] 2 AC 104 and *Mayor and Burgesses of the London Borough of Hounslow v Powell* [2011] UKSC 8, [2011] 2 AC 186. *Ghaidan* [2004] UKHL 30, [2004] 2 AC 557 was strictly speaking an Art 14 case piggybacking on Art 8; the issue being whether the relevant provision of the Rent Act 1977 could be interpreted to include same-sex couples. In one sense, what the House of Lords did in *Ghaidan* could be characterised as remedying a legislative oversight (the notion of same-sex couples not having been considered when the 1977 Act was passed).

[100] *McDonald* [2016] UKSC 28, [2017] AC 273 at [34]–[37], referring to *Pinnock* [2010] UKSC 45, [2011] 2 AC 104 at [45], [49] and [51]–[54], applied in *Powell* [2011] UKSC 8, [2011] 2 AC 186.

[101] *McDonald* [2016] UKSC 28, [2017] AC 273 at [29] and [38]; the matter had been left open in *Pinnock* [2010] UKSC 45, [2011] 2 AC 104 at [50].

the second, the constitutional roles of particular institutions; and the third, the character of the area of law and/or actors involved.

The first consideration – applicability – can be associated with the Supreme Court's conclusion that clear and authoritative Strasbourg guidance did not require proportionality analysis,[102] and that without such a requirement, Art 8 did not justify a different order from one 'mandated by the contractual relationship between the parties, at least where ... there are legislative provisions which the democratically elected legislature has decided properly represent the competing interests of private sector landlords and residential tenants'.[103] Art 8 thus imposed, in this instance, no requirement to develop national law. Key for present purposes is the *reason* why this was important. According to the Supreme Court, a different finding would have affected applicability, entailing rights 'effectively being directly enforceable as between private citizens so as to alter their contractual rights and obligations, whereas the purpose of the Convention is ... to protect citizens from having their rights infringed by the state'.[104] Having associated Convention rights with applicability against the state rather than private disputes, it was suggested that there was a 'fundamental difference between public sector landlords (who owe their residential tenants an article 8 duty) and private sector landlords (... who do not)'.[105]

The second, constitutional consideration can be associated with the Supreme Court's observation that a legislative framework was already in place based on Parliament's policy choices, thereby excluding a broader decision-making role for courts. Disputes about invasion of privacy arose from 'tortious or quasi-tortious relationships, where the legislature has expressly, impliedly or through inaction, left it to the courts to carry out the balancing exercise'.[106] In contrast, the parties in *McDonald*, while in a contractual relationship, were in one 'in respect of which the legislature has prescribed how their respective Convention rights are to be respected'.[107] On this view, the exclusion of a dynamic role for the court reflected the maintenance of a boundary between the legislature and the judiciary – a concern not manifested in the privacy cases.[108] More specifically, Lord Millett had already explained in *Harrow London Borough Council v Qazi* that national courts were 'merely the forum for the determination of the civil right in dispute between the parties'.[109] There was nothing further to investigate once the landlord had been

---

[102] *McDonald* [2016] UKSC 28, [2017] AC 273 at [47]–[59]. It was acknowledged that there was some support for the notion Art 8 might be engaged when a court was asked to make an order, but this did not translate into a requirement to consider proportionality.

[103] ibid at [40]. In addition to the Housing Acts 1980 and 1988, the Protection from Eviction Act 1977 was in issue.

[104] ibid at [41]. See also [37].

[105] ibid at [49].

[106] ibid at [46].

[107] ibid.

[108] Phillipson notes in relation to privacy that courts are keen to avoid 'judicial law-making ... that they consider plainly beyond their constitutional and institutional capacities': op cit fn 50 p 163.

[109] [2004] 1 AC 983 at [108] (cited in *McDonald* [2016] UKSC 28, [2017] AC 273 at [44]).

found entitled to possession, notwithstanding s 6 and Strasbourg's categorisation of national courts as part of the state.[110] Given the role of the state, it would be unsatisfactory if the national legislature could not create a scheme to protect private sector residential tenants without 'forcing the state to accept a super-added requirement of addressing the issue of proportionality in each case where possession is sought'.[111] This is, of course, a visibly constitutional proposition.

In association with the third area of law-related consideration, the Supreme Court appeared reluctant to reach a decision which would alter what it saw as an agreement-based contractual relationship concerning the property. It noted that the Strasbourg case law[112] did not assist tenants of privately rented properties, in part because stipulations concerning public authorities could not be 'confidently translated to cases involving private sector landlords seeking to enforce a contractual right to possession subject to legislative constraints'.[113] Even if a translation was possible, it would beg the question whether a national court could be *required* to consider the proportionality of making an order that was required 'by the contractual terms as softened by domestic legislation'.[114] As a general matter, there was a distinction between contractual arrangements made between private parties, including in *McDonald*, and cases such as *Campbell* in which 'the court can be required to balance conflicting Convention rights of two parties'.[115]

Seemingly combining factors associated with the second and third underpinning considerations, the judgment noted, *obiter*, while rejecting a role for HRA 1998, s 3, that in the context of the housing legislation, decisions by public authorities were viewed as distinct from those made by private landlords in part because the former were 'obliged to use their powers lawfully in accordance with the general principles of public law; it is open to a tenant to defend possession proceedings on the ground that the authority has acted unlawfully'.[116] In contrast, the (public law) concept of legality had no application to a private landlord, whose exercise of a discretion was not subject to *Wednesbury* unreasonableness review and who was 'entitled to recover possession of his property in accordance with

---

[110] ibid at [109] (cited in *McDonald* [2016] UKSC 28, [2017] AC 273 at [44]; see also [38]).

[111] ibid at [43]. [41] and [42] also discuss potential uncertainties which would result in the private sector. The Supreme Court noted, separately, at [45], that dismissing the s 6 argument did not preclude an argument in an appropriate future case that the housing legislation failed properly to protect Art 8 rights and that 'the legislature had not carried out its obligations under the Convention'.

[112] The Strasbourg cases discussed included *Di Palma v United Kingdom* (1986) 10 EHRR 149; *Wood v United Kingdom* (1997) 24 EHRR CD 69; *Connors v United Kingdom* (2004) 40 EHRR 9; *Blečić v Croatia* (2006) 43 EHRR 48; *McCann v United Kingdom* (2008) 47 EHRR 40; *Zehentner v Austria* (2009) 52 EHRR 22; *Mustafa and Tarzibachi v Sweden* (2008) 52 EHRR 24; *Ćosić v Croatia* (2011) 52 EHRR 39; *Kay v United Kingdom* [2011] HLR 13; *Orlić v Croatia* [2011] HLR 44.

[113] *McDonald* [2016] UKSC 28, [2017] AC 273 at [50]. See also [49], [51]–[56].

[114] ibid at [50]. Note also the observations at para [57] concerning *Mustafa and Tarzibachi v Sweden* (2008) 52 EHRR 24.

[115] *McDonald* [2016] UKSC 28, [2017] AC 273 at [46].

[116] ibid at [64], referring to *Wandsworth London Borough Council v Winder* [1985] AC 461; *Doherty v Birmingham City Council* [2009] 1 AC 367 at [69] (Lord Scott).

the law for whatever reason he likes'.[117] HRA 1998, s 6 did not apply 'to a private landlord, who is not obliged to act compatibly with the Convention rights'.[118]

Despite the visibility of the underpinning considerations in *McDonald*, at least three key uncertainties were unfortunately also evident. First, the *relative* importance of factors associated with each consideration was unclear; something which may – given the logically divergent nature of the considerations – affect the reach of Convention rights in future cases, and our understanding of horizontal effect generally. For example, an approach which specified that the subject matter – eg that a case concerned tort rather than contract – provided the key to determining whether Convention rights might apply, would handle matters differently from one which treated as decisive the constitutional issue of the presence (and nature) or absence of legislative involvement. At minimum, the first approach might entail a court focusing on how to identify a case as concerning tort rather than contract,[119] and the second on assessing the degree and nature of legislative intervention. In reality, though, each – if considered on its own – might sometimes respond differently to whether Convention rights applied. By mixing its treatment of these different considerations together and not offering a clear order of priority, *McDonald* invites future argument.

A second uncertainty is whether the emphasis placed by Lords Hoffmann, Nicholls and others in *Campbell* on the potential for the values or protections associated with Convention rights to extend into litigation between individuals can easily be reconciled with the later characterisation of the Convention in *McDonald* as something 'intended to protect individual rights against infringement by the state'.[120] Neither body of *dicta* was absolute, but it is hard to avoid the impression of a difference of focus. It is unclear whether this signals a deeper-level substantive disagreement concerning the applicability of human rights – in which case, a choice may be needed between competing approaches to this underpinning consideration – or simply the presence in different judgments of sometimes unduly general propositions which could usefully be brought closer together.

A third uncertainty, extending out of the first two, concerns how easy it will be to distinguish *McDonald* from other cases involving what David Mead characterises as publicly infused private law – that is, an 'essentially private law dispute [which] arises from a relationship that is underpinned or informed by statute'.[121] Mead

---

[117] *McDonald* [2016] UKSC 28, [2017] AC 273 at [64], referring to *Associated Provincial Picture Houses Ltd v Wednesbury Corporation* [1948] 1 KB 223. For discussion of the role of contract in judicial analysis of the vertical application of s 6, see Palmer (2007) 'Public, private and the Human Rights Act 1998: an ideological divide' *Cambridge Law Journal* 559, discussing *YL v Birmingham City Council* [2007] UKHL 27, [2008] 1 AC 95.

[118] *McDonald* [2016] UKSC 28, [2017] AC 273 at [66]. See also [67].

[119] Arguments are canvassed in Burrows (1998) *Understanding the law of obligations: essays on contract, tort and restitution* ch 1.

[120] *McDonald* [2016] UKSC 28, [2017] AC 273 at [37]; see also [41].

[121] Mead (2005) 'Rights, relationships and retrospectivity: the impact of Convention rights on pre-existing private relationships following *Wilson* and *Ghaidan*' *Public Law* 459 p 460.

was talking of *Ghaidan*, which the Supreme Court distinguished in *McDonald* by reference to the limits of reinterpretation. More complex, however, might be the bloc of cases, unmentioned in *McDonald*, in which statutory provisions governing contracts of employment between private parties *have* been interpreted in the light of Convention rights.[122] The Court of Appeal considered the Employment Rights Act 1996, covering unfair dismissal from (contractual) private employment, through this lens in *X v Y*,[123] *Copsey v WWB Devon Clays Ltd*[124] and *Turner v East Midlands Trains Ltd*,[125] engaging with the requirements of relevant rights.[126] Some commentators have questioned the practical utility of this approach, given that it has had little effect on outcomes.[127] The cases are significant for present purposes since it is not clear how we are to distinguish situations in which applicable legislation is deemed to have prescribed how Convention rights are to be applied in relation to a contract – excluding interpretation, according to *McDonald* – from those in which wide-reaching statutory provisions were read subject to Convention rights, as in the contract of employment cases. Possibilities might include the nature of the right in question, the general circumstances of the case, and (by analogy with *McDonald*) the extent to which relevant legislation allows for discretion by the decision-maker as opposed to being narrowly prescriptive.[128] Whatever the preferred approach, it looks as if the general uncertainties surrounding the limits to permitted reinterpretation under the HRA 1998, s 3[129] are finding an echo in this present uncertainty about when Convention rights may be invoked – probably not a welcome phenomenon from the standpoint of legal certainty, but not a surprise given the design of the HRA.

The Strasbourg Court rejected the applicant's Art 8 complaint when declaring the appeal from *McDonald* inadmissible in *FJM v United Kingdom*,[130] and in doing

---

[122] For general analysis of the employment cases, see Collins and Mantouvalou (2016) 'Human rights and the contract of employment', Freedland et al (eds), *The contract of employment*.

[123] *X v Y* [2004] EWCA Civ 662, [2004] ICR 1634. See also *Pay v Lancashire Probation Service* [2004] ICR 187.

[124] [2005] EWCA Civ 932, [2005] ICR 1789.

[125] [2012] EWCA Civ 1470, [2013] ICR 525.

[126] At Strasbourg level, see also *Pay v United Kingdom*, Application no 32792/05, 16 September 2008; (2009) 48 EHRR SE2; *Redfearn v United Kingdom*, Application no 47335/06, 6 November 2012; (2013) 57 EHRR 2. And see also the discussion of the ECtHR's decision in *Eweida v United Kingdom* [2013] 57 EHRR 8 in Hatzis' chapter herein at pp 241–42 for an example of how 'positive obligations' can provide a backdoor route to creating horizontal effect.

[127] Vickers (2004) 'Unfair dismissal and human rights' *Industrial LJ* 52; Collins and Mantavoulou (2013) '*Redfearn v. UK*: political association and dismissal' *MLR* 909; Mantouvalou (2008) 'Human rights and unfair dismissal: private acts in public spaces' 71 *MLR* 912; Mantavoulou and Collins (2009) 'Private life and dismissal' *Industrial LJ* 133.

[128] The first two factors might be associated with Mummery LJ's approach in *X v Y* [2004] ICR 1634 at [45], [49], [51]–[52]. Note also Rix LJ's potential exclusion, in the Art 9 context, relating to 'contracts freely entered into': *Copsey* [2005] EWCA Civ 392 at [62]. And see further Hatzis' chapter herein at pp 239–42.

[129] See Kavanagh (2009) *Constitutional review under the UK Human Rights Act* chs 2–5.

[130] Application no 76202/16, 29 November 2018, [2019] HLR 8. See the summary of national decision-making at [26] to [29].

so reinforced ambiguity concerning Art 8 and horizontal effect. The Court relied upon a point first highlighted in *Vrzic v Croatia*, that a private party at risk of losing their home and seeking a remedy was not automatically entitled to have the proportionality of repossession determined by an independent tribunal.[131] In such a situation, the balance between (competing) private parties' interests could potentially be struck by national legislation concerning the rights in issue. One unclear aspect of this vertical focus was that the Court seemingly echoed the differences of emphasis seen at national level, highlighting *both* that private as well as public interests had to be weighed in the horizontal context – affecting the balance in play – *and* that national legislation had tried to strike that balance, an issue going to the constitutional roles of different institutions: 'two private individuals or entities have entered voluntarily into a contractual relationship in respect of which the legislature has prescribed how their respective Convention rights are to be respected'.[132] The sense that abstract issues were in play but not fully explained was reinforced by the Court's much broader – yet unsupported – assertion, reminiscent of the Supreme Court, that:

> If the domestic courts could override the balance struck by the legislation in such a case, the Convention would be directly enforceable between private citizens so as to alter the contractual rights and obligations that they had freely entered into.[133]

E. Conclusion

Drawing together the arguments from this section, the criteria offered by Young and by Phillipson for categorising the operation of horizontal effect, particularly its strength, are helpful when classifying the approaches in the UK cases. Those cases also demonstrate that factors associated with the underpinning considerations identified in the preceding section are often central (singly or in combination) to a *full* understanding. We will see in the next section that they play an analogous role when analysing horizontal effect and the Charter.

The horizontal effect associated with the HRA 1998, ss 3 and 6 is indirect under the Young and Phillipson criteria.[134] The pre-existing parameters of Convention rights – their basic applicability – remain, in logic, the same from the standpoint of the Convention when entering into national law (unless the Strasbourg Court says otherwise). From a UK perspective, the focus is on ss 3 and 6 as the filters

---

[131] ibid at [41], invoking *Vrzic v Croatia*, Application no 43777/13, 12 July 2016, (2018) 66 EHRR 30 at [67].

[132] ibid at [42]; for assessment in the circumstances, see [43]–[46].

[133] ibid at [42]. Commentators have criticised *FJM* for the paucity of its reasoning, in particular concerning Art 8 and horizontal effect in previous housing possession cases: Boddy and Graham (2019) '*FJM v United Kingdom*: the taming of Article 8' *Conveyancer and Property Lawyer* 166; Vols (2019) 'European law and evictions: property, proportionality and vulnerable people' *European Review of Private Law* 719.

[134] Note also Leigh and Masterman op cit fn 43 pp 262–64.

through which Convention rights are given horizontal effect, albeit that relevant rights must be capable of assuming such effect – they must be applicable. The s 3 interpretive obligation operates (subject to what is deemed 'possible') whenever a statute and applicable Convention right interact in a horizontal case.

The meaning of s 6 as it applies to courts is more contentious. It officially encompasses the development of existing common law causes of action rather than the creation of new ones, but questions have arisen about whether effect is given to rights or to values and whether earlier constraints have been discarded. In horizontal common law litigation, Convention rights have varied in their visibility and effect, the strongest manifestation being in regard to invasion of privacy, and with the treatment of 'publicly infused' common law contractual provisions seemingly depending on the area in play. On one potential reading, the area of law in issue – judicial reluctance to rewrite contracts as opposed to developing privacy liability – is thus crucial; on another, the extent and degree of detail in which the legislature has either intervened or appears willing to do so is determinative. Each reading corresponds with a different underpinning consideration, opening the door to uncertainty in future cases while also illustrating the central part played by the considerations in shaping horizontal effect.

How should the UK cases be viewed overall? Phillipson offers a 'prosaic explanation'.[135] We should not treat the privacy cases 'as providing a general template for common law horizontality'.[136] Instead, the development of liability results from local circumstances, including the perceived existence of a problem and an apparent lack of legislative engagement, rather than 'the clear acceptance of any general model of horizontal effect'.[137] This explanation might be extended to *McDonald* given the role played there by the pre-existing local statutory scheme. A more radically pragmatic analyst troubled by the uncertainties associated with some cases might presumably go beyond Phillipson and suggest that courts are making wholly ends-oriented and situation-by-situation assessments of the desirability and practicality of using Convention rights horizontally, without troubling themselves to explore even Phillipson's 'prosaic' factors in depth.

Nonetheless, either a 'prosaic' or a wholly pragmatic explanation may seem incomplete in light of the frequent judicial *attempts* – even if inadequate in practice – to engage with underpinning considerations, particularly the characteristics of the right(s) in issue (applicability), general constitutional requirements, and the area of law in play. As such, a realistic but arguably more rounded explanation might be that since arguments about horizontal effect and Convention rights may well look somewhat open-ended when raised before a court, it is unsurprising that resulting decisions are often tied to rather general statements (concerning applicability, the constitutional landscape, and so on) associated with particular

---

[135] ibid at p 164.

[136] Phillipson op cit fn 50 p 163.

[137] ibid. Although note Phillipson's articulation elsewhere (with Williams) of the 'constitutional constraint' model, which is argued to fit with the existing judicial approach: Phillipson and Williams, op cit fn 94.

underpinning considerations. In consequence, a long-established common law position – for instance, that contracts rest on intentions, which are normally to be respected – may prove less amenable to refinement in the light of Convention rights than a more fluid concept like confidentiality. Similarly, the presence of visible legislative activity in an area may encourage a court, reflecting concerns about its constitutional remit, to be more reticent in its approach to the common law. This is not to say, that there can be *no* general model of horizontal effect; rather, any conceptualisation (including the explanation just advanced) is simply bound to be quite abstract, restricting its usefulness as a *practical* day-to-day guide to the case law.

III. Horizontal Effect under the Canadian Charter

The debate in Canada as to the horizontal effect of the Charter has been tied to the text of s 32(1). This applies the Charter:

(a) to the Parliament and government of Canada in respect of all matters within the authority of Parliament including all matters relating to the Yukon Territory and Northwest Territories; and

(b) to the legislature and government of each province in respect of all matters within the authority of the legislature of each province.

There is no express mention of courts, in contrast with the HRA 1998, s 6, but s 32 must be read alongside s 24, which expressly assigns (in very broad terms) juris-diction to many Canadian courts to provide remedies for unjustified breaches of Charter rights (lack of justification being measured by reference to s 1). Section 24 stipulates that 'Anyone whose rights or freedoms, as guaranteed by this Charter, have been infringed or denied may apply to a court of competent jurisdiction to obtain such remedy as the court considers appropriate and just in the circum-stances'. The nature and purpose of that remedial jurisdiction is elaborated (a little) in the 'supremacy' provision found in the Constitution Act 1982, s 52(1), which underpins the Charter: 'The Constitution of Canada is the supreme law of Canada, and any law that is inconsistent with the provisions of the Constitution is, to the extent of the inconsistency, of no force or effect'. By analogy with the inclusion of courts in the HRA 1998, s 6, the express references to legislatures and governments in s 32 have focused attention on relevant boundaries, including whether matters falling outside the ambit of 'governmental action' are affected by the Charter.

Specific practical differences include the absence from the Charter of a direct equivalent to Art 8 of the Convention, which may help to explain how the focus on privacy seen in UK cases has not been evident in Canada[138] – a point perhaps reinforced by the fact that several Canadian provinces had enacted privacy

---

[138] See Reiter (2009) 'Privacy and the Charter' *Canadian Bar Review* 119 pp 120–22.

statutes with horizontal as well as vertical effect by the time the Charter entered into force.[139] Unlike in the UK, a general approach to the operation of horizontal effect has also been articulated by the Supreme Court, in *Dolphin Delivery*,[140] although – as in the UK – judicial treatments have been criticised for vagueness.[141]

It will be argued in this section that divergences between the human rights measures and constitutional structures of the two jurisdictions exist alongside analogous considerations underpinning the operation of horizontal effect in each.

A. The *Dolphin Delivery* Decision

At issue in *Dolphin Delivery* was the legality of secondary picketing in a trade dispute between private actors, with a company seeking to tie its application for an injunction to prevent a union from secondary picketing to substantive claims based on the common law torts of inducing breach of contract and civil conspiracy (despite the existence of expansive statutory regulation of labour relations at both the national and provincial levels, the applicable national legislation had omitted to address the matter in issue).[142] The litigation brought into question the role – if any – in these circumstances of freedom of expression and association as protected under s 2 of the Charter, given that the union argued that its rights under these headings should bind private sector actors. Three aspects of McIntyre J's judgment are relevant in explaining the Supreme Court's conclusion that the union could not invoke the Charter directly as a defence against the company's claim.

First, McIntyre J noted that the drafting of s 32(1) referred *specifically* to the executive or administrative branches of government, alongside the legislature – not the whole governmental apparatus of the state – and did so whether those institutions' actions were invoked in public or private litigation. State action in reliance on statutory or common law authority would thus be unconstitutional if it infringed a Charter right, while the Charter 'will apply to the common law ... only in so far as the common law is the basis of some governmental action'.[143] However, it did not apply to the common law 'between private parties'.[144]

---

[139] See Hunt and Shirazian (2016) 'Canada's statutory privacy torts in Commonwealth perspective' *Oxford University Comparative Law Forum*, available at https://ouclf.iuscomp.org/canadas-statutory-privacy-torts-in-commonwealth-perspective/.

[140] [1986] 2 SCR 573. It is labelled a 'seminal ruling' on the topic by Barendt (2007) 'The United States and Canada: state action, constitutional rights and private actors' in Oliver and Fedtke (eds), *Human rights and the private sphere: a comparative study*. For analysis, see Slattery (1987) 'The *Charter's* relevance to private litigation: does *Dolphin* deliver?' (1987) *McGill LJ* 905; Gibson (1993) 'The deferential Trojan horse: a decade of Charter decisions' *Canadian Bar Review* 417 pp 425–26, 429–31. For strong criticism, see Manwaring (1987) 'Bringing the common law to the bar of justice: comment on the decision in the case of *Dolphin Delivery Ltd*' *Ottawa LR* 413.

[141] For example Weinrib and Weinrib op cit fn 33 pp 44–46. Etherington describes the Court's reasoning as 'cryptic': (1987) 'Notes of cases' 66 *Canadian Bar Review* 818 p 825.

[142] *Dolphin Delivery* [1986] 2 SCR 573 at 583–88. For a summary of the issues see at 582. On injunctions and s 1 of the Charter see at 588–92.

[143] ibid at 599.

[144] ibid.

The prominence accorded here to the text of s 32(1) is analogous to the attention paid to the wording of the HRA 1998, s 6 in the UK case law,[145] although commentators have debated the adequacy of McIntyre J's reading of the legislature's intent.[146] McIntyre J seemingly focused on institutional identity, for example, rather than competence to legislate – notwithstanding that the latter might be thought to have been encompassed in the word 'matters' in s 32(1) and the national legislature had the power to enact measures overriding the common law with respect to secondary picketing.[147]

Rather confusingly, McIntyre J *also* used institutional identity as the basis for the broader and starker proposition that 'the Charter does not apply to private litigation'.[148] This latter *dictum* appears to exclude *any* litigation between actors falling outside s 32(1), not *just* litigation based on common law, yet no basis was offered to correlate institutional concerns with the subtle differences between the two positions. The broader and starker position is also difficult to reconcile with two other points: first, given its starkness, with the Supreme Court's later acceptance (demonstrated in cases discussed below) of the role of Charter *values* in interpreting legislation in horizontal cases; and secondly, and *per se*, with McIntyre J's apparent acceptance that some examples of litigation between private parties (including in one accepted case) – however inadequate the basis for their identification – turned on the authority of a statute and properly attracted Charter scrutiny.[149]

More generally, *Dolphin Delivery*'s focus is rather different from that adopted by UK courts in applying the HRA 1998. Under the Charter, governmental action, whether relying on statute or common law, opens the door to scrutiny using Charter rights; under the HRA 1998, reinterpretation of legislation or common law, and challenges to public authorities' actions, require the prior presence of Convention rights.

A second aspect of McIntyre J's judgment which deserves attention is the significance attached to general constitutional considerations relating to courts, although (as we will see below) the Supreme Court's position on this issue shifted. McIntyre J stressed that the Charter would apply: 'Where … exercise of, or reliance upon, governmental action is present and where one private party invokes or relies upon it to produce an infringement of the Charter rights of another'.[150] While the

---

[145] The role played by drafting is emphasised by Saunders (2005) op cit fn 28 pp 199–200.

[146] See for example Gibson (1986) *The law of the Charter: general principles* pp 112–15; Fader (1997) 'Reemergence of the Charter application debate: issues for the Supreme Court in *Eldridge* and *Vriend*' 6 *Dalhousie J Leg Stud* 187 pp 197–203.

[147] Nor that provincial legislatures could do so insofar as labour disputes fell within provincial jurisdiction (see the chapter by Ewing herein).

[148] *Dolphin Delivery* [1986] 2 SCR 573 at 597.

[149] The case considered in *Dolphin Delivery* ibid at 600–02 was *Re Blainey and Ontario Hockey Association*, 26 DLR (4th) 728, 54 OR (2d) 513, [1986] OJ No 236 (dismissal of application to appeal: 58 OR (2d) 274).

[150] *Dolphin Delivery* [1986] 2 SCR 573 at 602–03.

term 'governmental action' was difficult to define,[151] it did not include application of a court order. Courts were bound by the Charter, but also by all law. Their duty was 'to apply the law, but in doing so they act as neutral arbiters, not as contending parties involved in a dispute'.[152] Furthermore, to 'regard a court order as an element of governmental intervention necessary to invoke the Charter would … widen the scope of Charter application to virtually all private litigation'.[153]

The third aspect requiring attention is McIntyre J's statement that 'Where … private party "A" sues private party "B" relying on the common law and where no act of government is relied upon to support the action, the Charter will not apply'.[154] This seemingly tied the Charter's applicability to the source of law – common law or statute – in play.[155] Nonetheless, McIntyre J went on to say that:

> [T]his is a distinct issue from the question whether the judiciary ought to apply and develop the principles of the common law in a manner consistent with the fundamental values enshrined in the Constitution. The answer to this question must be in the affirmative. In this sense … the Charter is far from irrelevant to private litigants whose disputes fall to be decided at common law.[156]

Analogous elements were later evident in *McKinney v University of Guelph* (hereafter *McKinney*). La Forest J began with the text of s 32: 'The exclusion of private activity from the Charter … was a deliberate choice which must be respected. We do not really know why this approach was taken'.[157] Among the explanations canvassed was the nature or applicability of constitutional rights:

> Historically, bills of rights … have been directed at government. Government is the body that can enact and enforce rules and authoritatively impinge on individual freedom. Only government requires to be constitutionally shackled to preserve the rights of the individual.[158]

La Forest J was also concerned that the subjection of all private action to constitutional review would diminish the realm of individual freedom and reopen many areas of settled law. Cory J cited with approval the suggestions that it might be tantamount to setting up an alternative tort system and seriously interfere with freedom of contract,[159] points reminiscent of McIntyre J's observation in *Dolphin Delivery* that if the Charter could preclude a court enforcement order from being made: 'it would seem that *all* private litigation would be subject to the Charter'.[160]

---

[151] ibid at 600–02.
[152] ibid at 600. For a pre-*Dolphin Delivery* argument for the inclusion of courts, see Gibson op cit fn 146 pp 95–96.
[153] *Dolphin Delivery* [1986] 2 SCR 573 at 600.
[154] ibid at 603.
[155] Hogg op cit fn 34 para 37.2(g).
[156] *Dolphin Delivery* [1986] 2 SCR 573 at 603.
[157] [1990] 3 SCR 229 at 262. As in *Dolphin Delivery*, the 'matters' element did not attract attention.
[158] *McKinney* [1990] 3 SCR 229 at 262.
[159] ibid at 262–63.
[160] *Dolphin Delivery* [1986] 2 SCR 573 at 600–01; emphasis added.

While maybe involving an exaggerated description of the consequences for private law,[161] Cory J's comments seemingly involve, by analogy with the HRA 1998, a combination of underpinning considerations: namely, the nature of rights (applicability) and of the Charter, a concern about which areas of the common law should be regulated by rights (on one view, seemingly maintaining a space within which contract and tort might operate unhindered), and a view of the legislature's proper role in balancing (through legislation) rights and private common law freedoms.[162]

Nonetheless, while *Dolphin Delivery* remains good law, the decision's practical reach – in terms of the extent to which legal relations between ostensibly 'private' parties are *not* regulated by the Charter – has been moderated in the three ways now considered.

B. Defining 'Governmental'

Firstly, the Supreme Court subsequently held that certain court actions counted as 'governmental' within s 32(1), notwithstanding McIntyre J's exclusion of the court order from that category in *Dolphin Delivery*. In *R v Rahey* (hereafter *Rahey*), the Court concluded that a trial judge's behaviour in conducting a criminal trial could breach Charter rights,[163] and in *British Columbia Government Employees' Union v British Columbia* (hereafter *British Columbia*), judicial enforcement of an injunction granted in relation to picketing during industrial action was found to engage Charter arguments.[164]

On a wider view, these decisions might also be thought generally to qualify the second highlighted aspect of McIntyre J's *Dolphin Delivery* judgment by accepting that the text of s 32(1) does not invariably exclude courts. Delivering the leading judgment in *British Columbia*, Dickson CJ (joined by Lamer, Wilson, La Forest and L'Heureux-Dube JJ) emphasised that *Dolphin Delivery* required the Charter's exclusion 'where the common law is invoked with reference to a purely private dispute'.[165] The present case, however, was different:

> At issue here is the validity of a common law breach of criminal law and ultimately the authority of the court to punish for breaches of that law. The court is acting on its own motion and not at the instance of any private party. The motivation for the court's action is entirely 'public' in nature, rather than 'private'.[166]

---

[161] In this regard, it is interesting that in *Vriend v Alberta* [1998] 1 SCR 493 the majority rejected at [107] and [108] an argument categorised as resting on another type of exaggeration as to consequences.

[162] Barendt op cit fn 140 pp 417–18.

[163] *Rahey* [1987] 1 SCR 588.

[164] *British Columbia* [1988] 2 SCR 214.

[165] ibid at 243.

[166] ibid at 243–44.

The two judgments have thus prompted Peter Hogg to suggest that *Dolphin Delivery* is best read as confined to (and thus as excluding) court orders *where they were based upon* the common law in litigation between private parties.[167] In turn, Dale Gibson argues that, following the later cases, 'whatever McIntyre J might have intended by his *Dolphin dicta* about the meaning of 'government', courts are subject to Charter obligations for most, if not all purposes'.[168]

A still bolder reading might draw attention to the importance, for Dickson CJ's reasoning, of the emphasis placed in the Charter text on the judicial protection granted to rights and freedoms that were guaranteed: protection which would become illusory if access to courts was hindered, impeded or denied by picketing.[169] Such a concern for the practical protection of Charter rights need not be limited, an ambitious theorist might argue, by the need to accord a strict interpretation to 'governmental action' when contemplating the future application of s 32(1).

However, a narrower interpretation is also possible. On its facts, *Rahey* concerned *only* state action: nothing horizontal was in play. Furthermore, while *British Columbia* involved industrial action, the argument concerned the legality of an injunction issued by a provincial judge to prohibit the picketing of *court houses*, where such picketing would inevitably impede and restrict access to the courts and undermine the administration of civil and criminal justice, as well as potentially attracting liability for criminal contempt.[170] On this basis, Dickson CJ's identification of a 'public motivation' here could provide a basis not only for distinguishing his treatment of courts from that in *Dolphin Delivery*, but even for arguing that the earlier decision still represented the generally authoritative position, to which *British Columbia* merely represented an exception.

Whichever view one prefers, the debate highlighted here is important because the extent – if any – to which courts are excluded must reflect, or presuppose, a particular conception of their constitutional role, alongside a view of the role of rights, in relation to private law: issues identified in the first section of the chapter as underpinning considerations which are central to our treatment of horizontal effect.[171]

---

[167] Hogg op cit fn 34 para 37.2(f).

[168] Gibson (1993) op cit fn 140 p 430: For criticism of *Dolphin Delivery*'s position on courts, see Manwaring op cit fn 140 pp 438–43.

[169] *British Columbia* [1988] 2 SCR 214, 228–30.

[170] ibid at 231–33, 236–37. McIntyre J sought to distinguish *Dolphin Delivery* on its facts, but not rationale, at 250–52, arguing that the claimant was not in fact invoking a Charter right which required to be balanced given that the conduct was unlawful.

[171] Glenn associates the initial exclusion of courts with factors unique to Canada's federal constitutional structure: (1995) 'The common law in Canada' *Canadian Bar Review* 261 pp 280–81.

C. Legislative Omissions

A second moderating element relates, as the Supreme Court demonstrated in *Vriend v Alberta*, to omissions by legislative bodies: demarcating the boundaries of s 32(1) may produce Charter-related consequences for non-state bodies as a result.[172]

One of the claimants was dismissed from employment at a private sector university due to his non-compliance, as a gay man, with the institution's policy against non-heterosexual practices. As the Alberta legislature had repeatedly failed to include sexual orientation among the grounds of discrimination proscribed under relevant provincial legislation (known at the time as the Individual's Rights Protection Act or IRPA), he was unable to file a discrimination claim against the university with the Alberta Human Rights Commission.[173] The questions arose whether the absence of sexual orientation unjustifiably infringed the right to non-discrimination under s 15(1) of the Charter, whether the omission constituted a 'matter within the authority' of the Alberta legislature and was subject to Charter analysis pursuant to s 32(1), and whether sexual orientation could be read into the IRPA as an extra ground by the court.

Cory J (in joint reasons with Iacobucci J) emphasised that *Vriend* was:

> [N]ot a case about employment discrimination as distinct from any other form of discrimination that occurs within the private sphere and is covered by provincial human rights legislation. Insofar as the particular situation and factual background of the appellant Vriend is relevant to establishing the issues ... it is the denial of access to the complaint procedures of the Alberta Human Rights Commission that is the essential element of this case and not his dismissal.[174]

This categorisation of the key issue – ultimately identified as the constitutional validity of the exclusion of sexual orientation (as a proscribed ground *and* from the complaint procedures) – was crucial. It enabled Cory J to reject the claim that applying the Charter to the IRPA amounted to applying it to private activity, contrary to *Dolphin Delivery*.[175] While the IRPA *targeted* private activity and had an effect on it, such effect was, he suggested, *indirect* and need not remove the statute from the Charter's purview.[176] It was possible 'to distinguish between "private

---

[172] *Vriend* [1998] 1 SCR 493. See also the earlier but less direct analysis in *Re Blainey and Ontario Hockey Association* 26 DLR (4th) 728, 54 OR (2d) 513, [1986] OJ No 236.

[173] Cory J set out details of the relevant legislative history and provisions at *Vriend* [1998] 1 SCR 493 [2]–[10]. The first IRPA was enacted in 1973 after being introduced in 1972; the substantive provisions were periodically amended, including in 1996 after the case began, and the statute was eventually relabelled the Human Rights, Citizenship and Multiculturalism Act.

[174] ibid at [46]; see also [47], and Major J at [193].

[175] ibid at [65]–[66], also citing *Tremblay v Daigle* [1989] 2 SCR 530 and *McKinney* [1990] 3 SCR 229 (where the Charter was 'applied' to legislation).

[176] *Vriend* [1998] 1 SCR 493 at [65]. Cory J also suggested that an (unspecified) unacceptable result would follow if legislation which regulated private activity was for that reason alone immune from Charter scrutiny.

activity" and "laws that regulate private activity". The former is not subject to the Charter, while the latter obviously is".[177] Here, the challenge was to the constitutionality of the IRPA *as legislation*, not to the *acts of the university* or any other private entity. The mere fact that it concerned the IRPA's under-inclusiveness – that is, its exclusion of one group – was not enough to place the situation beyond s 32(1). The reference to 'matters' in the text did not imply that a positive act by the legislature was necessary, and such a narrow reading would have prioritised form over substance in reading the statute.[178]

The constitutional architecture associated with the Charter played a crucial underpinning role in determining that the IRPA's under-inclusiveness was unconstitutional by reference to s 15(1) and (by a majority) that sexual orientation should be read in.[179] Cory J stressed that such judicial deference as was due to legislative choices was relevant when assessing the justifiability of a measure by reference to s 15(1), *not* as a basis for determining that s 32(1) did not apply and that Charter review was excluded.[180] Iacobucci J (in joint reasons with Cory J) suggested by reference to the Charter that 'courts in their trustee [of rights] or arbiter role must perforce scrutinize the work of the legislature and executive not in the name of the courts, but in the interests of the new social contract that was democratically chosen'.[181] In upholding the constitution, courts had been 'expressly invited to perform that role by the Constitution itself'.[182] In similar vein, Cory J noted that 'it is not the courts which limit the legislatures. Rather, it is the Constitution, which must be interpreted by the courts'.[183]

Two sets of issues deserve attention here. The first concerns the solidity of the reasoning in *Vriend*.[184] Logically, Cory J's distinction between private activity and laws regulating such activity enabled *Vriend*'s reassertion of *Dolphin Delivery* to be paired with its acceptance of differential treatment of the vertical and horizontal, such acceptance being implicit in the Supreme Court's agreement that the employment dispute with the university lay beyond the Charter's direct reach and that there were limits to what counted as 'matters' falling within s 32(1). However, little explanation was offered for how the activities/laws distinction could reliably be

---

[177] ibid at [66].

[178] ibid at [59]–[61]; note also the hypothetical questions concerning omissions canvassed at [62]–[64]. Ewing notes in his chapter herein (pp 216–18) that the Supreme Court pursued a similar technique in *Dunmore v Attorney General for Ontario* [2001] 3 SCR 1016, reading agricultural workers into Ontario's Labour Relations Act even though the legislature had determined after consideration not to include them.

[179] *Vriend* [1998] 1 SCR 493 [67]–[104], [107] (Cory J), [108]–[128], [143]–[179] (Iacobucci J, with reasons shared by Cory J); [183]–[187] (L'Heureux-Dube J), [192]–[202] (Major J, dissenting as to remedy).

[180] ibid at [53]–[55].

[181] ibid at [135].

[182] ibid at [136]; see also, generally, [130]–[142], [176].

[183] ibid at [56].

[184] A further unanswered question in the case is whether the substantive nature of the rights in issue is relevant. Cory J emphasised the general importance of equality and dignity (*Vriend* [1998] 1 SCR 493 [67]–[69]) but did not connect the matter to horizontal effect.

drawn, and its robustness may be challenged by the simultaneous presence of an apparently close *prima facie* connection between the two (by reference to *Vriend*, was the core concern – analytically – *really* the constitutionality of the legislation or the legality of the university's action?) and divergent consequences – for the identity of the defendant and whether a remedy was available given *Dolphin Delivery*'s exclusion of 'private litigation' – depending on the categorisation applied.

A related point is whether, despite the references to *Dolphin Delivery*, the concern voiced in that case against widening the scope of Charter litigation (discussed earlier) might in practice be *undermined* by allowing litigants to challenge under-inclusive legislation where direct action against a private employer is precluded. The invocation of *Dolphin Delivery* – concerned on its facts with common law regulating private activity – might also suggest that Hogg's argument that a line can defensibly be drawn between statutes and common law governing such activity,[185] the former falling within s 32(1) and the latter outside, continues to carry weight. Whether this is blurred by the Supreme Court's use of values-based reasoning – considered below – is an open question.

The second set of issues concerns how far *Vriend* should be seen as Canada-specific. Cory and Iacobucci JJ associated their judgments with Canada's particular constitutional architecture, thus demonstrating the force of constitutional factors as a consideration underpinning the possibility and/or operation of horizontal effect. Canadian legislatures – at both federal and provincial level – are directly bound by s 32(1), and unconstitutional (including Charter-incompatible) legislation may be challenged. Nonetheless, what was described above as McIntyre J's broad and stark proposition in *Dolphin Delivery* excludes the Charter from private litigation. These points help delimit where *Vriend* applies in practice, and also illustrate divergences from the position in the UK.

In the UK, Convention-incompatible exclusions from the scope of legislation may be directly addressed in horizontal proceedings due to HRA 1998, s 3, requiring – as in *Ghaidan* (discussed earlier) – a Convention-compatible outcome to be reached between private litigants through 'reading in', provided this is possible.[186] *Dolphin Delivery* seemingly precludes such a practice in Canada, however. At the practical level, by using s 32(1) of the Charter to rectify omissions from legislation in (vertical) proceedings, *Vriend* may reduce the range of situations in which an exclusion may appear to 'bite' when it prevents the use of Charter arguments in the horizontal context.[187] Nonetheless, as *Vriend* itself demonstrates, when 'reading in' occurs in proceedings against the Government, the practical (including remedial) consequences for a litigant aggrieved about their treatment

---

[185] Op cit fn 34.

[186] Op cit fn 43.

[187] Hypothetical questions about what might constitute an unconstitutional legislative omission – for example, whether a deliberate or accidental refusal to include, or even to legislate *per se*, might generate a different response – thus seem likely to remain matters specifically for Canadian constitutional law (in relation to which Cory J's rather robust treatment of matters is interesting: *Vriend* [1998] 1 SCR 493 [167] and [168]).

in the horizontal context – for example, in being dismissed from employment – are likely to be indirect. As a further distinction, HRA 1998, s 4, reflecting the Westminster Parliament's legislative supremacy, results in a declaration of incompatibility where legislation is irretrievably incompatible with Convention rights, including in horizontal proceedings, leaving Parliament to resolve matters.

While the practical relevance of *Vriend* is thus obvious in Canada, there is no easy translation to horizontal proceedings involving Convention rights in the UK.[188] What *is* common to both jurisdictions is more analytical: namely, the part played by national constitutional features in shaping horizontal effect in each.

D. Charter Values

The third moderating element has been the invocation of Charter values. As noted, McIntyre J accepted in *Dolphin Delivery* (the third highlighted aspect of his judgment) that in litigation between private parties, common law principles should be applied and developed consistently with constitutional values, including those found in the Charter.[189] While the grant of an injunction against secondary picketing was held not to contravene such values in *Dolphin Delivery*, the Supreme Court elsewhere developed the common law relating to (for example) expressive activity to be consistent with its understanding of what they required.[190]

In *Hill v Church of Scientology of Toronto* (hereafter *Hill*), the Supreme Court further explained the role of values.[191] Having determined that 'governmental action' did not include a Crown-employed attorney seeking damages in a common law defamation action,[192] Cory J focused on *Dolphin Delivery* to see whether the common law needed to be changed to ensure compliance 'with the underlying values upon which the Charter is founded'.[193] An appropriate balance was found to exist between the values of protection of reputation and freedom of expression, and the adoption of a US-style 'actual malice' approach was deemed unnecessary – although, as we will see below, the Court has since developed the law.

---

[188] A further inhibition, in relation to the legislature's failure to act, may arise from the prohibition on judicial evaluation of 'proceedings in Parliament' further to Parliamentary privilege: *R v Chaytor* [2010] UKSC 52, [2011] 1 AC 684.

[189] *Dolphin Delivery* [1986] 2 SCR 573 at 603.

[190] For example, *Dagenais v Canadian Broadcasting Corporation* [1994] 3 SCR 835 at 864–68, 874–78 (Lamer CJ, supported by Sopinka, Cory, Iacobucci and Major JJ), effectively analogous to *Dolphin Delivery* [1986] 2 SCR 573 in terms of litigants. Interestingly, McLachlin J's concurring judgment instead discussed matters (at 940–51) in the language of rights, while also focusing on the application of the Charter to judicial activity.

[191] *Hill* [1995] 2 SCR 1130. *Hill* is discussed as a libel case in Loveland's second chapter in this volume; see especially pp 157–64 herein.

[192] *Hill* [1995] 2 SCR 1130 at [76]–[79]. For a strong criticism of that conclusion see Loveland's chapter at pp 163–64 herein.

[193] *Hill* [1995] 2 SCR 1130 at [82].

Cory J noted that the judicial obligation was 'simply a manifestation of the inherent jurisdiction of the courts to modify or extend the common law in order to comply with prevailing social conditions and values'.[194] Since the Charter represented:

> [A] restatement of the fundamental values which guide and shape our democratic society and our legal system … it is appropriate for the courts to make such incremental revisions to the common law as may be necessary to have it comply with the values enunciated in the Charter.[195]

Emphasising the limits to the judicial role, however, Cory J noted that courts must not go further than necessary when taking account of Charter values, and must leave far-reaching changes to the legislature: a position associated by Saunders with boundary-drawing between the judiciary and legislative bodies,[196] in other words reflecting the underpinning consideration concerning institutions' proper constitutional roles. The judgment's references to values and incremental development also suggest analogies, where – as we have seen – both terms are used. Nonetheless, Cory J was not entirely clear about whether Charter rights and principles were synonymous, or whether there were sometimes differences of meaning between the two.

Hill strongly reiterated the distinction between government and private parties in relation to human rights, in doing so highlighting the underpinning consideration concerning the applicability of rights. For the Supreme Court, *Dolphin Delivery* had associated the Charter with the constitutional duties the state owed citizens, generating rights-based challenges.[197] In contrast, 'Private parties owe each other no constitutional duties and cannot found their cause of action upon a Charter right … Charter rights do not exist in the absence of state action'.[198] Hence, the private litigant could rely only on Charter *values*, and in litigation between private parties the Charter applied to the common law only as far as it was inconsistent with those values. Furthermore, the exercise conducted under s 1 of the Charter to see whether, when governmental action was challenged, the restriction of the right concerned could be justified, involved differences from the equivalent exercise in the horizontal context. The latter involved a 'conflict between principles. Therefore, the balancing must be more flexible'.[199] In horizontal cases, 'Charter values, framed in general terms, should be weighed against the principles which underlie the common law. The Charter values will then provide the guidelines for any modification to the common law which the court feels is necessary'.[200]

---

[194] ibid at [91].
[195] ibid at [92].
[196] Saunders (2005) op cit fn 28 p 200.
[197] *Hill* [1995] 2 SCR 1130 at [93]–[94].
[198] ibid at [95].
[199] ibid at [97].
[200] ibid. As was made clear at [98], the onus applicable in a Charter right-based challenge also did not translate directly over. For normative argument as to how balancing might be done, see Weinrib and Weinrib op cit fn 33 pp 57–59.

While serving to constrain the role of values, the significance of the area of law in play as an underpinning consideration may have also played a part. Cory J highlighted the distinct place of private law litigation when noting that care had to be taken 'not to expand the application of the Charter beyond that established by s 32(1), either by creating new causes of action, or by subjecting all court orders to Charter scrutiny'.[201]

Charter values shaped the Supreme Court's later decision in *Retail, Wholesale and Department Store Union, Local 558 v Pepsi Cola Canada Beverages (West) Ltd* (hereafter *Pepsi Cola*),[202] in which it was held that picketing was generally lawful at common law unless a tort or crime was involved, something dubbed the 'wrongful action' model.[203] The case concerned the legality of secondary picketing of private business premises by a trade union and thus fell within the third previously highlighted aspect from McIntyre J's *Dolphin Delivery* judgment. McLachlin CJ and LeBel J (giving judgment for the Court) employed the 'more flexible' balancing approach between principles and values articulated in *Hill*,[204] and were clear that the *right* to freedom of expression protected under s 2(b) of the Charter could not be directly invoked. Expression constituted 'a fundamental Canadian value. The development of the common law must therefore reflect this value. Indeed, quite apart from the Charter, the value of free expression informs the common law'.[205] Applying 'more flexible' balancing, the Court was clear that 'if we are to be true to the values expressed in the Charter our statement of the common law must start with the proposition that free expression is protected unless its curtailment is justified'.[206] The 'wrongful action' model was the most capable, among the potential approaches, of conforming with this Charter-mandated methodology.[207] It allowed for: 'a proper balance between traditional common law rights and Charter values'.[208]

In reaching this conclusion, the Court emphasised both the importance of expression – whether as a right in cases against government bodies, or as a value – and the fact that s 2(b) sometimes allowed for its legitimate qualification where the Charter directly applied.[209] This carried over horizontally. When interpreting the common law, 'The starting point must be freedom of expression. Limitations are permitted, but only to the extent that this is shown to be reasonable and demonstrably necessary in a free and democratic society'.[210]

Unless expression is to be understood quite differently when operating as a horizontal common law value and when serving under s 2(b) as a right against

---

[201] *Hill* [1995] 2 SCR 1130 at [95].
[202] *Pepsi Cola* [2002] 1 SCR 156.
[203] The model is accepted at ibid at [3] and explained at [62]–[64].
[204] ibid at [22], applying *Hill* [1995] 2 SCR 1130 at [96]–[98].
[205] *Pepsi Cola* [2002] 1 SCR 156 at [20].
[206] ibid at [67].
[207] ibid at [66]–[68].
[208] ibid at [74]. The Court's assessment is set out in detail at [73]–[82], [101]–[107] and [111]–[113].
[209] ibid at [32]–[36].
[210] ibid at [37].

government, it presumably makes sense to assume that there will be *some* similarities and cross-overs between the two contexts. Unfortunately, apart from loose
references to 'more flexible' horizontal balancing, neither *Hill* nor *Pepsi Cola*
explains in detail how far we can *also* expect permitted balances and justifications
for restricting expression to vary in each context, given the differing constitutional
roles of the actors (and/or activities) in play.[211]

The horizontal effect seen in *Pepsi Cola* was seemingly indirect and weak in
terms of Young's and Phillipson's criteria, while the *extent* to which values might
enable the development of the common law horizontally remains open to debate.
At a practical level, argument is clearly possible about how far *Pepsi Cola* entailed
merely a shift of emphasis, or instead a more fundamental change.[212] The 'wrongful
action' model seemingly offered greater protection to the expressive role of secondary picketing than was available under one previous case law approach, labelled
the 'illegal *per se*' model.[213] However, several earlier cases had already qualified
that approach by recognising pragmatic exceptions.[214] The Supreme Court also
stressed that 'wrongful action' would still 'catch most problematic picketing – ie
picketing whose value is clearly outweighed by the harm done to the third party'.[215]
In addition, 'wrongful action' might entail analogous risks of circularity or arbi-
trariness to those seen under the other models: for example, secondary picketing
would be unlawful if it was tortious, but tort liability required unlawfulness.[216]

By reference to the underpinning consideration concerning general constitutional requirements, the Supreme Court also tried to highlight the constraints
applicable to its role. *Dolphin Delivery* had not, it was suggested, reached a final
decision on the legality of secondary picketing, the status of which remained
unsettled.[217] In *Pepsi Cola*, the Court thus described itself as merely 'clarify[ing]
the common law given two strands of conflicting authority, each with some claim
to precedent'.[218] Since the judicial role had constitutional limits, change to the
common law should be 'Incremental'.[219] However, common law provisions could
and should be judicially developed to reflect social, moral and economic needs:
'it does not grow in isolation from the Charter, but rather with it'.[220] Nonetheless,
in line with *Hill*, 'Proposed modifications that will have complex and far-reaching
effects are in the proper domain of the legislature'.[221] On the facts, and doubtless

---

[211] Note also Loveland's analysis in ch 5 of this volume. Within *Pepsi Cola*, compare [2002] 1 SCR 156
at [32] and [80].
[212] For further analysis, see the chapters by Ewing and Loveland in this volume.
[213] *Pepsi Cola* [2002] 1 SCR 156 at [47]–[61], [105], [117].
[214] ibid at [56]–[61].
[215] ibid at [106]. A practical example is recognised at [117].
[216] ibid at [105].
[217] *Pepsi Cola* [2002] 1 SCR 156 at [16], [43].
[218] ibid at [16].
[219] ibid.
[220] ibid at [19]; see also [17].
[221] ibid; see also at [22] (invoking *Hill* [1995] 2 SCR 1130 at [96] and [107].

given this complex balance, the provincial legislature's failure to regulate second-ary picketing was not synonymous with an intent to approve the common law position and block judicial development.

The Supreme Court was somewhat bolder in *Grant v Torstar Corporation* (hereafter *Torstar*).[222] In regard to a defamation suit by a private individual concerning allegations in a newspaper article of political impropriety, it accepted that the common law should be modified to recognise a new defence of responsible communication on matters of public interest.[223] Assessment of the law's content rested squarely on Charter values. According to McLachlin CJ:

> The fundamental question of principle is whether the traditional defences for defama-tory statements of fact curtail freedom of expression in a way that is inconsistent with Canadian constitutional values. Does the existing law strike an appropriate balance between two values vital to Canadian society – freedom of expression on the one hand, and the protection of individuals' reputations on the other?[224]

This conclusion was reached by reference both to comparative authority and 'the perspective of principle'.[225] The latter involved giving adequate weight to the constitutional values in play, and led to the conclusion that:

> When proper weight is given to the constitutional value of free expression on matters of public interest, the balance tips in favour of broadening the defences available to those who communicate facts it is in the public's interest to know.[226]

McLachlin CJ seemingly acknowledged that this went beyond *Hill* in substance. In the earlier case, the Supreme Court had accepted the common law's general conformity with Charter values and rejected a modification of liability to adopt the US 'actual malice' rule, instead undertaking 'a modest expansion of the recognized qualified privilege for reports on judicial proceedings'.[227]

McLachlin CJ's acknowledgement invokes the underpinning consideration going to constitutional considerations. She noted that *Hill* had not 'close[d] the door to further changes in specific rules and doctrines'.[228] Instead, *Hill* accepted that the common law 'though not directly subject to *Charter* scrutiny where disputes between private parties are concerned, may be modified to bring it into harmony with the *Charter*'.[229] Furthermore, it was implicit in the judicial duty to adapt the common law to reflect the changing social, moral and economic fabric,

---

[222] *Torstar* [2009] 3 SCR 640; see the discussion at pp 169–74 herein.

[223] *Torstar* [2009] 3 SCR 640 at [7]; see also [46].

[224] ibid at [41]; see also [42]. Abella J suggested an analogous balance at [143].

[225] ibid at [65]; see also [86]. The rationales for protecting expression, their application to the common law position, the need for a balance and arguments for and against the new defence were considered at [47]–[64].

[226] ibid at [65]. Comparative approaches were considered at [66]–[85].

[227] ibid at [45]; see also [46].

[228] ibid at [46]; at [57] and [106], *Hill* [1995] 2 SCR 1130 was seemingly further confined.

[229] *Torstar* [2009] 3 SCR 640 at [44], citing *Hill* [1995] 2 SCR 1130 at [97].

that courts 'will, from time to time, take a fresh look at the common law and re-evaluate its consistency with evolving societal expectations through the lens of *Charter* values'.[230]

This statement implies that judicial interpretation of the common law may evolve – though to what extent is unclear – in response to the non-static character of (judicially identified) Charter values: arguably a bolder position than the statements in *Hill* and *Pepsi Cola* about 'incremental' development. Interestingly, McLachlin CJ also accepted that 'the proposed change to the law should be viewed as a new defence'.[231] This was in preference to categorising it as an evolution of *existing* defences – at face value the more 'incremental' approach. Furthermore, the Supreme Court spelt out the substantive and procedural details of the new defence's operation in an *extremely* comprehensive and detailed fashion,[232] arguably resembling an act of legislation *more than* a mere reinterpretation. *Torstar* thus seemingly entailed a stronger view of the court's institutional role than had previously been seen.

In 2007, Eric Barendt suggested that to require consistency with Charter values 'is a much weaker requirement than the scrutiny of laws limiting the exercise of Charter rights'.[233] If one applies Young's and Phillipson's criteria, a values-based reinterpretation approach would certainly seem to be weaker than a requirement of consistency with rights. In addition, the fact that courts do not inevitably count in private contexts as 'governmental' within s 32 might be thought to impose a weaker sense of obligation than that associated with HRA 1998, s 6, which applies for all purposes. Turning to the development of private law, Lewis Klar suggested – not long after *Hill* and invoking the caution seen in that case – that despite McIntyre J's 'concession' in *Dolphin Delivery* concerning reinterpretation of the common law, 'it would be fair to say that the *Charter* has not played much of a role in tort law judgments'.[234]

However, *Torstar* seemingly points in a stronger direction. Hogg suggests that both this case and *Pepsi Cola* gave greater weight to the value of freedom of expression, qualifying previous common law positions and the reach of *Hill*. As such, 'the exclusion of the common law from Charter review is not particularly significant'.[235] The extent to which the Charter has reshaped litigation, including of a horizontal variety, within family law – in Canada a branch of private law – has

---

[230] *Torstar* [2009] 3 SCR 640 at [46], citing *R v Sullivan* [1991] 3 SCR 654 at p 670 (Iacobucci J); see also *Dunmore v Attorney General for Ontario* [2001] 3 SCR 1016 at [26] (Bastarache J).

[231] *Torstar* [2009] 3 SCR 640 at [95]. See also [90]–[94].

[232] ibid at [97]–[135], [140] (McLachlin CJ), [142]–[144] (Abella J). At [3] and [39], loose association of values and principles to the vertical context, similar to that seen in *Hill* [1995] 2 SCR 1130 is also visible.

[233] Barendt op cit fn 140, p 425; see also p 421.

[234] Klar (2001) 'Judicial activism in private law' *Canadian Bar Review* 215 p 217.

[235] Hogg op cit fn 34 para 37.2(g). Note also Harding and Knopf (2013) 'Constitutionalising everything: the role of "*Charter* values"' *Review of Constitutional Studies* 141.

also been a matter of much academic controversy.[236] However, there is seemingly less evidence than in the UK – not least given the lower profile which horizontal effect has come to assume over the years (as noted in the chapter's introduction) – to found a clear claim that the impact of Charter values depends upon the area of private law in play,[237] thus preventing the assertion that the latter underpinning consideration plays a definite role.

E. Conclusion

In summary, the text of the Charter, as a part of Canada's broader constitutional architecture, has been central in shaping horizontal effect and produces certain Canada-specific features. This is particularly seen in the role accorded in *Dolphin Delivery* to 'governmental action' as the lynchpin for the application of s 32. A key additional point is the Supreme Court's insistence that Charter values, applied in private common law litigation, entail a different approach from that found when dealing with Charter rights. Furthermore, the use made of legislative exclusions in *Vriend* is not easily translatable to the different constitutional environment of the UK, while the values-related approach may attract the designations 'weak' and 'indirect' when applying Young's and Phillipson's classifications.

These matters concern practical features. When it comes to considerations underpinning horizontal effect, Canadian law seemingly flags up some *analogous* questions to those seen in the UK, relating to the applicability of human rights and to the constitutional roles of institutions (the significance of the nature of private law or branches thereof being more ambiguous). The commonality of these considerations in two constitutionally distinct jurisdictions might perhaps be considered indicative when drawing overall conclusions about the character of horizontal effect.

IV. Overall Conclusions

This chapter has highlighted the importance of underpinning considerations concerning national constitutions (including the roles of courts and legislatures within them), the nature of human rights, legal texts and particular areas of law in shaping the horizontal effect of human rights or values, in association (to differing extents) with the HRA 1998 and the Charter. This hopefully helps demonstrate the

---

[236] See, generally, Taylor's chapter herein, op cit; Harvison Young (2001) 'The changing family, rights discourse and the Supreme Court of Canada' *Canadian Bar Review* 749: Leckey (2007) 'Family law as fundamental private law' *Canadian Bar Review* 69.

[237] For argument supporting an ambitious general approach, see Weinrib and Weinrib op cit fn 33 pp 64–67, 71.

relevance of these considerations, alongside the criteria advanced for categorising and measuring the extent of horizontal effect, when analysing the phenomenon. In comparing Canada with the UK, what should be clear is that significant differences in constitutional architecture, tied more specifically to differences of wording between s 32(1) of the Charter and the HRA 1998, s 6, have encouraged divergences in the judicial focus when discussing horizontal effect: for example, through the threshold role attached in Canada to what is 'governmental'.

Nonetheless, this has been coupled with an ability in *both* systems to think – albeit sometimes unclearly – by reference to direct and indirect *horizontal effect*, rights and values, and balances between competing interests, and to reason by reference to similar underpinning considerations, including applicability and appropriate institutional roles. It is on these foundations that comparative analysis contributes to understanding both the idea of horizontal effect and the legal systems concerned.

5

Private Law, Public Law, Libel Law

IAN LOVELAND

From a Canadian constitutional law perspective, 1867 is most memorable for the enactment of the BNA. From a British viewpoint, the year's key domestic initiative was the passage of Disraeli's electoral reform legislation. For the initial purpose of this chapter, however, 1867's most noteworthy event was the publication of an article in *The Times* on 13 February. The article contained an accurate summary of parliamentary proceedings in which the integrity of a Mr Wason was substantially traduced. Mr Wason was legally barred from bringing defamation proceedings against either his critics or the publisher of *Hansard*,[1] and so sued Mr Walter, a proprietor of *The Times* instead.

Wason likely thought his prospects of success very good. In 1867, English libel law was a very claimant-friendly construct.[2] Damage to reputation was presumed by mere publication of defamatory factual material. The primary defence was to prove (and the burden of proof lay on the defendant) that the defamatory material was true. Alternatively, the defendant could invoke the fair comment defence by proving that that defamatory material expressed opinion, not fact (ie something not provable as true or false) on a matter of public interest, whereupon the burden would shift to the claimant to prove that the defendant was motivated by malice. In respect of factual material that was not true nor comment, in very limited circumstances defendants might invoke a defence of privilege, rooted either in statute or common law.

'Absolute privilege' – ie an indefeasible defence – attached to parliamentary and court proceedings. 'Qualified privilege' was an effective if not indefeasible defence. If the defendant persuaded the court that the publication was made on a privileged 'occasion', he or she would defeat the claim unless the claimant proved that the publication was made in circumstances of 'actual malice'; that the defendant knew

---

[1] Speeches of the members of the Commons and Lords could not found a libel action because of the statutory exclusion provided by Art 9 of the Bill of Rights 1689 and the publishers of *Hansard* were similarly protected by the Parliamentary Papers Act 1840.
[2] See generally Loveland (2000) *Political libels* ch 1.

the information was false or was reckless as to its falsity, and was motivated by a desire to cause damage to the claimant.

In terms of its *effect*, qualified privilege placed substantial doctrinal and evidential burdens on the claimant. However, in terms of its *reach* it was very narrow. A relevant 'occasion' existed only in circumstances where the publisher and recipient had a reciprocal duty to share the information. This essentially required a pre-existing intimacy, be it professional or personal, between the parties. Clichéd examples would be a father writing a letter to his daughter to tell her that her fiancée was a charlatan, or a former employer writing a reference for a former employee to a prospective employer reporting that the employee was a bully or thief. There was no assumption that publication to 'all the world' – which meant, despite the literal sense of the phrase, any person other than the dutybound recipient(s) – could attract qualified privilege.[3]

The doctrinal peg on which the defence then hung, and the reason for it, had been formulated in 1834 in *Toogood v Spyring*: qualified privilege would attach to statements

> fairly made by a person in the discharge of some public or private duty, whether legal or moral, or in the conduct of his own affairs, in matters where his interest is concerned ... [S]uch communications are protected for the common convenience and welfare of society: and the law has not restricted the right to make them within any narrow limits.[4]

In relation to widespread dissemination of material about politicians in the early/mid-nineteenth century, the 'common convenience and welfare of society' principle proved of very limited assistance to defendants. During the first election held after the passage of the 1832 Great Reform Act, the defendant in *Duncombe v Daniel*[5] had, via letters published in a London newspaper, accused Duncombe (a candidate for election to the Commons) of fraud. Daniel's attempt to bring the material within the *Toogood* principle on the basis that he had a duty to publish such material and the electors[6] a duty to consider it was unsuccessful. The court concluded that 'However large the privilege of electors may be, it is extravagant to suppose that it can justify the publication to all the world of facts injurious to a person who happens to stand in the situation of a candidate'.[7]

The court's assumption that a person could 'happen' – as if by chance – to seek election to the Commons rather than to do so through a deliberate choice to enter

---

[3] So in my above example if the father pinned a copy of the letter to a noticeboard in the fiancée's golf club the 'occasion(s)' (ie making the information available to anyone who passed by the noticeboard) would not be privileged, even though the content of the information remained unchanged. 'Occasion' is a poorly chosen label. What is really in issue is the identity of the audience to whom the information is made accessible.

[4] (1834) 1 CM&R 181 at 193.

[5] (1837) 8 Car and P 222; discussed in Loveland op cit fn 2 pp 19–20.

[6] Who then of course comprised only a tiny fraction of the (male) adult population.

[7] (1837) 8 Car and P 222 at 229.

the public sphere of governance is a curious one. Similarly, the 'all the world' label was a hyperbolic legal fiction in the context of 1830s London. The 'world' in issue was the readership of the relevant newspaper. By the 1830s, many parts of Britain – and especially London – were awash with newspapers, journals and pamphlets disseminating all manner of conservative and radical political information. But insofar as *Duncombe* (notwithstanding its roots in empirical fictions) correctly stated the common law – a common law which Parliament evinced no inclination to change – publishers published 'facts injurious' to political actors at their peril.

I. *Wason v Walter* (1868): A Tentative Recognition – Soon Forgotten in English Law – of 'Political Libels'

The court's decision in *Wason v Walter* was authored by Cockburn CJ. As a judge, Cockburn is most likely remembered for his (to modern eyes) illiberal definition of obscenity in *R v Hicklin*.[8] But prior to joining the bench in 1856, Cockburn had run his practice at the bar, much of which was concerned with electoral law,[9] alongside a political career. He was a Liberal party MP for 10 years in the 1850s and 1860s, serving as both Solicitor General and Attorney General.[10]

It is hard to resist the inference that *Wason* was influenced, if not driven, by Disraeli's electoral reform legislation. Although the 1832 statute has been garlanded with the label of the 'Great Reform Act', the 1867 legislation enfranchised many more people (just men, of course) than its predecessor, and represented a substantial further step towards legal expression of the political theory that the legitimacy of the government system rested on the consent of (significant numbers) of the governed. Cockburn's judgment spoke very clearly to those values. Few members of even the recently enfranchised middle classes would regularly read *Hansard* itself, but in Cockburn's view the 'common convenience and welfare of (a slowly democratising) society' required that newspaper recirculation of such information should attract qualified privilege. It was not the 'occasion' of publication that was important, but the substance of the information. And it was not predominantly the 'right' of the publisher to publish that was thereby protected, but the 'right' of the public (in effect 'all the world') to receive the information:

> Where would our confidence be in the government of the country or in the legislature by which our laws are framed … – where would be our attachment to the constitution under which we live – if the proceedings of the great council of the realm were shrouded in secrecy and concealed from the knowledge of the nation …

---

[8] (1868) LR 3 QB 360. See the discussion in Beattie and Phillipson's chapter herein.
[9] Although most famously he had been the successful defence counsel in *R v McNaghten* (1843) 8 ER 718.
[10] Lobban (2004) 'Cockburn, Sir Alexander James Edmund, twelfth baronet' *Oxford Dictionary of National Biography*.

[Every] member of the educated portion of the community from the highest to the lowest looks with eager interest to the debate of either house, and considers it a part of the duty of the public journals to furnish an account of what passes there.[11]

Cockburn expressly recognised that his judgment was altering the common law, and took care to justify both the general principle that it was appropriate for the courts to do so and the application of that principle to this specific issue:

Whatever disadvantages attach to a system of unwritten law, and of these we are fully sensible, it has at least this advantage, that its elasticity enables those who administer it to adapt it to the varying conditions of society, and to the requirements and habits of the age in which we live, so as to avoid the inconsistencies and injustice which arise when the law is no longer in harmony with the wants and usages and interests of the generation to which it is immediately applied ...

[W] who can doubt that the public are gainers by the change, and that, though injustice may often be done, and though public men may often have to smart under the keen sense of wrong inflicted by hostile criticism, the nation profits by public opinion being thus freely brought to bear on the discharge of public duties?[12]

Curiously perhaps, given the steady onward march of statutory reform which, step by step, created an almost universal franchise by 1928, Cockburn's methodology and its potential to further alter the boundaries of English libel law in respect of 'political' information – the 'discharge of public duties', as he put it – disappeared virtually without trace from the English legal landscape during the next 100 years. This is perhaps because the judgment was narrowly construed as doing no more than providing an exception to the generally applicable libel law presumption that the reporting of a libellous comment was itself libellous; the exception arising because the speeches published in *Hansard* were themselves absolutely privileged and so their accurate repetition and/or summation should be protected at least to the extent of attracting qualified privilege. A wider construction of Cockburn's opinion, that he was presenting the common law as a mechanism that should regularly revisit the boundaries of libel law in respect of political matters as societal understandings about the legitimate basis of the governmental system evolved, did not achieve any great currency in English judicial circles.[13]

Parliament occasionally stepped into the field to extend qualified privilege to accurate reportage of the proceedings of various public bodies, but neither legislators nor the courts showed any enthusiasm for the idea that the print or broadcast media should enjoy the protection of qualified privilege for stories dealing with political or other public interest issues.

---

[11] (1868) LR 4 QB 73 at 89–90.
[12] ibid at 93–94.
[13] *Wason* is of course an early example of what Canadians would style a 'living tree' approach to the task of judicial lawmaking; see *Edwards v Canada* [1930] AC 124.

II. *Wason v Walter*: A Tentative Recognition – Seized upon and Built upon in American Law – of 'Political Libels'

In contrast, Cockburn's judgment enjoyed a high profile in several US state jurisdictions, where its inherent principle was stretched far beyond its initially limited reach to provide a rationale for extending qualified privilege at state common law and/or state constitutional law to newspaper articles dealing not just with libels found in summaries or critiques of official records of the proceedings of governmental bodies, nor even just to such libels and those involving narrowly political questions (ie the opinion and behaviour of elected or appointed government officials or candidates for such roles), but also to stories dealing with much broader public interest issues.[14]

A. Innovation as State Common Law: *Coleman v McClennan* (1908) and *Press Co v Stewart* (1888)

The best example is the Kansas Supreme Court's 1908 decision in *Coleman v McClennan*,[15] in which the defendant newspaper owner had run an article accusing the claimant, then the State's Attorney-General, of corruption. Burch J devoted considerable attention to *Wason*, and then reasoned:

> [P]araphrasing this language, it is of the utmost consequence that the people should discuss the character and qualifications of candidates for their suffrages. The importance to the State and to society of such discussions is so vast and the advantage derived are so great that they more than counterbalance the inconvenience of private persons whose conduct may be involved, and occasional injury to the reputation of individuals must yield to the public welfare.[16]

The most expansive application of the principle is the Pennsylvania case of *Press Co Ltd v Stewart*.[17] The libel in *Stewart* was an irreverent newspaper article which questioned the competence of a man running a journalism school. There was nothing 'political' in the governmental sense about the story, but the Pennsylvania Supreme Court nonetheless accepted Press Co's submissions that qualified privilege should apply:

> If we are asked why this article is so privileged, I answer because it was proper for public information. The plaintiff was holding himself out to the world as a teacher and guide

---

[14] A selection is reviewed in Loveland op cit fn 2 ch 3. In addition to those discussed here, see especially *Ambrosious v O'Farrell* (1905) 199 Ill App 265 and *Ogren v Rockford Star* (1925) 237 Ill App 349 (Illinois); *Briggs v Garrett* (1886) 2 ATL 513; *State v Balch* (1884) 31 Kan 465 (Kansas); *Salinger v Cowles* (1922) 191 NW 167.

[15] (1908) 98 Pac 281.

[16] (1908) Pac 281 at 286.

[17] (1888) 119 Pa 584.

> of youth ... This gave him a quasi-public character. Whether he was a proper person to instruct the young, and whether his school as a proper place for them to receive instruction, were matters of importance to the public, and the Press was in the strict line of its duty when it sought such information, and gave it to the public.

Such innovation – focused as in *Wason* on the nature of the information not the 'occasion' of publication – had been widely but by no means universally adopted in state jurisdictions, whether by legislation or judicially engineered alteration to state common or constitutional law, by the early 1960s. Such initiatives were state-specific in origin and territorial effect; even as late as the 1940s (and by 1926 the US Supreme Court had accepted that the substance of the First Amendment constrained the states through the mechanism of the Fourteenth Amendment)[18] the Supreme Court categorised libel alongside obscenity and 'fighting words' as speech not raising First Amendment issues.[19] And then in the early 1960s, *Coleman* was given extensive and approving consideration in the US Supreme Court's judgment in *Sullivan v New York Times*.[20]

B. And Innovation as National Constitutional Law: To *Sullivan v The New York Times* (1964)

Sullivan is too well known to require more than brief mention here.[21] Its *ratio decidendi* was that the publication of information relating to the political conduct of elected government officials could not found liability in libel unless the claimant proved that the information was false and that it was published with 'actual malice', by which was meant that the defendant knew the information was false or was recklessly careless in assuming it to be true.[22]

The *Sullivan* defence – applicable through the First and Fourteenth Amendments to all state and national defamation law – was more expansive than the traditional qualified privilege defence in that it could apply to publication to 'all the world'. The moral rationales underpinning the judgment was that the American political tradition properly understood demanded that citizens had not just an entitlement but a responsibility constantly to evaluate the adequacy of their governing institutions and the people elected to staff them, and that the press had a vital role to play in facilitating that process. The 'balance' struck in *Sullivan* was tripartite: the reputations of political figures; the entitlement of publishers to publish; and –most importantly – the entitlement of the public to consume (and ideally evaluate) the information. Orthodox libel law unacceptably deterred or 'chilled'

---

[18] *Gitlow v New York* (1925) 268 US 652.
[19] *Chaplinsky v New Hampshire* (1942) 315 US 568.
[20] (1964) 376 US 255.
[21] See generally Loveland op cit fn 2: Lewis (1991) *Make no law* ch 5: Kalven (1964) 'The New York Times Case: a note on the central meaning of the First Amendment' *Supreme Court Review* 267.
[22] To be proved to an enhanced standard of 'convincing clarity'.

the dissemination of such information. The *Sullivan* majority accepted that its actual malice test would inevitably result in publication of some false information. But that was presumed a price worth paying to reduce the amount of 'true' information that might otherwise be suppressed.

III. Traditional Perspectives on 'Political Libels' in England and Canada in the Near *Sullivan* Era

It was obviously not open to either Canadian or British courts in that era to lend any reform to libel law a national 'constitutional' status in normative terms. But in both jurisdictions, there was no normative impediment to prevent amendment of the common law in the *Sullivan* direction. Nor is there any obvious reason to think that the moral values underpinning *Sullivan*, essentially the premise that the legitimacy of the governmental system rested on the informed consent of the population, were less pertinent to British and Canadian society than to the US. But the *Sullivan* rationale had had in the 1950s, and continued to have in the 1960s and 1970s, no significant bite in either jurisdiction.

A. In Canadian Law – A Provincial Matter Concerning 'Property and Civil Rights'?

Under the terms of the BNA 1867, civil defamation law within Canada was presumptively a matter reserved to provincial jurisdiction within the 'property and civil rights' provision of s 92(13).[23] Other than in Quebec, the Provinces initially retained English common law as the basis of their defamation provisions. In principle it would have been possible for the various Provinces (only four in 1867, but 10 by 1950) to have adopted quite different libel law regimes in respect of political or public interest libels. By the 1930s, such differentiation was clearly visible in the libel laws of American states, spanning the range from complete prohibition on suit even being brought for some types of political libel, through the application of an orthodox or modified qualified privilege defence being applied to political/ public interest speech to simple replication of English common law.

In its early constitutional jurisprudence, the Canadian Supreme Court displayed considerable interest in and engagement with US constitutional ideas, although that enthusiasm was never matched in Privy Council judgments on Canadian constitutional issues.[24] It was not until the 1980s, in early cases dealing

---

[23] Criminal libel laws were a Dominion matter, per BNA 1867, s 91(27).

[24] cf for example the Privy Council's judgment in *R v Russell* (1882) 7 AC 829 on the important question of when the national Parliament could use its general 'peace order and good government' power in s 91, and the Canadian Supreme Court's previous judgment on the point in *Fredericton (City) v R* (1880) 3 SCR 505.

with the interpretation and application of the Charter,[25] that the Canadian Court's initial interest reawakened. In the libel context, that trend was nicely illustrated by a cluster of 1950s and 1960s cases which – with one very limited exception – attached no consideration at all either to US authority or to the arguments which shaped it. In each case, the Court issued a brief, unanimous opinion authored by Cartwright J.

i. Douglas v Tucker *(1952)*

The litigation in *Douglas v Tucker*[26] had an obvious political hue. During the 1948 provincial election campaign Douglas, then the Premier of Saskatchewan,[27] made speeches – and arranged for their press publication – suggesting that Tucker, leader of the Liberal opposition, was involved in fraudulent economic activities. Among the defences Douglas advanced was that the publication attracted qualified privilege because it was made:

(a) by way of refutation of an allegation by the plaintiff which would injure the defendant, his Government, and the Co-operative Commonwealth Federation and with the sole desire of protecting as it was the defendant's duty to protect, the interests of his Government, those of the party of which he is leader, and his own interests.

(b) to citizens of the Province of Saskatchewan who had a legitimate interest in the election campaign then proceeding and in the matter referred to by the defendant which was one of its principal issues. The words were spoken in good faith and in the honest belief that they were true and without malice toward the plaintiff.[28]

The Supreme Court promptly dismissed this argument. It relied squarely on *Duncombe*:

[33] *Duncombe v. Daniell* is cited as an authoritative statement of the law in Gatley on Libel and Slander (*supra*) at pages 251 and 278 and in Odgers on Libel and Slander, (*supra*), at pages 171 and 246. The principle which it enunciates, that the privilege of an elector will be lost if the publication is unduly wide, has been applied repeatedly, see for example: *Anderson v. Hunter, Bethell v. Mann* and *Lang v. Willis*.

[34] The view that a defamatory statement relating to a candidate for public office published in a newspaper is protected by qualified privilege by reason merely of the facts that an election is pending and that the statement, if true, would be relevant to the question of such candidate's fitness to hold office is, I think, untenable.

---

[25] See *Law Society of Upper Canada v Skapinker* [1984] 1 SCR 357 (on general interpretive techniques); *Hunter v Southam* [1984] 2 SCR 145 (on such techniques and the specific issue of 'unreasonable' searches and seizures of documents; *Big M Drug Mart* [1985] 1 SCR 295 (on religious freedoms).

[26] [1952] 1 SCR 275.

[27] Douglas led a party called the Co-operative Commonwealth Federation (the forerunner of the New Democrat Party). Douglas offers his own account of the proceedings at Thomas (ed) (1984) *The making of a socialist: recollections of T. C. Douglas* pp 260–62. Tucker's accusations did not derail the Government's electoral prospects. At the election Douglas's CCF won 31 of the legislature's 52 seats. Tucker's Liberals won 19.

[28] [1952] 1 SCR 275 at [15].

Tucker's counsel apparently made no resort to the case law of the US jurisdictions where such an argument had been regarded not just as tenable, but compelling. He had perhaps taken the view that to do so would be futile. However, the three authorities referred to at para [33] of the judgment are not especially weighty supports for the orthodox position.

Anderson v Hunter[29] is an 1891 five-line judgment of the Scottish Court of Session in a slander case, and so necessarily one where mass media dissemination was not in point. *Bethell v Mann* – a 1919 English High Court judgment – occupies a half page in the *Times Law Reports*.[30] It certainly concerned a party political issue; the libel being a pamphlet circulated to local electors by the Labour opponent of a Liberal candidate for the Commons. The entirety of the Court's consideration of the qualified privilege issues is this: 'The Lord Chief Justice said that the fact that the leaflet was distributed broadcast [sic] would of itself prevent the occasion of the publication being held privileged'.[31] *Lang v Willis*[32] was of more recent vintage (1934), although it was an Australian case which was yet one more stage in the bitter factional in-fighting which plagued the New South Wales Labour party in the 1920s and 1930s. Its relevance to *Tucker* is minimal. Firstly, it was also a slander case, so 'all the world' publication was again not in issue. Secondly, the case did not turn on common law qualified privilege – the point was not even pleaded at trial – but on an obscure provision (s 5) in the New South Wales Defamation Act 1912.[33] It is hard to believe Cartwright J had read the case; more likely he just adopted segmented references to it in counsel's submissions.

Douglas was, all in all, a distinctly unimpressive exercise in legal reasoning.

ii. Globe and Mail Ltd v Boland *(1960)*

Cartwright J also delivered the Court's similarly flimsy judgment eight years later in *Globe & Mail Ltd v Boland*.[34] Mr Boland was an Independent Conservative candidate in the 1957 federal election. He had organised a stunt in which a supposedly former Communist revealed that the then Liberal Government was infiltrated by communists. *The Globe and Mail* denounced the stunt as McCarthyite scaremongering, calling it a 'disgusting performance' designed to mislead voters and 'a degradation to whole democratic system of government in Canada'.

---

[29] (1891) 18 SLR 467.
[30] [1919] *The Times* 29 October.
[31] ibid.
[32] (1934) 52 CLR 637.
[33] The New South Wales legislature had shown remarkable phlegmatism in s 5 of the 1912 Act in accepting (by re-enacting a provision dating from 1847) that the rough and tumble of political argument in the State was habitually so fierce and so rooted in personal abuse, and so many politicians were presumptively seen by the wider public as scoundrels, that having one's honour, honesty or competence traduced by one's political opponents in the run-up to an election might not inflict any meaningful damages on a politician's reputation. Both Willis and Lang were such scarred political figures in 1934 that likely anything defamatory either said about the other would fall within s 5. See generally Nairn (1995) *The Big Fella: Jack Lang and the Australian Labour Party 1891–1949* chs 12–13.
[34] [1960] SCR 203.

The trial judge accepted that qualified privilege attached to such an article. Although *Wason* was not cited, the judge (Spence J) had concluded:

> Surely no section of the public has a clearer duty to publish, for the information and guidance of the public, political news and comment, even critical comment, during a Federal Election in Canada than the great Metropolitan daily newspaper such as the Defendant. Just as certainly the public, every citizen in Canada, has a legitimate and vital interest in receiving such publications.

The Ontario Court of Appeal had upheld that analysis.

Reversing the Court of Appeal, Cartwright J again invoked *Duncombe* and also found great assistance in a passage from the Privy Council judgment in *Arnold v the King Emperor* which had concluded that journalists enjoyed no greater protection in defamation proceedings than ordinary citizens.[35] One might suggest that Cartwright there entirely misses the point, which is that the information and its audience and not its publisher should be foremost in the court's mind.[36]

Boland is however notable for making a foray into American libel jurisprudence. Cartwright J was apparently convinced that accepting the defendant's argument would actually undermine the 'common convenience and welfare of society' because it would discourage worthy people from seeking public office. He adopted a similar view expressed by Taft J in 1893 in *Post Publishing Co v Hallam*.[37] Taft had offered no evidence to support that supposition in *Hallam*, and Cartwright offered none in *Boland*. That may well be because the proposition is unprovable. But what Cartwright also omitted was any allusion to judicial statements (albethey similarly un-evidenced) pointing in the opposite direction. *Coleman* offers an apposite example:

> Without speaking for the other states in which the liberal rule applies [ie qualified privilege for political information], it may be said that there at least men of unimpeachable character from all political parties present themselves in sufficient numbers to fill the public offices and manage the public institutions.[38]

iii. Banks v The Globe and Mail

The article complained of in *Banks*[39] was published in May 1957. Mr Banks was the director of the Seafarers International Union, a trade union which represented

---

[35] (1914) 30 TLR 462.

[36] The libel in *Arnold* was written and published in a newspaper by an experienced journalist, and was 'political' in a narrow sense in that it accused a British Imperial official of corruption. But in the context of Canada in 1960, reliance on *Arnold* as an authority is not immediately compelling. That is in (small) part because the case was a criminal libel prosecution, not a civil action. The (much) larger part is that this was not litigation arising in a country (India) that – qua British colony – even pretended to have a democratic basis to its governmental system.

[37] (1893) 59 Fed 540. *Hallam* is a federal district court decision, and so had very limited precedential value.

[38] (1908) 98 Pac 281 at 289.

[39] [1961] SCR 474.

many maritime workers. The article accused him inter alia of engaging in a deliberate strategy to undermine the viability of the Canadian shipping fleets, of having an extensive criminal record in the US and of having committed various crimes in Canada. At trial, *The Globe and Mail* successfully pleaded qualified privilege. The trial judge, in another *Wason-esque* charge to the jury, held that the scope of qualified privilege was dynamic and expanding:

> It is difficult to conceive a matter in which the public would be much more interested in the year 1957 than the most important topic of industrial relations ... There is no more efficient organ for informing the public and for disseminating to the public intelligent comment on such matters of public interest, than a great metropolitan newspaper.[40]

That reasoning was rejected in the Supreme Court as perfunctorily as it had been in *Douglas* and *Banks*. Cartwright J again delivered the sole judgment. He relied straightforwardly on his own opinions in those cases, and again invoked *Arnold*, to reach the same conclusion:

> [29] The decision of the learned trial judge in the case at bar, quoted above, appears to involve the proposition of law, which in my opinion is untenable, that given proof of the existence of a subject-matter of wide public interest throughout Canada without proof of any other special circumstances any newspaper in Canada (and *semble* therefore any individual) which sees fit to publish to the public at large statements of fact relevant to that subject-matter is to be held to be doing so on an occasion of qualified privilege.

iv. Jones v Bennett *(1968)*

Before *Jones v Bennett*[41] was decided in 1968 *Sullivan* – and several subsequent US Supreme Court decisions[42] – had confirmed that in that jurisdiction the proposition rejected in *Banks* was entirely tenable. But it seems that for Cartwright, now Chief Justice, and his colleagues, *Sullivan* and the ideas on which lay were not just unpersuasive but not even worthy of serious consideration.[43]

Bennett was the then Premier of British Columbia. Jones, the chairman of a government body, the Purchasing Commission,[44] was accused but acquitted of taking bribes. Jones declined government invitations to resign, and was eventually dismissed by the extraordinary device of what was essentially an Act of Attainder.[45]

---

[40] Quoted at ibid at [20].

[41] [1969] SCR 277.

[42] *Garrison v Louisiana* (1964) 379 US 64; *Rosenblatt v Baer* (1966) 383 US 75; *Curtis v Butts; Associated Press v Walker* (1967) 388 US 130.

[43] Canadian legal journals seemed not much interested either. The only contemporaneous piece exploring *Sullivan's* possible relevance to Canadian law seems to be Weller (1967) 'Defamation, enterprise liability and freedom of speech' *U of Toronto LJ* 278. (There were of course many fewer such journals then than there are now.)

[44] An executive agency with extensive statutory responsibilities for public procurement.

[45] Splendidly titled, with not quite perfect accuracy, 'An Act to Provide for the Retirement of George Earnest Pascoe Jones 1965'. The Act's effect (per s 2(3)) was retrospective; available at www.bclaws.ca/civix/document/id/consol18/consol18/00_65063_01.

Jones took exception to a speech by Bennett in which Bennett somewhat cryptically said of the matter in a speech to his party members, 'let me just assure of this: the position taken by the government is the right position'.

Jones convinced the trial court that the words implied he was corrupt, notwithstanding his acquittal. On appeal, the British Columbia Court of Appeal had accepted the defence of qualified privilege was made out, evidently on the basis of an unintended concession by Jones's counsel. On further appeal, the Supreme Court indicated that it might have been willing to consider (but likely would not have accepted) the argument that that privilege could attach to a speech made only to party members on political matters even if there was no pending election.[46] However, the Court declined to address that point since it also accepted that Bennett had intended that the speech would be reported in newspapers. Consequently, following its own judgments in *Tucker* and *Boland,* and in a decision intellectually skimpy even by the not very exacting standards set in those cases, the Court concluded simply that

> it must be regarded as settled that a plea of qualified privilege based on a ground of the sort relied on in the case at bar cannot be upheld where the words complained of are published to the public generally ...[47]

Sullivan did not engage the Court's attention, nor is there any indication that it was invoked by Bennett's counsel[48] to suggest that existing common law rules might be revisited.

B. A Curious Complacency ?

It is unsurprising that the Canadian Supreme Court decided these cases (even the post-*Sullivan Bennett*) without considering American authorities and ideas. As noted above, the Court's early flirtation with US jurisprudential ideas quickly disappeared. More surprising perhaps is the very limited – even feeble – nature of the judgments' treatment of freedom of political expression as an indigenously Canadian constitutional value. The cause for surprise is that in the 1950s the Court – led on the issue by Ivan Rand[49] – produced several judgments significantly extending the protection afforded to free expression against provincial intrusion. Most of those judgments were directed against the activities of the DuPlessis regime

---

[46] Which conclusion would slightly have extended the *Duncombe* principle.

[47] [1969] SCR 277 at 285.

[48] John Pippinette QC, apparently widely regarded as one of Canada's foremost post-war counsel. See Henderson (2004) 'Book notes: *John J. Robinette, peerless mentor: an appreciation,* by George D. Finlayson' *Osgoode Hall LJ* 541.

[49] While Rand is a celebrated figure in Canadian legal circles, second perhaps only to Bora Laskin in the ranks of 'great' Canadian constitutional law scholars, he and his work are little known here. For a corrective see Kaplan (2009) *Canadian maverick: the life and times of Ivan C Rand,* and especially ch 4 therein. Rand sat in *Douglas,* but had retired before the later cases were heard.

in Quebec, especially, although not entirely, in respect of its fierce attacks on Jehovah's Witnesses in the province.[50] The judgments are notable for the way in which the Court, adopting a method similar to Cockburn's in *Wason*, drew on principles of political theory – of constitutional morality if you will – to structure its conclusions.

R v Boucher[51] is perhaps the best known case.[52] In *Boucher*, the Supreme Court lent a very narrow character to the crime of sedition, providing not only that the crime required the incitement of violent conduct, but also that such conduct be directed against governmental targets. For present purposes, *Boucher* is notable for the methodology that some members of the Court deployed; the particularistic nature of sedition as a crime was derived from much more pervasive values. So, for Ivan Rand:

> Freedom in thought and speech and disagreement in ideas and beliefs, on every conceivable subject, are of the essence of our life. The clash of critical discussion on political, social and religious subjects has too deeply become the stuff of daily experience to suggest that mere ill-will as a product of controversy can strike down the latter with illegality … Similarly in discontent, affection and hostility: as subjective incidents of controversy, they and the ideas which arouse them are part of our living which ultimately serve us in stimulation, in the clarification of thought and, as we believe, in the search for the constitution and truth of things generally.[53]

These sentiments seem consistent with *Sullivan's* approach to libel law. That they did not spill over into Canadian libel jurisprudence might be explained on the superficial basis that the aforementioned Quebec judgments arose in cases that in form as well as substance involved actions initiated by governmental bodies against private individuals, and in criminal rather than civil proceedings, whereas *Douglas* et al were civil actions that – as a matter of form at least – were between individuals. Such an argument is hardly compelling in substantive terms. That a criminal prosecution for seditious libel might be a less effective deterrent to the dissemination of political information by a newspaper than a civil suit for libel is not an especially contentious proposition. Douglas and Boland were both politicians suing over stories about their political activities: to characterise them as 'private citizens'[54] in that context is simplistically misleading.

[50] The case in this context best known to English public lawyers is likely *Roncarelli v DuPlessis* [1959] SCR 121, which while instructive as to the gross venality of DuPlessis's administration was decided on quite mundane administrative law principles (taking account of an irrelevant consideration and/or bad faith) rather than abstract constitutional law reasoning.

[51] [1951] 1 DLR 657.

[52] The other notable decisions are *Saumur v City of Quebec* [1953] 2 SCR 299; *Chaput v Romain* [1955] SCR 834; *AG of Quebec v Begin* [1955] SCR 593, [1955] 5 DLR 394 and – DuPlessis's target here being leftist radicals rather than Jehovah's Witnesses – *Switzman v Elbling* [1957] SCR 285. For an overview see Laskin (1966) 'Our civil liberties' *Queens Quarterly* 455.

[53] [1951] 1 DLR 657 at [85].

[54] The label might more (but not wholly) defensibly be attached to *Jones* and *Banks*.

C. In English Law – For and Against the *Wason* Principle

With very few exceptions, the English courts took a similarly unreceptive view of suggestions that political information be subject to a more benevolent libel law regime. Two cases sitting at different ends of the spectrum merit attention here.[55] The first is Pearson J's 1960 judgment in *Webb v Times Publishing*;[56] the second the Court of Appeal's 1984 decision in *Blackshaw v Lord*.[57]

i. Webb v Times Publishing

Webb concerned an accurate *Times* summary of court proceedings in Switzerland which suggested the claimant was guilty of a murder of which he had been acquitted in England. The subject matter was not 'political' in a party sense, but could readily be seen as raising a broader 'governmental issue'. Such reports of court proceedings in Britain enjoyed a statutory qualified privilege. In extending that protection at common law to reports of foreign court proceedings, the High Court could be seen as simply replicating a narrow understanding of *Wason* in respect of a different category of 'official information'. But Pearson J's judgment also lends itself to characterisation as endorsing the broad reading of *Wason*, a case to which he expressly referred. Most notably Pearson J defined the 'balance' the law should strike as being between the audience's consumption interest and the claimant, not the publisher's publication interest and the claimant's reputation: '[A]nd most important, there is what may be called the balancing operation – balancing the advantages to the public of the reporting of judicial proceedings against the detriment to individuals of being incidentally defamed'.[58]

As in *Wason*, what was important was not the 'occasion' of the article's publication, but its subject matter:

> One has to look for a legitimate and proper interest as contrasted with an interest which is due to idle curiosity or a desire for gossip ... There is thus a test available for deciding whether the subject-matter is appropriate for conferring privilege ... Sometimes a report of foreign judicial proceedings will have intrinsic world-wide importance, so that a reasonable man in any civilised country, wishing to be well-informed, will be glad to read it, and would think he ought to read it if he has the time available ... That is the present case.[59]

The suggestion that the reasonable person *ought* to keep herself informed about 'English affairs', and should be able to rely upon the press to provide such information even if might turn out to be false, obviously echoes the values underlying *Wason* and *Sullivan*. But even as late as the mid-1980s, it was far from being accepted as an orthodoxy in English law.

---

[55] The era is analysed more thoroughly in Loveland op cit fn 2 ch 6.
[56] [1960] 2 QB 535.
[57] [1984] 1 QB 9 (CA).
[58] [1960] 2 QB 535 at 561.
[59] ibid at 569.

ii. Blackshaw v Lord

Blackshaw offered the interesting spectacle of the High Court accepting an expansive reading of *Wason* and *Webb* and being promptly overruled by the Court of Appeal. The libel, an article by Lord in the *Daily Telegraph*, concerned a claim that a senior civil servant (Blackshaw) wasted large sums of public money through incompetence. The trial judge (Caulfield J) accepted that qualified privilege applied: it was 'beyond argument' the article addressed an issue that 'It would be the duty of the press to bring it to the attention of the public and any right thinking person ... who was interested in the running of the country would want to know those facts'.[60]

The Court of Appeal saw no force in that contention. In reviewing what it considered the relevant authorities – including *Webb*, but not *Wason* – it could not find any support for the suggestion that qualified privilege could attach to 'all the world' publication of such material, albeit that circulating it to MPs might well be so protected: 'No privilege yet attaches to a statement on matter of public interest believed by the publisher to be true in relation to a matter in which he has exercised reasonable care'.[61] There is nothing to suggest that the Court of Appeal would have taken a different view if the claimant had been a minister rather than a civil servant.

Webb was read very narrowly, much as *Wason* had been read (in England though not in the US) for much of the previous 100 years; ie being simply a fair summary of an 'official' source of information. If the *Telegraph* was to avail itself of qualified privilege, it could not rely on its own investigative reporting, but would have to await the publication of some kind of governmental report or inquiry reaching the conclusions it had reached itself, and then accurately report those conclusions.

The judgment placed no weight on the public's interest in knowing that such maladministration might have occurred. As such it would fit very comfortably into Canada's *Douglas* line of authority. Indeed, the law on this point up to the 1980s is a nice illustration at a micro-level of the broader suggestion that Canada and Britain did indeed have 'constitutions similar in principle'.

IV. And the Charter Makes no Difference – *Hill* *v Church of Scientology*

Sulllivan was perhaps an 'easy case' as a vehicle for constitutionalising libel law reform. The suit was essentially just another weapon used by racist Southern politicians to frustrate the desegregation of public education facilities mandated

---

[60] ibid.
[61] [1984] 1 QB 9 at 26.

by *Brown v Board of Education* and *Cooper v Aaron*.[62] For proponents of the idea that the Charter might be deployed to impose *Sullivan*-esque reform on defamation law, the defendant in *Hill* was, in contrast, an unhappy flag-bearer. While it is likely safe to assume the crank status of Scientology had no bearing on the Court's reasoning and conclusion, it is also perfectly credible to assume, given the evidence adduced at trial, that Mr Hill would have won his case even if faced by a *Sullivan* defence.

The gist of the libel was the accusation that Mr Hill, a government lawyer, had deliberately connived in releasing privileged communications between the Church and its lawyers, communications ordered to be sealed by a court in one set of proceedings to a judge hearing another case, in order to discredit the Church. The evidence in the libel action indicated that the Church had already inspected the sealed documents and established that no tampering or release had occurred before the libellous accusation was made. That Mr Hill should have succeeded, and recovered quite substantial damages, is not in any sense – even a *Sullivan* sense – objectionable. What is objectionable about the Supreme Court's judgment is the intellectual poverty, in several respects, of its reasoning on the constitutional question of whether Ontario's libel law had to be amended to render it consistent with the 'values' inherent in s 2 of the Charter.[63]

A. On Horizontal Effect – From Charter Rights to Charter Values

The above reference to 'Charter values' rather than 'Charter rights' arises because *Hill* was characterised by the Court as litigation between 'private' parties on a point purely of common law. As such, per *Dolphin Delivery*,[64] the interference which Ontario's libel laws worked on the defendants' freedom of expression could not breach s 2 of the Charter per se. Rather, the Charter was relevant to the case because its 'values' might require the Court to alter the content of the common law.

The general defensibility of that rationale has been explored in Nick Bamforth's chapter in this volume.[65] For present purposes, and accepting the 'correctness' of the proposition, we might note simply the Court's ostensibly very surprising

---

[62] Respectively (1954) 347 US 438 (*Brown 1*), (1955) 349 US 295 (*Brown 2*), (1958) 358 US 1 *Cooper*. For comment see inter alia Tushnett (1994) *Making civil rights law* ch 18; Woodward (1966) *The strange career of Jim Crow* pp 154–81: Blaustein and Ferguson (1973) 'Avoidance, evasion and delay', in Becker and Feeley (eds.) *The impact of Supreme Court decisions*.

[63] [1995] 2 SCR 1130. The sole judgment was written by Cory J, and concurred in by the other members of the Court; (then La Forest, Gonthier, McLachlin, Iacobucci and Major JJ).

[64] *RWSDU v Dolphin Delivery* [1986] 2 SCR 573.

[65] In addition to Bamforth's discussion in ch 4 above, see also in this volume the chapter by Hatzis at pp 235–42; and Taylor's account of the curious priority given by the Court to 'values' rather than 'rights' in the context of family law and religious freedom.

conclusion (at [77]) that the fact that the national government was funding Hill's claim had no bearing on whether or not the suit acquired a s 32 character. That conclusion is prima facie risible in theory and was unexplored as a matter of evidence. If Mr Hill had to run the risk of bearing the costs of a failed action, would he have taken it, against an opponent with very substantial resources? That seems most unlikely. Without that government funding – which was made available by what was surely a governmental decision in the s 32 sense – the claim would probably never have been brought. It is, however, a conclusion that typifies the whole thrust of the Court's judgment.

B. The Value of Reputation

Cory J began his analysis of the apparently competing Charter values by considering the importance of reputation. Whether being accused of professional malpractice by the Church of Scientology – an organisation which hardly enjoys in either Canadian or British society the status of a voice of record or reason even on matters concerning little green people from galaxies far, far away in times long, long ago – would much damage one's professional or social standing is one might think debatable. But of course, the common law has never required the damage inflicted by a libel to be empirically proven: the assumption is and has always been for the claimant a happy (and for the defendant an unhappy) fiction. Nonetheless, the Court's observation that the Church's libel cast severe aspersions on Mr Hill's professional integrity is uncontentious, as is the wider proposition that to accuse a person of inter alia dishonesty, violence, racism, misogyny or child abuse may inflict significant damage on that person. Nor is there any difficulty in sustaining the proposition that it is perfectly proper for the law – be it statute or common law – in a modern democratic society to regard one's (good) reputation as matter deserving of legal protection when that society decides what is meant by the notion of freedom of expression.

However, what is quite bizarre about the Court's reasoning in *Hill* is the route followed to reach this destination. Section 1 of the Charter tells us of course that interferences with Charter rights are permissible if inter alia such interferences are 'demonstrably justifiable in a free and democratic society'. Why then begin a search for the value of reputation – as Cory J did – with visits to the *Old Testament*, pop into the (chronologically undefined) 'Roman era', alight briefly on the feudal Teutons and Normans, pass through England's Star Chamber, end with the observation that '[119] The character of the law relating to libel and slander in the 20th century is essentially the product of its historical development up to the 17th century …', but not then ask, 'How much weight should we give that history?'.

We might as credibly say that: 'The character of the law relating to libel and slander in the 20th century is essentially the product of societies where – inter alia – notions of democratic governance were non-existent; in which women were effectively the chattels of men; where non-white people could be bought and sold as slaves; and in which the forcible colonisation of foreign lands and the genocide of indigenous colonial populations was widely considered a perfectly legitimate tool of foreign policy and commercial development'.

Interrogating one of Cory J's sources perhaps serves to make the point. At [112] he refers (indirectly, as the quote is taken from *Carter-Ruck on libel and slander*) to Exodus 22:28: 'Thou shall not revile the gods, nor curse the ruler of thy people'. What this command (from God via Moses to the children of Israel) presumably means is that we not question whatever belief systems pass for society's one true religion (on pain of death, since we should surely read 22:28 alongside 22:20: 'He that sacrificeth unto any god, save unto the LORD only, he shall be utterly destroyed') and one must not seek to question, let alone change the basis of the governmental system.[66] By the by, we might note that 22:29 requires everyone to hand over their first-born son to God (but not daughter, since the vengeful God of Exodus does not really consider women to be people); and on the normalcy of the pain of death as a social regulator in *Exodus*'s moral compass, we might recall that, per 22:18, 'witches' should be put to death, as should, per 22:19, anyone who 'lieth with a beast'.[67] And when one has finished with the putting to death of witches and sexual 'deviants', one can take a break and enjoy the fruits (literally and metaphorically) of the ethnic cleansing and geno-cide of the Amorites, the Hittites, the Perizzites and the Canaanites which one's God has promised (per 23:23, and 23:27–23:31) to carry out on one's behalf. One could go on – and on – to make similar observations about the 'Roman era', about Teutonic or Norman feudalism, et al. The point is simply that judges engaged in a juridic exercise based on the balancing of competing values, should be alert to the danger of overloading one side of the scales by piling it up with weights drawn uncritically from contexts in which notions of democratic governance play no part in constructing social morality. Accept by all means that the protection of reputation is an important value in modern society, but root its protection in societal contexts consistent with, rather than abhorrent to, those the Charter was designed to protect.

The balancing exercise undertaken by Cory J in *Hill* took an inappropriately simplistic approach to discerning the value of reputation and so lent that value an improperly burdensome weight. And in the context of a judicial exercise purportedly rooted in assessing the balance between competing forces, that is a problematic misstep to take.

---

[66] So 23:20 'Behold, I send an Angel before thee, to keep thee in the way, and to bring thee into the place which I have prepared'. 23:21 'Beware of him, and obey his voice, provoke him not; for he will not pardon your transgressions: for my name is in him'.

[67] 'Lie', one assumes, in the sexual rather than mendacity (defamation-relevant) sense.

C. The Value of Untrue Speech

On the other side of the Court's scales, the question weighed was how much worth lay in promulgating *false* speech. By 1995, the Court had decided several free expression cases which identified s 2's 'underlying values':[68]

> (1) seeking and attaining the truth is an inherently good activity; (2) participation in social and political decision-making is to be fostered and encouraged; and (3) the diversity in forms of individual self-fulfilment and human flourishing ought to be cultivated in an essentially tolerant, indeed welcoming, environment not only for the sake of those who convey a meaning, but also for the sake of those to whom it is conveyed.

The *Hill* Court could not see that any of those values would be served by extending greater protection to political libels. At [109], invoking *Boland*, Cory J asserted that:

> Certainly, defamatory statements are very tenuously related to the core values which underlie s. 2(*b*). They are inimical to the search for truth. False and injurious statement cannot enhance self-development. Nor can it ever be said that they lead to healthy participation in the affairs of the community. Indeed, they are detrimental to the advancement of these values and harmful to the interests of a free and democratic society.

We might for the moment accept that the 'core values' underlying s 2 were well-rooted in the Canada of 1960 when *Boland* was decided. But the proposition that false statements are 'inimical' to the 'search for truth' and 'healthy participation in the affairs of the community' is manifestly preposterous. A trite hypothetical scenario supports that point. A local newspaper published a story that politician A took a bribe from land developer X to smooth the passage of X's latest building project. The story prompts huge public concern and further press and then police investigation of A's activities. It transpires that A did not take a bribe from X. The story was false. But the investigations that only occurred because of the story reveal that A did in fact take bribes from developers Y and Z, and that developer X had paid such a bribe to politicians B and C.

Indeed, that the (even deliberate) propagation of false material might aid the truth and participation values was accepted by the Court *three years earlier* in *R v Zundel*,[69] in which Canada's retention of the obscure English offence of propagating false news was held incompatible with the Charter:

> The first difficulty results from the premise that deliberate lies can never have value. Exaggeration – even clear falsification – may arguably serve useful social purposes

---

[68] *Ford v Quebec* [1988] 2 SCR 712 ((Quebec's French-only signage law): *Irwin Toy v Quebec* [1989] 1 SCR 927 (television advertising targeting children); *Rocket v Royal College of Dental Surgeons* [1990] 2 SCR 232 (medical profession advertising); *R v Keegstra* [1990] 3 SCR 697 (hate speech); *R v Zundel* [1992] 2 SCR 731 (Holocaust denial); *R v Butler* [1992] 1 SCR 452 (obscenity). The quotation comes from *Irwin* at 976 per Dickson CJ and Lamer and Wilson JJ.

[69] [1992] 2 SCR 731 at 754–55.

linked to the values underlying freedom of expression. A person fighting cruelty against animals may knowingly cite false statistics in pursuit of his or her beliefs and with the purpose of communicating a more fundamental message, e.g., 'cruelty to animals is increasing and must be stopped'. A doctor, in order to persuade people to be inoculated against a burgeoning epidemic, may exaggerate the number or geographical location of persons potentially infected with the virus ...

Zundel was a 4:3 judgment, with Cory J (joined by Gonthier and Iacobucci JJ) among the dissentients. The dissent upheld the offence – then in s 181 of the Criminal Code – in part because it criminalised wilful (ie known) falsehoods. It is perhaps surprising that this point eluded all of the judges in *Hill*, including McLachlin J who authored the majority opinion in *Zundel*.

Hill's primary shortcoming, however, is exemplified by para [140] of the judgment:

(e) Conclusion: Should the Law of Defamation be Modified by Incorporating the Sullivan Principle?

[140] The *New York Times Co. v. Sullivan*, supra, decision has been criticized by judges and academic writers in the United States and elsewhere. It has not been followed in the United Kingdom or Australia. I can see no reason for adopting it in Canada in an action between private litigants. The law of defamation is essentially aimed at the prohibition of the publication of injurious false statements. It is the means by which the individual may protect his or her reputation, which may well be the most distinguishing feature of his or her character, personality, and, perhaps, identity. I simply cannot see that the law of defamation is unduly restrictive or inhibiting. Surely it is not requiring too much of individuals that they ascertain the truth of the allegations they publish. The law of defamation provides for the defences of fair comment and of qualified privilege in appropriate cases. Those who publish statements should assume a reasonable level of responsibility.

That shortcoming is that para [140] sets up the question before the court as a binary issue – the publisher's right to publish versus the claimant's right to repu-tation. That ignores altogether the interest of the audience (actual and potential) in receiving, evaluating and deciding how to respond (if at all) to the informa-tion. The omission is beyond trite, and not simply because that latter interest is manifestly the one underlying the reasoning in *Sullivan*. It is also because the Canadian Supreme Court had already (and repeatedly) recognised the importance of the audience interest to s 2 analysis. That value is central to the analysis in *Ford* (Valerie Ford's two-word shop sign (*laine* – wool) was a benefit to the non-French speaking wool-buying public); in *Irwin Toy* (adults might well want to know what new toys they could buy for their children); and in *Rocket* (a dentist's customers might wish to know about her specialised skills or services).

We might leave para [140] with the observation that its final sentence makes no sense at all in the light of Cory J's reasoning, which at no point countenanced the possibility that a distinction might validly be drawn between deliberate, reckless, negligent and innocent falsehood. 'A reasonable level of responsibility' is not what Ontario libel law imposed. 'Reasonable responsibility' sounds like a negligence test. What Ontario's law imposed was 'strict responsibility'. 'Reasonable responsibility' would require a significant change to the law, albeit one that would be much less significant than adopting the orthodox qualified privilege test. The church perhaps overplayed its hand in its pleadings. The substantive leap from *Douglas* to *Sullivan* is vast. There are many points in between which would enhance – to very varying degrees – the protection afforded to disseminators of libellous political material.[70]

i. And Demonising Sullivan

Whatever the failings of the church's legal advisers – and their conduct of the litigation apparently left much to be desired – the Court seemed unwilling to countenance filling the gap. Cory J presented the choice before it as the status quo or *Sullivan*. And since his portrayal of *Sullivan* could best be described as feeble and selective misrepresentation, that the judgment opted for the status quo is hardly surprising.

So, as one example, Cory J referred to academic critiques critical of *Sullivan* but did not treat with any supporting the judgment. Similarly, at [135], Cory J invoked the US Supreme Court's decision in *Gertz v Robert Welch*[71] as a stick with which to beat *Sullivan*, noting that in *Gertz* the Court observed, 'There is no constitutional value in false statements of fact'.[72] What Cory J omits to mention is that in the passage following the above quotation the Court explained why it was nonetheless necessary to extend some – and some substantial – protection to such false statements.[73] Nor does Cory J acknowledge that *Gertz* did not overrule *Sullivan*. Certainly *Gertz* narrowed the scope of post-*Sullivan* extensions to the public figure route to the *Sullivan* defence (here that a lawyer's involvement qua professional in legal proceedings arising out of a political controversy did not make that lawyer a *Sullivan* public figure). *Gertz* also made it very clear that the *Sullivan* rationales should not apply to 'private' figures. But *Gertz* also introduced two very important additional and generally applicable obstacles to successful libel claims. Firstly, *Gertz* required that state law had to set at least a negligence standard (with the evidential burden on the claimant) as to falsity in *all* libel actions, irrespective of the defendant's identity. And secondly, in *all* libel actions punitive damages could only be recovered if the *Sullivan* test was met.

[70] cf Tingley's contemporaneous critique 'Reputation, freedom of expression and the tort of defamation in the United States and Canada: a deceptive polarity' *Alberta LR* 620 especially at 645–47. See also Boivin (1997) 'Accommodating freedom of expression in the common law of defamation' *Queens LJ* 230: Ross (1996) 'The common law of defamation fails to enter the age of the Charter' *Alberta LR* 117.

[71] (1974) 418 US 323.

[72] ibid at 340.

[73] In an example of poor practice, Cory took his reference to *Gertz* from a second-hand source, namely White J's very *Sullivan*-sceptical judgment in *Dun & Bradstreet Inc v Greenmoss Builders Inc* (1985) 472 US 749.

Cory's treatment of *Sullivan* and of – to borrow from then extant Charter s 2 jurisprudence – its 'underlying values', was distinctly shabby. But to that point of course, so had been its treatment in British law.

V. But Perhaps the ECHR does Make a Difference? From *Blackshaw* to *Reynolds* – And *Jameel*

By the early 1990s, there were indications in the ECtHR's case law that English libel law might breach Art 10 ECHR because it drew no meaningful distinction between defamatory material relating to political or governmental issues and purely private matters. The suggestion arose most clearly in *Lingens v Austria*,[74] in which the ECtHR observed:

> [42] … The limits of acceptable criticism are accordingly wider as regards a politician as such than as regards a private individual. Unlike the latter, the former inevitably and knowingly lays himself open to close scrutiny of his every word and deed by both journalists and the public at large, and he must consequently display a greater degree of tolerance.

The ECtHR did not specify just what this 'greater degree of tolerance' might entail in terms of defences to defamation actions. *Lingens* concerned Austrian criminal defamation law, which imposed strict liability on defendants. But the obvious implication of the above-quoted passage was that domestic defamation law should recognise a meaningful distinction in terms of defences between 'political' and non-political libels. The Court repeated the principle on several occasions in the next few years in case (both criminal and civil) arising in various jurisdictions.[75]

In the early 1990s in *Derbyshire County Council v Times Newspapers*,[76] the Court of Appeal had drawn on Art 10 to conclude that a government body could not bring a libel action, a conclusion endorsed (though in reliance on American and commonwealth authorities) by the House of Lords. However, neither court had indicated that politicians as individuals could not bring such actions, nor that they might face more effective defences should they do so.[77] That question was eventually broached in *Reynolds v Times Newspapers*.

---

[74] (1986) 8 EHRR 407.

[75] See also *Barfod v Denmark* (1989) 11 EHRR 493; *Oberschlik v Austria* (1991) 19 EHRR 389; *Castells v Spain* (1992) 14 EHRR 445; *Thorgeirson v Iceland* (1992) 14 EHRR 843.

[76] [1992] QB 770 (CA); [1993] AC 534 (HL). Discussed in Cumberbatch (1994) 'The quiet revolution in freedom of speech: a comment on Derbyshire CC v Times Newspapers Ltd' *NILQ* 219: Loveland (1994) 'Defamation of government: taking lessons from America ?' *Legal Studies* 206.

[77] A point noted and relied on by Cory J in *Hill* at [1995] 2 SCR 1130 [137].

A. The *Reynolds* Defence

Albert Reynolds, Ireland's former Taoiseach, sued over a story in the London edition of the *Sunday Times* which accused him of lying to the Dáil. At trial and in the Court of Appeal,[78] the *Sunday Times* had unsuccessfully argued that qualified privilege should attach to the story, drawing both on the House of Lords' judgment in *Derbyshire* and the *Lingens* line of ECtHR case law. That conclusion was reversed on further appeal.

The ratio of the majority judgment in the House of Lords in *Reynolds*[79] and the reasoning underlying is too well known to require more than a brief account here. At first sight, *Reynolds* appeared to offer a curious tweak to the established qualified privilege defence. Crudely put, the defence seemed to be that if it was in the 'public interest' that the information in issue be published to 'all the world', then the publisher could not be liable in defamation if he/she/it established that the article's production and publication were carried out in accordance with a standard of 'responsible journalism'.

On the first 'public interest' issue, the *Reynolds* defence initially appears more favourable to media defendants than orthodox qualified privilege, inasmuch as it alters the traditional 'occasion' test from one of 'what is the information and to whom is it published' to one of 'is the information something that can properly be published to all the world'. Lord Nicholls' leading judgment had a certain circularity in defining this notion of public interest. It might include – but was not limited to – political information in the *Sullivan* sense: all matters of 'public concern' might fall within the defence. A list of factors would be relevant to answering this case-specific question;[80] among them the seriousness of the allegation in terms of its impact on the claimant's reputation, the significance of the public interest issue, the source of the information, and the urgency of the need to publish.

The defendant would still bear the burden of proof on this point, as in qualified privilege. However, on the second issue, *Reynolds* appears much less favourable to the defendant than orthodox qualified privilege. This is because the defendant retains the burden of proof – to show the publication was 'responsible journalism' – whereas under qualified privilege it is for the claimant to prove 'malice'.

That distinction per se suggests that styling the *Reynolds* defence as a form of privilege was misconceived. Furthermore, it seems that the defence collapses aspects of the first and second issues into each other. This becomes evident when one considers the illustrative factors listed by Lord Nicholls to which a court might have regard when deciding if a 'public interest' matter has arisen. Some of these factors – such as '3. The source of the information … 4. The steps taken to verify

---

[78] [1998] 3 WLR 862.
[79] [2001] 2 AC 127.
[80] ibid at 205.

the information ... 7. Whether comment was sought from the defendant' – obviously go to the issue of the defendant's 'culpability' in publishing false information. Under traditional qualified privilege, those would be matters for the claimant to raise and prove. But to complicate matters further – and again to depart from the orthodox privilege defence – *Reynolds* rather suggested that the defendant would have to prove only that he/she/it acted reasonably in the light of prevailing journalistic standards – ie a negligence test.

While the new defence had obvious complexities in its detail, it did appear to be driven by the Court's concern to underline the increased importance of providing protection for press discussion of political matters.[81] *Wason* and *Webb* were invoked in Lord Nicholls' reasoning,[82] as was the line of ECtHR authority flowing from *Lingens*.[83] Lord Nicholls had begun his analysis from an unusual position in the English libel law context, taking as his starting point the need for the common law to assist electors in making informed choices about who should govern their country. Towards the end of his judgment he offered a short passage which attracted much press attention, his opinion opening a new legal era for conscientious investigative journalism:

> Above all, the court should have particular regard to the importance of freedom of expression. The press discharges vital functions as a bloodhound as well as a watchdog. The court should be slow to conclude that a publication was not in the public interest and, therefore, the public had no right to know, especially when the information is in the field of political discussion. Any lingering doubts should be resolved in favour of publication.[84]

Despite this rhetoric, which would not be out of place in *Sullivan*, Lord Nicholls and his colleagues expressly disavowed any idea of importing that defence into English law. The Court likely did not appreciate *Sullivan's* roots in *Wason*, although its primary concern seemed to be that as 'malice' in the *Sullivan* sense was difficult for a claimant to prove, a *Sullivan* rule would result in too much false information entering the political arena.

From the perspective of media defendants publishing information which the public had 'a right to know', and more importantly of their readers, *Reynolds* marked a distinct improvement on the orthodox position. The defence was however confused and confusing in conceptual terms.[85] It also appeared to have a

---

[81] It is perhaps important to remember that Mr Reynolds won the case notwithstanding the new defence. This was primarily because the *Times* had published a quite different version of the article in its Irish edition, a version which did not impute dishonesty to Mr Reynolds, and because it has not given him an opportunity to respond to the allegations. Given the first point, Mr Reynolds might well have won under a *Sullivan* regime as well.

[82] ibid at 204, where Lord Nicholls invokes – without citation – Cockburn's reference to the elasticity of the common law and its capacity to adapt to modern conditions.

[83] ibid at 203–04.

[84] ibid at 205.

[85] cf Loveland (2000) 'A new legal landcape? Libel law and freedom of political expression in the United Kingdom' *EHRLR* 476: Williams (2000) 'Defaming politicians: the not so common law' *MLR* 748.

less significant impact in practice that the House of Lords had evidently intended. This perceived problem was recognised by the House of Lords, and addressed in unusually forthright terms five years later in *Jameel v Wall Street Journal Europe*.[86]

B. Clarifying *Reynolds* in *Jameel*

The claimant in *Jameel* was a Saudi company which the *Wall Street Journal* identified as being on a list of organisations with suspected terrorist ties. The story was said to be based on information from anonymous US and Saudi government officials, and the claimant was not invited to comment on the story before publication. Those two factors, both explicitly identified in Lord Nicholls 10-point list, had led the trial court to find the *Reynolds* defence did not apply, and that decision was upheld in the Court of Appeal.[87]

In reversing that judgment, several members of the House of Lords issued what was in effect a rebuke to the lower courts in general – and to the trial judge in *Jameel*, Eady J, in particular – for misapplying the *Reynolds* principle. Lord Hoffmann perhaps made the point most clearly. Referring to the 10 points, he cautioned that they

> are not tests which the publication has to pass. In the hands of a judge hostile to the spirit of Reynolds, they can become ten hurdles at any of which the defence may fail. That is how Eady J treated them ...[88]

The accusation of judicial 'hostility' was oversimplistic. The *Reynolds* defence can readily be seen as poorly conceived and poorly formulated. The Court made some limited efforts to clarify the defence's doctrinal character in *Jameel*, suggesting that it should be seen as a new 'public interest defence' rather than a bastardised form of qualified privilege. In a more practical vein, the Court also stressed that articles containing defamatory allegations had to be read as a whole; it was not appropriate for a trial court to treat such allegations in isolation. Relatedly, the judgment indicated that greater weight ought to be given to the defendant's editorial judgment in deciding that a story should be run.

Reynolds and *Jameel* had been decided alongside near contemporaneous developments in Australia and New Zealand, both triggered by cases brought by the former New Zealand Prime Minister David Lange. In *Lange v Atkinson*,[89] New Zealand's Court of Appeal embraced the more doctrinally straightforward – and for defendants much more useful – innovation of extending qualified privilege in its orthodox form to 'all the world' publications which addressed the claimant's

---

[86] [2006] UKHL 44, [2007] 1 AC 359.

[87] [2003] EWHC 37 (QB), [2004] EMLR 11, [2005] EWCA Civ 74, [2005] QB 904.

[88] [2006] UKHL 44, [2007] 1 AC 359 at [56].

[89] [2000] 3 NZLR 385. See Barber and Young (2001) 'Political libel in New Zealand' *LQR* 175; Atkin (2001) 'Defamation law in New Zealand "refined" and "amplified"' *Common Law World Review* 237; Loveland op cit fn 2 pp 159–63.

current or prospective fitness to hold elected political office. In Australia, the High Court modified the common law in *Lange v Australian Broadcasting Corporation*[90] to introduce a variant of qualified privilege in respect of material 'concerning government and political matters that affect the people of Australia'.[91] The effect of the modified defence would however be less a favourable to defendants than the New Zealand variant: it would be for the defendant to prove that he/she/it had a reasonable basis to believe the material was true and had taken appropriate steps to establish that it was indeed true. The *Lange* judgments provided valuable source material above and beyond that provided by *Reynolds* for Canadian courts when offered the opportunity to reconsider *Hill*.

VI. Second (and Third) Thoughts on whether the Charter makes a Difference

A differently composed Canadian Supreme Court compared to its *Hill* predecessor sat in *Simpson v Mair*[92] in 2007: only McLachlin (by 2007 as Chief Justice) sat in both cases.[93] The defendant Rafe Mair hosted a controversy-driven radio talk show, during which he suggested that Simpson, a prominent anti-gay rights campaigner, was engaging in hate-provoking activities which might lead to violence.

The defamatory material was treated as comment rather than fact, and so the central issue before the Supreme Court was whether the requirement in Canadian law that a person could not avail herself of the fair comment defence unless his comment was one a reasonable person could have made was consistent with Charter values.[94] The issue was resolved in Mair's favour, insofar as the Court held that fair comment could be applied even if only a person with prejudiced or exaggerated views could honestly express such an opinion. But for present purposes, the judgment's significance lay its hint that *Hill* was ripe for reconsideration.

Mair's counsel had pleaded – anticipating that the material might be characterised as fact – that Canadian law should modify *Hill* and accept what was styled a 'responsible journalism' defence modelled on (the above-mentioned) developments in Britain, Australia and New Zealand. While noting that this question would have to await 'another appeal', Binnie J (giving the leading judgment) briefly reviewed the relevant authorities (*Reynolds* and *Lange* (Australia) and *Lange* (New Zealand), and concluded the passage by saying that Canadian law would 'necessarily evolve' and that what would be in issue would be the scope of any such privilege and the location of the burden of proof.

---

[90] (1997) 189 CLR 520, (1997) 71 AJLR 818. On *Lange*, and its place within the radical approach taken by the High Court to freedom of expression issues in the 1990s see Loveland op cit fn 2 pp 147–50.
[91] ibid at 833 per Brennan J.
[92] [2008] 2 SCR 420.
[93] Bastaraches, Binnie, LeBel, Fish, Abella, Charron and Rothstein JJ also sat.
[94] This being – again – a 'horizontal' action.

Judgment in *Mair* was handed down on 27 June 2008. Barely a year later, the Supreme Court heard argument both in *Cusson v Quan et al*[95] and in *Grant v Torstar Corporation*.[96]

A. In Canada: The Responsible Communication Defence in *Cusson* and *Grant* (2009)

The claimant in *Cusson* was an Ottawa police officer who had, on his own initiative, gone to New York immediately after the Twin Towers attack to offer assistance to American rescue teams. *The Ottawa Citizen* newspaper subsequently ran several articles about Mr Cusson, which portrayed his activities very unflatteringly. At trial, the defendants unsuccessfully ran justification and fair comment defences. The trial judge rejected their assertion that qualified privilege attached to the articles. Mr Cusson recovered $100,000 against *The Citizen*.

The claimant in *Grant v Torstar Corporation* was an Ontario property magnate with close ties to the then provincial Premier, Mike Harris, and Harris' Ontario Progressive Conservative party. Grant was seeking permission for a controversial land development, opposed by many local residents, who feared Grant was using his political influence to bypass normal zoning constraints. *The Toronto Star* reported on the controversy, in an article which included a comment from a local resident that 'became the centrepiece of the litigation':[97] "'Everyone thinks it's a done deal because of Grant's influence – but most of all his Mike Harris ties," says Lorrie Clark, who owns a cottage on Twin Lakes'. Grant sued both *The Star* and Ms Clark, the latter settling before trial. The alleged sting was that Grant bribed Harris to smooth the path of Grant's proposed development. *The Star* ran two innovative defences: first that the Charter required that qualified privilege attach to the story; second, alternatively, that the Charter required a *Reynolds*-type defence of 'responsible journalism' for such stories, which would succeed if the defendant persuaded the court that the issue was a matter of public interest and that he/she/it had exercised reasonable care in establishing the truth of any allegations made. The trial court considered both defences precluded by *Hill*; Grant won the suit and recovered substantial damages.

i. Appeal in Ontario

The Ontario Court of Appeal's judgment in *Cusson*[98] is a curious and/or ingenious decision in several respects, especially concerning what it tells us about notions of 'dialogue' in Charter jurisprudence and how such 'dialogue' might impact on

[95] [2009] SCC 62.
[96] [2009] SCR 64.
[97] [2009] SCR 64 at [16].
[98] (2007) 87 OR (3d) 241.

orthodox notions of judicial hierarchies.[99] The citizen raised two grounds of appeal: that the trial judge was wrong to reject the (pleaded) qualified privilege defence; and that it could invoke (although it had not pleaded at trial) a 'responsible journalism' defence.

The Court of Appeal, in a judgment by Sharpe JA, accepted that the 'responsible journalism' defence, modelled on the *Reynolds/Jameel* principles, could now properly be regarded as required by s 2. That conclusion was inspired by the observation that not just the UK but also Australian and New Zealand courts had recently accepted that their respective constitutions demanded more effective defences for in libel suits involving political or public interest material:

> [122] While evolution of the law of defamation has produced a variety of solutions in different jurisdictions, the evolution away from the common law's traditional bias in favour of the protection of reputation is strikingly uniform. The … traditional common law standard unduly burdens freedom of expression and have all made appropriate modifications to achieve a more appropriate balance between protecting reputation on the one hand and the public's right to know on the other.

Sharpe J was also influenced[100] by several post-*Hill* first instance judgments in Ontario and other Canadian provinces in which courts countenanced the availability of qualified privilege in cases involving publication to 'all the world':

> [71] … [O]ne can hardly quarrel with the proposition that the law of qualified privilege is in a state of "evolution" and "flux" and considerably more nuanced than would appear from a literal reading of the *Douglas v Tucker* line of cases …

More significantly, the factor which Sharpe J considered had to be balanced against the claimant's reputation was not the publisher's right to inform, but the audience's right to be informed:

> [129] Under the traditional common law regime, society makes a clear choice to forego a certain level of exposure, scrutiny and criticism on matters of public interest in the name of protecting individual reputation. That choice sacrifices freedom of expression to the protection of reputation to a degree that today cannot be sustained as consistent with Charter values.

Since the Tucker line of cases had been approved in *Hill*, the Court of Appeal could not simply discard them because of their pre-Charter origins:

> [130] … The *Douglas v. Tucker* line of cases was decided some 50 years ago in a very different legal context, one that gave preponderant consideration to protection of reputation. These cases bear the mark of the pre-Charter past, an era less concerned about the right of free expression and the need for open, vibrant political debate.
>
> [132] That, of course, does not mean that we can or should simply ignore the *Douglas v. Tucker* line of decisions. Likewise, we must respect the Supreme Court's ruling in *Hill v. Scientology*. …

---

[99] See the discussion in the introductory chapter above.
[100] ibid at [63]–[71].

Rather than 'ignore' these cases, Sharpe JA asked what was the precise proposition they supported? In his view, *Hill*'s ratio in dismissing *Sullivan* was that Charter values did not require extension of the traditional qualified privilege defence to political information. The *Tucker* line also rested on that premise. But *Hill* was not authority that less protective amendment was precluded. That is strictly speaking correct. The Church had pleaded only qualified privilege, rather than a selection of less effective defences. And since *Jameel* indicated that *Reynolds* was not a mani-festation of qualified privilege, but a new, freestanding common law principle, *Hill* did not preclude Canadian courts adopting a similarly novel defence:

> [133] Our task, it seems to me, is to interpret and apply the earlier decisions in light of the Charter values at issue and in light of the evolving body of jurisprudence that is plainly moving steadily towards broadening common law defamation defences to give appropriate weight to the public interest in the free flow of information.

However, the Court of Appeal's judgment treads on less stable ground in suggest-ing that that Cory J also implicitly endorsed the responsible journalism idea in his comment at [138] that 'surely it is not requiring too much of individuals that they ascertain the truth of the allegations they publish'. Sharpe JA's conclusion that this comment is 'entirely consistent with what the *Reynolds-Jameel* defence aims to achieve' might have some force if we slotted in the italicised addendum: '*that they take reasonable steps to try to ascertain ...*'. However those words are not there, a negligence-based defence was never discussed in *Hill*, and *Hill* concluded with the stark observation at [144] that 'the common law of defamation complies with the underlying values of the Charter and there is no need to amend or alter it'.

Notwithstanding that statement, the Ontario Court of Appeal did amend the law. Its 'responsible journalism' defence while not following *Reynolds/Jameel* 'in a slavish or literal fashion' endorsed the principle enunciated in those cases:

> [143] ... The defence rests upon the broad principle that where a media defendant can show that it acted in accordance with the standards of responsible journalism in publishing a story that the public was entitled to hear, it has a defence even if it got some of its facts wrong ...

> [144] To avail itself of the public interest responsible journalism test a media defendant must show that it took reasonable steps in the circumstances to ensure that the story was fair and its contents were true and accurate ...

The Court of Appeal was playing rather fast and loose here with traditional notions of precedent and judicial hierarchy, albeit expecting that the Supreme Court might now be ready to modify *Hill*. That expectation was likely reinforced by the Supreme Court's judgment some six or so months later in *Mair*.

But before that Supreme Court opportunity arose, the Ontario Court of Appeal also issued judgment in *Grant*.[101] None of the *Cussan* judges sat in *Grant*.

---

[101] [2008] 92 OR (3d) 561.

The *Grant* bench approved both the reasoning and conclusions reached in *Cussan* and remitted the matter for a new trial. Its formulation of the new defence, rooted firmly in consideration of *Reynolds* and *Jameel*, was:

> [43] ... [T]he essence of the defence is that the matter reported is of public interest, that it was appropriate in that context to include the defamatory statement as part of the story, and that the publisher took reasonable and fair steps, given the defamatory statement, to verify the story including giving the subject of the story a chance to respond before publishing it.

Both *Cussan* and *Grant* were appealed to the Supreme Court, which used *Grant* as the vehicle to revisit *Hill*.

ii. In the Supreme Court

McLachlin CJC's leading judgment in *Grant*[102] broadly approved both the reasoning and result that Sharpe JA had offered in *Cusson*. She also adopted Sharpe JA's suggestion that *Hill*'s ratio rejected *Sullivan* specifically, and not liberalising reform per se; while *Hill* was 'an affirmation of the common law of defamation's general conformity with the Charter, it does not close the door to further changes in specific rules and doctrines'.[103] The door not being closed, a 'fresh look'[104] could properly be taken. Again echoing Sharpe JA's opinion, McLachlin CJC saw the 'tentative forays' post-*Hill* taken by provincial courts in giving an extended reach to qualified privilege and the liberalising trends in the case law of other Commonwealth countries as justification for taking such a look.

While the observation might sound fatuous, the place from which one begins a journey, and the amount of time one spends there, may have a significant bearing on where one ends up. In *Hill*, Cory J had begun his balancing analysis from the start point of protecting reputation, and wallowed indulgently in several democratically deficient swamps in doing so. In *Grant*, McLachlin CJC's 'argument from principle' (at [41] onwards) starts with the importance of freedom of political expression, rooting that value not in the Old Testament or the 'Roman era' (since one would not find it there) but in Ivan Rand's 1950s jurisprudence and the core rationales or underlying values of s 2, which she styled as '(1) democratic discourse; (2) truth-finding; and (3) self-fulfilment'[105] These issues are

---

[102] [2009] SCR 64. The Court was unanimous, save for a brief concurrence by Abella J (para [142] et seq) relating to the respective roles of the judge and jury in applying the new defence.

[103] ibid at [46]. McLachlin CJC was generous in her treatment of *Hill*, noting also at [57] that: 'The statement in Hill (at para [106]) that "defamatory statements are very tenuously related to the core values which underlie s.2(b)" must be read in the context of that case'. That context presumably being that the defendants in *Hill* knew their statements were false. For reasons relating one assumes both to questions of institutional prestige and legal certainty, Supreme Courts in many jurisdictions seem most reluctant to overrule their own decisions, even when those decisions are, as in *Hill*, palpably ill-founded.

[104] ibid at [46].

[105] ibid at [47].

explored in [41]–[57]. The countervailing value of protecting reputation is set up in [58]–[60].

Were one to take quantity as one's guide to the relative importance of those competing values, reputation would seem much the inferior. More important perhaps is the qualitative presumption that underlies points (1) and (2); namely that it is the *audience's interest* in receiving the information rather than the writer/speaker's interest in disseminating it that is the central concern here:

> [48] *First and foremost*, free expression is essential to the proper functioning of demo-
> cratic governance. As Rand J. put it, 'government by the free public opinion of an open
> society ... demands the condition of a virtually unobstructed access to and diffusion of
> ideas': *Switzman*, at p. 306; [emphasis added].

That starting point led McLachlin CJC on a judicial journey to recent develop-ments in several Commonwealth jurisdictions, with most attention being directed to *Reynolds* and *Lange* in Australia and New Zealand.[106] The combination of indigenous (contemporary) Canadian principle and Commonwealth authority persuaded McLachlin CJC that a new defence – and not an extension of qualified privilege – was required which closely followed Sharpe JA's lead in *Cussan*:

> [98] ... First, the publication must be on a matter of public interest. Second the defend-
> ant must show that the publication was responsible, in that he or she was diligent in
> trying to verify the allegations, having regard to all the relevant circumstances.

Much like the House of Lords in *Reynolds*, McLachlin CJC felt unable to offer any definitive guide to what might be a 'public interest' matter. Her most help-ful suggestion was that issues currently regarded as triggering the fair comment defence would likely be public interest matters. This categorisation would go beyond governmental and political matters:

> [104] ... Whenever a matter is such as to affect people at large, so that they may be
> legitimately interested in, or concerned at, what is going on; or what may happen to
> them or others; then it is a matter of public interest on which everyone is entitled to
> make fair comment ...

As to the assessment of whether publication was 'responsible', McLachlin CJC appeared to borrow heavily from Lord Nicholls' list methodology in *Reynolds*, offering[107] an interactive melange of seven factors (all with multiple subparts) to which a trial court should have regard: the seriousness of the allegation in terms of its effect on the claimant's reputation, the importance in a public interest sense of the material in issue, the reliability of the publisher's source(s) and whether or not the claimant had been afforded the opportunity to comment on any allegations prior to publication were all matters that would weigh heavily in the balance.

---

[106] Save for a brief reference to *Sullivan* (and only in the context of what *Hill* decided), she did not engage with US libel jurisprudence.
[107] At [110]–[121].

McLachlin CJC's judgment was perhaps a little better informed than Lord Nicholls' opinion in *Reynolds* as to the empirical effects of such an alteration of the law, in that she drew on (or at least alluded to) several academic sources which had investigated that issue;[108] she proceeded on the basis of informed surmise rather than complete guesswork. This criticism should not be overstated. There is no credible basis on which to predict – whether in Canada or Britain – how many 'true' stories would no longer be self-censored, or how much more (to coin a now topical phrase) fake news would be disseminated, or how many worthy candidates for elected or appointive government office would be deterred from seeking such posts[109] if the new defence were adopted.

The Supreme Court[110] also reversed the Court of Appeal in *Cussan* on the question of the availability of the new defence. McLachlan CJC's sole judgment recorded 'some difficulty'[111] in understanding the Court of Appeal's reasoning, given that it had in essence not just considered but also accepted the premise that a new (albeit unpleaded) defence should be available. The case was thus remitted for a new trial.

VII. Conclusions – A Judicial or Legislative Responsibility?

Grant was accorded a generally warm welcome in Canada's academic press.[112] This was primarily because of its doctrinal innovation. However, some significance was also attached to the fact that McLachlin CJC's judgment had been alert to a perceived flaw in the implementation of *Reynolds* and *Jameel* in the lower English courts; namely that Lord Nicholls' illustrative list was being construed as 10 obstacles which the defendant – who bears the burden of proof – would, one by one, have to surmount. The consequence of this was that the new defence was having a much less significant practical effect than the House of Lords had intended. As noted above, the post-*Reynolds* and pre-*Grant* judgment in *Jameel* had been widely welcomed as sending corrective instructions to the lower courts to avoid adopting a narrow reading of *Reynolds*, although it seemed *Jameel* had a limited effect. McLachlin was presumably concerned to impress upon Canadian provincial

---

[108] The most substantial being Kenyon (2004) 'Lange and Reynolds qualified privilege; Australian and English defamation law and practice' *Melbourne ULR* 406.

[109] The unreasoned assertion that many would be was an element of Cartwright J's above-discussed judgment in *Boland*.

[110] [2009] 3 SCR 712.

[111] ibid at [34].

[112] See for example Dearden and Wagner (2009–10) 'Canadian libel law enters the 21st century: the public interest responsible communication defence' *Ottawa LR* 351; Jobb (2010–11) 'Responsible communication on matters of public interest: a new defence updates Canada's defamation laws' *Journal of International Media and Entertainment Law* 195.

courts to avoid a similarly unwelcome gap emerging in Canada's post-*Grant* libel practice.

That problem in the UK was returned to by the Supreme Court in 2012 in *Flood v Times Newspapers*.[113] The claimant was a police officer who asserted that *The Times* had accused him of corruption. For present purposes, the case's significance lies in the Court's endorsement of the sentiments expressed in *Jameel*.

Lord Phillips' leading judgment approved the suggestion made in *Jameel* that to classify the *Reynolds* defence as 'privilege' was 'misleading'; a better term was simply 'public interest defence'.[114] More significantly perhaps, the Court again indicated that lower courts had continued to be less receptive than was desirable to the *Reynolds* defence, and should seek to be more so in future. None of the judges – nor counsel – saw any need to consider *Grant* or *Cussan*, nor to engage with any of the critical academic literature[115] which had reviewed *Reynolds*' doctrinal integrity and empirical effect. The intellectual insularity of *Flood* when compared to *Grant* is striking. It is certainly not a libel-specific phenomenon. As several contributions to this volume suggest, the Canadian Supreme Court casts its intellectual net much wider than its British counterpart when addressing contentious public law questions.[116]

As *Flood* progressed through the courts, the UK's Parliament was engaged in considering an overhaul of many of the traditional ingredients of defamation law, an overhaul which eventually resulted in the passage of the Defamation Act 2013. One feature of the 2013 Act was an explicit abolition (s 4(6)) of the *Reynolds* defence, and its replacement with a new statutory defence:

4. – Publication on matter of public interest

(1) It is a defence to an action for defamation for the defendant to show that—

(a) the statement complained of was, or formed part of, a statement on a matter of public interest; and

(b) the defendant reasonably believed that publishing the statement complained of was in the public interest.

Section 4 appears to enact a generous rather than narrow reading of *Reynolds*, echoing in both form and substance much of what was said in *Flood*. While s 4(2) directs courts to have regard to all the circumstances of the case in assessing the s 4(1) test, s 4(3) instructs the court in doing so to disregard the defendant's failure to try to verify the truth of the published material, and s 4(4) instructs the court to pay particular attention to the issue of editorial judgment.

---

[113] [2012] UKSC 11, [2012] 2 AC 273. For more extensive analysis see Tan (2013) 'The Reynolds privilege revitalised' *LQR* 27; Bennett (2012) 'Flood v Times Newspapers Ltd – Reynolds privilege returns to the UK's highest court' *Entertainment LR* 134; Dowrick (2012) 'Some brief thoughts on public interest: Flood v Times Newspapers Limited' *Communications Law* 98.

[114] ibid at [27] and [38].

[115] Lord Phillips referred briefly to passages in Gatley and Carter-Ruck's latest editions, works best classified as professional rather than academic in nature.

[116] See the chapters by Draghici and Easton above and Taylor and Hatzis below.

Although some of the initial commentary on the Act was sceptical about s 4's significance[117] – it can quite credibly be seen as removing *Reynolds* in form while relabelling it in substance – other more generic features of the 2013 Act may also work a liberalising effect on the publication of public interest material.[118]

The Act was also the result of an unusually exacting process of deliberation within Parliament, both on the *Reynolds* point and other aspects of libel law. It is certainly not fanciful to suggest that the intellectual quality of the legislative process leading to the 2013 Act was much enhanced by its reference to *Reynolds* and the rich vein of subsequent litigation which *Reynolds* triggered. Interaction between judicial and legislative lawmakers has become a normalised feature of Canada's constitutional landscape in the post-Charter era and is beginning to become established in the UK.[119]

Both jurisdictions have arrived, albeit by differing routes, at legal positions quite distinct from those which prevailed little more than 20 years ago, and which even though so hard fought in the courts appear to be acquiring a normalised moral status. The tangible difference that remains is of course that the UK Parliament might at any juncture through ordinary legislation restore the pre-*Reynolds* position. For a Canadian province to reject *Grant* is more problematic, since any such legislation would require a s 33 notwithstanding declaration. It is of course possible that provincial legislatures or courts might tweak aspects of *Grant* without breaching s 2, but there is no credible prospect that *Grant* will be reversed by amendment of the Charter, given the super-majorities that amendment would require. For that reason alone, one might defensibly conclude that since 1982 the suggestion that Canada and the UK still share constitutions that are 'similar in principle' is on the surface poorly founded in terms both of principle and practice. As one digs a little deeper, however, at least on the narrow point addressed in this chapter, similarities do emerge. And in chapter six, Gavin Phillipson and Tara Beattie dig down into the way in which the Canadian and the UK constitutions have addressed another contentious aspect of the law relating to freedom of expression – namely the regulation and criminalisation of pornography.

---

[117] Scott and Mullis (2014) 'Tilting at windmills: the Defamation Act 2013' *MLR* 87; Hooper, Waite and Murphy (2013) 'Defamation Act 2013 – what difference will it really make?' *Entertainment LR* 199.

[118] Notably the 'serious injury' requirement (s 1); the one-year limitation period and single publication rule (s 8); and the academic and scientific journal privilege (s 6).

[119] See especially Draghici's discussion of the to-ing and fro-ing between courts and the UK Parliament over the assisted suicide issue at ch 2 above.

6

Criminalising Pornography[1]

TARA BEATTIE AND GAVIN PHILLIPSON

The reform of pornography laws in the UK and Canada presents an intriguing pattern of striking similarity and strong contrast, which makes comparative analysis of particular interest. The starting point for comparison is that both juris- dictions have undergone relatively recent reform of what were originally Victorian conceptions of obscenity. Further, in both cases these reforms were driven at least in part by feminist campaigners seeking to reorient the law away from its historical concern with traditional moral values towards the recognition of the harm pornography is said to do to women. In both cases, the law was thus given a new ostensible focus: seeking to tackle pornography that portrays violent, degrad- ing or dehumanising sexual treatment of women and hence – it is said – causes a form of social harm.

However, the *means* of reform form a strong contrast. In the UK, reform has come almost exclusively from the legislative branch: traditional obscenity law[2] has been left in place but supplemented by new legislation, which has a new target – the *consumers* of 'extreme' pornography.[3] In Canada, there has been no federal legislative change in relation to adult pornography. What has changed – quite radically – is its judicial *interpretation:* in *Butler*[4] the Canadian Supreme Court recast the purpose and target of existing obscenity laws from simply explicit material that offends traditional moral values to that which threatens the human, equality or other Charter rights of individuals. Obscenity law in Canada has thus been subject to interpretive constitutional review with a distinctly feminist flavour. The lead- ing judgment of Sopinka J in *Butler* 'relied heavily upon the anti-pornography feminist discourse of theorists like Catharine MacKinnon and Kathleen Mahoney,

---

[1] The authors would like to thank Dr Kyle L Murray for comments on an earlier draft. All errors remain the authors' own. At the time of writing, Tara Beattie is a seconded official at the Council of Europe. The views and opinions expressed in this article are those of the authors and do not necessarily reflect the official position of the Council of Europe or its member states.
[2] The Obscene Publications Act 1959, discussed below at pp 180–182.
[3] pp 188–195 below.
[4] *R v Butler* [1992] 1 SCR 452 (hereafter '*Butler*').

who along with Linda Taylor' wrote the intervention by the women's group LEAF.[5] This makes comparative pornography regulation a potentially interesting case study for comparing the oft-debated respective strengths and weaknesses of judicial and legislative decision-making.

However, in both countries, the experience of how the new laws have turned out in practice has led to considerable discomfort among their feminist proponents. *Butler* was described at the time (perhaps with some hyperbole) as the 'best that any nation on earth has done so far to protect women from the harms of pornography'.[6] Twenty years later, a commentator observed that feminist supporters of *Butler* are now in the 'unpalatable position of having a legal framework labelled as feminist that is blamed for various negative outcomes but almost never applied to the kinds of materials that cause the most concern'.[7] As we will, see, that quote could equally be used to sum up the views of many British feminists on the UK's new pornography laws. It cannot be plausibly argued that either law has done anything significant to tackle the prevalence of sexual violence in society or the cultural values that sustain it. Indeed, we will contend that both laws show, in different ways, the futility and often the injustice of criminalising specific consumers or producers and distributors in one country, in light of the avalanche of material freely available online.

While we will thus argue that both laws may be regarded as failures from an anti-pornography feminist perspective, their strategies make another intriguing contrast. The UK approach has been to tackle narrow and tightly defined categories of pornography. This has avoided – to an extent – the problems associated with laws that rely on broad, subjective concepts, such as sexual material that is 'degrading or dehumanising', but at the risk of rendering the law at times absurdly specific and hence partial in application. Rather than seeking to prohibit pornography portraying sexual violence against *women*, the new law captures only the depiction of serious injury to certain body parts – namely, the anus, breasts or genitals. Indeed, the legislation, as passed, did not itself capture the paradigmatic form of violence against women with which feminists are concerned: rape. Amendments to capture 'rape pornography' were only added several years later.[8] In contrast, the Canadian approach sweeps extraordinarily broadly – capturing both material that mixes violence with sex, and material that is not violent but is 'degrading or dehumanising'[9] – with predictable results. Such vague terms invite those enforcing

---

[5] The Women's Legal Education and Action Fund; see Hernan (1998) 'Sounding the death knell for Butler? A review of B. Cossman, S. Bell, L. Gotell & B.L. Ross, Bad attitude/s on trial: pornography, feminism, and the Butler decision' 43 *McGill LJ* 955.

[6] Scales (1994) 'Avoiding constitutional depression: bad attitudes and the fate of Butler' *Canadian Journal of Women and the Law* 349 at p 363.

[7] Benedet (2015) 'The paper tigress: Canadian obscenity law 20 years after *R v Butler*' *Canadian Bar Review* 1 at p 3.

[8] pp 190–92 below.

[9] pp 184–88 below.

the law, particularly the police and customs officials, to import their own values. For example, at times such officials appeared to have been more ready to find gay and lesbian pornography 'degrading' or 'dehumanising' than the pornography aimed at heterosexual men that has generally been the main target of feminist campaigners, including those who influenced the decision in *Butler*.[10]

Both sets of reforms sought to mark a sharp departure with the old moralism of traditional obscenity laws. However, we find that a pervasive theme in both jurisdictions is one we term the 'ghosts of moralism'. Feminist campaigners may have aimed for a law with a clear focus on the harms to women said to be caused by pornography, but in both cases, more traditional moral concerns have stubbornly persisted. In the UK, this may be seen in two distinct ways: first in the thoroughly mixed-up rationales for the offence, in which feminist arguments were indiscriminately jumbled together with notions of disgust and abhorrence[11] – a jumble that then found its way into the substance of the offence; second, prosecutions have overwhelmingly targeted *not* the violent pornography highlighted by feminist campaigners, but pornography depicting bestiality – a category included seemingly out of simple moral disgust.

In Canada, the lingering influence of moralism has been more subtle. As we will see, the rationale for judicial reform was much more sharply and clearly articulated in terms of feminist principle and tackling gendered harms. But key elements of the offence – as reinterpreted – have reimported moralism via the notion of 'community standards'; that fiction in turn cloaks the imposition of a particular set of values *within* society – one that is fiercely contested by members of minority queer and 'kink' communities, for example – as the standards of the whole community. Even a later turn away from community standards and towards 'harm' can, upon closer inspection, dissolve into the more nebulous notion of harm to political values, which are highly contestable.

In what follows, we first briefly consider the traditional concept of obscenity common to both jurisdictions and the key feminist arguments that led to pressure for change. We then outline the reforms themselves – provisions of the Criminal Justice and Immigration Act 2008 in the UK and the decision of *Butler* in Canada, in each case examining the rationales advanced for reform. We then discuss how far each law fulfilled its feminist aims in practice, and how far its content is faithful to the aims of the feminist campaigners that helped produce it. We further consider the contrasting strategies of prosecuting distributors of pornography versus its consumers – and the pitfalls in each. Finally, we briefly survey the comparative influence constitutional and human rights-based considerations had on the reforms in each country.

---

[10] For example Benedet (2015) op cit fn 7 above pp 3, 37.
[11] pp 188–91 below.

I. The Roots of Pornography Offences: Obscenity

In both Canada and the UK, the principal provisions governing the supply of sexually explicit materials rely on the concept of 'obscenity', an old common law notion rooted in the idea of preventing depravity and corruption articulated in the nineteenth-century ruling of *Hicklin*.[12] That ruling centred on the notion of protecting the individual from moral harm, characterised as flowing from material that would 'deprave and corrupt' by provoking 'thoughts of a most impure and libidinous character'.[13] As Sopinka J commented in *Butler*:

> The *Hicklin* philosophy posits that explicit sexual depictions, particularly outside the sanctioned contexts of marriage and procreation, threatened the morals or the fabric of society. In this sense, its dominant, if not exclusive, purpose was to advance a particular conception of morality. Any deviation from such morality was considered to be inherently undesirable, independently of any harm to society.[14]

In the UK, the *Hicklin* test was codified in the Obscene Publications Act 1959 (OPA 1959),[15] which prohibits the publication for gain or possessing, with a view to publication, an article which tends, taken as a whole, to 'deprave and corrupt a significant proportion of those likely to see or hear it' (s 1(1)). It is clear from the leading decision in *DPP v Whyte*[16] that the aim of the law was to tackle moral corruption; hence no likelihood of any anti-social action flowing from consuming the obscene material was needed. Thus, Lord Cross wrote that 'influence on the mind is not merely within the law but is its primary target'[17] and Lord Pearson bluntly said that 'bad conduct may follow from the corruption of the mind, but it is not part of the statutory definition.'[18]

The question of whether a given item would have this corrupting effect was one for the jury. *DPP v Jordan*[19] held that:

> [I]t is for the jury to say whether the tendency of the material is such as to deprave or corrupt them, and for this purpose, in general, no evidence, psychological, sociological or medical may be admitted … The jury consider the material for themselves and reach their conclusion as to its effect. They cannot be told by psychologists or anyone else what the effect of the material on normal minds may be.[20]

---

[12] (1868) 3 QB 360. Curiously perhaps the 'illiberal' *Hicklin* test came at the same time and from the same judge – Cockburn CJ – as the distinctly 'liberal' judgment relating to political libels in *Wason v Walter* (1868) LR 4 QB 73; see Loveland's chapter at pp 145–46.

[13] (1868) 3 QB 360 at 371.

[14] [1992] 1 SCR 452 at 492.

[15] And reformed in 1964.

[16] [1972] AC 849 (HL).

[17] ibid at 873.

[18] ibid at 864.

[19] [1977] AC 699.

[20] ibid at 717.

Hence, in the UK expert evidence on this key point is generally inadmissible.[21] Thus, the whole operation of the law depends on whether juries or magistrates consider the material would produce a 'moral change for the worse' in those likely to encounter it, applying 'contemporary standards'.[22] Only the highly selective exercise of prosecutorial discretion keeps this wholly unbounded law within manageable limits. For example, it now appears clear that, de facto at least, the written word will not be prosecuted[23] and that prosecutions are only brought in relation to fairly extreme material.[24] There is also evidence of a recent move towards more 'harm'-based standards for prosecution, as the 2019 revision of the Crown Prosecution Service (CPS) Legal Guidance demonstrates.[25] Under the OPA 1959, it is a defence to a finding that a publication is obscene if it can be shown that 'the publication of the article in question is justified as for the public good in that it is in the interests of science, literature, art, learning or of other objects of general concern'.[26]

There is a central problem with a law that depends upon jurors applying 'contemporary standards' in society on sexual morality which, as we shall see, has also bedevilled the Canadian approach. As one of us has previously argued,[27] the 'deprave and corrupt' test made sense in a society in which there was a strong consensus as to substantive sexual morality, one based upon a puritanical interpretation of Judeo-Christian moral teaching: sex and sexual desire was morally permissible only in marriage, and homosexual sex was always wrong; to produce a publication likely to arouse *hetero*sexual desire was generally therefore to corrupt per se; any attempt to arouse homosexual desire was doubly so. In contemporary society, however, agreement as to appropriate sexual morality has fractured spectacularly, aside from a basic remaining consensus that sexual activity should be confined to consenting adults. There are some morally conservative groups (particularly those with traditional religious beliefs) who still think that only sex within heterosexual marriage is morally acceptable. Beyond that, there is a vast range of views based on personal preference, taste and ethical conviction. For example, the latter part of the twentieth century saw a rapid revolution in terms of attitudes towards, and the legal treatment of, homosexuality; a significant minority continue to take the view that consenting homosexual intercourse between adults is morally wrong, or at least repugnant, albeit perhaps something that should be

[21] An exception was provided for in *R v Skirving* [1985] QB 819, in which it was said that in cases concerned with alleged depravity and corruption arising from factors other than the sexual nature of the material, expert evidence will, exceptionally, be admissible, although the evidence can only be as to the effects of the behaviour described in the material, not as to the likely effects of the material itself.
[22] *Calder and Boyars* [1969] 1 QB 151.
[23] Fenwick and Phillipson (2006) *Media freedom under the Human Rights Act* at p 428.
[24] See eg Edwards (1998) 'On the contemporary application of the Obscene Publications Act 1959' *Criminal LR* 843.
[25] See CPS (revised January 2019) 'Legal guidance: obscene publications'.
[26] s 4. Similar defences apply to theatrical productions (Theatres Act 1968, s 3) and films (Criminal Law Act 1977, s 53(6)).
[27] This paragraph draws on Fenwick and Phillipson (2006) op cit fn 23 above p 433.

tolerated. Given the plethora of varying views as to what might be meant by moral corruption, to ask a jury to apply 'contemporary standards' to sexually explicit material is to ask of them the impossible. The law, as it has traditionally been used, has depended on little more than the unstructured intuitions of police officers, prosecutors and jurors as to what is morally beyond the pale in contemporary society. While modern prosecutorial standards have somewhat attenuated the risk of rampant use of 'contemporary standards', this lingering subjective test remains highly problematic.

Canadian obscenity law remains based on s 163 of the Canadian Criminal Code, under which 'any publication a dominant characteristic of which is the undue exploitation of sex, or of sex and any one or more of ... crime, horror, cruelty and violence, shall be deemed to be obscene'. What amounted to an 'undue' exploitation of sex was, pre-*Butler*, to be decided by the so-called 'community standards' test. In *Towne Cinema Theatres Ltd v The Queen*,[28] a decision of the Supreme Court of Canada, Dickson CJ said:

> The cases all emphasize that it is a standard of *tolerance*, not taste, that is relevant. What matters is not what Canadians think is right for themselves to see. What matters is what Canadians would not abide other Canadians seeing because it would be beyond the contemporary Canadian standard of tolerance to allow them to see it ... The operative standards are those of the Canadian community as a whole, but since what matters is what other people may see, it is quite conceivable that the Canadian community would tolerate varying degrees of explicitness depending upon the audience.[29]

Similarly to UK law, there is a 'public good defence', which applies if the defendant can establish that 'the public good was served by the acts that are alleged to constitute the offence and [that] the acts alleged did not extend beyond what served the public good'.[30]

Overall, Canadian law required the court to determine 'whether the sexually explicit material when viewed in the context of the whole work would be tolerated by the community as a whole'.[31]

A. Anti-Pornography Feminism and the Law

Feminist critiques of pornography offer a fundamentally different basis for pornography regulation from that outlined above, based not on morally conservative notions of 'obscenity', but on the harms that these materials are said to cause women. Although there are differences in emphasis between various feminist anti-pornography proponents, it is possible to identify several unifying threads:

---

[28] [1985] 1 SCR 494.
[29] ibid at 508–09.
[30] s 163(3), discussed in *Butler* [1992] 1 SCR 452 at 482–83.
[31] ibid at 486.

first, the thesis that, at least certain kinds of pornography hurt women as a class, or group (although individual women depicted in pornography may be harmed, too); second, that this harm occurs through changing or reinforcing social attitudes about gender, violence and sex; and third, this reinforcement is caused by normalising and eroticising inequality and violence.[32]

This strand of feminism reached its height during the so-called feminist 'sex wars' of the 1970s and 1980s. Emanating from North America, it was spearheaded by prominent American feminists, principally Andrea Dworkin and Catharine MacKinnon,[33] who focused on legal reform to respond to the perceived harms of pornography. The movement also sparked interest across the Atlantic, arguably inspiring activist groups like the UK's Campaign against Pornography. Dworkin and MacKinnon's attempts to introduce civil rights-based pornography regulation in the US were ultimately unsuccessful.[34] But feminist campaigners in Canada inspired by their work appeared successful in influencing legal change several years afterwards. In *Butler*,[35] the Supreme Court reinterpreted obscenity law standards in light of the principles of equality and human dignity, focusing on the degradation of and potential violence against women that may result from the spread of certain pornographic materials. The Court appeared to be strongly influenced by the legal intervention of LEAF, which had, in turn, been directly inspired by MacKinnon's work.[36]

During the late 1990s and at the turn of the century, anti-pornography rhetoric appeared to be dwindling. Yet there has been an arguable resurgence in response to rising concerns over the unprecedented ease of production, distribution and viewing of pornography, through modern technologies and the internet. In 2004, the sexually driven murder of Jane Longhurst – who was strangled to death during sexual activity – attracted high levels of media attention in the UK. During the trial, the defendant's 'extreme' or violent pornography viewing habits were emphasised.[37] In the wake of Longhurst's death, her family led an ultimately successful campaign to clamp down in England and Wales on 'extreme' and violent

---

[32] See, for example, MacKinnon (1984) 'Not a moral issue' *Yale Law & Policy Review* 321 at p 326: 'pornography institutionalizes the sexuality of male supremacy, which fuses the erotization of dominance and submission with the social construction of male and female. Gender is sexual. Pornography constitutes the meaning of that sexuality. Men treat women as who they see women as being'; McGlynn and Rackley (2014) 'Why criminalise the possession of rape pornography' Durham Law School Briefing Document at p 2: 'Rape pornography, and images of other forms of sexual violence, glorify and sexualise violence ... the proliferation and tolerance of such images, and the messages they convey, contribute to a climate in which sexual violence is condoned'.

[33] See eg Dworkin (1979) *Pornography: men possessing women*; MacKinnon (1987) *Feminism unmodified: discourses on life and law*.

[34] Most pertinently, the Indianapolis ordinance was declared unconstitutional in *American Booksellers Association v Hudnut* 771 F2d 323 (7th Cir 1985).

[35] [1992] 1 SCR 452.

[36] See Factum of the Intervener Women's Legal Education and Aid Fund at para 10.

[37] For a summary of the facts, see the Court of Appeal decision: *R v Coutts* [2005] EWCA Crim 52.

pornography, with a focus on online pornography.[38] In 2010, successful campaigns to amend the offence, thereby remedying the perceived omission of pornographic depictions of rape in England and Wales' law, were led by women's rights groups like Rape Crisis South London, and with the support of legal feminist academics Clare McGlynn and Erika Rackley.[39]

To this extent, it can be said that anti-pornography feminism has had a real impact on the legal regulation of pornography, on both sides of the Atlantic. The extent to which the resultant laws and practices have respected their feminist roots is another matter.

II. Changes in Direction

The rest of this chapter reveals that, in both jurisdictions, lawmakers and enforcers alike have failed to fully embrace this feminist ideology. The results may properly be regarded as unsatisfactory: while moral conservatives have been able to further clamp down on forms of 'aberrant' pornography, feminists are likely to regard the results with ambivalence at best.

A. Canada

As noted above, the decisive change to Canadian law came not via legislation but through reinterpretation of the legislative meaning of obscenity in the leading decision in *Butler*.[40] The Supreme Court had to consider whether Canadian obscenity law was compatible with the right to freedom of expression in s 2 of the Charter. This involved applying the s 1 general limitation clause, under which it must be determined whether limits on Charter rights are 'reasonable', 'prescribed by law' and 'can be demonstrably justified in a free and democratic society'.[41] The starting point was the rejection of the traditional aim of preventing moral harm. Sopinka J for the majority said that this aim:

> [I]s no longer defensible in view of the *Charter*. To impose a certain standard of public and sexual morality, solely because it reflects the conventions of a given community, is inimical to the exercise and enjoyment of individual freedoms, which form the basis of our social contract.[42]

---

[38] See eg 'Victim's mother in web porn plea' (4 February 2004, *BBC News*).

[39] See eg McGlynn and Rackley (2009) 'Criminalising extreme pornography: a lost opportunity' *Criminal LR* 245.

[40] [1992] 1 SCR 452 at 492.

[41] The Constitution Act 1982, Part I, Canadian Charter of Rights and Freedoms. On the Charter generally and the '*Oakes*' test in particular see Loveland's introductory chapter in this volume.

[42] [1992] 1 SCR 452 at 492.

At first instance, Wright J had held that legislation which seeks to proscribe a fundamental freedom must have as its objective a more precise purpose than simply to control the morals of society or to encourage decency. He said:

> The aim must be directed more specifically to objectives such as equality concerns, or other Charter rights, or particular human rights; otherwise, the basic freedoms in the Charter will be subject to restrictions that arise from very personal and subjective opinions of right and wrong that will be impossible to identify ... Examples of more precise aims or bases for restrictions will be ... the prevention of the circulation of pornographic material that effectively reduces the human or equality or other Charter rights of individuals.[43]

The question, as ever, was where to draw the line between merely sexually explicit material and that which promotes 'harm'. Wright J drew what was an explicable and relatively easy to apply distinction, suggesting that the law should catch:

> [O]nly those materials which contained scenes involving violence or cruelty intermingled with sexual activity or depicted lack of consent to sexual contact or otherwise could be said to dehumanize men or women in a sexual context.[44]

Under this approach, most other forms of pornography depicting nudity, masturbation, gay sex, group sex and incest would have been deemed non-obscene.[45] This would have given the newly interpreted law a degree of certainty and predictability, using categories of material that are *relatively* easy to apply. However, when the case came to the Supreme Court, Sopinka J gave a far more expansive definition of potentially obscene pornography:

> Pornography can be usefully divided into three categories: (1) explicit sex with violence, (2) explicit sex without violence but which subjects people to treatment that is degrading or dehumanizing, and (3) explicit sex without violence that is neither degrading nor dehumanizing.[46]

Sopinka J went on to explain the significance of material being placed in each of these categories:

> The courts must determine as best they can what the community would tolerate others being exposed to on the basis of the degree of harm that may flow from such exposure. Harm in this context means that it predisposes persons to act in an anti-social manner as, for example, the physical or mental mistreatment of women by men, or, what is perhaps debatable, the reverse. Anti-social conduct for this purpose is conduct which society formally recognizes as incompatible with its proper functioning. The stronger the inference of a risk of harm the lesser the likelihood of tolerance. The inference may be drawn from the material itself or from the material and other evidence. Similarly, evidence as to the community standards is desirable but not essential. The portrayal of

---

[43] (1989) 50 CCC (3d) 97 at 121.
[44] ibid.
[45] ibid at 124–25.
[46] [1992] 1 SCR 452 at 484.

sex coupled with violence will almost always constitute the undue exploitation of sex. Explicit sex which is degrading or dehumanizing may be undue if the risk of harm is substantial. Explicit sex that is not violent and neither degrading nor dehumanizing is generally tolerated in our society and will not qualify as the undue exploitation of sex unless it employs children in its production.[47]

What however, constitutes sufficient risk of harm that would lead certain types of material to be unacceptable? Sopinka J wrote:

> Some segments of society would consider that all three categories of pornography cause harm to society because they tend to undermine its moral fibre. Others would contend that none of the categories cause harm. Furthermore, there is a range of opinion as to what is degrading or dehumanizing ... Because this is not a matter that is susceptible of proof in the traditional way and because we do not wish to leave it to the individual tastes of judges, we must have a norm that will serve as an arbiter in determining what amounts to an undue exploitation of sex. *That arbiter is the community as a whole.*[48]

In this way, the notion of 'community standards of tolerance' becomes part of the test of 'harm' said to be caused by the material. We may note here the similarity of UK prosecutorial standards on when obscenity should be prosecuted: criminal activity, including the infliction of serious harm, may be considered obscene, but that this 'harm should be assessed applying contemporary social standards'.[49]

Sopinka J then cited the Report on Pornography by the Standing Committee on Justice and Legal Affairs,[50] which articulates key feminist concerns:

> The clear and unquestionable danger of this type of material is that it reinforces some unhealthy tendencies in Canadian society. The effect of this type of material is to reinforce male-female stereotypes to the detriment of both sexes. It attempts to make degradation, humiliation, victimization, and violence in human relationships appear normal and acceptable. A society which holds that egalitarianism, non-violence, consensualism, and mutuality are basic to any human interaction, whether sexual or other, is clearly justified in controlling and prohibiting any medium of depiction, description or advocacy which violates these principles.[51]

Sopinka J went on to find that the law, thus reinterpreted, was a proportionate restriction on freedom of expression as protected under the Charter:

> ... [T]his kind of expression [sexually explicit materials accompanied by violence, and those without violence that are degrading or dehumanizing] lies far from the core of the guarantee of freedom of expression. It appeals only to the most base aspect of individual fulfilment, and it is primarily economically motivated. The objective of the legislation, on the other hand, is of fundamental importance in a free and democratic society. It is aimed at avoiding harm, which Parliament has reasonably concluded will be caused

---

[47] ibid at 454.
[48] ibid at 484 (emphasis added).
[49] CPS (2019) op cit fn 25 above.
[50] MacGuigan Report (1978) at p 18:4.
[51] Cited at *Butler* [1992] 1 SCR 452 at 492–43.

directly or indirectly, to individuals, groups such as women and children, and consequently to society as a whole, by the distribution of these materials. It thus seeks to enhance respect for all members of society, and non-violence and equality in their relations with each other. I therefore conclude that the restriction on freedom of expression does not outweigh the importance of the legislative objective.[52]

Seemingly, then, Canadian law, with one judicial bound, was freed from the shackles of old-fashioned moralism and decisively reoriented towards the protection of the 'equality and dignity'[53] of disadvantaged groups in society, in particular women.

There was however a key problem in the *Butler* approach: it relied on the legal fiction that the arbiter of when material constitutes a sufficient risk of 'harm' to make the material beyond tolerance – was 'the community as a whole'. According to the judgment, such harm could come about by depicting 'degrading or dehumanising' sex, or sex with any degree of violence, even if mild and consensual. As one of us has previously argued:

> The obvious problem, of course, is that 'the community as a whole' consists in fact of a fractured range of diverse voices and views ... Inevitably it will be the judicial view of what 'the community' can tolerate that will in fact be used as the standard. It also seems odd that the actual, current standards of tolerance are used as the legal test; this means that rather than the law setting a standard of tolerance, it simply follows its perception of that of the average Canadian. This seems a strangely majoritarian view of human rights protection: courts are there not to protect inoffensive speech, which is not under threat in any event, but precisely that speech that does 'offend, shock or disturb' the average citizen. The noble idea of re-orienting the law on obscenity around the protection of fundamental constitutional values seems at this point to be in danger of collapsing into the mere reinforcement of majoritarian proclivities.[54]

Hence while rhetorically, the shift from the protection of morals to the prevention of harm is clear, in substance, the change is much less so. Harm to fundamental *values* of dignity and equality is not harm in the ordinary sense of the word and nor can it be empirically measured. As a subsequent Supreme Court decision honestly admitted, such 'social harms' are 'not ... fact[s] susceptible of proof in the traditional way ... Rather where the activities or material in question involve the degradation and objectification of women ... the law infers harm simply from that degradation and objectification.'[55]

Given both that the objection to the degradation of women is ultimately a moral one, but also that reasonable minds might differ as to what *constitutes* degradation and objectification, it is immediately apparent that the new Canadian position was in danger of simply resurrecting the very ghosts of moralism that the Supreme Court had ostensibly laid to rest.

---

[52] ibid at 509.
[53] ibid at 479.
[54] Fenwick and Phillipson (2006) op cit fn 23 at 455.
[55] *R v Mara* [1997] 2 SCR 630 at 651.

Moreover, this approach appears to pay scant regard to individual autonomy – the core right of the individual to decide what is valuable and fulfilling in life *for them* – which is meant to be a key Charter value.[56] It appears that erotic humiliation, for example, may be judicially deemed 'degrading' (and hence obscene) if 'most people' would find it 'humiliating'.[57] A situation in which people can be criminalised for distributing erotic material that those with congruent sexual preferences find arousing and liberating, on the basis that a judge thinks 'most people' would find it 'humiliating', does not seem to take autonomy seriously as a constitutional value.

B. New Legislation in England and Wales: Campaign, Consultation and Rationale

Following the campaign in memory of Jane Longhurst, ensuing debate in the House of Commons centred around the need for tougher measures against 'extreme' pornography, as a response to concerns that these kinds of materials could fuel sexual violence against women in society.[58] Shortly afterwards, the Home Office and Scottish Executive launched a public consultation on the introduction of an offence which would criminalise individuals found in possession of certain categories of 'extreme' pornography.[59] The consultation document appeared, however, to somewhat obfuscate the preceding campaigners' motivations for the offence. First, the document placed great emphasis on the fact that those individuals who were *depicted* within the materials may have been subject to violence and torture.[60] In this regard, it took a highly paternalistic approach, citing:

> [A] desire to protect those who participate in the creation of sexual material containing violence, cruelty or degradation, who *may* be the victim of crime in the making of the material, whether or not they notionally *or genuinely* consent to take part.[61]

The second, main basis for introducing the offence stemmed from 'a desire to protect society, particularly children, from exposure to such material … which may encourage interest in violent or aberrant sexual activity'.[62] This comes closer to the concerns shared by the offence's original campaigners, but with two

---

[56] See generally Dyzenhaus (1991) 'Obscenity and the Charter: autonomy and equality' 1 CR (4th) 367.

[57] *R v Hawkins* (1993) 15 OR (3d) 549 (CA) at [46]–[47]: 'Degradation may be found in sexually explicit material where people are depicted as … sexual playthings existing solely for the sexual satisfaction of others, or in subordinate roles in their sexual relationship with others, or in engaging in sexual practices that would, to most people, be considered humiliating'.

[58] *HCD* 18 May 2004 c 178 (Tim Loughton MP).

[59] Home Office and Scottish Executive (2005) 'Consultation: on the possession of extreme pornographic material'.

[60] ibid at para 5.

[61] ibid at para 34 (emphasis added).

[62] ibid.

significant deviations. First, the particular focus on children is potentially problematic: given that the offence targets individual possessors (and recalling that
the document noted that the biggest users of online pornography are children
and young people[63]), a possession offence risked primarily targeting precisely
the group it ostensibly sought to protect. Secondly, this rationale adds the aim of
tackling materials that may encourage an interest in 'violent *or aberrant*'[64] sexual
activity. The morally charged term – 'aberrance' – appears to have opened the door
for moral – as opposed to harm-based – judgments on pornography, and probably largely accounts for the appearance of 'bestiality' as an additional category
of proscribed material. Criminalising the portrayal of bestiality does not have an
obvious link with preventing harm to women and, indeed, feminist campaigners
expressed disappointment that it was included.[65] At various further points of the
consultation document, morally based justifications for the introduction of the
offence are emphasised and even favoured over harm-based or gender equality-
based arguments; for example, the proscribed categories are referred to as acts
which 'most people would find abhorrent'[66] and even 'repugnant'.[67] In fact, the
document concludes by asking consultees whether, even in the 'absence of conclusive research results as to its possible negative effects, there is some material which
is so degrading, violent or aberrant that it should not be tolerated',[68] concluding:
'although we recognise that accessing such material does not necessarily cause
criminal activity, we consider the *moral* and public protection case against allowing this kind of material sufficiently strong'.[69]

During the consultation stage, therefore, a significant part of the rationale for
introducing the offence appears to resemble something akin to the 'community
standards of tolerance' test found in Canadian obscenity law. There was comparatively less emphasis placed on the 'fuelling violence' arguments put forward by
feminist campaigners (apparently as the result of a lack of conclusive evidence for
this finding). Such concerns are diluted further by the consultation document's
reference to a smattering of further justifications, ranging from the direct harm
which may be caused to participants in these materials, to more directly 'disgust'-
based argumentation.

During the passage of the Criminal Justice and Immigration Bill, the rationale for the offence became further muddied. Arguments in favour of the offence
ranged from the images exceeding the community standards of tolerance by
their 'extreme' nature,[70] to the need to prevent harm to individuals, 'particularly

---

[63] ibid at para 6.
[64] ibid at para 34 (emphasis added).
[65] See eg McGlynn and Rackley (2009) op cit fn 39 above at pp 250–51.
[66] Home Office and Scottish Executive (2005) op cit fn 59 above at para 11.
[67] ibid at para 33.
[68] ibid at Annex A, Q2.
[69] ibid at para 52 (emphasis added).
[70] Public Bill Committee 16 October 2007, col 31 (Maria Eagle MP), available at publications.
parliament.uk/pa/cm200607/cmpublic/criminal/071016/am/71016s01.htm.

children' (although the nature of this harm was usually not elaborated upon),[71] and concerns that 'a smallish number of the population … might be susceptible to their behaviour being affected by viewing extreme pornography'.[72] Not infrequently, a combination of these rationales were used by the same person.[73] At the House of Lords stage, there was widespread criticism of the lack of scrutiny which the House of Commons had paid to the Bill.[74] Nevertheless, it was passed in May 2008.

Initial calls to add a 'rape pornography' amendment to the offence were rejected by the Ministry of Justice, on grounds that there was 'no evidence' to suggest that staged rape images involve 'any harm to the participants or causes harm to society at large'.[75] Given that the lack of evidence on these matters was evidently not found fatal in the passage of the original extreme pornography offence, this justification appears puzzling. Nevertheless, a later letter addressed to then-Prime Minister, David Cameron, calling for the material to be banned,[76] led to a change in policy, and a statement that the government intended to address this gap in the legislation.[77]

A governmental document setting out the case for change appeared to provide justifications for the amendment as diverse as those proffered for the original legislation: it was said that there was 'some evidence' that exposure to these kinds of materials could have a harmful effect on young people's attitudes, and that some men showed heightened aggression after exposure to violent pornography.[78] However, it also relied on the contention that most people would find these images 'disgusting and deeply disturbing'.[79] Finally, it argued that the amendment could play a symbolic role, signalling to society that images of sexual abuse, as well as sexual abuse itself, were not acceptable.[80] McGlynn and Rackley's argument that rape pornography causes 'cultural harm', by normalising and even sexualising violence against women within society, was cited with approval by the Joint Committee on Human Rights during its scrutiny of the relevant provisions within the Criminal Justice and Courts Bill.[81]

The resultant rationale for the extreme pornography possession offence (as amended) is much less clear than the argument, first put forward by campaigners,

[71] ibid.
[72] ibid.
[73] ibid.
[74] *HLD* 22 January 2008 cc 135, 139–40, 151 (Lord Henley, Lord Thomas of Gresford, Baroness Miller of Chilthorne Domer).
[75] Pearson, cited in 'Call to close "rape pornography website loophole"' (7 June 2013, *BBC News*).
[76] ibid.
[77] Cabinet Office 'Speech – the internet and pornography: Prime Minister calls for action' (22 July 2013, *GOV.UK*).
[78] 'Fact sheet: extension of the offence of extreme pornography (possession of pornographic images of rape and assault by penetration)' (2014) at para 6.
[79] ibid at para 7.
[80] ibid at para 8.
[81] Joint Committee on Human Rights (2014) 'Legislative scrutiny: Criminal Justice and Courts Bill: fourteenth report of session 2013–2014' at para 1.45.

that it fuels real-life instances of violence against women. While the legislative process certainly *considered* the issue of evidence of the harms of extreme pornography, this never seems to have been a determining factor. Consideration of the weak evidential basis for criminalising extreme pornography was often sidelined, or at the very least 'bolstered' by a range of morally based justifications, whether grounded on 'disgust' or 'tolerance', sending symbolic messages to the public about violence, or protecting children from corruption.[82] The development of McGlynn and Rackley's 'cultural harm' argument appears to well reflect the hybrid rationale for the offence: it *appears* to centre on harm-based concerns about fuelling violence against women, without actually going so far as to claim that the material causes this violence. Nor, indeed, does it make any clear claim about how exactly certain persons viewing extreme pornography, for example, somehow leads police and prosecutors not to take rape and other sexual offences as seriously as they might otherwise do.[83]

Above all, at no point does there appear to have been serious engagement with the question of whether, in the absence of clear indications of harms or violence against women (as traditionally understood), these morally based justifications are sufficient to criminalise individuals for merely *possessing* adult pornography – particularly where there has been no harm committed during the *production* of the material. This lack of engagement with the matter contrasts with the Canadian experience, and particularly the attempt to lay down stronger harm-based requirements for the criminal law in cases subsequent to *Butler*.[84] The issue of whether the legislation is based on a clear rationale is not a merely theoretical one: as the following subsection demonstrates, a lack of clear direction appears to have resulted in similarly unclear substantive aspects of the English and Welsh offence.[85] It may also be, in part, to blame for the problematic enforcement of the offence, considered below.[86]

i. The Offence as Enacted

This proposed new offence was a drastic roll-back on the measures proposed by campaigners and its supporters, which would have additionally introduced website-blocking powers and targeted payment and other services ancillary to the supply of pornography, among other things.[87] Further adjustments were made

---

[82] Admittedly, this last-mentioned justification is more ambiguous, in terms of whether it should be considered a harm-based justification. For one view on this see Feinberg (1987) *The moral limits of the criminal law volume 1: harm to others* at p 70.

[83] On this argument, see Rackley and McGlynn 'The cultural harm of rape pornography' (22 May 2015, *Free Speech Debate*).

[84] In particular *R v Labaye* [2005] 3 SCR 728 (hereafter '*Labaye*') discussed below.

[85] As well as that of the Northern Irish offence, which is identical.

[86] pp 198–200 below.

[87] See *HCD* 18 May 2004 cc 170–71 (David Lepper MP). These further proposals were later reflected in the Digital Economy Act 2010, Pt III, but were subsequently shelved: see Secretary of State for Digital, Culture, Media and Sport (16 October 2019) 'Online harms: written statement'.

to the content of the extreme pornography possession offence during its passage through Parliament. The provisions of the offence covering England, Wales and Northern Ireland are found in the Criminal Justice and Immigration Act 2008, ss 63–67 (CJIA 2008).[88]

One significant difference between the offence proposed within the Consultation, and the resultant enacted offence, is the breadth of sexually violent pornography covered. While the post-consultation Home Office proposal would have encompassed materials depicting 'serious sexual violence',[89] the Bill as presented (and subsequently enacted) restricted and divided this into two categories: an act which threatens a person's life; and an act which results, or is likely to result, in serious injury to a person's anus, breasts or genitals (CJIA 2008, s 63(1) (a)–(b)). Women's rights groups were quick to point out that this narrow concept of sexual violence created a gap in the offence, in particular, by excluding 'rape pornography' from its remit. The above-noted campaign to 'close the loophole'[90] resulted in a legal amendment and addition of CJIA 2008, s 63(7A), which covers rape and sexual assault by penetration.[91]

Looking more closely at the actual offence, CJIA 2008, s 63(1) makes it an offence for a person to be in possession of an extreme pornographic image. The requirement of a visual 'image'[92] renders the offence narrower than both UK and Canadian obscenity laws, which cover other media forms, including written text, audio recordings or cartoons. 'Pornography' is defined as material that is reasonably assumed to have been produced solely or principally for the purpose of sexual arousal (s 63(3)). This is judged according to the overall context in which the image is found, and is a question of fact for the jury to determine.[93] In addition to being considered pornographic, the image must be considered 'extreme', which follows a two-pronged test. First, the image must be considered 'grossly offensive, disgusting or of an obscene character' (s 63(5A)).[94] Secondly, it must depict acts, in an explicit and realistic way, which fall under s 63(7) or (7A). These are:

- an act which threatens a person's life;

- an act which results, or is likely to result in, serious injury to a person's anus, breasts or genitals;

---

[88] In Scotland, a similar possession offence was introduced in the Criminal Justice and Licensing (Scotland) Act 2010.

[89] Home Office (2006) 'Consultation on the possession of extreme pornographic material: summary of responses and next steps'.

[90] See 'Call to close "rape pornography website loophole"' (7 June 2013, *BBC News*).

[91] Through the Criminal Justice and Courts Act 2015, s 37.

[92] Defined further in CJIA 2008, s 63(8).

[93] On trial for indictment. See Ministry of Justice (2009) 'Possession of extreme pornographic images and increase in the maximum sentence for offences under the Obscene Publications Act 1959: implementation of ss. 63–67 and s.71 of the Criminal Justice and Immigration Act' (Circular No 2009/01) at para 10.

[94] ibid, para 3. It appears that this requirement was intended to ensure parity with the Obscene Publications Act 1959, considered above, which continues to provide a criminal offence for the production and distribution of obscene materials.

- an act which involves sexual interference with a human corpse;

- a person performing an act of intercourse or oral sex with an animal (whether dead or alive);

- an act which involves the non-consensual penetration of a person's vagina, anus or mouth with the other person's penis or other part of the other person's body or anything else.

For materials involving bestiality, or rape pornography, the persons or animals depicted therein must also be such that a reasonable person looking at them would think they were real (s 63(7)). For these materials, therefore, there is a double, 'realistic' standard that must be met, relating to both the act and the 'participants'.

The 'realistic' requirement(s) means that certain staged or simulated acts are covered by the offence. This was no oversight, but designed for the purpose of avoiding 'insuperable' evidential hurdles in determining that the acts actually took place.[95] The interpretation of this threshold in practice can be questioned, with some arguing that charges have been successfully brought against material which contains 'clearly and not especially realistically' staged acts.[96] However, from an anti-pornography feminist perspective, if the intention is to target 'cultural harm' caused by sexist and sexually violent imagery, then its 'realism' may be considered irrelevant.[97]

The final, and most novel, element of the offence is that it targets 'pure' possession (ie possession without intent to further distribute). Although 'possession' is not defined in the Act, it is now clear that it takes a similar approach to other possession offences, for example, in the case of drugs or child sexual abuse material.[98] Demonstrating 'possession' therefore entails a two-step test. First, the defendant must have 'custody and control' of the images. This significantly limits the potential applicability of the offence in the context of internet-based pornography: watching online streaming videos or merely viewing images online will usually not meet the threshold, since the content is not, without more, stored on hardware which can be said to be in the defendant's custody and control. Usually, this means the individual in question would have to deliberately download online material, in order for it to come into their custody and control. Once deleted, moreover, it will no longer be considered to be in their possession, unless they have the technical knowledge and means to retrieve it.[99] Secondly, there must be proof that the defendant knew of the materials' existence. They do not, however, need to know the precise nature of the content – in other words, they need not know that the

---

[95] Home Office and Scottish Executive (2005) op cit fn 59 above para 38.

[96] Attwood and Smith (2010) 'Extreme concern: regulating 'dangerous pictures' in the United Kingdom' *Journal of Law and Society* 171 at p 178.

[97] See Public Bill Committee (session 2013–2014) 'Criminal Justice and Courts Bill: written evidence submitted by End Violence against Women Coalition (CJC04)' at para 2.3, available at https://publications.parliament.uk/pa/cm201314/cmpublic/criminaljustice/memo/cjc04.htm.

[98] See *R v Ping Chen Cheung* [2009] EWCA Crim 2965 at [14].

[99] *R v Porter* [2006] 1 Cr App R 25.

images depict 'extreme pornographic' content.[100] In the case of *Ping Chen Cheung*, therefore, where the defendant was found with a collection of DVDs (some of which contained depictions of bestiality), the fact that the defendant claimed not to know about the content of the DVDs was irrelevant: knowing that he had been carrying DVDs was sufficient to shift the burden of proof on to the defendant to establish that he had not seen, and did not know or have cause to suspect, the content of the materials (a defence under s 65(2)(b)).

There is some ambiguity surrounding the possession test and the status of online images that have been stored on a device's cache system,[101] or automatically downloaded – for example, through phone messaging applications.[102] Online data (including images) can be automatically stored on a computer's hard drive within the cache. This renders that data available offline – in other words, within the individual's *physical* possession. Following the approach taken in cases involving possession of child sexual abuse materials, for an individual to be found liable for materials stored in the cache, it must be shown that they were aware of the existence of a cache of images.[103] The result is that the criminal liability of someone viewing extreme pornography online will depend on the rather arbitrary, dual matters of whether the material has been automatically stored in their device's cache (and not subsequently deleted – whether automatically or manually), as well as their individual level of IT knowledge. In relation to materials automatically downloaded to a device's memory, the case of *Okoro* has made clear that this is highly likely to constitute 'control and custody'. Applying the test of knowledge, a defendant need not know the content of the images; only that they received images as such.[104] In *Okoro*, therefore, the defendant's conviction for receiving unsolicited extreme images through WhatsApp was upheld. In light of this case law, we can seriously question the suitability of a possession offence when applied to the digital sphere. The rules surrounding automatic storage risk turning criminal liability into a game of Russian roulette, rather than a targeted approach to weeding out the most harmful of content (and prolific of users).

Material that has been classified by the video regulatory body, the British Board of Film Classification (BBFC), is excluded from the offence (s 64(1)) – unless certain images have been 'extracted' from the classified work, for the (reasonably assumed) purpose of sexual arousal (s 64(3)(b)). GIFs, memes and video clips extracted from even classified films could therefore fall under the offence. In addition, it is a defence to show that the defendant had a legitimate reason for possessing the image (s 65(2)(a); for example, for the purpose of conducting official police work), or where they were sent the image without prior request, and did

---

[100] [2009] EWCA Crim 2965 at [15].

[101] On cache systems, see further Park, Lang and James (2017) 'Possession of child exploitation material in computer temporary internet cache' *Journal of Digital Forensics, Security and Law* 7.

[102] *R v Okoro (Cyprian)* [2019] 1 WLR 1638, which involved images downloaded automatically through WhatsApp.

[103] *Atkins v DPP* [2000] 1 WLR 1427 at 1440.

[104] *R v Okoro (Cyprian)* [2019] 1 WLR 1638 at 1648.

not keep it for an unreasonable amount of time (s 65(2)(c)). Finally, s 66 provides a defence for individuals who have consensually and directly participated in the depicted acts (catering for 'homemade' pornography), as long as it can be shown that there was no infliction of non-consensual harm, that any portrayed 'corpse' was not, in fact, a corpse, or that any portrayed non-consensual penetration was, in fact, consensual. On the other hand, an individual who directly participated in apparent depictions of bestiality will not be able to avail themselves of the s 66 defence, even where they can show that the 'animal' (or sexual act performed upon or by it) was not real. There is no obvious justification for this anomaly.

Those found guilty of an offence under the subsections concerning portrayal of life-threatening acts, serious injury to specified body parts, or 'rape pornography' will be subject to up to three years' imprisonment. For the remaining acts – necrophilia and bestiality – a maximum sentence of two years' imprisonment can be imposed. Those who receive a sentence of above two years' imprisonment will also be made subject to statutory notification requirements; that is, they will be registered as sex offenders and subject to a number of related restrictions.[105]

III. Criminalising Pornography: Feminist Success, or Damp Squib?

It is a trite but nonetheless important observation that shifts in legal doctrine, whether through the enactment of new legislation or judicial reinterpretation of existing legal norms, may prove to have limited, partial or unexpected effects in practice. This phenomenon is evident in both the UK and Canada in respect of their pornography laws.

A. Canada

LGB groups have argued that pornography made for them may be particularly important, since it affirms and celebrates their sexuality, and may assist them in developing it, in a hostile or unsympathetic, certainly heterosexual-dominated, environment.[106] It was particularly unfortunate, therefore, that one of the high-profile targets of the new *Butler*-style obscenity law were the owners of Little Sisters,[107] a lesbian and gay bookshop, which carried a range of sexually explicit material aimed at the gay community generally. It was found that:

> Customs officials had not only wrongly delayed, confiscated, destroyed, damaged, prohibited or misclassified materials imported by the appellant on numerous occasions,

---

[105] Sexual Offences Act 2003, Sch 3, para 35A, as inserted by CJIA 2008, Sch 26, para 58(2).
[106] *Little Sisters and Art Book Emporium v Canada* [2000] 2 SCR 1120 at [247].
[107] ibid.

but that these errors were caused 'by the systemic targeting of Little Sisters' importations in the [Vancouver] Customs Mail Center'.[108]

As Binnie J for the majority observed:

The administration of the [customs legislation] was characterized by conduct of Customs officials that was oppressive and dismissive of the appellants' freedom of expression. Its effect ... was to isolate and disparage the appellants on the basis of their sexual orientation.

In short, as the trial judge had concluded, 'untrained Customs officials were too quick to equate homosexuality with obscenity'.[109]

The case merely demonstrated the obvious: the more broad and open-ended the definitions used by the law are, the more discretion is vested in the enforcement authorities. A definition that uses terms such as 'degrade or dehumanise' is wide open to abuse, simply because such judgments will inevitably be coloured by the personal standards and tastes of the individuals making the judgments. The *Little Sisters* case was by no means an isolated incident: further cases include *Scythes*, involving lesbian erotica, discussed further below;[110] and the detention by customs officers of gay male pornography, some in short story form, destined for Glad Day Bookshop, which the judge found 'dehumanising' and hence obscene, because there was no suggestion of 'real meaningful human relationships', just casual sex with strangers, 'involving oral and anal sex with excessive descriptions which are degrading'.[111]

Thus pornography aimed at the LGB community became an unintended but significant target of the 'new' law. But what of the material that feminists hoped and expected it to catch? A study examining a 15-year period after *Butler* (1998–2012) could find 'only three judicial decisions and one jury verdict in obscenity cases involving pornography that was alleged to be violent or degrading to women'.[112] Only one of these eventually resulted in conviction (with a lowered sentence on appeal);[113] three resulted in acquittals.[114] *Butler* thus appears to have proved a rhetorical, but not a substantive, victory for anti-pornography feminists.

Moreover, the same study notes that in most of the cases charged during this period, the material was discovered 'in the course of some other investigation' (including in relation to child sexual abuse material), or after specific complaints were made from the members of the public, 'some of whom wondered if they might have viewed internet recordings of rapes or murders'.[115] In other words,

---

[108] ibid at [1] and [40] (Binnie J).
[109] ibid at [37].
[110] Below at pp 201–203.
[111] *Glad Day Bookshop v Deputy Minister of National Revenue (Customs & Excise)* [1992] OJ 1466 at [81] and [102].
[112] Benedet (2015) op cit fn 7 above p 18.
[113] *R v Smith* (2005) 76 OR (3d) 435, (2005) 198 CC (3d) 399 (CA).
[114] *R v Price*, 2004 BCPC 103; *R v Latreille*, 2007 QCCA 1330; *Remy Couture* (22 December 2012, unreported).
[115] Benedet (2015) op cit fn 7 above pp 20–21.

policing of the obscenity offence, post-*Butler*, has been more the result of hazard, than of active pursuit.

Meanwhile the Supreme Court decision in *Labaye*[116] did two things that tightened up the law. First, it was much clearer than *Butler* that harm had to manifest in concrete terms. *Butler* was expressed primarily in terms of harm but, as argued above, the notion of harm employed remained often highly abstract and closer to the notion of harm to values, than to anything more concrete.[117] Second, *Butler* had equivocated on the issue of *evidence* of harm, allowing it to be assumed in cases involving violent material and watered down to deference to the legislature's 'reasoned apprehension of harm' in relation to non-violent but degrading pornography.[118] *Labaye* both recast harm in much more narrow terms and demanded real evidence of causality:

> If the harm is based on predisposing others to anti-social behaviour, a real risk [of] … this effect must be proved. Vague generalizations that the sexual conduct at issue will lead to attitudinal changes and hence anti-social behaviour will not suffice. Attitudes … are not crimes, however … disgusting. What is required is proof of links, first between the sexual conduct at issue and the formation of negative attitudes, and second between those attitudes and a real risk of anti-social behaviour.[119]

This may have made police and prosecutors more hesitant to bring cases, given the uncertainty surrounding what might constitute the required evidence of causation of harm.

However, the core problem remained the continuing influence of the community standards test, which has seriously limited the feminist potential of Canadian obscenity law. The test originally came about because the statutory wording which, as noted above, defines as obscene the 'undue' exploitation of sex, led to judges invoking the notion of community standards in order to avoid being seen as simply applying their own standards. As seen, the Supreme Court in *Labaye* sought to recast the offence as being about harm but, out of deference to the original purpose of the legislature, felt unable to jettison the role of community standards. Instead, its function was altered. Rather than acting as the arbiter of moral acceptability it now acts as a kind of gateway through which the harm argument has to pass: instead of the court simply deciding whether material is harmful, it has to decide whether the degree of harm posed by the material is such that Canadians would not tolerate other Canadians viewing it. This then leads to the problem that the very prevalence of violent or dehumanising pornography – which of course would *increase* the harm, on the anti-pornography feminist account – leads to the

---

[116] *R v Labaye* [2005] 3 SCR 728.

[117] pp 185–88 above.

[118] pp 185–86 above.

[119] *Labaye* [2005] 3 SCR 728 at [58]. The case actually concerned the archaic offence of 'keeping a common bawdy-house' (hence the reference to 'sexual conduct'), but in doing so, it directly relied on and applied the *Butler* test. See also Loveland's critique of the Supreme Court's use of 'evidence' in political libel cases; pp 150–54 and 157–64.

conclusion that Canadians seemingly do tolerate the harms of such porn, because they are apparently consuming it in large numbers.

Thus in *Price*, the court refused to convict because 'the contents of the [materials alleged to be obscene], coupled with their widespread availability, satisfies [the judge] that Canadians, for better or for worse, tolerate other Canadians viewing explicit sexual activity coupled with graphic violence'.[120] As one feminist commentator despairingly notes, 'the men accused in these cases have secured acquittals by pointing to the prevalence of misogynistic sexually violent material as part of the mainstream. The community standards test has allowed the pervasiveness of pornography to become its own defence'.[121] This turns the feminist argument on its head: it is precisely community standards on gender and sex that pornography is said to damage; and yet, they are being used to judge the very pornography that has – on the anti-pornography feminist analysis – so damagingly distorted them.

B. England and Wales: Early Indications

A decade after the Act's introduction, the number of prosecutions brought for possession of extreme images appears to still be in a state of flux. The number initially rose year-on-year,[122] reaching its peak in 2016–17 with nearly 2,000 prosecutions.[123] This number almost halved in 2018–19, to 1,075 prosecutions.[124] In spite of this volatility, it is clear that the offence has been more successful, purely in terms of uptake, than its Canadian counterpart. It is worth looking into these figures in a little more depth, however. This figure does not take into account the 'rape pornography' amendment under s 63(7A). Since its enactment, prosecutions under subsection 7A have risen from three (2015–16) to a modest 28 (2018–19).[125] Data also suggests that the vast majority of prosecutions and convictions are being secured for 'bestiality': according to research by McGlynn and Bows, conducted through freedom of information requests to police forces across England and Wales, this constitutes 85 per cent of charged cases;[126] rape pornography, by contrast, makes up only one per cent.[127]

There are a number of possible explanations for the offence's disproportionate use against depictions of bestiality: one is its definitional ease. The other subsection (7) categories use relative or open-ended terms, such as 'likely', 'serious risk' and 'life-threatening'. Meanwhile, the 'rape pornography' provision entails an

---

[120] *R v Price* 2004 BCPC 103, at [99].
[121] Benedet (2015) op cit fn 7 above p 28.
[122] With the exception of 2012–13, where there was a minor decrease.
[123] Crown Prosecution Service (2019) 'Violence against women and girls report (2017–2018)' p A50.
[124] ibid, p A53.
[125] ibid.
[126] McGlynn and Bows (2019) 'Possessing extreme pornography: policing, prosecutions and the need for reform' *The Journal of Criminal Law* 473 at p 481.
[127] ibid.

examination of whether an image portrays non-consensual activity – this may be impossible to determine, where the surrounding context of a still image or short clip is lacking. By contrast, the definition of bestiality (sexual activity with an animal) is relatively straightforward to apply. Difficulties in categorisation of acts may therefore account for some of this discrepancy.

It also cannot be ruled out that the comparative social taboo attached to bestiality has had an influence on its high prosecution and conviction rates. In other words, given widely held attitudes of disgust vis-à-vis bestiality, those involved in law enforcement and judicial processes may instinctively feel that such materials should be criminalised. It should be underlined, in this context, that that the CPS charging practice for extreme pornography possession appears to be quite discretionary.[128]

By contrast, and as noted in the Canadian context, depictions of sexual violence against women are so widespread (and attract such widespread acceptance) that law enforcement and jurors alike may be hesitant to condemn them as criminal.[129] This fundamentally puts into question the efficacy of the criminal law as a tool for tackling widespread and socially embedded regressive attitudes: rather than tackling them, it may risk being used to further enforce them. If the criminal justice system is itself a source of gendered harms and attitudes, using it to prosecute pornography risks replicating and reinforcing sexist outcomes rather than tackling them.

Regardless of the explanations for it, once the disproportionately high rates of prosecution for bestiality are excluded, enforcement in both jurisdictions is more comparable. Both have seen extremely low prosecution rates for materials that could be seen as contrary to principles of gender equality.

When it comes to equality of enforcement, the extreme pornography offence appears to have suffered from the same substantial 'teething problems' encountered by its Canadian counterpart. It is disturbing to note that one of the early cases brought under the offence related to images depicting consensual homosexual group sex.[130] At trial, the case turned on whether acts like 'fisting' and 'urethral sounding'[131] were considered to be extreme, on the basis of being likely to result in 'serious injury'. This was despite the fact that, just several months previously, a jury had acquitted a defendant under the OPA 1959, on grounds that videos containing acts of fisting, among other things, were *not* considered obscene[132] (recall that the extreme pornography possession offence was intended to be in parity with the obscenity standards of the OPA 1959). The defendant was acquitted (not without

---

[128] CPS (updated 10 September 2019) 'Legal guidance: extreme pornography': when determining whether prosecutions should be brought for cases involving 'serious injury', in particular, a number of public interest considerations should be borne in mind. Consent to prosecute must be granted by the Director of Public Prosecutions.
[129] Benedet (2015) op cit fn 7 pp 25–28.
[130] *R v Walsh* (8 August 2012, unreported).
[131] The insertion of an object into the urethra.
[132] *R v Peacock* (6 January 2012, unreported).

serious reputational damage), and the CPS Guidance has since been amended.[133] Yet the case serves as another concerning example of pornography laws potentially being used in accordance with problematic, hetero-normative standards, rather than – as had been intended – to fight against them.

Conviction rates also appear to be very low, when compared to the number of prosecutions brought under CJIA 2008, s 63. According to a freedom of information request, there were just 405 convictions in the entire period between 2009–14.[134] This might further support the argument that there is a lack of certainty as to the materials deemed to fall under the offence. Given the level of stigma attached to conviction for such an offence, this discrepancy is a cause for concern: those who are found innocent of any criminal wrongdoing may nevertheless have their livelihoods – and lives – ruined by highly public criminal investigations and court hearings which centre on their private sexual fantasies. Indeed, there have been a number of high-profile reports of individuals losing their jobs, facing health problems and/or familial breakdowns, and becoming the target of harassment and attacks, as the result of (ultimately unsuccessful) criminal investigations into whether they were in possession of extreme pornography.[135]

Echoing the Canadian experience, research suggests that the majority of prosecutions are brought *in addition* to other, primarily sexual, offences.[136] In a significant number of Court of Appeal judgments involving extreme pornography possession offences, convictions for possession of child sexual abuse material had also been secured.[137] Moreover, usually the number of extreme pornography images in these cases paled in comparison to the numbers of child sexual abuse images found to be in the defendant's possession; an extreme example is *R v Southwell*, which involved 76,000 indecent images of children, compared to 26 extreme pornographic images.[138] It also appears that the extreme images were not infrequently discovered during the course of investigations into other crimes (eg child sexual abuse images).[139] This use of the offence – as a 'bolt-on' to other, more serious criminal charges, and where the extreme material has been found (often coincidentally) in the course of reactive policing – seriously brings into question the commitment of those enforcing and pursuing it as an offence in its own right.

In conclusion, we can say that the first decade of the offence's enforcement in England and Wales reveals it to have been far from a feminist success. In most

---

[133] See CPS (2019) op cit fn 128 above.
[134] See Antoniou and Akrivos (2017) *The rise of extreme porn* at p 203. Again, the vast majority of convictions were brought on grounds of bestiality under CJIA 2008, s 63(7)(d).
[135] See, for example Roberts 'Simon Walsh: How bodged arrest and "profoundly damaging" false charges have ruined my City Hall career' (14 August 2012, *Evening Standard*) and Peachey 'Six months on bail – for being sent spoof video of a 'tiger' having sex, that was really a man in a tiger suit' (26 October 2014, *Independent*).
[136] McGlynn and Bows (2019) op cit fn 126 above pp 486–87.
[137] See recently *R v Weall* [2019] EWCA Crim 1166; *R v Connor* [2019] EWCA Crim 234; *R v Al Mahmood* [2019] EWCA Crim 788; *R v Wilkinson* [2019] EWCA Crim 641.
[138] [2012] EWCA Crim 2882.
[139] Antoniou and Akrivos (2017) op cit fn 134 above.

instances, there has been no attempt whatever actively to target those, for example, repeatedly viewing pornography depicting rape or serious violence. Rather, most prosecutions have resulted from extreme images which have 'turned up' during investigations for other offences. Instead, the offence has been used in a manner which reinforces problematic attitudes in relation to materials which attract 'disgust' (overwhelmingly, bestiality), while leaving almost untouched potentially problematic depictions of violence and non-consensual activity. It also appears to be enforced in a way which attracts the least amount of resistance (namely, as a 'bolt-on' to other offences, or as the collateral of unrelated investigations), rather than with an eye to the transformative, women's rights-enhancing purpose which feminist proponents hoped it would have. When we look at the record of actual prosecutions, it seems that 'moral disgust' has comprehensively 'trumped' feminist principle. As discussed above, the very aims of those introducing the legislation seemed to be an uneasy mixture of feminist concern and moral disgust. This confused rationale is likely a contributing factor to the offence's subsequent, problematic implementation.

C. Radically Feminist in Substance?

A comparison of the substance of both jurisdictions' offences can be helpfully illuminated by a case study. In the Canadian case of *R v Scythes*,[140] *Bad Attitude* (a lesbian sex magazine) published a short, erotic work of fiction, under the title of 'Wunna my fantasies'. The story concerns a female perpetrator, who follows another woman into the shower, grabs her, ties her up, slaps her and pulls her hair. The victim 'succumbs' and the two have seemingly consensual sex. It was found to have breached the Canadian obscenity test, in the wake of *Butler*'s equality-based interpretive gloss.[141] One can see how the story could be considered problematic, from an anti-pornography feminist perspective. It describes initial non-consensual violence (albeit minimal) and restraint, which, on that basis, could be viewed as degrading. The story's conclusion with apparently consensual sex could, additionally, be seen to reinforce problematic attitudes about women's enjoyment of subjection to coercion in a sexual context. The gender of the perpetrator does not necessarily change this.[142]

---

[140] [1993] OJ 537.

[141] The case may have been decided differently today, in light of *Labaye*.

[142] This is not intended to dismiss arguments relating to the transgressive potential of 'queer' pornography (on this, see further Stychin (1995) *Law's desire: sexuality and the limits of justice*). The explanation above gives one plausible interpretation, only – an anti-pornography feminist one. For an alternative reading of 'Wunna my fantasies', see Ross, '"It's merely designed for sexual arousal": Interrogating the indefensibility of lesbian smut' in Bell, Cossman, Gotell and Ross (1997) *Bad attitude(s) on trial: pornography, feminism and the Butler decision*.

It is clear, however, that possession of 'Wunna my fantasies' would not consti-tute an offence under the law of England and Wales.[143] In the first place, the extreme possession offence covers only realistic and explicit *images*. This appears to result, in part, from the fact that law reform was motivated by an increase in online and predominantly visual pornographic material.[144] There also appears to be a wider presumption that visual materials have more of an impact on the recipient.[145] It is further clear that the somewhat porous rationale for the offence may have had an influence in restricting the offence to images: if the purpose of the offence is, at least in part, to prevent and stop the circulation of depictions of real-life violence against women, then limiting the law to realistic images appears to be more readily justifiable.[146] The restriction is less clear, however, if the aim is to tackle materials which may fuel later acts of violence against women, including by having some kind of general, deleterious effect on cultural attitudes to women, consent and sexual violence. No evidence was presented at any stage of the English and Welsh legislative process, which would suggest that realistic, explicit images have a greater impact on recipients than other forms of materials (or even than other forms of images).[147]

Additionally, 'Wunna my fantasies' would not fall under any of the listed acts under the extreme pornography offence. In spite of the victim being clearly and repeatedly assaulted, the violence would not come anywhere near the high thresholds of an act likely to result in 'serious injury' to the breasts, anus or genitals; nor would any of the acts be considered 'life-threatening'. Although fisting is involved during the later sexual act, it appears clear, after *Walsh* and the CPS Legal Guidance as amended, that this would not reach the necessary threshold for likely serious injury: at any rate, the fact that fisting takes place is hardly the reason why feminists might take issue with the piece. Finally, given that the later sexual acts appear to take place consensually (with the 'victim' even instructing the perpetrator), it seems highly unlikely that the material would be eligible to be considered to fall under s 63(7A) (sexual assault by non-consensual penetration). Therefore, although there are elements of sexual violence and non-consent throughout the narrative, the English and Welsh offence's narrow list of categories would restrict consideration of the story as a series of individual acts, which do not reach the required, 'extreme' threshold for the offence by themselves. Such an approach appears to be a poorly adapted method for considering the effects which material may have upon its audience.

---

[143] Nor the rest of the UK. Further, it would also be unlikely to fall under the OPA 1959.

[144] Although, in that case, the further threshold that the images must be 'realistic' is not immediately obvious.

[145] Fenwick, (2017; 5th edn) *Fenwick on civil liberties and human rights* at p 402.

[146] Of course, audio-recordings or written entries may also record a real-life crime, but their veracity may be more difficult to determine than in the case of photographic evidence.

[147] Indeed, in their written evidence on the amending Bill, the End Violence Against Women Coali-tion noted, with criticism, that 'the requirement for the image to be "explicit and realistic" will exclude a great deal of imagery that is, nevertheless, harmful in that it promotes violence', including cartoons: See Public Bill Committee (session 2013–2014) op cit fn 97 above.

Moreover, the offence's preoccupation only with acts that reach the 'extreme' end of the spectrum of violence or non-consensual activity is a questionable standard, if the aim is to tackle materials which may fuel misogyny and acts of violence against women, more broadly. The focus on 'extremity' makes more sense, however, if the offence's rationale also incorporates a desire to tackle serious, real-life crimes to those depicted in the images, or to tackle materials which the majority of society might deem 'aberrant' – bearing in mind that the very concept of 'extremity' revolves around a deviation from the norm.[148] Once more, therefore, we see that the broad and confused rationale for the extreme pornography offence may have influenced (and, indeed, diluted) its anti-pornography feminist credentials in substance. At the same time, even on the 'extreme' end of the spectrum, the s 63 offence is lacking: it would not, for example, capture the possession of pornography showing even the most gruesome sexual torture of a woman, so long as it did not injure her anus, genitals or breasts, or threaten her life. Among the long list of potential gaps would therefore be, for example, gross forms of sexual torture involve the cutting or branding of the buttocks, which (assuming they were unlikely to reach the 'life-threatening' threshold) would not fall within the offence.

If the UK position seems in some ways under-inclusive, the Canadian has the opposite problem. As just seen, the new-style Canadian law led to the prosecution of a small-circulation lesbian publication because of an erotic fantasy involving comparatively mild themes of (initial) non-consent with some minimally rough sex.[149] This, while Canadians are completely free to read the vast swathes of erotica dealing with fantasies of rape and other forms of sexual violence freely available online.[150] Indeed, considering the most explicit scenes of the torture, mutilation and murder of women found even in mainstream, popular films such as *Hostel*, *Saw* or *American Pscyho*, the impugned content of 'Wunna my fantasies' looks vanilla indeed. This makes such offences look not only *unjust* but *ineffective* – given the prevalence of (sexual) violence in both mainstream films and in pornography and erotica freely available online, does anyone really believe that convicting a tiny handful of rather randomly selected people could plausibly make any difference to general cultural attitudes towards sex and gender?

IV. Broader Comparative Perspectives

A significant difference between the Canadian and UK offences lies in which actor they target. While the Canadian offence targets the producer, distributor or disseminator, the UK offence introduced the novel element of targeting the

---

[148] On this see eg Dymock (2013) 'Criminalising extreme pornography: five years on – Dymock on the question of regulating pornography: is criminalisation the answer?' (22 May 2013, *Inherently Human*).

[149] pp 201–02 above.

[150] eg *Literotica.com* lists 26,538 stories in the category of 'Non-Consent/Reluctance', 36,279 in the category of BDSM and 49,513 in the category of 'Incest/Taboo'.

consumer (or 'possessor'). It is worth considering which offence is best placed to target the harm envisioned by anti-pornography feminists. Presumably, the aim of law enforcement in this area would be to discourage and reduce the amount of damaging pornography in circulation, or, at the very least, to 'send a clear message'[151] against the sexist and sexually violent messages it may contain, with the goal of thereby promoting a culture of gender equality and non-violence against women.

A. Targeting Publication/Distribution *versus* Possession

On the one hand, a production/distribution-based offence faces clear limitations in tackling the global phenomenon of online pornography, which may frequently have been produced and hosted extra-territorially. According to one analysis, 86 per cent of the world's pornographic web pages are hosted in the US and the Netherlands. The UK hosts a mere seven per cent of all pages, while Canada lays claim to a paltry 0.3 per cent.[152] In the consultation document, the UK Home Office and Scottish Executive sought to justify their proposal of a possession offence on precisely this basis.[153] Canada's 'interpretive gloss' upon its traditional, obscenity-based 'production/distribution' offence is therefore severely limited in its ability to tackle the reality of the modern-day (online) pornography market. Its application to territorial producers and distributors – a tiny fraction of the global market – massively constrains its ability to affect the amount of material in circulation, and readily accessible to Canadians through the internet. If the ready availability of violent, degrading or dehumanising pornography is a serious problem, this is quite simply not a serious method of tackling it.

Yet the UK's possession-based offences are also problematic. Most significantly, targeting individual possessors arguably does not get to the heart of the 'harm' (on this feminist view) caused by extreme pornography. Throughout their works on the subject, McGlynn and Rackley make clear that the 'cultural harm' of extreme pornography, by definition, goes beyond the attitudes and behaviours of the individuals who personally watch (or possess) these materials: it impacts on *culture*.[154] Accordingly, those who produce and disseminate extreme pornography are, surely, more obviously 'responsible' (if anyone is to be considered so on an individual basis) for any of its culturally harmful effects.[155] Individual recipients

---

[151] McGlynn, quoted in 'Academics back ban on rape porn' (22 July 2013, *The Northern Echo*).

[152] See data compiled by the filtering company Metacert in Walsh (2015) 'Why the UK government is wrong to think it can control 93% of all pornography' (3 August 2015, *Metacert Blog*).

[153] Home Office and Scottish Executive (2005) op cit fn 59 above para 22.

[154] See eg Rackley and McGlynn (2015) fn 83 above; (2014) 'Why criminalise the possession of rape pornography?' *Durham Law School Briefing Document*; fn 39 above, pp 256–58.

[155] Images criminalised by the possession offence should also be criminalised under the OPA 1959, which does target producers and disseminators of pornography. This is subject, however, to the same significant jurisdictional limitations that were outlined earlier.

of material, on the other hand, play a less obviously culpable role in the creation, modification or enforcement of culture at large.

In reply, it might be argued that certain material which glorifies or advocates rape or serious sexual violence against women is analogous to, or a form of, hate speech against women.[156] However, that in itself provides no rationale for prosecuting mere possession; neither UK nor Canadian hate speech laws make it an offence merely to read hateful material: the offence consists of inciting others to hatred, or 'promoting hatred'.[157] Hence, the speaker, not the audience, is the target. This possession offence looks like the equivalent of prosecuting those who pick up leaflets left by a racist speaker, regardless of whether they applaud the racist message or greet it with vocal and passionate opposition.

Notwithstanding the individual possessors' tenuous influence upon 'cultural harm', a number of further, pragmatic justifications have been offered for extending the criminal law to them. First, it could be argued that targeting possessors disrupts the supply-demand chain for this material.[158] As seen, it is difficult for any individual jurisdiction to directly tackle the amount of online extreme pornography in circulation (the supply) but, according to this thesis, targeting domestic consumers may lower demand and thereby reduce the incentive for producing and disseminating this content in the first place. This justification is based on several questionable assumptions. The most obvious is that it appears to forget the very premise on which it is based: online pornography is a global market, upon which the UK, individually, has a very limited influence. This applies just as much to its domestic consumer market, as it does to its domestic producers and distributors. Even assuming that the law would deter some in the UK from possessing pornography, this would not realistically have a significant impact upon the global demand – and supply – of material.[159] It should also be recalled that the offence's limitation to 'possession' excludes perhaps the most common forms of online pornography access, including streaming and merely 'viewing' images online.[160] Finally, applying a capitalistic supply-demand theory seems dubious, when large amounts of pornographic materials are accessible for free.

Secondly, some of the feminist literature has argued that criminal law may play a symbolic or educative role.[161] On this theory, extreme pornography possession offences may send a message, backed by the authority of the criminal law, that

---

[156] One of the feminist supporters of *Butler*, Kathleen Mahoney, makes precisely this argument: Mahoney (1992) '*R v Keegstra*: a rationale for regulating pornography?' *McGill LJ* 242.

[157] See the UK Public Order Act 1984, s 18 and (as amended) the Canadian Criminal Code, s 319.

[158] Home Office and Scottish Executive (2005) op cit fn 59 above para 23.

[159] Though it is possible this would lead to less exposure for those in the UK, which might, in turn, have some indirect impact on national culture. This, however, is separate to the argument about the supply-demand chain.

[160] Unless, of course, these viewed images are automatically stored on the cache, as discussed above.

[161] See eg McGlynn and Rackley (2017) 'Image-based sexual abuse' *Oxford Journal of Legal Studies* 534 at pp 552–53.

sexual violence against women is not tolerated in society.[162] This justification is problematic in light of the offence's current form and implementation: its focus on 'extremity', the inclusion of obscenity and disgust standards, and its continued, overwhelming enforcement against depictions of bestiality, among other things, send no clear message about gender equality.[163]

More fundamentally, we should be sceptical about pragmatic justifications for imposing sanctions on individuals who are not centrally responsible – or culpable – for the 'harm' in question.[164] Merely targeting domestic possessors because of technical difficulties in getting hold of extra-territorial producers and distributors appears cynical – and, frankly, lacking in imagination. It should also be recalled that the harm in question (ie from an anti-pornography feminist perspective) is abstract and causally diffuse: it concerns itself with a range of potential harms to women as a group which certain kinds of pornography might influence, through changing or reinforcing social attitudes. Even if it was accepted that possessors played some culpable part in this process, labelling them as 'sex offenders' (and punishing them as such) seems inappropriate. The possession offence therefore also raises serious questions about its rational connection and proportionality to the harm envisioned.

We can conclude that both jurisdictions' target groups come with serious limitations, both in terms of reducing the amount of perceived, problematic material in circulation, and more broadly, in tackling the potential messages and influence that these materials may have. The Canadian approach of merely targeting distributors and producers is anachronistic and ill-suited to the modern pornography landscape. The UK approach, on the other hand, risks not just impotency (from a feminist perspective), but also constituting a disproportionate interference in the lives of individuals.

It is outside the scope of this chapter to give detailed consideration to alternative regimes for tackling materials (pornographic or otherwise) that may undermine gender equality. It should be clear, however, that measures which aim to reduce the production and circulation of harmful online content should ideally take a global approach, favouring international co-operation and harmonisation. The primary aim should be to tackle production and distribution directly. In the absence of an agreed global approach, a much more limited, country-specific action that could be taken would be requiring internet service providers to geo-block access from within the territory to sites hosting certain forms of extreme pornography.[165] For example, blocking access to sites that truly glorify and advocate sexual violence would be both a more serious attempt to tackle the problem, and a non-punitive one.

---

[162] McGlynn (quoted in 2013) fn 151 above.

[163] See eg Cowen (2016) 'Briefing paper – nothing to hide: the case against the ban on extreme pornography' *Adam Smith Institute* at pp 11–12.

[164] See the discussion at pp 193–95 above. In theory the offence applied online could catch someone who stumbles across an illegal image in a collection of otherwise lawful images on a website, and looks away, repelled, forgetting at the time that a copy may now be stored on their computer's cache.

[165] Indeed, this was one of a package of such measures contained within the Digital Economy Act 2017, Pt III, as well as within HM Government (2019) 'Online harms white paper'.

Rather than ruining the life of individual users – who may themselves pose no risk of perpetrating damaging social attitudes – such a step could prevent hundreds of thousands of users from accessing this content.[166] Finally, if the ultimate goal is to tackle potentially harmful social attitudes, the most obvious means of doing so would be widespread educational programmes and sustained awareness-raising measures.

B. The Role of Constitutional/Human Rights Considerations

As we have seen, the entire process of reform through reinterpretation in Canada was driven by the Supreme Court's interpretation of the Charter. The Court's primary focus was on the equality and dignitarian rights of women and others portrayed in pornography, but the case law is also notable for the careful proportionality analysis by which it was determined that the obscenity laws, as recast by the Supreme Court, were a justifiable restriction (under s 1) on the right to freedom of speech. Indeed, the initial impetus for reform came from the clear finding by the majority in *Butler* that old-fashioned concerns about the adverse moral impact on individuals and society did not provide a justification under the Charter for the continued use of obscenity laws against sexually explicit material.[167] Hence in Canada, whatever one thinks of the soundness of the reasoning and the results of the *Butler* decision, it is clear that rights-based arguments flowing from the Charter were situated front and centre of the debate.

By comparison, human rights law has barely figured in the UK debate. This is despite the fact that, under the Human Rights Act 1998 (HRA 1998), all legislation must be interpreted compatibly with the rights identified in Sch 1 of the Act,[168] including Art 3 (prohibition of torture) and Art 14 (prohibition of discrimination), on the one hand, and Art 8 (respect for private life) and Art 10 (freedom of expression) on the other. All public authorities must also act compatibly with these rights.[169] During parliamentary scrutiny of the 2014 amendment to add 'rape pornography' to the possession offence, the Joint Committee on Human Rights made a short, factual claim that the measure was equality-enhancing.[170] Few others in England and Wales have sought to frame feminist arguments about extreme pornography's potential harms to women explicitly within the language of human rights.

More strikingly still, there has been virtually no engagement at all with the serious interferences with human rights that are posed by this offence, which

---

[166] We suggest this as a possibility that could be an improvement on the possession offence; whether it could work in practice would depend upon a number of factors not considered here.

[167] pp 184–87 above.

[168] HRA 1998, s 3(1); the applicable rights in the European Convention on Human Rights are defined in s 21.

[169] HRA 1998, s 6(1); there are exceptions in s 6(2) where incompatible legislation requires or clearly mandates action incompatible with the Convention rights.

[170] Joint Committee on Human Rights (2014) op cit fn 81 above para 1.45.

criminalises people in relation to an intimate area of their private lives. While concerns about the offence's grave impact on the private lives of those targeted by it have been occasionally raised throughout the reform debates,[171] it has generally been answered by a vague reference to the need for proportionality. Restrictions on the (usually commercial) production or distribution of pornography are considered primarily through the framework of freedom of expression (Art 10), wherein it usually ranks as relatively 'low-value' speech.[172] This may have encouraged the view that criminal sanctions for pornography are not generally a cause for major concern in human rights. However, this fails to recognise the significance of this offence catching individual *possession*, and hence impacting primarily on the private sexual lives of individuals. There is some recognition of this point in the current Legal Guidance produced by the CPS, which states simply that, having regard to Art 8 of the Convention, the threshold for prosecuting cases under CJIA 2008, s 67(3)(b) ('serious injury') 'should be a high one'.[173] However, a number of cases bring into question how high this threshold is in practice,[174] and it is curious and unsatisfactory that the legal guidance restricts explicit human rights considerations to only one category of 'extreme' acts. In reported cases, meanwhile, discussion of the offence's impact upon the human rights of those caught by it appear to be entirely lacking. This is all the more troubling given that, on the face of it, what we have here is an extremely serious intrusion into private life. Moreover, as detailed throughout this chapter, it appears difficult to claim that the offence is 'necessary in a democratic society' as Art 8(2) requires, given that it is very hard indeed to point with confidence to any real countervailing benefit to society in criminalising the group (mere 'possessors') targeted by this legislation.

Admittedly, the European Court of Human Rights has traditionally provided little further guidance in this area, tending to take a 'hands-off' approach when considering countries' pornography regulation schemes.[175] There is some evidence of a growing interest in change at the European level, with increasing focus on gender and human rights-based harms of pornography.[176] As one of us has argued elsewhere, however, caution must be exercised to ensure that this is done in a robust and balanced manner.[177] The highly intrusive nature of the UK's possession offence should not be overlooked in these emerging human rights debates.

---

[171] See eg *HLD* 22 January 2008 c 160 (The Earl of Onslow).

[172] *Butler*, fn 52 above; *Belfast City Council v Miss Behavin' Ltd* [2007] 1 WLR 1420 at 1426 (Lord Hoffmann).

[173] CPS (2019) op cit fn 128 above.

[174] See discussions of cases, fn 134 above.

[175] See further Johnson (2014) 'Pornography and the European Convention on Human Rights' *Porn Studies* 299 at p 316.

[176] See the Concurring Opinion of Judge Pinto de Albuquerque in *Pryanishnikov* (Application no 25047/05) judgment of 10 September 2019; Resolution 1835(2011) of the Parliamentary Assembly of the Council of Europe on violent and extreme pornography; Parliamentary Assembly of the Council of Europe (2019) Motion for a resolution on gender aspects and human rights implications of pornography.

[177] Beattie (2019) '*Pryanishnikov v Russia* (App No 25047/05), judgment of 10 September 2019 – setting the foundations for human rights discourse on pornography' 6 *European Human Rights LR* 654.

V. Conclusions

The comparative analysis undertaken in this chapter has been a tapestry of similarity and contrast. The two jurisdictions have each taken an area of law bequeathed by Victorian sexual moralism and sought to take it in a new direction, replacing concerns for moral corruption with a seeming determination to tackle the influence of material thought to threaten the interests of women in dignity, equality and freedom from violence. In each case, however, the application of the law has done very little to further these goals. In practice, the law has in both countries too often veered back into the well-trodden path of reinforcing majoritarian moral and disgust-based sentiment. What we have termed the 'ghosts of moralism' have not only exercised a powerful hold over prosecutorial and police practice in enforcing these laws; they have also resulted in offences that in their mixed content (the jumbled categories of forbidden material in England and Wales) and their doctrinal intricacies (the lingering influence of 'community standards' in Canada) are thoroughly compromised in their purported pursuit of egalitarian goals. Indeed, the enforcement of these laws against those with minority sexual preferences and tastes has turned them at least at times into an engine for *inequality*, in which the distaste of 'most people' for a minority sexual practice can morph into a reason for punishing it. If these laws are meant to uphold and reinforce human dignity, then, to this extent, both countries seem to have lost sight of individual autonomy as a key dignitarian value. As one member of a minority sexual community states: 'The things that seem beautiful, inspiring and life-affirming to me seem ugly, hateful, and ludicrous to most other people.'[178] Sadly, the law in both the UK and Canada has allowed itself at times to become little more than a tool for the enforcement of majoritarian proclivities on those whose sexual tastes seem merely ugly to others.

What is surprising about our comparison is the way in which each country pursued reform through such markedly different means: in the UK, through brand new legislation, setting out specific and narrow categories of material that it is prohibited to possess; in Canada, by judicial interpretation of existing law, using broad concepts like 'degrading and dehumanising', thereby catching a potentially wide swathe of sexually explicit material.[179] The contrast in reliance upon constitutional, or human rights, guarantees, has also been stark: while the UK's human rights approach is notable only for its general absence, arguments grounded in the Canadian Charter were front and centre of reform.[180] And yet in both countries, each of the mixed rationales, the mixed legal content and the thoroughly mixed

---

[178] Califia (1988) *Macho Sluts* at p 9.

[179] The same distinction is evident in relation to political libel laws; see ch 5 herein.

[180] The absence is also anomalous in the light of the centrality of human rights arguments within the UK's response to other issues analysed in this volume; see especially Draghici's chapter on assisted dying; Easton's discussion of the prisoner voting rights laws, Loveland's critique of political libel law and Hatzis's and Taylor's respective critiques of various laws relating to freedom of religious expression and behaviour.

results of the new legal directions taken in criminalising pornography have been strikingly similar, strikingly disappointing.

In neither jurisdiction has a really forensic examination of the available evidence, in the attempt *not* simply to engage in sentiment-driven law reform, played a major role. However, insofar as experience has differed here, the comparison throws up a perhaps mild surprise: a common strength of legislatures is often said to be their ability to gather a wide range of evidence so as to produce better policy than can a court, informed only by the arguments that counsel may choose to make, in a bilateral dispute.[181] However, what we have found is that, in the UK, politicians showed little concern for harm and evidence-based arguments and, as we have seen, actually supported moves to widen the scope of the possession offence in 2015. In Canada, by contrast, judicial reform has, over time, tightened and narrowed the law, attempting at least to move it away from protecting majoritarian sentiment and towards a far greater concern with harm and evidence. While this attempt has been only a partial success, it contrasts sharply with the UK experience.

---

[181] Tomkins (2005) *Our Republican Constitution* at pp 27–29.

7

'Labouring under the Canadian Constitution' Revisited

KD EWING*

I. Introduction

In this chapter I revisit an article I wrote jointly with Tim Christian in 1988, entitled 'Labouring under the Canadian Constitution'.[1] One of the purposes of writing our article was to consider a trilogy of labour cases decided by the Supreme Court of Canada in the context of British proposals for a Bill of Rights, which at the time were gathering support on the centre-left. The article was published in the same year that Charter 88 was launched and a few years before Liberty's proposed Bill of Rights. This was a time when the Thatcher assault on civil liberties was at its peak, trade unions reeling from the policing of the miners' strike, the ban on trade unions at GCHQ, and three major pieces of legislation eating away at their rights to organise, bargain and strike. One of our concerns was to urge caution on the part of those British trade unions that saw a Canadian-style Charter of Rights as an answer to their prayers, given the approach of the Supreme Court in the three labour cases decided in quick succession in 1987.[2]

These cases followed a predictable lack of engagement by common law courts to labour rights at the time, leading us to conclude that a Bill of Rights of the kind then proposed in Britain would be not only counterproductive but also ineffective. As a result, we concluded that trade unions would be better advised to campaign politically for a better framework of labour law under a progressive government than rely on courts and litigation to free them from growing restraint. As coincidence would have it, 1988 was the same year in which a new saviour arrived on the British scene, in the form of Jacques Delors, who as President of the European

* My thanks to Peter Barnacle, who was counsel to the Saskatchewan Federation of Labour at the time of *Saskatchewan Federation of Labour v Saskatchewan* 2015 SCC 4, discussed below. I remain responsible for views expressed and the errors to be found in the pages that follow.

[1] Christian and Ewing (1988) 'Labouring under the Canadian Constitution' *Industrial LJ* 73.
[2] *Reference re Public Service Employee Relations Act, Labour Relations Act and Police Officers Collective Bargaining Act* (1987) DLR (4th) 161; (hereafter *Alberta Reference*). This was followed by the Supreme Court in *Public Service Alliance of Canada v Canada* (1987) 38 DLR (4th) 249 (hereafter *PSAC*), and *Government of Saskatchewan v Retail, Wholesale & Dept Store Union, Locals 544, 496, 635 and 955* (1987) 38 DLR (4th) 277 (hereafter *RWDSU*).

Commission gave his famous speech to the TUC announcing Social Europe.[3] The promise that under EC law every worker would be protected by a collective agreement was rhetorical rather than realistic, but it was enough to persuade hitherto sceptical British trade unionists that the solution to their problems lay in the new political direction that was being charted in Europe, with Jacques Delors' commitment to lead in the following year to the EU Charter of the Fundamental Rights of Workers, and an Action Plan to go with it.

In the end, of course, this was not the answer either, the effective application of EC law depending to a large extent on receptive Member States willing to support the development of social rights at EC level, and to implement them in a purposive way at national level. We now know that the benefits of EC and subsequently EU law are contestable. But they did not stop the attack on trade unions, nor under a Labour government did they lead to trade union rights being fully restored to anything near where they were pre-Thatcher. So does the human rights/labour rights approach as pursued by Canadian trade unions have a renewed appeal? It is not revealing too much at this stage to say that the labour trilogy of the 1980s has given way to a new optimism – a new labour trilogy, reaching its apotheosis in the *Saskatchewan Federation of Labour* (hereafter *SFL*) case in which the Supreme Court capped the repudiation of the trilogy 30 years earlier by holding that the freedom of association includes the right of trade unions to strike.[4]

That was a huge leap forward, which invites placing an additional introductory marker, namely the growing importance of international treaties in human rights and constitutional litigation at national level. The importance of these treaties is particularly notable in some jurisdictions in the Westminster tradition which have dualist systems in which courts have traditionally eschewed giving domestic legal effects to international law.[5] In Canada and the UK the wall separating national and international law is crumbling, with the recent labour cases in Canada's Supreme Court providing evidence of that collapse as the Court integrates the standards of the International Labour Organisation (ILO) into its dynamic constitutional jurisprudence. If the original labour trilogy of the 1980s was a cause for pessimism on the part of the labour movement, is the new approach of the Supreme Court a cause for optimism and engagement, an optimism reinforced by the progressive development of remarkably similar jurisprudence of the Strasbourg Court?

Indeed, it is a striking feature of Canadian developments that they track an almost identical path to that cut by the ECtHR in the development of jurisprudence under ECHR Art 11.[6] It is true that the language of the Convention and

---

[3] Delors (1988) *1992: the social dimension* (address by President Delors at the TUC – Bournemouth, 8 November 1988).

[4] *Saskatchewan Federation of Labour v Saskatchewan* 2015 SCC 1, [2015] 1 SCR 245.

[5] See *Reference Re Weekly Rest in Industrial Undertakings Act, Minimum Wages Act and Limitation of Hours of Work Act* [1937] AC 326; *Re Alberta Union of Public Employees and Alberta* (1980) 120 DLR (ed) 590; on which see Bendel (1981) 'The international protection of human rights: a Canadian case study' *Ottawa LR* 169.

[6] See Ewing and Hendy (2010) 'The dramatic implications of *Demir and Baykara*' *Industrial LJ* 2. See also the articles by Peter Barnacle referred to at fn 86 below.

the Charter is different. The ECHR expressly mentions trade unions in Art 11(1) in contrast to the lack of any mention in the Charter's s 2(d), a textual difference that could potentially make it more difficult for the Supreme Court to keep pace with the Strasbourg Court. It is perhaps a measure of the progressive nature of the Supreme Court's recent jurisprudence that it has not only kept up with Strasbourg developments, but in some respects has gone beyond them. Some significant judicially inspired restraints on trade unions produced by the Strasbourg judges have no parallel in Canada.[7] So while the middle of the journey has been different, both Courts have moved from a position of a general denial of trade union rights to one of equivocal embrace. As we will see, however, the equivocation is very important.

Yet although the landscape has changed dramatically, it is not clear that different circumstances necessarily lead to different conclusions, albeit that the reasons for these conclusions may have changed. In what follows, I begin by contextualising the discussion with a brief account of labour law in Canada, the potential role of the Charter to underpin the system, and the Supreme Court's unwillingness in the labour trilogy in the 1980s initially to engage. This is followed by an examination of the slow journey to *SFL*, in which the Supreme Court finally recognised the right to strike as an integral feature of freedom of association, having also recognised a right to organise and a right to bargain collectively en route. Why then would there be cause for anything other than unalloyed joy, recent developments surely confounding the claims Tim Christian and I made in 1988? That is one of the key questions to be explored in the pages that follow, in which it is contended – perhaps paradoxically – that the 'progressive' jurisprudence nevertheless vindicates the original scepticism in 'Labouring under the Canadian Constitution'.

II. Labour Law and the Charter

Labour law is primarily a provincial matter in Canada, unlike in the US, and although there is a federal labour law jurisdiction, this has a relatively limited scope.[8] There are important differences between the Canadian jurisdictions, though the structure is basically the same, with what is referred to as a 'Wagner-style' collective bargaining system, supplemented by minimum standards legislation. The system takes its name from Senator Robert Wagner, who is credited with having played a prominent role in the enactment of what is the National Labor Relations Act of 1935, a US federal statute that formed the basis for the regulation of labour relations in Canada after the Second World War, albeit with important improvements.

---

[7] Notably *Young, James and Webster* [1981] ECHR 4, and its progeny. Compare *Lavigne v Ontario Public Service Employees Union* [1991] 2 SCR 211.

[8] See for example *Toronto Electric Commissioners v Snider* [1925] AC 396; *Canadian Pacific Railway v Attorney General of British Columbia* (Empress Hotel) [1950] AC 122; *Reference re Validity of Industrial Relations and Disputes Act (Stevedores)* [1955] SCR 529.

Wagner is nevertheless widely recognised by labour lawyers as a flawed model that creates too many obstacles to establishing effective collective bargaining arrangements. These flaws have been confirmed by the experience of other common law jurisdictions that have adopted and tried largely in vain to improve Wagner's bequest.

The essence of the Wagner model is as follows. In order to secure bargaining rights for a particular bargaining unit within an enterprise, a union must be certified as a bargaining agent. Certification is possible only if the union has first demonstrated majority support in an election of the workers in the bargaining unit in question. In some Canadian jurisdictions, majority support could be established as an alternative to an election by 'card check', whereby the union demonstrates to the relevant administrative agency (usually a labour relations board, of which the Central Arbitration Committee would be a close parallel in the UK) that a majority of workers in the bargaining unit are members of the union. This has many advantages over the US system of mandatory ballots, which provide the employer with a better opportunity to disrupt the union by hostile and intimidatory campaigning against certification, often with the assistance of external labour consultants (sometimes referred to as 'union busters'), who are extremely effective.[9]

Once a union is certified, the employer and the trade union are expected to enter into collective bargaining with a view to creating a collective agreement to regulate terms and conditions of employment for the workers in the bargaining unit. The agreement will be for a fixed number of years, and will apply to all the workers in the bargaining unit in question, including non-members. However, by virtue of what is referred to as the 'Rand formula' (after the judge – Ivan Rand – who was its author in 1946), in some Canadian jurisdictions all members of the bargaining unit will be required by the collective agreement to make a payment in lieu of union membership if they are not already members of the union. In return, these employees will enjoy the benefits of the agreement and the uplift it will typically provide, as well as a right to be fairly represented by the union, usually in relation to grievance, discipline and dismissal. The latter are important features of collective agreements in systems where historically there has often been no statutory protection against unfair dismissal.

Under this system the right to strike is heavily circumscribed, with industrial action normally forbidden during the lifetime of the collective agreement, which is a legally binding contract between employer and union, unlike in the UK.[10] Indeed, the whole purpose of the Wagner model is to maintain industrial peace, which the collective agreement is intended to create for the length of the agreement, with an expectation that any disagreements about the terms of the agreement will be

---

[9] Gould (1993) *Agenda for reform: the future of employment relationships and the law*, esp ch 9.

[10] See *Ford Motor Co Ltd v AUEFW* [1969] 2 QB 303; Trade Union and Labour Relations (Consolidation) Act 1992, s 179. For the transformative implications of the collective agreement in the Canadian system in contrast, see *McGavin Toastmaster Ltd v Ainscough* [1976] 1 SCR 718.

resolved by procedures established by the agreement itself.[11] It is only when the agreement ends and the parties are negotiating a new agreement that either side is entitled to resort to industrial action as a way of imposing its will (lock-outs in the case of employers, and strikes in the case of unions). That said, Canadian jurisdictions are generally unwilling unconditionally to respect the right to strike even in these limited circumstances, and governments in various jurisdictions have taken steps of various kinds to frustrate trade union action.

Nevertheless, the structure just described has been fairly stable throughout Canada since the end of the Second World War. But this is not to deny tensions in its operation as evolving economic arrangements have led to pressures of various kinds for change. So issues arise because some categories of workers are excluded from these statutory systems, or because the threshold for being certified as a bargaining agent is too high, or because as an anti-inflation device collective agreements are temporarily frozen with renegotiation of terms forbidden. Otherwise, there are also issues about restrictions on an already narrowly circumscribed right to strike, whether in the form of statutory bans for certain categories of worker, or ad hoc measures legislating strikers back to work – a uniquely Canadian solution to the adverse impact of industrial action. Exclusions, qualifications and restrictions of these various kinds are by no means unusual, and the introduction of the Charter in 1982 raised questions about the extent to which the post-war statutory model would now be better protected by the new constitutional guarantees.

These were perhaps optimistic questions, given that there was no inclusion of labour rights in the Charter, which is a compendium of civil and political, not social and economic rights. Rigidly maintaining this distinction, in the first labour trilogy the Supreme Court by a majority revealed no desire to advance labour rights on the back of s 2(d)'s protection for freedom of association.[12] As a result, statutory restrictions on public sector strikes in Alberta were held by the majority to be beyond the reach of the Charter (*Alberta Reference*), a decision then applied to federal legislation extending the life of collective agreements (*PSAC*), and subsequently back to work legislation in Saskatchewan as the blunt response to a dairy workers' strike in the mid-1980s (*RWDSU*). It seemed little consolation that the Chief Justice (Dickson) wrote a strong dissent in *Alberta Reference* (joined by Justice Wilson).[13] But it was to be an important dissent, the history of labour engagement with the Charter being in part the history of how that dissent became the majority position in *SFL*.

---

[11] On the Wagner model and its Canadian significance, see *Health Services and Support – Facilities Subsector Bargaining Assn v British Columbia*, 2007 SCC 27, [2007] 2 SCR 391.

[12] The Supreme Court took the view that the Charter protection of freedom of association was protection for an individual rather than a collective right, and did not extend to inherently collective action of the kind undertaken by trade unions: *Alberta Reference* (1987) DLR (4th) 161 at 219 et seq (McIntyre J). See discussion in Christian and Ewing fn 1 above pp 80–82.

[13] Justice Wilson was in due course to write another powerful pro-union judgment in *Lavigne v Ontario Public Service Employees Union* [1991] 2 SCR 211. It is an approach with which British labour lawyers are unfamiliar.

III. *Dunmore*: Turning the Tide

The process of change began fairly gingerly in *Dunmore v Ontario*,[14] which concerned the removal of agricultural workers from the coverage of the Ontario Labour Relations Act (LRA), with the result that they had no right to organise, bargain or strike. Not only were these workers denied the benefits of the legislation, the amending legislation also declared void all collective agreements negotiated on behalf of agricultural workers while the LRA was applicable to them, and more remarkably enacted that any collective agreement concluded by the voluntary recognition of the union by the employer outside the statutory procedure would also cease to apply. Following the labour trilogy, an application to the courts by farm workers to challenge their exclusion nevertheless seemed hopeless. In an important first step in a new direction, however, the Supreme Court held by a majority that s 2(d) was now to be construed 'to protect the full range of associational activity contemplated by the *Charter* and to honour Canada's obligations under international human rights law'.[15]

To do this, it would be necessary to extend the meaning of s 2(d) beyond that set out in *Professional Institute of the Public Service of Canada v Northwest Territories (Commissioner)*.[16] In that case, Sopinka J distilled principles established in the first labour trilogy to mean that the Charter had recognised four separate propositions concerning the coverage of s 2(d):

> [F]irst, that s.2 (d) protects the freedom to establish, belong to and maintain an association; second, that s.2(d) does not protect an activity solely on the ground that the activity is a foundational or essential purpose of an association; third, that s.2(d) protects the exercise in association of the constitutional rights and freedoms of individuals; and fourth, that s.2(d) protects the exercise in association of the lawful rights of individuals.[17]

These were rights of individuals, which did not recognise any autonomous right of organisations such as trade unions. In a notable step forward, however, it was held in *Dunmore* that:

> [B]ecause trade unions develop needs and priorities that are distinct from those of their members individually, they cannot function if the law protects exclusively what might be 'the lawful activities of individuals'. Rather, the law must recognize that certain union activities – making collective representations to an employer, adopting a majority political platform, federating with other unions – may be central to freedom of association even though they are inconceivable on the individual level.[18]

This did not mean that the essential features of the labour trilogy would be reversed, but it did mean that certain unspecified 'collective activities must be recognized if

---

[14] [2001] SCR 91.
[15] ibid at [13].
[16] [1990] 2 SCR 367.
[17] ibid at pp 401–02.
[18] *Dunmore v Ontario* [2001] SCR 91 at [17].

the freedom to form and maintain an association is to have any meaning'.[19] The obvious question here is this: what activities? In its early jurisprudence the ECtHR had said something similar, holding that it was enough that trade unions were permitted means by which their voice could be heard, without protecting any particular form of trade union conduct.[20] Taking a slightly different approach, the Court in *Dunmore* said that although there was no duty to have in place 'right to organise' laws, the exclusion of vulnerable groups where such rights did exist could lead to a breach of the Charter s 2(d). But it was also said unhelpfully that while 'the exclusion of agricultural workers from the *LRA* substantially interferes with their fundamental freedom to organize', it did not follow that these workers were entitled to the full protection of the LRA.[21]

As we have seen, there are three core labour rights: the right to organise; the right to bargain; and the right to strike. *Dunmore* was concerned only with the first; the Supreme Court was constrained at the time by the labour trilogy from going any further until the trilogy was overruled. According to Bastarache J, the minimum required to give effect to the Supreme Court's cautious reappraisal was 'a regime that provides agricultural workers with the protection necessary for them to exercise their constitutional freedom to form and maintain associations',[22] which meant that

> the statutory freedom to organize in s.5 of the LRA ought to be extended to agricultural workers, along with protections judged essential to its meaningful exercise, such as freedom to assemble, to participate in the lawful activities of the association and to make representations, and the right to be free from interference, coercion and discrimination.[23]

The aforementioned s 5 provides that 'Every person is free to join a trade union of the person's own choice and to participate in its lawful activities'.

As already suggested, however, it was 'misguided' to think that 'minimum legislative protection cannot be extended to agricultural workers without extending full collective bargaining rights'.[24] On this the Court was quite specific: its decision did not require 'the inclusion of agricultural workers in a full collective bargaining regime, whether it be the *LRA* or a special regime applicable only to agricultural workers'.[25] Although the Court perhaps squeezed as much as it could from the space left by the labour trilogy, the decision was nevertheless an uncomfortable attempt to navigate between Canada's international obligations and the constitutional legacy of the labour trilogy. It is thus a notable feature of *Dunmore* that Canada's international human rights obligations in the labour field were

---

[19] ibid.
[20] See *National Union of Belgian Police v Belgium* [1975] ECHR 2; *Swedish Engine Drivers' Union v Sweden* [1976] ECHR 2; and *Schmidt and Dahlstrom v Sweden* [1976] ECHR 1.
[21] *Dunmore v Ontario* [2001] SCR 91 at [48].
[22] ibid at [67].
[23] ibid.
[24] ibid.
[25] ibid at [68].

comprehensively canvassed by the majority,[26] and it is a notable feature of these obligations that they went very much further than the Court felt able to go. Indeed, ILO standards mandated precisely what the majority rejected, ie the extension of full collective bargaining rights to agricultural workers.

Nevertheless as Bastarache J pointed out, ILO Convention 87 – ratified by Canada in 1972 – provides by Art 2 that 'workers and employers, *without distinction whatsoever*, shall have the right to establish and … to join organisations of their own choosing', and that only members of the armed forces and the police may be excluded. These 'broadly worded provisions' confirmed that 'discriminatory treatment implicates not only an excluded group's dignity interest, but also its basic freedom of association',[27] a point 'further confirmed by the fact that Article 2 operates not only on the basis of sex, race, nationality and other traditional grounds of discrimination, but on the basis of <u>any</u> distinction, including occupational status'.[28] The latter point was reinforced in the specific context of agricultural workers by ILO Convention 11 – to which notably reference was made despite Canada not having ratified it. Convention 11 could not be more clear in its reference to a duty to 'secure to all those engaged in agriculture the same rights of association and combination as to industrial workers'.[29]

IV. *BC Health Services*: Repudiating the First Labour Trilogy

Dunmore was an important first step in breaking free from the labour trilogy and in acknowledging the importance of international labour conventions, even if the Court was unwilling to go all the way towards full compliance with the treaties in question. A much bigger step in this direction was taken in *BC Health Services and Support v British Columbia*[30] (hereafter *Health Services*), which was concerned not with the removal and exclusion of a defined category of workers from the collective bargaining process, but with – inter alia – the statutory annulment of collective agreements negotiated for workers who were very definitely included. Here the Court now expressly repudiated that aspect of the labour trilogy that collective bargaining was excluded from constitutional protection, holding that the grounds advanced in the earlier decisions 'do not withstand principled scrutiny and should be rejected'.[31]

---

[26] ibid at [16], [27].

[27] ibid.

[28] ibid, referring to Swepston (1998) 'Human rights law and freedom of association: development through ILO Supervision' *International Labour Review* 169.

[29] ILO Convention 11 (Rights of Association (Agriculture) Convention, 1921) Art 1.

[30] *BC Health Services and Support – Facilities Subsector Bargaining Assn v British Columbia*, 2007 SCC 27, [2007] 2 SCR 391.

[31] ibid at [22].

One reason for the repudiation is that the exclusion of collective bargaining from Charter protection was 'inconsistent with Canada's historic recognition of the importance of collective bargaining'.[32] According to McLachlan CJC, 'the history of collective bargaining in Canada reveals that long before the present statutory labour regimes were put in place, collective bargaining was recognized as a fundamental aspect of Canadian society', adding that historically, it emerges as the most significant collective activity through which freedom of association is expressed in the labour context.[33] The willingness to imply a right to bargain collectively based on Canadian identity is not to be underestimated. Apart from distinguishing Canada from the US in treating collective bargaining as a constitutional issue, the Court is making another – more profound – statement of difference with the US, namely that Canada is a social liberal society, based on 'human dignity, equality, liberty, respect for the autonomy of the person and the enhancement of democracy'.[34]

Apart from reasons based on national identity, the Supreme Court was strongly influenced by the fact that 'collective bargaining is an integral component of freedom of association in international law, which may inform the interpretation of Charter guarantees'.[35] Thus, although 'the incorporation of international agreements into domestic law is properly the role of the federal Parliament or the provincial legislatures', Canada's international obligations can nevertheless 'assist courts charged with interpreting the *Charter*'s guarantees'.[36] This takes us back to Dickson CJC's powerful dissent in the *Alberta Reference* (expressly acknowledged in *Health Services*), and it picks up a thread woven into *Dunmore*, where the Court felt constrained to take into account 'international human rights' standards, by which at this stage it meant only relevant ILO Conventions.[37] Nevertheless, in addition to ILO Conventions 11 and 87, the Court in *Dunmore* was also guided unusually by ILO Convention 141 – another unratified treaty – dealing with rural workers, providing specifically for the right to organise to anyone 'engaged in agriculture, handicrafts or a related occupation in a rural area'.[38]

This acknowledgment of the importance of international standards was carried to a new level in *Health Services*, with the court relying heavily on an expanded range of treaties to which Canada was a party to justify its decision that collective bargaining was now protected by the Charter.[39] The treaties in question included the ICCPR and the ICESCR, though neither expressly refers to collective bargaining. Reference was also made to ILO Convention 87 and the ILO Declaration of

---

[32] ibid at [20].

[33] ibid at [41] and [66].

[34] ibid, at [81]. In relation to 'enhancement of democracy', the contribution was to workplace democracy (ibid at [82]). This was a long distance from the decision in *PSAC* 30 years earlier.

[35] ibid at [20].

[36] ibid at [69].

[37] *Dunmore v Ontario* [2001] SCR 91 at [27].

[38] ILO Convention 141 (Rural Workers' Organisations Convention, 1975) Art 2(1).

[39] *BC Health Services and Support – Facilities Subsector Bargaining Assn* [2007] 2 SCR 391 at [69]–[79].

the Fundamental Rights of Workers of 1998, the reference to the former drawing academic criticism on the ground that the promotion of collective bargaining is governed by ILO Convention 98 and not Convention 87, Canada not having ratified Convention 98 at the time.[40] Needlessly, much was made of this pointless distinction, for it is clear from the ILO Constitution that Canada has obligations to promote collective bargaining (of which it has been reminded repeatedly by the ILO Freedom of Association Committee), obligations reinforced by the ILO Declaration of Philadelphia of 1944 (which was not referred to by the Court). These obligations exist independently of Conventions 87 and 98.[41]

But whether or not the Court was right to rely on Convention 87 (which Canada had ratified), as a source of the right to bargain collectively, the point for present purposes is that the reference to ILO standards (which also set the minimum standard for trade union rights in the ICESCR and the ICCPR) makes clear that the standard below which it ought not to be possible to fall is the standard set by the ILO. That standard is developed in a comprehensive jurisprudence of two specialist ILO committees, the Freedom of Association Committee (CFA) (applicable to Canada by virtue of membership of the ILO),[42] and the Committee of Experts (which will now supervise Canada's compliance with ILO Convention 98, since ratification in 2017).[43] Notably, the CFA subsequently held that the legislation annulling collective agreements that was being challenged in *BC Health Services and Support* was a breach of ILO standards. Although this was not referred to in *Health Services*, the matter was revisited by the court subsequently in *Ontario v Fraser*,[44] where it was pointed out that:

> The decision rendered by the ILO Committee on Freedom of Association ('CFA'), in the conflict between the employees of the B.C. health services and the government of British Columbia, concerned the very conflict that formed the factual background of the decision in *Health Services*. After applying Convention No. 87 and noting that Canada had not ratified *Convention (No. 98) concerning the application of the principles of the right to organise and to bargain collectively*, 96 U.N.T.S. 257 ('Convention No. 98'), the CFA concluded that the action of the government of British Columbia violated the employees' right to freedom of association. It stated that the unilateral cancellation of collective agreements 'may have a detrimental effect on workers' interests in unionization, since members and potential members could consider it useless to join an organization the main objective of which is to represent its members in collective

---

[40] Langille (2006–2007) 'Can we rely on the ILO?' *CLELJ* 273; Langille (2009) 'The freedom of association mess: how we got into it and how we can get out of it' *McGill LJ* 177.

[41] See Ewing and Hendy (2012) 'Giving life to the ILO – two cheers for the Supreme Court' in Faraday, Fudge and Tucker (eds), *Constitutional labour rights in Canada: farm workers and the Fraser case* ch 11.

[42] ILO (2018) *Compilation of decisions of the Committee on Freedom of Association* (6th edn).

[43] On which see, ILO (2012) 'Giving globalisation a human face: general survey on the fundamental conventions concerning rights at work in the light of the ILO Declaration on Social Justice for a Fair Globalization, 2008'.

[44] [2011] SCR 3.

bargaining, if the results of bargaining are constantly cancelled by law' (Report No. 330 (2003), vol. LXXXVI, Series B, No. 1, at para. 304).[45]

This reference subsequently in *Fraser* to the CFA's comments to justify the approach in *Health Services* was made in response to a strong dissent by Rothstein J in the *Fraser* case. Armed with the scholarly writings of Brian Langille,[46] Rothstein J argued that the Court had been mistaken to rely on a treaty that Canada had not ratified at the time, which in any event 'conceives of collective bargaining as being a process of "voluntary negotiation" that is fundamentally distinct from the model of collective bargaining incorporated in the Wagner model'.[47] Rothstein J was not persuasive, nor was his critique; neither was that of Langille. That said, it is hard to exclude the possibility that both Rothstein and Langille had an effect in diluting the content of Charter protection of freedom of association. The annulment by the Court of the offending legislation in *Health Services* was arguably the high-water mark of the Charter's engagement with labour rights, from which there has been a notable regression in relation to the constitutional protection for collective bargaining in particular. So although a decision of great importance for labour standards globally, *Health Services* was soon revealed to be fragile and vulnerable, reinforcing the quiet scepticism of progressive labour lawyers at the time about its real and lasting impact.

V. *Fraser*: Two Steps Forward, One Step Back

Health Services nevertheless appeared initially to be the complete vindication of those who saw the virtues of constitutional protection of labour rights, and thought that the scepticism on display in 'Labouring under the Canadian Constitution' was misplaced. That being the case, this might well have been the time for a recantation. Recantation, however, would have been a mistake. For just as the sceptics in 1988 could not see far enough into the future to imagine *Health Services* 20 years later, nor would Charter supporters have been able to anticipate the speed with which the Supreme Court would backtrack from that new landmark moment, or how what was to become the homespun constitutional protection of freedom of association would be counterproductive and regressive. The dangers were to become very clear in *Ontario v Fraser*,[48] the third in what was in effect a second trilogy of labour cases, in which the Court appeared to take a step back from *Health Services* (the other two cases in this second trilogy being *Dunmore* and *Health Services*).

---

[45] ibid at [94].
[46] See articles referred to in fn 40 above.
[47] *Ontario v Fraser* [2011] SCR 3 at [249].
[48] [2011] SCR 3.

At issue in *Fraser* was the Agricultural Employees Protection Act 2002 (AEPA 2002), which had been passed to give effect to the *Dunmore* case discussed above. But in providing a system of collective representation, the Act continued to exclude farm workers from the scope of the Ontario Labour Relations Act and introduced a different and diluted form of worker representation instead. This gave an employees' association the right to make representations to an employer about terms and conditions of employment, the employer being required to 'listen to the representations if made orally, or read them if made in writing'. The 2004 Act was of course enacted before the *Health Services* decision, and the best that could be said is that the Ontario legislature did the minimum required to implement *Dunmore*. Yet although *Dunmore* fell some way short of the new standard set in *Health Services*, AEPA 2002 was nevertheless upheld in *Fraser*, despite a strong dissent from Justice Abella.

This is an issue Alan Bogg and I addressed in a co-authored article following the Supreme Court decision in *Fraser*.[49] There we pointed out that unlike *Dunmore* and *Health Services*, *Fraser* was a step back, however much the Court might protest that implicit in the right to make representations was a duty that they be considered in good faith. There is a qualitative difference between the right to *make representations* about terms and conditions of employment, and the right to *negotiate* terms and conditions of employment, which is what collective bargaining typically entails.[50] Indeed, as the Court itself had recognised in *Health Services* (of which it was reminded by Abella J in *Fraser*):

> [T]he right to bargain collectively protects not just the act of making representations, but also the right of employees to have their views heard in the context of a meaningful process of consultation and discussion … *[T]he right to collective bargaining cannot be reduced to a mere right to make representations.*[51]

Other details to emerge from *Fraser* were to reinforce the sense of scepticism about the constitutional protection of labour rights by litigation. In a notable passage in the majority decision, it was pointed out that by the time of the Supreme Court hearing in *Fraser*, there had not been a single example of a procedure being established under AEPA 2002 since enactment.[52] The legislation was wholly ineffective, yet still was held by the majority to meet the new test set in *Health Services*. And despite reaffirming the view that 'Charter rights *must* be interpreted in light of

---

[49] Bogg and Ewing (2012) 'A (muted) voice at work? Collective bargaining in the Supreme Court of Canada' *Comparative Labor Law and Policy Journal* 379.

[50] ILO Convention 98, Art 4 requires as follows: 'Measures appropriate to national conditions shall be taken, where necessary, to encourage and promote the full development and utilisation of machinery for *voluntary negotiation* between employers or employers' organisations and workers' organisations, with a view to the regulation of terms and conditions of employment by means of collective agreements' (emphasis added).

[51] [2007] 2 SCR 391 at [114], cited by Abella J in her dissenting judgment in *Fraser* [2011] SCR 3 at [50] (author's emphasis).

[52] See also the critical essays in Faraday, Fudge and Tucker fn 41 above.

Canadian values and Canada's international and human rights commitments',[53] if the decision was consistent with these values (on which others are better placed to comment), it was nevertheless clearly inconsistent with international commitments. This was made clear by the ILO Freedom of Association Committee following a complaint by the United Food and Commercial Workers Union (UFCW), though it is unfortunate that the Committee's report was published after rather than before the Supreme Court decision in *Fraser*.

True, the CFA welcomed 'the finding of the Supreme Court in *Fraser* that agricultural employers have the duty to consider employee representations in good faith'.[54] Nevertheless, the CFA was of the opinion that 'this duty, whether implied or explicit, is insufficient to ensure the collective bargaining rights of agricultural workers under the principles of freedom of association'.[55] Here the Committee recalled that 'collective bargaining implies an ongoing engagement in a give-and-take process, recognizing the voluntary nature of collective bargaining and the autonomy of the parties', and noted that AEPA 2002's 'duty to consider employee representations in good faith, which merely obliges employers to give a reasonable opportunity for representations and listen or read them – even if done in good faith, does not guarantee such a process'.[56] After noting that AEPA 2002 would need to be amended to 'ensure respect' for ILO principles, the CFA continued by expressing concern about:

> [T]he relevancy of the simple provisions permitting representations in the AEPA, given that there does not appear to exist any successfully negotiated agreement since the Act's adoption in 2002, nor has there been any indication of good faith negotiations. The Committee therefore continues to consider that the absence of any express machinery for the promotion of collective bargaining of agricultural workers constitutes an impediment to one of the principal objectives of the guarantee of freedom of association. The Committee also observes that there appear to be no provisions recognizing the right to strike of agricultural workers, which would inevitably impact on the ability of agricultural workers to bring about a meaningful negotiation on a list of claims. In this regard, the Committee recalls that it has always recognized the right to strike by workers and their organizations as a legitimate means of defending their economic and social interests and highlights that the agricultural sector does not constitute an essential service in the strict sense of the term [see Digest, op. cit., paras 521 and 587].[57]

Although informed by human rights law and by ILO standards in particular, the Supreme Court in *Fraser* nevertheless appears to have developed a uniquely and peculiarly Canadian judicial conception of freedom of association that does not comply with these international principles. Yet the CFA decision in the UFCW complaint against Canada is an important reminder that ILO principles are *international* principles. This means that while there might be scope for flexibility in the

---

[53] *Fraser* [2011] SCR 3 at [92].
[54] ILO (2012) *Freedom of Association Committee, Report No 363, Case 2704 (Canada)* at [398].
[55] ibid.
[56] ibid.
[57] ibid at [399].

manner of their implementation, in terms of their substantive content they must nevertheless be applied consistently across the different national jurisdictions to which they apply. It is not for domestic courts any more than it is for national governments and parliaments to dilute these principles, which are minimum, not aspirational, standards. Canada's constitutional protection of collective bargaining rights as developed in *Dunmore* and *Fraser* was exposed as having no regulatory effect and was in danger of being a deception, hardly likely as a result to inspire confidence in the purpose or value of constitutional litigation.

VI. Contradiction Reinforced: The Police Cases

The first point to emerge from *Health Services* was that although the annulment of collective agreements and restrictions on collective bargaining in that case were held to violate the Charter, the Supreme Court nevertheless made clear that the right to bargain collectively did not imply protection of a particular model of collective bargaining, and in particular did not fossilise the Wagner system in Canada.[58] This was reinforced by *Fraser*, where we discovered that what was implied was an opaque standard that did not necessarily comply with minimum ILO standards, this gap between international standards and constitutional law reinforced subsequently by what has been referred to as the second labour trilogy (though it is in fact at least the third trilogy of labour cases).[59] We begin this account of the 'third trilogy' with *Mounted Police Association of Ontario v Ontario*[60] (hereafter *Mounted Police*) and *Meredith v Canada*[61] (hereafter *Meredith*) before considering *SFL* in the following section. The first two cases were concerned with different aspects of collective bargaining arrangements in the police service.

The latter decisions were significant for a number of reasons, not least for emphasising the growing gap between international and constitutional law in Supreme Court jurisprudence. Positively, it might be argued that they reveal the latter to be more comprehensive than the former in the sense that ILO freedom of association conventions expressly exclude the police and the armed forces, to the extent that it is up to countries individually to decide how best these categories should be protected, if at all.[62] We know now that RCMP officers are entitled to the Charter's 'right of employees to associate in a meaningful way in the pursuit of collective workplace goals'.[63] *Mounted Police* established that the latter right implies a process which includes 'an acceptable measure of employee choice and

---

[58] A point that the Court was at pains to emphasise repeatedly.

[59] By my reckoning the first trilogy consists of the cases referred to in n 1 above; the second consists of *Dunmore*, *Health Services*, and *Fraser*; and the third consists of *Meredith*, *Mounted Police* and *SFL*, all discussed in this and the following section.

[60] (2015) SCC 1, [2015] 1 SCR 3.

[61] (2015) SCC 2, [2015] 1 SCR 125.

[62] ILO Convention 87 (Freedom of Association and Protection of the Right to Organise Convention, 1948) Art 9(1).

[63] *Meredith* (2015) SCC 2, [2015] 1 SCR 125 at [25].

independence to ensure meaningful collective bargaining'.[64] The Pay Council established under provincial legislation failed to meet that standard because it denied police officers the right to choose their representatives. So far, so good.

In reaching this decision, the majority (6:1) made clear by implication that while the Charter standard developed by the Supreme Court may be informed by international standards, it is nevertheless not bound by them. Thus, what is striking is that in a judgment grounded in a principled analysis of the purpose and content of freedom of association in the labour context, there was no reference to international standards by the majority, and no reference to the laws and practices of other 'free and democratic' societies as is common when assessing whether a restriction can be justified. It was left to Rothstein J in dissent to point out that the approach adopted by the Government in this case was 'consistent with international instruments regarding freedom of association'.[65] He added by way of explanation that while 'international conventions and covenants do not prevent domestic law from granting associational rights to police forces', the wording of those instruments reflected 'the fact' that governments 'may find it reasonable to restrict such rights', citing not only ILO Convention 87, but also ICESCR Art 8, and the ICCPR Art 22.

The issue in *Meredith* was not the choice of 'bargaining' representative as in *Mounted Police*, but a statutorily imposed 'rollback of scheduled wage increases from the previous Pay Council recommendations accepted by the Treasury Board',[66] a step taken by the federal Government in response to the global financial crisis. The case was heard around the same time as *Mounted Police*, but unlike in the latter case, the appellants in *Meredith* did not challenge the constitutionality of the Pay Council process. Instead, their concern was with the failure to engage the process before pay cuts were imposed by the Government. In other words, the appellants were seeking to rely on a process that had been found to be constitutionally defective, an application on their part which the Supreme Court, in this case, was willing to accept. This is because despite its defectiveness, the Pay Council was still an 'associational activity', the issue for the Court being whether the statutory rollback was a substantial interference with the activity in question. To have denied the appeal to be heard because the Pay Council process was constitutionally defective would presumably have allowed the Government to benefit from its own unconstitutional arrangements.

The Government's case on the point taken by the Supreme Court was that while 'wages are an important issue', the cuts were 'time-limited in nature, were shared by all public servants, and did not permanently remove the subject of wages from collective bargaining'.[67] This was accepted by a majority as sufficiently distinguishing *Meredith* from *Health Services*, where the impugned legislation was said to have 'introduced radical changes to significant terms covered by collective agreements previously concluded'.[68] In *Meredith*, in contrast, the capped increases

---

[64] *Mounted Police* (2015) SCC 1, [2015] 1 SCR 3 at [95].
[65] ibid at [267].
[66] (2015) SCC 2 at [26].
[67] ibid at [27].
[68] ibid at [28].

were 'consistent with the going rate reached in agreements concluded with other bargaining agents inside and outside of the core public administration and so reflected an outcome consistent with actual bargaining processes'.[69] This, however, was not a full answer to the appellants' case, the critical point addressed by Abella J in dissent being the unilateral imposition of pay cuts:

> [62] The unilateral rollback of three years of agreed-upon wage increases without any prior consultation is self-evidently a substantial interference with the bargaining process. This conduct was precisely what led this Court in *Health Services* to find an unjustified infringement of s.2(d). I have difficulty seeing the distinction between that case and this one. The fact that the rollbacks were limited to a three-year period does not attenuate the key fact that they were unilateral. Nor does the fact that consultation was possible on other more minor compensation issues minimize the severity of the breach.

> [63] The failure to engage in *any* discussion meant that the RCMP was denied its right to a meaningful negotiation process about wages, a central component of employment relationships generally and particularly for RCMP members whose other benefits – pensions, disability benefits, paid time off, and service pay – were tied to their wage amounts.

For all its protestations to the contrary,[70] in *Meredith* the Supreme Court majority appeared to take a further step back from *Health Services*. There the Court was not concerned with the scope or substance of 'collective bargaining' procedures (as it had been in *Dunmore*, *Fraser* and *Mounted Police*), but with their outcome, striking down legislation that invalidated collective agreements and prohibited collective bargaining on prescribed issues. In *Meredith* the Court held that for there to be a breach of s 2(d) in relation to state interference with outcomes, 'there has to be a substantial interference, with the bargaining process'.[71] Here it was held that a pay cut imposed unilaterally in breach of an already defective procedure in response to the global economic crisis did not meet that threshold. This is not to say that governments should be prevented by the Charter from dealing with economic crises or other emergencies. But that is why we have limitations clauses: it should not be left to s 2(d) to take the strain by reading down the substance of rights in order to avoid having to engage with s 1.

VII. *Saskatchewan Federation of Labour*: Final Repudiation of the First Labour Trilogy or Flattering to Deceive?

This brings us to the *SFL* case,[72] which has, for some, gone a long way to restore confidence in the Supreme Court as an actor in the development of labour rights.

---

[69] ibid.

[70] ibid at [28]–[29].

[71] ibid at [4].

[72] 2015 SCC 1, [2015] 1 SCR 245. For background, see Ewing (2014–15) '"The lady doth protest too much, methinks" – the right to strike, international standards and the Supreme Court of Canada' *Canadian Labour and Employment LJ* 517.

Moving beyond collective bargaining, the Court appeared to deliver a final blow to the first labour trilogy by holding that the right to strike is now also constitutionally protected, with the result that sweeping restrictions on the right to strike in Saskatchewan's essential services were struck down. The effect of the latter was to encourage employers and unions in designated essential services to negotiate an essential services agreement to ensure the continued delivery of services during a strike or lock-out. Where agreement was not possible, essential services employees could be prohibited from participating in any work stoppage and required to continue to work under the terms of the most recent collective agreement.

Giving the lead judgment in *SFL*, Abella J held that the 'right to strike is an essential part of a meaningful collective bargaining process in our system of labour relations', a conclusion 'supported by history, by jurisprudence, and by Canada's international obligations'.[73] Referring to the Charter values of 'human dignity, equality, liberty, respect for the autonomy of the person and the enhancement of democracy' identified in *Health Services* above, Abella J added that:

> The right to strike is essential to realizing these values and objectives through a collective bargaining process because it permits workers to withdraw their labour in concert when collective bargaining reaches an impasse. Through a strike, workers come together to participate directly in the process of determining their wages, working conditions and the rules that will govern their working lives … The ability to strike thereby allows workers, through collective action, to refuse to work under imposed terms and conditions. This collective action at the moment of impasse is an affirmation of the dignity and autonomy of employees in their working lives.[74]

The case is thus uncompromising, though so too so is the direct link between the right to strike and collective bargaining. In an enigmatic and revelatory passage, Abella J also concluded that 'the right to strike is not merely derivative of collective bargaining, it is an indispensable component of that right. It seems to me to be the time to give this conclusion constitutional benediction'.[75]

Having thus created a new judicial indulgence for the right to strike, Abella J made clear that the right applied to public sector as well as private sector employees, adding that while 'public sector employees who provide essential services undoubtedly have unique functions which may argue for a less disruptive mechanism when collective bargaining reaches an impasse', nevertheless 'they do not argue for no mechanism at all'.[76] In reaching this conclusion, the majority were influenced again by Canada's international obligations. After referring to a number of international treaties in which the right to strike is expressly mentioned, Abella J added that:

> Besides these explicit commitments, other sources tend to confirm the protection of the right to strike recognized in international law. Canada is a party to the International

---

[73] 2015 SCC 1, [2015] 1 SCR 2451 at [3]. These points were developed at length in a judgment notable for the heavy reliance on scholarly writings, including in particular the compelling legal history of Judy Fudge and Eric Tucker.
[74] ibid at [54].
[75] ibid at [3].
[76] ibid at [4].

Labour Organization (ILO) *Convention (No. 87) concerning freedom of association and protection of the right to organize*, ratified in 1972. Although *Convention No. 87* does not explicitly refer to the right to strike, the ILO supervisory bodies, including the Committee on Freedom of Association and the Committee of Experts on the Application of Conventions and Recommendations, have recognized the right to strike as an indissociable corollary of the right of trade union association that is protected in that convention.[77]

This is not to say that restrictions cannot be placed on strikes in essential services. But the ILO has made it clear that where such restrictions are imposed, some form of independent binding arbitration must be introduced to resolve disputes, which was not the case in the impugned Saskatchewan legislation. Yet although of great symbolic importance, closer examination of the *SFL* decision reveals what by now is more than a nagging doubt about the developing jurisprudence of the Supreme Court despite its promising reboot in *Dunmore* and *Health Services*. Thus, it is a major concern that in acknowledging the right to strike as constitutionally protected, the Supreme Court restricted the context of the right to a right associated exclusively with collective bargaining ('not merely derivative of collective bargaining', but 'an indispensable component of that right').[78] This, however, is not the ILO standard as developed by the *CFA*:

> 763. While purely political strikes do not fall within the scope of the principles of freedom of association, trade unions should be able to have recourse to protest strikes, in particular where aimed at criticizing a government's economic and social policies.
>
> 766. The right to strike should not be limited solely to industrial disputes that are likely to be resolved through the signing of a collective agreement; workers and their organizations should be able to express in a broader context, if necessary, their dissatisfaction as regards economic and social matters affecting their members' interests.[79]

Again, the Supreme Court flatters to deceive. In addition, however, the *SFL* case was not only about the banning of strikes in Saskatchewan's public services, but also the introduction of new rules to dilute the Province's Wagner collective bargaining model in the private sector. This would be achieved in a number of ways, including by a requirement that a trade union could trigger a ballot for certification as a bargaining agent by an employer only after it had first been able to demonstrate that it had the support of 45 per cent of the employees in the bargaining unit in a petition for this purpose. Although upheld as being Charter compliant by the Saskatchewan Court of Appeal,[80] this aspect of the statutory changes had been found by the ILO CFA also to breach ILO freedom of association principles as being 'excessively difficult to achieve'.[81] The Government was thus requested to

---

[77] ibid at [4].

[78] Also, 'The test, then, is whether the legislative interference with the right to strike in a particular case amounts to a substantial interference with collective bargaining'; ibid at [78].

[79] ILO (2018) 'Compilation of decisions of the Committee on Freedom of Association'.

[80] *R v Saskatchewan Federation of Labour* [2013] SKCA 43, (2013) 361 DLR(4th) 132.

[81] ILO Freedom of Association Committee, Report No 356, Case 2654 (Canada) (2012) at [379].

'ensure that the provincial authorities take the necessary measures to amend the Trade Union Act so as to lower the 45 per cent support requirement for beginning the process of a certification election'.[82]

Notwithstanding ILO concerns that the new requirements would be 'excessively difficult',[83] Abella J dismissed this aspect of the appeal – in only four paragraphs of a majority decision of 104 paragraphs – on the ground that the amendments '[did] not substantially interfere with the freedom to freely create or join associations'.[84] But recalling the Court's view that the right to strike is tied to collective bargaining as an indispensable component, what she also did was to put the newly recognised right to strike beyond the reach of the great bulk of the Province's private sector workers. It is not a right that can be exercised independently of the collective bargaining process, yet the requirements for securing certification as a bargaining agent have been set at an implausibly high level. This much-celebrated decision is thus based on two violations of ILO standards, these relating to the circumstances in which the right to strike is acknowledged and the conditions to be met before it can be exercised. As a Charter protected activity, it remains an activity accessible not to the many but only to a few.

VIII. Conclusion

Returning to 'Labouring under the Canadian Constitution', the question is whether we misjudged the potential of constitutional protection for labour rights. What we may have misjudged is the dynamic nature of constitutional interpretation and the slow-burning impact of the powerful and persuasive dissent for a future generation.[85] This has been the unanticipated development in Canada, where in a series of carefully positioned steps the Supreme Court has moved gradually but inexorably to repudiate the first Labour trilogy and to elevate the groundbreaking dissent of Dickson CJC in the *Alberta Reference*. The process is all the more fascinating for having been mirrored in the jurisprudence of the ECtHR, which has reached much the same position, by much the same route, at about much the same time, but without much acknowledgement by one court of the other.[86] The way in which the Supreme Court has embraced international labour rights – and not only those to be found in ILO instruments – is genuinely remarkable.

---

[82] ibid.

[83] ibid.

[84] 2015 SCC 1, [2015] 1 SCR 245 at [100].

[85] For example, Lord Atkin's famed dissent in *Liversidge v Anderson* [1942] AC 206.

[86] See Barnacle (2004) '*Dunmore* meets *Wilson and Palmer*: interpretation of freedom of association in Canada and Europe' *Canadian Labour and Employment LJ* 142; and Barnacle (2012) 'Convergence revisited: Canadian and European judicial approaches to freedom of association and their implications for a constitutional right to strike' *Canadian Labour and Employment LJ* 419.

Nevertheless, it is not clear whether and if so to what extent 'the landscape has changed with the constitutionalization of Charter principles'.[87] The problem is not the embrace, but its awkward nature, *as the Court operates well below minimum standards set by international law*, despite claims endorsed in *SFL* that 'the Charter should be presumed to provide at least as great a level of protection as is found in the international human rights documents that Canada has ratified'.[88] As we have seen, this is manifestly not the case in relation to collective bargaining, where after a promising start (*Dunmore* and *BC Health Services*), the Supreme Court has constitutionalised a standard that: (i) requires activity falling short of ILO standards in terms of the process to be conducted (*Fraser*); (ii) allows for the outcomes of even a defective process to be unilaterally revoked by the employer without any consultation or negotiation (*Meredith*); and (iii) permits high thresholds for bargaining status that will put it out of reach in the face of aggressive employer resistance (*SFL*).

At least in relation to (i) and (iii) we know that the constitutionalised position violates ILO standards, not least because the CFA has told us so. In the absence of any complaint to the CFA affecting *Meredith*, we can only speculate about (ii), but it seems inconceivable that the unilateral rollback of collective agreements would be acceptable to the ILO supervisory bodies, being an expression of the very power that collective bargaining is designed to contain.[89] The danger in relation to (i) and (iii) in particular is that they will provide deregulatory space for Conservative governments to dilute to the constitutional minimum (dialogue rather than the international standard of negotiation), with consequences discussed in *Fraser* (that is to say no regulatory coverage), and anticipated by *SFL* (diminishing levels of coverage because of thresholds known by the experience of other jurisdictions to be prohibitive). There is now a real risk of Canada sinking freely to US levels, where there is less than ten per cent collective bargaining density in the private sector.

The other issue relates to the way in which *governments and legislatures grudgingly implement even these diluted standards*,[90] a concern exposed initially by *Fraser* and now *SFL*. Under the new essential services legislation introduced in Saskatchewan, there is no definition of an essential service, which is to be determined by the employer and appropriate trade unions, on the basis of 'what services are *essential for their respective organizations*'.[91] If the parties are unable to agree about which workers are essential service workers for these purposes, the decision is to be made by the Labour Relations Board sitting as the Essential Services

[87] See Blackett (2018) '"This is hallowed ground": Canada and international labour law', Canada in International Law at 150 and Beyond, Paper No 22 (April 2018), available at www.cigionline.org/sites/default/files/documents/Reflections%20Series%20Paper%20no.22%20Blackett.pdf.

[88] (2015) SCC 2, [2015] 1 SCR 125 at [64], citing *Davito v Canada (Public Safety and Emergency Preparedness)* [2013] 3 SCR 157 at [23].

[89] ibid at [67] (Abella J dissenting).

[90] Saskatchewan Essential Employment (Essential Services) Amendment Act, 2015 (SS 2015, c 31), amending Saskatchewan Employment Act 2013 (SS 2013, c S 15-1, Pt VII).

[91] Saskatchewan Party Caucus, 'Government Introduces New Essential Services Legislation', 15 October 2015.

Tribunal. This means potentially that all public employment is either an essential service or includes at least some workers who perform essential services.[92] In contrast, the ILO standard confines essential services to those workers whose action would 'endanger the life, personal safety or health of the whole or part of the population';[93] that is to say *services that are essential for the community not essential to the enterprise.*

The courts cannot be blamed for the way their decisions are implemented by governments and legislatures, though the foregoing experience does nevertheless reinforce concerns about the effectiveness of litigation even when decisions are partially favourable. *SFL* has led to complex legislation, which by the Government's own admission may not comply with ILO standards.[94] But more than that, the legislation invites contestation by employers about the role of different categories of workers, and lengthy tribunal litigation to resolve the contest. This will not only postpone by some time the start of any proposed industrial action, but will also reinforce the advantage of the employer by giving more time for contingency planning. As is perhaps inevitably the case, the *SFL* decision thus simply led to legislation that has created a need for further litigation – and further engagement with the ILO – to determine whether the category of essential services is too broad, and whether the procedures for determining who is an essential service worker are excessive.

Suboptimal standards and problems of implementation may not seem like much of a 'benediction'. Yet that is the least of it, a more urgent concern being the counterproductive nature of the litigation and its impact. The fact that the right to strike is restricted to collective bargaining has major implications for the extent of its enjoyment by all workers, beyond the permitted restraints in the case of essential services. This in turn brings us back to the weak conception of collective bargaining and the permissively high thresholds to be met before any meaningful collective bargaining can be established. There may be a right to strike, but in practice only for the 30 per cent or so Canadians who currently manage to

---

[92] In fact, the Saskatchewan legislation applies to employees of a public employer, defined in turn to mean those employers who provide an *essential service to the public* (s 7-1(1)(f)). The employer can be public or private sector, and there is otherwise no definition of what is an essential service.

[93] ILO, *Compilation of decisions of the Committee on Freedom of Association* fn 42 above at [1417].

[94] Note the Saskatchewan Government's communication to the ILO, where it says that 'The parties are now required to negotiate *what they consider to be essential services*; for this purpose, *guidance can be sought* from the ILO definitions': ILO (2016) *Freedom of Association Committee, Report No 380, Case 2654* (Canada) (2016), at [20] (emphasis added). In other words, the legislation could go beyond the ILO definition, which is not binding. These concerns were confirmed by the only decision of the Essential Services Tribunal at the time of writing. In *University of Saskatchewan v Canadian Union of Public Employees, Local 1975* LRB File No 015-19, 27 June 2019, the Tribunal was guided but not bound by the ILO definition of an essential service, in a decision which makes it clear that some university staff can be characterised as performing an essential service, which appears to go well beyond established ILO jurisprudence faithfully outlined by Justice Abella in *SFL*: see [92]. The ILO Committee of Experts was thus surely premature in welcoming the legislation with 'satisfaction': ILO Committee of Experts, Observation on Convention 87 (Canada) (adopted 2016, published 2017). Available on ILO website.

overcome the barriers to securing it, barriers which the Supreme Court in *SFL* has indicated may be raised to levels subsequently reaffirmed by the CFA as being 'excessively difficult to achieve'.[95] If the Supreme Court has created a new constitutionally protected right to strike (albeit of limited scope), it has also endorsed the means to contain its operation.

---

[95] ILO *Freedom of Association Committee, Report No 380, Case 2654* fn 94 above at [26]. Indeed, as the Committee pointed out, the level of support required to trigger a ballot may be greater than the level of support in the ballot itself.

8

Wearing Religious Symbols

NICHOLAS HATZIS

Legal cases on wearing religious symbols are a subcategory of religious exemptions claims. All such claims raise the issue of a conflict between religious conviction and legal obligation: the religious claimant seeks exemption from a rule which prevents him or her from doing what their religion requires or compels them to perform what their religion forbids. The basis of the claim is that since religious commitment is a person's view of the ethical life, a liberal state which leaves space for individual choice should not coerce citizens into acting against their beliefs. At one level, this is an argument about the intrinsic value of a certain system of morality. At another, it is about political practice, in the sense that a liberal state has good instrumental reasons, such as maintaining social peace, promoting political involvement and social inclusion and encouraging cooperation among individuals and social groups, not to ask citizens to abandon their view of what kind of life is worth living in order to participate in the political community.

Wearing religious symbols raises particularly interesting issues because in many faiths symbols and clothing are core aspects of practice and ritual. Moreover, the religious individual who appears publicly in attire which signifies a religious affiliation is making a statement to the world about the values they embrace and the life choices that define their identity and view of themselves.

This chapter explores how courts in Canada and the UK have approached the question of the limits that constitutional law places on the power of government bodies and legislatures to dictate what religious symbols can be worn publicly. This issue has latterly prompted significant political and legal controversy in both Canada and the UK. Like the topics explored in the chapters by Easton and Draghici, the controversy over religious dress and symbols has been intensely argued over a quite short period. And as with the questions of prisoners' votes and assisted dying there has been, more so in Canada than in the UK, a notable shift in judicial analysis of the matter in that time.

The first section of this chapter sets the scene by exploring how the law in each jurisdiction has defined the notion of 'religion' as a constitutionally protected principle.[1] Section II explores the way in which Canadian and British[2] courts have treated governmental attempts to justify interference with a person's right to wear religious symbols. Section III addresses the issue of neutrality and the right of non-believers not to be exposed to religious symbols when interacting with public officials – an issue which has had much greater prominence in Canada than in the UK. The chapter concludes by discussing the ECtHR's judgment in *SAS v France*[3] and assessing to what extent Canada's Supreme Court is likely to adopt similar reasoning – with similar results – in the forthcoming litigation prompted by Quebec's recently enacted legislation imposing a partial ban on dress that covers the face.

I. Assessing Religious Motivations

When a claimant asks to be allowed to wear religious symbols in public the first question to be determined in each jurisdiction is what types of belief or behaviour are 'religious' as opposed to non-religious or secular in character. If a constitutional or human rights provision (for present purposes primarily Art 9 ECHR and s 2 of the Charter) protects freedom of 'religion', or an anti-discrimination statute provides exemptions for 'religious' organisations, courts need to determine whether a particular act or organisation is religious in character and, therefore, can benefit from the protection of the law.

In everyday life we can usually form an intuitive view of whether a belief or practice is religious, but defining religion for the purpose of determining the content of legal rights will not always be straightforward, particularly for claims on the borders of mainstream religious phenomena.[4] The definition of religion is a threshold question which arises at the first stage of religious freedom claims as courts will determine the religious character of an activity or belief before assessing the Government's reasons for interfering with it.[5]

A. What is a Religious Belief or Practice? Canadian Judgments

To British observers, the Supreme Court's acceptance that the beliefs and actions which led to Malcom Ross being dismissed from his job as a high school teacher

[1] The predominant provisions being s 2 of the Charter and Art 9 ECHR. Section 2 is something of an omnibus provision, as it includes freedom of expression, assembly, and association as well as freedom of conscience and religion.

[2] Including for these purposes the ECtHR.

[3] (2015) 60 EHRR 11.

[4] On the various approaches to judicial definition of religion in the US context see Greenawalt (2006) *Religion and the Constitution: free exercise and fairness* ch 8.

[5] Greenawalt (1984) 'Religion as a concept in constitutional law' *California LR* 753 at p 755.

were 'religious' for s 2 purposes might 'intuitively' seem far-fetched. Ross had for many years promulgated rabidly anti-Semitic conspiracy theories in pamphlets, in local newspapers, and on local radio. In *Ross v New Brunswick School District*,[6] however, the Supreme Court accepted that such beliefs were properly classed as religious:

> 70 In arguing that the order does infringe his freedom of religion, [Ross] respondent submits that the Act is being used as a sword to punish individuals for expressing their discriminating religious beliefs. He maintains that '[a]ll of the invective and hyperbole about anti-Semitism is really a smoke screen for imposing an officially sanctioned religious belief on society as a whole which is not the function of courts or Human Rights Tribunals in a free society'. In this case, the respondent's freedom of religion is manifested in his writings, statements and publications. These, he argues, constitute 'thoroughly honest religious statement[s]' and adds that it is not the role of this Court to decide what any particular religion believes.
>
> 71. I agree with his statement about the role of the Court. In *R. v. Jones*, [1986] 2 S.C.R. 284, I stated that, assuming the sincerity of an asserted religious belief, it was not open to the Court to question its validity ...[7]

The Court explained the basis for this conclusion more fully in *Syndicat Northcrest v Amselem*.[8] Although *Anselem* is not about wearing religious symbols on one's person, the judgment is very relevant for the discussion here because of the way it construed freedom of religion and the function of religious symbols. The claimants, Orthodox Jews, were co-owners of apartments in a mansion block in Montreal. The co-ownership syndicate prevented them from placing in the balconies of their apartments individual sukkahs (temporary tents or huts) to celebrate the festival of Sukkot as the building's by-laws prohibited all constructions on balconies, suggesting instead the erection of a communal sukkah in the garden. The Superior Court dismissed the claim that the prohibition violated their religious freedom under the Quebec and Canadian Charters because it concluded that only interferences with a practice 'required by the official teachings'[9] of a religion are caught by the relevant provisions. The judge took the view that the correct interpretation of the biblical

---

[6] [1996] 1 SCR 825.

[7] The Supreme Court had initially expressed a disinclination to fashion an objective test for religious belief in *Edwards Books v R* [1986] 2 SCR 713 because of the evidential difficulties it presented, but in terms which can readily be broadened to embrace a more substantive principle: 'In my view, state-sponsored inquiries into any person's religion should be avoided wherever reasonably possible, since they expose an individual's most personal and private beliefs to public airing and testing in a judicial or quasi-judicial setting ...', per Dickson CJ at [142]. The religious belief in issue in *Jones* was much more mainstream than in *Ross*, the defendant being a fundamentalist Christian who wished to home-school his children to save them from the (in his 'religious' view) corrupting influence of a secular education. The relevant passage of La Forest J's opinion is at [20]: 'Assuming the sincerity of his convictions, I would agree that the effect of the *School Act* does constitute some interference with the appellant's freedom of religion. For a court is in no position to question the *validity* of a religious belief, notwithstanding that few share that belief. But a court is not precluded from examining into the sincerity of a religious belief when a person claims exemption from the operation of a valid law on that basis. Indeed it has a duty to do so ...' (original emphases).

[8] [2004] 2 SCR 551.

[9] ibid at [21].

commandment to erect a sukkah was that it did not matter where it was erected, thus the communal sukkah was enough to satisfy the claimants' religious needs. A majority of Quebec's Court of Appeal upheld the judgment.

The Supreme Court allowed the claimants' appeal. It started by affirming earlier judgments which had adopted 'an expansive definition of freedom of religion, which revolves around the notion of personal choice and individual autonomy and freedom'.[10] Such a definition prioritises a 'personal or subjective conception'[11] of the right which encompasses both mandatory and voluntary instances of religious practice. Therefore, there is no need for a religious claimant to demonstrate that a religiously motivated act he or she wishes to perform is required by the doctrine of their religion or that others in their community share their belief, nor is it necessary to invoke the authority of religious leaders or experts. Consequently, the fact that not all Orthodox Jews shared the view that individual sukkahs were necessary was irrelevant for deciding whether the claimants fell within the scope of the provisions on religious freedom.

The Supreme Court also emphasised that courts should not involve themselves in assessing the relative merits of competing notions of orthodoxy and necessity within particular religious belief systems. The trial judge in *Anselem*[12] had heard evidence from competing expert witnesses as to the necessity of an individual rather than communal sukkah being used. The Supreme Court considered such inquiries inappropriate, given that the entitlement Mr Anselem sought to protect was manifestly one of individual belief.[13]

The only appropriate test, the Supreme Court continued, was sincerity. If courts were satisfied that a claim was sincerely motivated by religious reasons, the right to freedom of religion was engaged. It summarised the position as follows:

> Freedom of religion consists of the freedom to undertake practices and harbour beliefs, having a nexus with religion, in which an individual demonstrates he or she sincerely believes or is sincerely undertaking in order to connect with the divine or as a function of his or her spiritual faith.[14]

i. R v NS

Seen from the perspective of the debate concerning the Charter's horizontal effect, *Anselem* is in doctrinal terms a rather curious decision.[15] Its analysis of the substance of what is religious has been considered authoritative even though it was made in the context of a case where the claimed interference with religious

---

[10] ibid at [40]. The leading early cases on the point being *R v Big M Drug Mart* [1985] 1 SCR 295; and *Edwards Books v R* [1986] 2 SCR 713.
[11] [2004] 2 SCR 551 at [40].
[12] [1998] RJ 1892.
[13] [2004] 2 SCR 551 at [19]–[25], [43] per Iacobucci J.
[14] ibid at [44].
[15] See pp 18–20, and 126–131 herein.

belief came from a private actor rather than a government body, and in a context where that private actor was exercising a choice rather than applying a statutory requirement.[16] That distinction is perhaps of more significance in relation to the justification element of judicial analysis, which is considered further below. But while *Amselem* has been particularly influential on the question of what counts as religiously motivated conduct falling within the scope of freedom of religion within s 2, that position has not always impressed itself upon lower courts.

An obvious example of this is the first instance judgment in *R v NS*. The appellant, a Muslim woman, wished to give testimony wearing her niqab against two men who had allegedly sexually assaulted her. At a preliminary pre-trial hearing,[17] the presiding judge held that her religious belief was not sufficiently strong to justify her being permitted to give evidence in her niqab, because in the past she had removed the niqab to be photographed by a female photographer for her driver's licence and admitted that, if necessary, she would remove it for identification purposes when crossing the border.

That conclusion was overturned on an initial appeal,[18] which decision was in turn sustained in the Ontario Court of Appeal.[19] In both courts the positon adopted was that it was not appropriate for a court to calibrate the 'strength' of a 'sincere belief'.

That conclusion was endorsed in the Supreme Court.[20] The Court held that the trial judge had failed to apply *Amselem* correctly: what was required was a showing of sincerity, not strength of belief. The fact that an individual may have not always been consistent in her religious adherence, did not, as such, negate her sincerity. The Supreme Court noted that:

> [I]nconsistent adherence to a religious practice may suggest lack of sincere belief, but it does not necessarily do so. A sincere believer may occasionally lapse, her beliefs may change over time or her belief may permit exceptions to the practice in particular situations. Departures from the practice in the past should also be viewed in context; a witness should not be denied the right to raise [a religious freedom claim] merely because she has made what seemed to be a compromise in the past in order to participate in some facet of society.[21]

While the Supreme Court did not express itself in such explicit terms, its point about inconsistent adherence implies the endorsement of a certain of view of religious freedom and the value of autonomy which underlies it. Autonomy, as an element of political morality, requires that people have adequate options to choose from when they decide how to live.[22] The outcome of the successive choices they

---

[16] *Stricto sensu*, the claim was brought under the Quebec Charter which is vertically and horizontally effective rather than under the Canadian Charter.

[17] The hearing is not formally reported, but is briefly summarised in *R v NS* [2012] 3 SCR 726 at [4].

[18] (2009) 95 OR (3d) 735 before Marrocco J in the Ontario Superior Court of Justice.

[19] 102 OR (3d) 161.

[20] [2012] 3 SCR 726.

[21] ibid at [13].

[22] Raz (1986) *The morality of freedom* p 373.

make is a life of their own creation. But autonomy does not require some sort of overarching unity in one's life.[23] Most people will choose various, and sometimes conflicting goals, reconsider earlier decisions and revise their life plans. An autonomous life involves incompatible desires, divergent pursuits and inevitable compromises. Some believers may structure their life around religious devotion in a way which achieves a very high degree of cogency and unity; others will experience and express their religiosity in a less comprehensive manner, with doubts, second thoughts, regrets and inconsistencies. In the latter case the ethical importance of having made a free choice about how to live is not lesser than in the former, and, as the Supreme Court correctly held, it should not be denied the protection of the law.

There is one caveat to be added to this analysis. The Supreme Court's initial religious freedom jurisprudence does contain a curious anomaly. This anomaly is that an interference with religious freedom will not amount to a breach of s 2 if its effect is 'trivial or insubstantial'. This principle was established prior to *Anselem*,[24] and is invoked there as an orthodoxy.[25] As has been suggested in the previous chapters in this volume, Charter jurisprudence generally reserves questions regarding the effect of the breach of a Charter right to the s 1 justification analysis, and specifically to the 'minimal impairment' element of that enquiry.[26] The 'trivial or insubstantial' test essentially transfers an aspect of that inquiry into the first stage of analysis,[27] and as such lends a rather unusual character to this particular 'fundamental freedom'.

B. What is a Religious Belief or Practice? British Judgments

The most prominent British case on the wearing of religious dress followed an approach similar to *Amselem*, but was less emphatic in adopting a sincerity test.[28] The issue before the House of Lords in *R(SB) v Governors of Denbigh High School*[29]

---

[23] ibid pp 370–71.

[24] The concept stems from *R v Jones* [1986] 2 SCR 284 at [28] per LaForest J. The interference in issue was not that Jones was not permitted to home-school his children, but that if he wished to do so he had to register his school with the relevant provincial authorities and submit to evaluation of the adequacy in both an educational and safeguarding sense of the provision made for the children who attended. Such interference was classed as 'minimal' or 'peripheral' by the trial judge and so not inconsistent with s 2; a view which LaForest endorsed. See also *Edwards Books v R* [1986] 2 SCR 713 at [97].

[25] [2004] 2 SCR 551 at [62], [64] and [75].

[26] See inter alia pp 12–18, 32–36, 79–82, and 171–174 above.

[27] Or – if you prefer – adds an additional second stage of analysis prior to justification. However classified, the notion imposes the burden of proof on the complainant.

[28] For a helpful review of the various approaches taken to the definition of 'religion' for legal purposes prior to enactment of the HRA 1998, see Sandberg (2018) 'Clarifying the definition of religion under English law: the need for a universal definition' *Ecclesiastical LJ* 132.

[29] [2006] UKHL 15, [2007] 1 AC 100. The copious list of authorities presented to the House of Lords reveals that neither counsel thought any useful guidance might be drawn from the Canadian cases discussed above.

(hereafter *Begum*) was a claim by a Muslim high school student girl who had not been allowed to wear a jilbab (a coat-like garment covering the head and the entire body) at school. The House of Lords did not accept that the fact that only a minority of Muslims thought that wearing the jilbab was a religious requirement meant that Ms Begum's belief that she had to do so was outside the protection of the Human Rights Act (HRA 1998), Sch 1, Art 9. ECHR. Lord Bingham held that Ms Begum's wish to wear the jilbab:

> [W]as not the less a religious belief because her belief may have changed, as it probably did, or because it was a belief shared by a small minority of people. Thus it is accepted, obviously rightly, that article 9(1) is engaged or applicable ... [A]ny sincere religious belief must command respect, particularly when derived from an ancient and respected religion.[30]

Similarly, Lord Hoffmann concluded that 'wearing a jilbab to a mixed school was, for her, a manifestation of her religion. The fact that most other Muslims might not have thought it necessary is irrelevant'.[31]

Like *Amselem*, *Begum* establishes that at the first stage of the inquiry in religious exemptions cases, it is not necessary for the claimant to demonstrate the objective validity of her religious belief. This is particularly important for claims about wearing religious symbols as religious dress is often linked to subtle issues of doctrine and the history of specific religious communities, and reflects different approaches to what is required of the believer even within the same belief system.

Begum was more specific application of a principle that the House of Lords enunciated two years earlier in *R (Williamson) v Secretary of State for Education and Employment*,[32] a case about parents who sent their children to religious schools which practised corporal punishment.[33] Lord Nicholls stated that courts may inquire whether the belief is 'genuinely held' but:

> [E]mphatically, it is not for the court to embark on an inquiry into the asserted belief and judge its 'validity' by some objective standard such as the source material upon which the claimant founds his belief or the orthodox teaching of the religion in question or the extent to which the claimant's belief conforms to or differs from the views of others professing the same religion. Freedom of religion protects the subjective belief of an individual.[34]

However, one might note that neither Lord Bingham nor Lord Hoffmann in *Begum* thought that Ms Begum's 'genuinely held' religious belief had been interfered with, because she could have worn her preferred dress at another school or attended a single-sex school where she would not have considered it necessary

---

[30] ibid at [21].
[31] ibid at [50].
[32] [2005] UKHL 15, [2005] 2 AC 246.
[33] Teachers are now – *qua* teachers – whether in state or private schools forbidden from inflicting corporal punishment per the Education Act 1996, s 548.
[34] [2005] 2 AC 246 at [22].

to wear a jilbab. There is an obvious blurring here with the issue of justification, which neither judge seemed quite to appreciate. Thus Lord Hoffmann observed that for Ms Begum to change schools 'might not have been entirely convenient for her', particularly when her sister was remaining at Denbigh High, but people sometimes have to suffer some inconvenience for their beliefs'.[35]

That conclusion is perhaps akin to the Canadian Supreme Court's doctrine that 'trivial and insubstantial' interferences with religious belief do not breach s 2, even if the affected person sincerely considers that they do. In either jurisdiction, 'sincerity' of belief may not always be enough to establish interference with belief.

There have been some notable post-*Begum* judgments (rather like the first instance judgment in *R v N* in Canada), in which lower British courts seem not to have accepted 'sincerity' as sufficient to found a religious belief at all. Two decisions in particular – both postdating *Begum* – merit attention. The first is the High Court's judgment in *R (Playfoot) v Governing Body of Millais School.*[36]

i. R (Playfoot) v Governing Body of Millais School

Ms Playfoot was a high school student who wanted to wear a purity ring at school as a manifestation of her Christian commitment to celibacy before marriage.[37] The school rejected her request because the school had a general prohibition on wearing jewellery. The court held that an act will count as a manifestation of religion only if there is an intimate link between the act and the belief it allegedly manifests, and that this link was missing in the claimant's case: 'Whatever the ring is intended to symbolise, it is a piece of jewellery'.[38] There was no doubt that the claimant's view about pre-marital sex arose from her religious beliefs; rather, the decisive fact was that the wearing of the ring itself, which had some symbolic significance, was not closely enough linked to the religious beliefs to satisfy the threshold requirement of 'religion'. Thus manifestation of religion requires more than an act invested with symbolic meaning, even if that meaning can be attributed to an individual's religious beliefs. The court concluded that since wearing the ring was not a religious act, Art 9 was not engaged.[39]

---

[35] [2007] 1 AC 100 at [50].

[36] *R (Playfoot) v Governing Body of Millais School* [2007] EWHC 1698 (Admin), [2007] HLRR 34.

[37] On the American origins of the belief see Rosenbloom (2005) 'A ring that says No, not yet' *New York Times* 8 December 2005, available at www.nytimes.com/2005/12/08/fashion/thursdaystyles/a-ring-that-says-no-not-yet.html.

[38] ibid at [29].

[39] The conclusion was perhaps surprising, given that the presiding judge was Michael Supperstone QC, who has considerable eminence in public law – and especially discrimination law – as both a practitioner and author (cf his Supperstone, Goudie and Walker (2017, 6th edn) *Judicial review*). For further discussion *of Playfoot* see Bacquet (2008) 'School uniforms, religious symbols and the Human Rights Act 1998: the "purity ring" case' *Education Law* 11; Horne (2008) 'Focus on article 9: religious rights in an increasingly secular society' *Judicial Review* 101. It may be that Supperstone was driven on this point by a finding of fact that Ms Playfoot did not regard wearing the ring as religious *obligation*, but 'merely' as a *choice*: [2007] HRLR 34 at [23].

Playfoot was not pursued to the higher English courts, nor to the ECtHR. Its strength as an authority is perhaps not very compelling.

ii. Eweida v British Airways

A related but different question is whether wearing a religious symbol, although religiously motivated, is a mandatory aspect of the claimant's religion. As noted above, Canada's Supreme Court does not see any proper role for courts to evaluate 'orthodoxy' in this context. It has simply adopted the position that religious freedom is engaged when a claimant's subjective understanding of their religious belief and its practice requirements is interfered with. This view focuses on how the claimant experiences his or her religious faith and the obligations it imposes on them, without requiring the corroboration of doctrinal orthodoxy.

In contrast, recent British authority suggests that such judicial investigation is appropriate, and that only practices mandated by official religious dogma should attract the protection of the law. In this view, the claimant's religious motivation in wearing a symbol is not enough: there also needs to be a strong or substantial enough link between her motivation and the established doctrine of a religious community.

The leading authority on the point is *Eweida v British Airways*,[40] which concerned the refusal to allow the claimant to wear a small visible cross at work. British Airways set a dress code for its employees which prohibited all neck adornments in order to promote its corporate image, so it was a neutral rule which did not target religious practice as such. Rather, it was the disparate effect it had on employees wearing religious symbols which formed the basis of an indirect discrimination claim. The Court of Appeal held that the claimant's wish to wear the cross was based on a personal understanding of what was required of practicing Christians which was not supported by the official doctrine of the Church, nor was it shared by other Christians. The Court had no doubt that the claimant was sincere and that her wish was based on her religious beliefs.[41] It concluded, however, that anti-discrimination law does not protect the solitary believer who suffers negative treatment at work because they adhere to a personal view of the requirements of religious practice.

Eweida had been argued as a discrimination law case per the Employment Equality (Religion of Belief) Equality Regulations 2003 (SI 2003/1660) reg 3 rather than as an Art 9 matter. This was presumably because British Airways could not sensibly be seen as a 'public authority' or a body performing a 'public function' per HRA 1998, s 6.[42] Like *Anselem*, the litigation was initially a horizontal rather than vertical action.

---

[40] [2010] EWCA Civ 80, [2010] ICR 890, [2009] ICR 303 in the Employment Appeal Tribunal.
[41] Per Sedley LJ at [37]: 'Neither Ms Eweida nor any witness on her behalf suggested that the visible wearing of a cross was more than a personal preference on her part. There was no suggestion that her religious belief, however profound, called for it.'
[42] See the chapter by Bamforth in this volume.

Ms Eweida subsequently raised the matter before the ECtHR, which found a violation of Art 9 ECHR.[43] After explicitly rejecting the view that only mandatory aspects of one's religion are covered by the right to religious freedom, the Court held that the domestic judgment did not struck a fair balance between the claimant's right to manifest her beliefs and the respondent's wish to project its corporate image. Most notably, perhaps, the ECtHR in something of a departure from its previous case law, indicated that a state could be under a positive obligation to fashion laws which adequately protected workers' religious freedoms in a private employment relationship; and in a passage which suggested the *Begum* 'inconvenience' (or *Anselem* 'trivial') analysis might not be appropriate in this context, observed that:

> Given the importance in a democratic society of freedom of religion, the Court considers that, where an individual complains of a restriction on freedom of religion in the workplace, rather than holding that the possibility of changing job would negate any interference with the right, the better approach would be to weigh that possibility in the overall balance when considering whether or not the restriction was proportionate.[44]

iii. Conclusion

While *Williamson's* reference to the 'genuine' nature of the belief is useful, and very similar to *Amselem*, the explicit adoption of the sincerity test expounded in the latter case is perhaps preferable. With its origins in the First Amendment case law of the US Supreme Court, sincerity is a familiar standard in constitutional law adjudication and might be easier for lower courts to apply.

As Loveland and Beattie/Phillipson have suggested in their chapters in this collection,[45] Canada's Supreme Court has been wary of uncritically applying First Amendment ideas to resolve Charter problems in the field of freedom of expression. That wariness has been similarly evident in the Court's religious freedom jurisprudence.[46] In *Anselem*, however, the Canadian Supreme Court cited, in support of its conclusion the judgment of the US Supreme Court in *Thomas v Review Board of the Indiana Employment Security Division*,[47] which concerned the refusal of a Jehovah's Witness to work in a factory which produced parts for military tanks. The state authorities rejected his request for an unemployment benefit because they concluded that his unemployment was voluntary. The Supreme Court held that this was a violation of the claimant's First Amendment right to the free exercise of religion. The fact that his interpretation of pacifism,

---

[43] *Eweida v United Kingdom* [2013] 57 EHRR 8.
[44] ibid at [83].
[45] pp 157–63, 172–74 and 184–87 above.
[46] See for example the Court's rejection in *Edwards Books v R* [1986] 2 SCR 713 at [85]–[89] of the 'evolving purpose doctrine' favoured by the Warren Court, through which the US Supreme Court upheld State Sunday observance laws passed originally for religiously discriminatory motives on the basis that by the 1960s the laws were fulfilling a purely secular purpose.
[47] (1981) 450 US 707 (1981).

a well-known doctrine of Jehovah's Witnesses, was stricter than that adopted by other members of the community was irrelevant. Intra-faith differences, the Court held, are not uncommon and it is not for judges to decide which view is doctrinally correct. Its oft-quoted conclusion was that 'courts are not arbiters of scriptural interpretation'.[48]

A possible objection is that the sincerity standard, which privileges the subjective experience of religious commitment over doctrinal orthodoxy, is too permissive. Skilful individuals will always find ways to present their claims as aspects of a religious outlook when trying to avoid compliance with a law they dislike. But even if the claim is sincere, and the claimant honestly believes that what he or she wants to do is their religious duty, the law cannot accommodate every personal understanding of religion. Unless each claim is assessed against a set of official or, generally accepted, religious duties imposed by a specific religion it will be impossible for judges to draw any limits. Then the right to exercise religion will be in danger of collapsing into a general, undifferentiated right to freedom, a right to do as one pleases.

There is merit in this objection, but the concern should not be exaggerated. Satisfying the sincerity requirement does not necessarily mean that the claimant will succeed – only that the claim can proceed to the next stage of the enquiry where the court will assess the reasons for the Government's interference with the individual's religiously motivated conduct and perform a proportionality (or similar) analysis. In this model, most of the moral and legal work is performed at this second stage. Conversely, if sincerity is replaced by a stricter standard, such as compliance with the official dogma of an organised religion, the first stage of the enquiry becomes a potent filtering mechanism which allows considerably fewer cases to reach the proportionality stage.

There are least two cogent reasons to opt for a sincerity standard. First, its focus on the believer's subjective understanding of religion better corresponds to at least some of the values that underpin and justify the legal protection of religious practice. Rights give rise to duties in the sense that the right-holder's interests are reasons for imposing a duty on others.[49] Assertions about the existence of a right are intermediate steps in practical reasoning which link duties to values. When we address specific questions about what one has to do, we may not refer explicitly to those values and proceed instead from arguments about rights, treating them as reasons grounding certain obligations. Yet, the ultimate reasons justifying the imposition of duties are the values underpinning the rights which operate at this intermediate level.[50] Thus, the claim that X has a right to perform religious act Y implies that there is a value which justifies a rights-based duty not to interfere with Y.

---

[48] ibid at 715–16.
[49] Raz op cit at 166. For an argument that the relationship between rights and values is reciprocal in the sense that rights also shape the values that justify them see Harel (2014) *Why law matters* ch 2.
[50] ibid at 180–81.

It is for this reason that the concept of religion is *legally* significant: of the many empirical manifestations of religion in human life, the law will protect only those which can be normatively justified. Cecile Laborde has identified several legally relevant dimensions of religion, of which three are particularly pertinent for questions about wearing religious symbols: religion as a conception of the good life; as a conscientious moral obligation; and as a key feature of identity.

The first is underpinned by the values of liberty and autonomy, and the second and third by the value of integrity.[51] A sincerity test is more likely adequately to capture and protect those values rather than a test which evaluates the claimant's beliefs against the official dogma or the prevailing views and practices in a religious community. Individuals who wish to appear publicly in a way which denotes their religious affiliation usually feel that this is an element which gives meaning and substance to their life; it makes it a life of their own choice, one that is worth living. Similarly, they will often feel that, having opted for a life of religious commitment, they have an obligation to conduct themselves in a certain way because it is the right thing to do. Having thus exercised their capacity to make choices they develop an identity, a sense of who they are, and this includes wearing the symbols of their religious commitment. The emotional and moral foundations of such choices, and the identity they create, will be by necessity personal to the individual concerned. It is the believer's own understanding of religion and the meaning it has for him or her as moral agent what structures their life and identity. As *Amselem* demonstrates, the sincerity test is a better reflection of the subjective nature of religious belief and practice in comparison to a test which relies on sacerdotal approval or majoritarian consensus.

The second reason which supports the sincerity test is that it makes it unnecessary for courts to assess doctrinal issues and intra-faith disagreements.[52] As noted above, in *Amselem* the claimant and the respondent had called as witnesses before the Superior Court rabbis who gave conflicting evidence about the requirement for individual sukkahs, and the judge concluded that the interpretation of the biblical commandment by the claimant's witness was 'too subjective'.[53] The Supreme Court considered such an inquiry improper. Similarly, in *Begum*, the Court of Appeal discussed in detail the views of several religious leaders and scholars and noted that there were serious disagreements about what was the required form of dress for Muslim girls but, unlike the Superior Court, it did not take sides. Instead, Brooke LJ noted that since the claimant's religious belief that she had to wear the jilbab at school was sincere, it was not the business of the court to evaluate its legitimacy.[54] Judges have no expertise on matters of religious doctrine and it would be

---

[51] Laborde (2015) 'Religion in the law: the disaggregated approach' *Law and Philosophy* 581 pp 594–98.

[52] I discuss adjudication and intra-faith differences in more detail in Hatzis (2011) 'Personal religious beliefs in the workplace: how not to define indirect discrimination' *MLR* 287 pp 295–99.

[53] [2004] 2 SCR 551 at [23].

[54] [2005] EWCA Civ 199.

not merely inappropriate but plainly absurd to expect them to understand, and pronounce on, the minutiae of dogmatic debates, particularly in religiously plural societies with a multitude of religious groups and beliefs.

This is not to suggest that a sincerity test answers all the difficulties which arise in adjudication of religious exemptions claims. Deciding whether a claimant honestly believes what he or she says they believe may involve complex assessment and lead to arbitrary decisions.[55] The main danger is that decision-makers will reject claims based on religious practices with which they are not familiar, thus placing minority and non-traditional religions at a disadvantage. Whether we are ourselves religious or not, we are culturally attuned to the prevailing, traditional expressions of religious commitment. We tend to think about what it means to be religious, and the demands it makes on the believers' lives, through the perspective of the religious phenomena we encounter in the society in which we live, and they are usually those of the majority. Further, an enquiry into sincerity, if too intrusive, may undermine the very essence of the right to exercise religion. Thus the Canadian Supreme Court emphasised that under the Canadian Charter the court's role when applying the sincerity test:

> [I]s intended only to ensure that a presently asserted religious belief is in good faith, neither fictitious nor capricious, and that it is not an artifice. Otherwise, nothing short of a religious inquisition would be required to decipher the inner-most beliefs of human beings.[56]

Those concerns notwithstanding, sincerity avoids the need to evaluate the religious belief itself and prioritises the believer's subjective understanding of religion, which makes it morally attractive and easier for judges to administer than competing tests.

II. Justification (or Balancing?)

The second issue assessed here is how courts in the UK and Canada deal with the competing interests in religious dress cases. Like most jurisdictions, both systems have opted for a form of balancing of interests. The alternative would have been a kind of categorization – the adoption of clear lines that would have excluded certain instances of wearing religious symbols from the protection of the law. The obvious consequence of that approach would be that the justification stage of analysis would never be reached.

A. A Categorisation Approach?

An argument in favour of categorisation was tried before the Canadian Supreme Court and rejected in *NS*, the case about a witness's testimony while wearing a niqab.

---

[55] See the discussion in Greenawalt op cit fn 5 at pp 109–10.
[56] [2004] 2 SCR 551 at [52].

One question for the Court was whether to adopt a rule that would always require witnesses in criminal trials to give testimony with their faces uncovered. The majority opinion by McLachlin CJ framed the issue as one where two constitutional rights – religious freedom of the witness, fair trial rights of the accused – are in conflict. Courts, she continued, should, first, try to reconcile the rights through accommodation and, if this is not possible, perform, a balancing exercise on a case-by-case basis.[57] Taking into account the specific characteristics of each case is the only way to ensure that rights are not limited more than is actually necessary. The example she gave was that of uncontested and uncontroversial evidence, where there is no pressing need for a witness to remove her face cover. The conclusion was that judges should decide, through balancing, each case on its own merits and, if there is a 'real and substantial'[58] threat to the fairness of the trial, witnesses should be required to remove the niqab.

A categorical approach was favoured by LeBel and Rothstein JJ. They took the view that in addition to the right of the accused effectively to cross-examine witnesses, and the need for judges (and in some cases juries) to observe their demeanour and form an opinion as to their credibility, the case gave rise to a broader constitutional concern about the openness of judicial proceedings and the function of 'the trial as an act of communication with the public at large'.[59] Wearing the niqab undermines communication because it 'shields the witness from interacting fully with the parties, their counsel, the judge and, where applicable, the jurors',[60] so it is necessary to have a 'clear rule'[61] that witnesses cannot testify with their faces covered.

The effect of categorisation is that 'all the important work in litigation is done at the outset'.[62] Certain types of conduct are completely excluded from constitutional protection at the threshold stage and never make it to the stage of judicial evaluation, with the main advantages being clarity, predictability and ease of application by decision-makers. Balancing as such does not necessarily lead to greater protection for rights.[63] It avoids, though, the rigidity of categorisation and allows for a much broader range of interests to be taken into account in a context-sensitive manner. This may be particularly important for the issue of wearing religious symbols because relevant cases arise in various environments under very different conditions such as in employment in the public and private sectors, education at all levels, court proceedings or simply in the public space of our cities. A balancing

---

[57] *R v NS* [2012] 3 SCR 726 at [52].

[58] ibid at [28].

[59] ibid at [76].

[60] ibid at [77].

[61] ibid at [78]. For criticism that this approach disadvantages marginalised social groups see Bhabha (2013) 'R v NS: what is fair in a trial? The Supreme Court of Canada's divided opinion on the niqab in the courtroom' *Alberta LR* 871.

[62] Sullivan (1992) 'Post-liberal judging: the roles of categorization and balancing' *University of Colorado LR* 293.

[63] See the discussion in ibid at pp 306–09 and Tsakyrakis (2009) 'Balancing: an assault on human rights?' *International Journal of Constitutional Law* 468.

approach has the potential to lead to more nuanced decisions and, since it involves judicial weighing up, requires the government to articulate clearly the interests which justify interference with freedom of religion and show that they outweigh the reasons for protecting it.

In constitutional adjudication generally, there are conflicts between constitutional rights (for example, speech versus privacy) and conflicts between constitutional rights and some legitimate interest that the government is pursuing (for example, national security, the integrity of the judiciary and so forth). The second paragraph of Art 9 ECHR is a typical example of a provision which lists what can be a legitimate aim justifying a restriction. Some religious freedom cases involve a clash with another right – the typical example is equal treatment. Cases on religious symbols in the UK and Canada arise mainly in education or employment contexts and usually involve a conflict with a legitimate interest. In education cases, the interest invoked to restrict religious freedom is a safe and/or peaceful school environment.

The most striking example of such a case is *Multani v Commission Scholaire Marguerite Bourgeoys*.[64] Mr Multani was a male Sikh high school student who wished to go to school wearing a kirpan (a small metal dagger) and was prevented from doing so because the school board considered the kirpan a weapon. In employment cases, the interest relied on by defendant employers is the effective functioning of the business or the service, and the projection of a corporate image (as in *Eweida*). But sometimes defendants also invoke the rights of others as reasons justifying a restriction on religious symbols. In *Begum* this appears to be the main reason: protecting other Muslim girls from the pressure to wear the niqab.[65]

B. Constitutional Law or Administrative Law – Settling the Standard for Justification

A particularly interesting issue which has arisen in both jurisdictions – and which is central to the justification inquiry – is what is the correct standard of review of administrative decisions which impinge on constitutional rights.[66] The House of Lords and the Canadian Supreme Court have held, in *Begum* and *Multani* respectively, that the standard of administrative law – reasonableness – is not appropriate for cases involving freedom of religion claims. The more detailed discussion can be found in *Multani* where the Quebec Court of Appeal had adopted administrative

---

[64] [2006] 1 SCR 256.

[65] Such considerations highlight the difficulties inherent in the singular antagonist/balancing dichotomy adopted by the Canadian Supreme Court; see further pp 14–16 and 261–62 in this volume. Ms NS on one view experiences the state as 'singular antagonist' if a judge orders Ms NS to remove her niqab, but the judge does so because she is seeking to protect the entitlements of defendants and so is, on another view, balancing competing interests.

[66] See Hickman (2016) 'Adjudicating constitutional rights in administrative law' *University of Toronto LJ* 121 (comparing the approaches of Canadian and UK courts).

law reasonableness as the standard for assessing the decision of the school. By contrast, Charron J, writing for the Supreme Court majority, stressed that the issue at stake was whether the decision was compatible with the Charter and thus a 'correctness standard'[67] was applicable. She held that presenting questions about the substantive scope of constitutional rights as if they were administrative law issues:

> [C]ould well reduce the fundamental rights and freedoms guaranteed by the *Canadian Charter* to mere administrative law principles or, at the very least, cause confusion between the two ... the fact that an issue relating to constitutional rights is raised in an administrative context does not mean that the constitutional law standards must be dissolved into the administrative law standards. The rights and freedoms guaranteed by the *Canadian Charter* establish a *minimum* constitutional protection that must be taken into account by the legislature and by every person or body subject to the *Canadian Charter*. The role of constitutional law is therefore to define the scope of the protection of these rights and freedoms.[68]

Having thus defined the correct approach to claims which raise issues of constitutional rights, Charron J carried out a proportionality analysis under s 1 and concluded that while ensuring safety at school was an important and legitimate objective, the absolute prohibition was disproportionate, impairing the claimant's religious freedom more than was necessary.[69]

The same concern about a possible conflation of the different standards of administrative and constitutional law is displayed in *Begum*. The Court of Appeal, like the Court of Appeal in *Multani*, had focused on the fairness of the decision-making process of the school. But the House of Lords held that what is called for under the HRA 1998 is not an assessment whether 'a challenged decision or action is the product of a defective decision-making process, but ... whether, in the case under consideration, the applicant's Convention rights have been violated'.[70] This requires an approach which, Lord Bingham said 'must go beyond that traditionally adopted to judicial review in a domestic setting'[71] and requires a 'value-judgment, an evaluation'[72] by the Court.

A different view was taken by two members of the Canadian Supreme Court, Deschamps and Abella JJ, in *Multani*. While agreeing with the majority on the outcome, they reached their conclusion by applying an administrative law analysis.

---

[67] [2006] 1 SCR 256 at [20].

[68] ibid at [16] (original emphasis).

[69] In contrast, as the Court noted in *Multani* (at [62]–[65]) a blanket ban on the wearing of kirpans during commercial air travel has been held readily justifiable under s 1; see *Nijjar v Canada 3000 Airlines Ltd* (1999), 36 CHRR D/76 (Can Trib). A more nuanced judgment upheld the prohibition on a particular defendant wearing a kirpan during his trial; in large part it seems because in the trial in question the defendant was charged with assault; *Hothi v R* [1985] 3 WWR 256 (Man QB) (affirmed [1986] 3 WWR 671 (Man CA)).

[70] [2007] 1 AC 100 at [29].

[71] ibid at [30].

[72] ibid. Subsequent cases affirmed this approach; see the discussion in Hickman op cit fn 66 at pp 130–32.

The underlying idea in their judgment is that constitutional review should be reserved for norms 'of general application, such as a statute or regulation'.[73] Decisions made by administrative bodies in specific cases, which lack that element of generality, are to be assessed by administrative law standards even if they raise human rights questions. Thus they held that the school's decision was unreasonable because it had failed to take into account the fact that the kirpan would be in a wooden sheath sewn inside a cloth envelope which the student would wear under his clothes, an arrangement which addressed the school's safety concerns. Further, they noted that the school board, while emphasising the value of security, had failed properly to consider the fundamental values of religious freedom and equality and the fact that the kirpan was a religious object.

The *Multani* minority relied on a 'categorical'[74] distinction between rules of general applicability and administrative decisions in specific cases. The result is that the method for assessing interferences with religious freedom becomes contingent on the *source* of the interference: if it is a statute or generally applicable regulation, proportionality is the appropriate standard for evaluating substantive correctness; if it is an administrative measure or decision, the court should use reasonableness to assess the procedure followed by the decision-maker. This approach has been righty criticised as simplistic and unworkable in the context of a modern administrative state where statutory provisions, administrative regulations and policy instruments form a complex network of rules which affect individual liberty.[75] Its defects are particularly evident in the minority's conceptualisation of what is at stake in different types of judicial review: 'The justification of the infringement [in constitutional law] is based on societal interests, not on the needs of the individual parties. An administrative law analysis is microcosmic, whereas a constitutional law analysis is generally macrocosmic'.[76]

At a trivial level, the microcosmic/macrocosmic distinction is correct, if what is meant is that the claimants in *Multani* and, similarly, in *Begum*, were concerned with the way the exercise of delegated authority by the school boards affected the practice of their religion. But it is unclear what the distinction is supposed to establish, particularly in relation to the other point in the excerpt above, namely that constitutional law analysis concerns societal interests while administrative law analysis is about individual interests. Is this supposed to be an empirical truth, a description of actual judicial practice in a specific jurisdiction at a certain time?

---

[73] [2006] 1 SCR 256 at [85].

[74] Gratton (2008) 'Standing at the divide: the relationship between administrative law and the Charter post-*Multani*' *McGill Law Journal* 477 at p 509. See also Poole (2005) 'Of headscarves and heresies: the Denbigh High School case and public authority decision making under the Human Rights Act' *Public Law* 685 (criticising the procedural approach of the Court of Appeal in *Begum* as excessively formalistic). For a more favourable view of the procedural approach see Mullan (2006) 'Administrative tribunals and judicial review of Charter issues after *Multani*' *National Journal of Constitutional Law* 19; Meade (2012) 'Outcomes aren't all: defending process-based review of public authority decisions under the Human Rights Act' *Public Law* 61.

[75] Gratton op cit fn 74 at pp 509–11.

[76] [2006] 1 SCR 256 at [132].

Or is it a conceptual truth, a statement about the essential properties of constitutional and administrative law review and how they must be understood? Either way, how is the line to be drawn between the two types of interests?

The main weakness of the minority opinion is that it obscures the moral aspect of constitutional rights. In religious exemptions cases, an argument is made that a prohibited activity in which the individual wishes to engage (or their refusal to engage in a mandatory activity) is a legally protected instance of the right to religious freedom. This is a deontological claim about what aspects of personal liberty the state is constitutionally bound to respect; it requires a normative assessment of the content of the contested decision; and cannot be addressed by means of ordinary reasonableness review which concerns the process by which the decision was reached.

By contrast, the majority in *Multani* brings this normative question into focus. I suggest that the best way of understanding its approach is as a reflection of what Alon Harel has described as the intrinsic value of binding constitutionalism.[77] 'Binding constitutionalism', he argues, 'is characterised by the constitutional entrenchment of pre-existing moral and political rights-based duties' and

> its value is grounded in the fact that constitutional entrenchment of moral and political rights is in itself a form of public recognition that the protection of rights is the state's *duty* rather than merely a discretionary gesture on its part, or that it is contingent upon its own judgments concerning the public good.[78]

Thus the value of constitutional rights does not depend on the potential good results their entrenchment might produce; what valorises them is their function as a public recognition of the fact that the state has a duty to protect individual freedom.

This does not mean that constitutionally entrenched legal rights are the only way to protect the underlying moral rights or a necessary condition for their protection. It is possible that an enlightened, benign, state refrains from violating rights because it thinks this is the right thing to do or will better promote public good or ensure social stability and so forth. This approach is protective of rights without being grounded in a constitutionally imposed duty to protect them. In such a state, though, the protection of rights depends on the attitudes, tendencies and views of a government which has no duty to respect them; in this sense, citizens 'live at the mercy of their legislatures'.[79] By contrast, constitutional entrenchment signifies 'the shared understanding' that rights 'bind the legislature and it is not free to act otherwise'.[80]

This is likely the concern underlying Charron J's point that the minority's procedural approach may 'reduce' the Charter rights to 'mere administrative law principles'.[81] The difference between the two methodologies is that when a

---

[77] Harel op cit fn 49 ch 5.
[78] ibid at p 149 (original emphasis).
[79] ibid at p 169. Harel focuses on legislatures as potential violators of rights but his analysis is equally applicable to potential violations by administrative authorities.
[80] ibid at p 182.
[81] [2006] 1 SCR 256 at [16].

governmental decision impinges on a fundamental freedom we expect the court to engage in a form of moral reasoning and make, in the words of Lord Bingham, a 'value-judgment'.[82] It is not enough to ask whether the process used by the organ which interfered with what is (allegedly) a protected instance of a right was adequate or reasonable. It is also necessary to explore what is the moral content of the right, and this cannot depend on the source of the interference with it. As Lord Hoffmann noted in *Begum*, what is important for human rights review is not the process adopted by the decision-maker, but 'the result: was the right to manifest a religious belief restricted in a way which was not justified under article 9(2)'.[83]

The procedural approach of the minority opinion in *Multani* fails properly to acknowledge that s 2(a) of the Canadian Charter enshrines a rights-based duty to respect religious freedom. The fact that it upheld the claim following a process-based review is not a substitute for answering the normative question arising in the case, namely whether wearing the kirpan at school was an instance of the consti-tutional right to exercise one's religion. Constitutional analysis and administrative review are not interchangeable because they perform, from a moral point of view, a different function. Even if 'the mechanisms of administrative law are flexible enough to make it unnecessary to resort to the justification process under s 1 of the Charter when a complainant is not attempting to strike down a rule or law of general application',[84] the public recognition, in the form of rights adjudication, that claims about religious practice concern the *constitutional* right to religious freedom is itself morally valuable.[85]

C. Justification as a Constitutional Law Exercise

Once the proportionality stage has been reached, both jurisdictions perform a similar exercise of weighing up competing interests. When assigning justification

---

[82] [2007] 1 AC 100 at [30].

[83] ibid at [68]. Baroness Hale made a similar point in *Belfast City Council v Miss Behavin' Ltd* [2007] UKHL 19, [2007] 1 WLR 1420 at [31], a case concerning freedom of expression: 'The role of the court in human rights adjudication is quite different from the role of the court in an ordinary judicial review. In human rights adjudication, the court is concerned with whether the human rights of the claimant have in fact been infringed, not with whether the administrative decision-maker properly took them into account.'

[84] [2006] 1 SCR 256 at [126].

[85] The Canadian Supreme Court has not applied the *Multani* approach consistently and in a subse-quent case, *Doré v Barreau du Québec* [2012] 1 SCR 395, it adopted the procedural approach of the minority in *Multani*, holding that administrative decision makers have an obligation to take into account the Charter and that the Court would only perform a reasonableness review of their decision without assessing independently whether it violates the Charter. However, it stated that reasonable-ness review and proportionality review are in a relationship of 'conceptual harmony' (at [31]). More recently, in *Loyola High School v Québec (Attorney General)* [2015] 1 SCR 613, the Court performed a proportionality review to hold that a decision of the Education Minister not to exempt a Catholic School from a requirement to teach religion in a neutral manner was unreasonable; three members of the Court, who concurred in the result, explicitly relied on the Charter as the basis of assessing the Minister's decision.

arguments for interference with 'valuable' religious beliefs and behaviour, the Canadian model, at least on its face, appears more neat and clear in its structure than that adopted in Britain. This is in part because the Supreme Court has expressly recognised a hierarchy of value in respect of various types of religious belief for the purposes of determining the required rigour of s 1 scrutiny. The concept initially appeared in the well-known hate speech free expression case *R v Keegstra*.[86] The virulently antisemitic 'religious' beliefs of Mr Ross were so lacking in value that on the basis of a very relaxed view of the evidential base the court was able to sustain the conviction.

Few s 2 cases fall within that caveat. In litigation involving mainstream beliefs, the Supreme Court has held that courts should begin their proportionality assessment by asking whether there is a connection between the restriction on religious freedom and the objective pursued by it.[87] The second stage is about 'minimal impairment' of the right being restricted: the restriction must be narrowly tailored so that rights are impaired no more than necessary. It is at this necessity/minimal impairment stage that most of the moral work is done; although in religious expression cases that general principle is somewhat compromised by the presumption that trivial interferences will not breach s 2 in any event.

Interestingly, *Multani* linked proportionality to the concept of 'reasonable accommodation' and stated at there is a 'logical correspondence'[88] between the two. This point seems to emphasise further the need for exploration by courts of the moral content of constitutional rights. A formalistic approach to the issue of the range of options available to the government when it restricts the right to wear religious symbols is not enough. Instead, accommodation analysis needs to mirror the proportionality test. Put differently, the ultimate question underlying both concepts is what is the content of religious freedom in conditions of political morality such as those prevailing in a liberal democratic state which respects individual rights.

When the weighing up of interests is performed, a common theme in Canada and the UK is the court's assessment of how the defendant approached the claim for a religious exemption to begin with. There is a tendency, exemplified by the House of Lords ruling in *Begum*, to defer too quickly to the judgment of administrative decision-makers if it can be demonstrated that they engaged in a discussion with the claimant and acted in a thoughtful way. Of course, being thoughtful, and engaging in a discussion with the student and the family, is the right thing – this is what a school board should do. Further, it is reasonable to think that a sensitive and thoughtful school board is more likely to reach the morally correct decision than a board which is indifferent or insensitive. However, it would be a mistake for courts to place too much emphasis on the school's readiness to engage with religious claimants. The question which calls for judicial determination is whether

---

[86] [1990] 3 SCR 697.
[87] [2006] 1 SCR 256 at [49].
[88] ibid at [53].

a pupil has a right to go to school wearing a religious symbol. And a school board may be thoughtful and serious and sensitive, and still reach the wrong decision about what religious freedom requires.

In this respect, *Begum* can be contrasted to *Multani*. In *Multani* the defendants had discussed the situation with the family, had taken the claimant's concerns into account and had offered some accommodation – they were willing to allow him to wear a non-metal dagger. The Court was not persuaded. Instead, it examined in detail the board's argument that the kirpan would make the school environment unsafe, rejected it and concluded that the board had failed to appreciate the religious symbolism of the kirpan and the importance of religious freedom.

III. Religious Symbols and Public Officials

In religious symbols cases, as in most cases concerning constitutional rights, the Government is relying on some kind of public interest as a legitimate aim justifying a restriction on an individual's religious freedom. Canada provides the less common example of a case where the Government is defending the public use of religious symbols by individuals against a challenge by another individual who claims that this violates a constitutional obligation of religious neutrality.

The leading case on the point is case is *Grant v Canada (Attorney-General)*.[89] A group of citizens who had links with the Royal Canadian Mounted Police challenged a decision to allow Sikh police officers to wear their turbans instead of the hat which was part of the uniform. They argued that the

> constitutional guarantee of freedom of religion is breached when members of the public are forced to interact with or confront police officers who are wearing, as part of the uniform of the state, a religious symbol which demonstrates the officer's allegiance to a religious group different from that to which the particular member of the public belongs.[90]

The Government responded that allowing the turban to be worn was a protection of individual liberty in a pluralistic, democratic state and made it possible for members of the Sikh community to seek employment with the police force.

The essence of the claimants' thesis is that the right to religious freedom includes a right to be 'free from' religion when engaging with the state.[91] The idea that there is a negative aspect to legal norms protecting religious freedom is certainly not novel. It is linked to the principle that basic rights are bilateral so the freedom to act includes within its scope a freedom not to act.[92] The rule that

---

[89] [1994] FCJ No 1001.

[90] ibid at [77].

[91] See Roberts (2017) 'Is there a right to be 'free from' religion or belief at Strasbourg?' *Ecclesiastical Law Journal* 35; Weiler (2013) 'Freedom of religion and freedom from religion: the European model' *Maine LR* 760; Dorfman (2012) 'Freedom from religion', available at ssrn.com/abstract=2176079.

[92] Nickel (1998) 'Why basic liberties are bilateral' *Law and Philosophy* 627.

immediately flows from this principle is that individuals cannot be compelled to profess belief in a religion or participate in religious worship, rituals or activities against their will. Thus the US Supreme Court has held that a state law requirement that all public officials declare their belief in the existence of God violated the First Amendment.[93] In a similar vein, the ECtHR has interpreted religious freedom under Art 9 as precluding an obligatory religious oath for members of Parliament.[94]

The claim in *Grant* goes considerably further than protection from direct compulsion. A democratic state, the argument runs, needs to be equally hospitable to people of all faiths and no faith at all, and the only way to achieve this is to insist that it does not include anything that might show, or be interpreted as showing, support for a particular religion or for religion in general as opposed to non-religion. This obligation is breached if a public official is allowed to demonstrate a religious affiliation while performing his or her duties. It is this final move which helps frame the issue as an interference with the claimants' freedom: the religious affiliation of the individual public official is projected on the state of which he or she is an employee and is construed as a signal of the state's endorsement of a religious view. For this argument to succeed it is necessary to obliterate the distinction between the governmental employee and the government itself so that the latter can be identified with any message emanating from the former.

The Federal Court of Canada distinguished the case from an earlier one where the Ontario Court of Appeal had held that daily prayer and Bible readings at schools violated religious freedom.[95] The rationale for that conclusion was that, although a pupil or their parents could request an exemption, the reality of the school environment was that 'the peer pressure and the classroom norms to which children are acutely sensitive … are real and pervasive and operate to compel members of religious minorities to conform with majority religious practices'.[96] Further, the requirement for an application for exemption was as such problematic because it 'compel[led] students and parents to make a religious statement'.[97]

That element of compelled participation in religious activity was absent from *Grant*. The Court explained the position as follows:

> In the case of interaction between a member of the public and a police officer wearing a turban, I do not see any compulsion or coercion on the member of the public to participate in, adopt or share the officer's religious beliefs or practices. The only action demanded from the member of the public is one of observation. That person will be required to observe the officer's religious affiliation. I cannot conclude that observation alone, even in the context of a situation in which the police officer is exercising his

---

[93] *Torcaso v Watkins* (1960) 367 US 488.

[94] *Buscarini v San Marino* [2000] 30 EHRR 208.

[95] *Zylberberg v Sudbury Board of Education (Director)* 1998 65 OR (2d) 641 (CA) cited in *Grant* [1994] FCJ No 1001 at [82].

[96] ibid.

[97] ibid.

law enforcement powers, constitutes an infringement of the freedom of religion of the observer.[98]

So, the morally relevant classification is coercion: where the effect of a rule or practice is to coerce, directly or indirectly, an individual to perform a religious act or make a religious declaration, the negative aspect of religious freedom has been infringed; if coercion is missing, the rule or practice is constitutional. The role of judges is to evaluate the facts of each individual case and classify the impugned measure as coercive or non-coercive. Since the Court concluded that observing the officer's turban is not coercive, the Government's decision to allow him to wear it while on duty was within its discretion to set rules on how people with very different viewpoints about what is a good life should interact with each other.

The issue has yet to arise in the British context, but has prompted litigation before the ECtHR. This coercion-focused analysis of religious symbols resembles the reasoning of the Grand Chamber of the Strasbourg Court in the second *Lautsi*[99] case, which concerned crucifixes in state schools. Initially the Second Section had unanimously ruled that their display in classrooms could be interpreted as endorsement of Christianity by the state and, thus, violated Art 2 of Protocol 1 (on the right of parents to ensure that the education of their children is in conformity with their religious and philosophical beliefs) taken together with Art 9. The Grand Chamber reversed, holding that the organisation of the school environment and setting of the curriculum fall within the margin of appreciation of national governments. The important test, the Court asserted, is whether the state is involved in indoctrination: if it is not, the Court will not interfere with national choices as to what is being displayed in schools. Crucifixes

> confer on the country's majority religion preponderant visibility in the school environment. That is not in itself sufficient, however, to denote a process of indoctrination on the respondent State's part and establish a breach of the requirements of Article 2 of Protocol No. 1.[100]

The claims in both *Grant* and *Lautsi* rest on the idea that the state should be neutral in relation to conceptions of the good. This includes the choice among different religious viewpoints or between religion and non-religion. Neutrality is a notoriously elusive concept and there is not much agreement as to what obligations it entails for contemporary democracies, or even whether it is a valid principle of political morality. In any case, the Grand Chamber agreed with the Second Section that states have an obligation to be neutral but found that the crucifix is a 'passive symbol and this point is of importance in the Court's view, particularly having regard to the principle of neutrality ... It cannot be deemed to have an influence

---

[98] ibid at [84]. Had *Grant* been decided after *Anselem* it may be that the court would have found such 'observation' to be 'trivial' or 'insubstantial' and as such insufficient to trigger any interference with the observers' s 2 entitlement.

[99] *Lautsi v Italy* [2012] 54 EHRR 3.

[100] ibid at [71].

on pupils comparable to that of didactic speech or participation in religious activities'.[101] Like the Federal Court in *Grant*, the Grand Chamber was classifying certain activities as being outside the discretion afforded to the Government, using indoctrination as the morally salient factor.

It is debatable whether indoctrination is the right standard and, if it is, whether a crucifix on the walls of state schools, in addition to conferring great visibility to Christianity, can also be an element of, or contribute to indoctrination. But it is important to note that the version of neutrality espoused by the claimants in *Grant* encompassed any interaction with a public official in the performance of his duties and was, therefore, much more stringent than that of the *Lautsi* claimants. In the latter case, the endorsement of Christianity was an official decision of the state itself; in the former, the link between Sikhism and the Government was indirect and attenuated, the result of looking at a policeman's turban. Even if *Lautsi* was wrongly decided, it does not follow that negative religious freedom should preclude all manifestations of religious affiliation. From a British perspective, the ruling in *Grant* appears preferable to an absolute prohibition on wearing religious symbols while on duty, an approach which would have been more at home in French *laïcité* or American strict separation of church and state under the Establishment Clause of the First Amendment. *Grant* makes a persuasive case that multicultural societies have good reasons to allow visibility of religion in public spaces, provided that the equal civic status of all, religious and non-religious alike, is not compromised.

The quest for extreme secularism which was rejected in *Grant* has recently resurfaced with Quebec's Bill 21.[102] Passed in June 2019, it declares Quebec to be a lay state and prohibits public sector employees from wearing religious symbols when discharging their functions. Section 6 defines a religious symbol as 'any object, including clothing, a symbol, jewellery, an adornment, an accessory or headwear, that (1) is worn in connection with a religious conviction or belief; or (2) is reasonably considered as referring to a religious affiliation'. This is a very broad definition which covers not only well-known religious symbols, such as the kippah, the cross or the veil, but anything that might reasonably create the impression that it relates to religious belief. The National Council of Canadian Muslims and the Canadian Civil Liberties Association challenged the law on federalism grounds and applied for a stay pending a judgment on the merits but their

---

[101] ibid at [72]. See the discussion in Kyritsis and Tsakyrakis (2013) 'Neutrality in the classroom' *International Journal of Constitutional Law* 200 (criticising the Court for failing to give effect to the principle of neutrality) and Leigh and Ahdar (2012) 'Post-secularism and the European Court of Human Rights: or how God never really went away' *MLR* 1064 (praising the Court for not adopting a strict rule of church–state separation).

[102] An Act Respecting the Laicity of the State. The text is available at www2.publicationsduquebec. gouv.qc.ca/dynamicSearch/telecharge.php?type=5&file=2019C12A.PDF. The Act invokes the 'notwithstanding clause' (s 33) of the Canadian Charter of Rights and Freedoms, which allows the legislature to declare that the law is applicable notwithstanding the Charter's provisions on human rights and, therefore, precludes judicial review on this ground.

application was refused because the judge held that the continuing operation of the law would not cause irreparable harm.[103]

IV. Conclusion

The concept of equal civic status has latterly been called into question by the ECtHR's judgment in *SAS v France*.[104] France's Loi no 2010-1192 of October 11, 2010 Art 1 provides that 'Nul ne peut, dans l'espace public, porter une tenue destinée à dissimuler son visage'.[105] Although loi no 2010-1192 makes no explicit reference to niqabs or burqas, its legislative history[106] indicates that its promoters' primary target was women who adhered to a strand of Islam that required them to keep their faces covered in public, either by a burqa or niqab.

The ECtHR had no difficulty in concluding that the so-called 'burqa ban' engaged Art 9. It was also unpersuaded by the 'threat to public safety' justification that France offered to sustain the law.[107] The Court did however accept this justification as a legitimate aim:

> [T]he voluntary and systematic concealment of the face is problematic because it is quite simply incompatible with the fundamental requirements of 'living together' in French society ... [and] systematic concealment of the face in public places, contrary to the ideal of fraternity, ... falls short of the minimum requirement of civility that is necessary for social interaction.[108]

On the question of whether the law was a proportionate means to achieve that legitimate aim, the Court categorised the issue as one of general policy, in respect of which a state should enjoy a wide margin of appreciation for laws enacted through a democratic process. The law could therefore properly be seen as necessary in a democratic society.[109]

---

[103] Hak c. Procureure générale du Québec 2019 QCCS 2989, available at www.canlii.org/fr/qc/qccs/doc/2019/2019qccs2989/2019qccs2989.html. Subsequently, the Court of Appeal gave the claimants leave to appeal the judge's decision on interim relief.

[104] (2015) 60 EHRR 11.

[105] 'No one shall, in any public space, wear clothing designed to conceal the face.' The French text is available at www.legifrance.gouv.fr/affichTexte.do?cidTexte=JORFTEXT000022911670&categorieLien=id. Per Art II(1), 'l'espace public est constitué des voies publiques ainsi que des lieux ouverts au public ou affectés à un service public'. Various exceptions – not including religious beliefs, are identified in Art II(2): 'si la tenue est prescrite ou autorisée par des dispositions législatives ou réglementaires, si elle est justifiée par des raisons de santé ou des motifs professionnels, ou si elle s'inscrit dans le cadre de pratiques sportives, de fêtes ou de manifestations artistiques ou traditionnelles'. Breach of the law is a criminal offence, subject to a maximum penalty of a euro 150 fine.

[106] Discussed succinctly in Adentire (2015) 'Has the European Court of Human Rights recognised a legal right to glance at a smile?' *LQR* 43. And see (2015) 60 EHRR 11 at [149].

[107] ibid at [139].

[108] Per the explanatory notes to the law; cited at ibid at [141].

[109] ibid at [153]–[159].

The judgment has unsurprisingly attracted strong criticism from legal commentators.[110] That no such law has been enacted in Britain nor by Canada's national Parliament indicates that there is an important point of convergence within the two jurisdictions which implies a similar understanding of how public space is constituted and what are the values of political morality underlying the arrangements for living together in a community. The similarity can probably be explained by the fact that both systems share a political and cultural tradition, shaped by classical liberalism, which recognises that citizens should enjoy a large degree of personal independence in making decisions about their lives and views with suspicion the state's attempts to coerce people to live in a certain way.

However, in October 2017 the National Assembly of Quebec passed a law imposing a partial prohibition on face covering.[111] The law – colloquially referred to as Bill 62 – which mainly catches Muslim headgear such as the niqab and the burqa, applies in the context of giving or receiving public services. The law is, therefore, less intrusive than its French equivalent, but is still very wide in scope, covering all government departments and agencies, municipal agencies and publicly funded bodies including hospitals and other health services, schools and public transport.

The Quebec legislature's justification for adopting the law seems to be what has been described as 'secular equality':[112] the idea that public space should be free from the presence of religion in order to ensure that every citizen is treated with the same respect. In this view, religious symbols, even if worn by private individuals, are seen as elements which undermine neutrality.

How the law will be applied in practice remains unclear. Even Quebec's Justice Minister who sponsored it was unable to explain what it requires. Her initial position was that the prohibition on face coverings was applicable whenever a citizen was receiving public services: 'The point of Bill 62 is having the face uncovered during the duration of the service and while the service is being rendered by the employee and being received by the citizens'.[113] However, following criticism over

---

[110] Adentire op cit fn 106 notes that the judgment was not premised on any existing authority (ibid at 46) and suggesting that its logic points towards the bizarre conclusion that all individuals might be placed under a legal duty to be sociable towards each other (ibid). The analysis by Cumper and Lewis (2018) 'Empathy and human rights: the case of religious dress' *Human Rights LR* 61 to the effect that the ECtHR lacked the judicial imagination properly to understand the detriment that compliance with the law would work on affected women has distinct echoes of the critique made by Horwitz ((1996) 'The sources and limits of freedom of religion in a liberal democracy' *University of Toronto Faculty LR* 1) of the Canadian Supreme Court's initial religious freedom jurisprudence as inadequately aware of the severity of the consequences for some litigants of having their religious beliefs overridden. Although Horwitz's analysis was not among the various academic sources invoked by the Court in *Multani*, the Court's reasoning was notably astute in identifying how important wearing the kirpan was for Mr Multani.

[111] An Act to Foster Adherence to State Religious Neutrality and, in particular, to Provide A Framework for Requests for Accommodation on Religious Grounds in Certain Bodies. The text is available at http://www2.publicationsduquebec.gouv.qc.ca/dynamicSearch/telecharge.php?type=5&file=2017C19A.PDF.

[112] Laborde (2012) 'State paternalism and religious dress code' *International Journal of Constitutional Law* 398.

[113] Authier (2017) 'Bill 62 would mean no face coverings on the bus, Minister confirms' *The Montreal Gazette* 17 October 2017.

the effects of the law on Muslim women, a few days later she changed her mind stating that it was relevant only at the moment of identification and interaction with a public employee. Therefore, people may be required to uncover their faces for identification purposes but would still be allowed to use public transport or walk around a library or sit at a hospital waiting room with their faces covered.[114]

The law has been challenged on constitutional grounds by the National Council of Canadian Muslims and the Canadian Civil Liberties Association. Pending judgment, the Quebec Superior Court granted, in December 2017, an interim stay until the publication by the government of guidelines on how the law will be enforced.[115] The guidelines were published in May 2018,[116] and the claimants argued that they were inadequate for preventing irreparable harm to Muslim women. In June 2018 the Court granted a second stay, until a decision on the merits, with the judge saying that the law appears to violate of the Charter.[117] Now Bill 21 on the laicity of the state, discussed above, also provides in s 8 that individuals receiving services from public agencies should have their face uncovered if interacting with the agencies' personnel.

It is very likely that the case will reach the Supreme Court which will thus have the chance to revisit its existing case law on wearing religious symbols. *SAS v France* – which upheld a law much more restrictive of religious freedom than Bill 62 – will likely be prayed in aid by the Quebec Government but on the basis of the existing authority, it is difficult to imagine that the Supreme Court will be persuaded that such a measure can be justified under s 1. As Loveland notes in chapter five, the intolerance displayed by the DuPlessis governments in Quebec in the 1950s towards the Province's Jehovah's Witnesses prompted an innovative and forceful response from the Supreme Court in the form of a common law constitutionalism in respect of religious and political expressive freedom.[118] There would be an ironic symmetry if Bill 62 led the Supreme Court to invoke the Charter to offer Quebec's latest flirtation with religious intolerance a similarly hostile reception. Should the matter ever arise in Britain, one might hope that such a judgment would assist the UK's Supreme Court in concluding that while such a law would not breach Art 9 ECHR, it could be regarded as incompatible with HRA 1998, Sch 1, Art 9.

---

[114] Authier (2017) 'You can ride the bus with a face covering, Quebec Justice Minister insists' *The Montreal Gazette* 24 October 2017.

[115] *National Council of Canadian Muslims v Attorney General of Quebec* [2017] QCCS 5459, available at www.canlii.org/en/qc/qccs/doc/2017/2017qccs5459/2017qccs5459.pdf.

[116] Stouter-Martin (2018) 'Bill 62: Quebec releases criteria for requesting, granting religious accommodation' (9 May 2018), available at www.cbc.ca/news/canada/montreal/quebec-bill-62-guidelines-accommodations-1.4655620.

[117] *National Council of Canadian Muslims v Attorney General of Quebec* [2018] QCCS 2766 available at www.canlii.org/en/qc/qccs/doc/2018/2018qccs2766/2018qccs2766.pdf.

[118] pp 154–156 above.

9

Raising Children in Accordance with Unorthodox Religious Beliefs

RACHEL TAYLOR

Nicholas Hatzis's analysis in chapter eight of the ways in which the British and Canadian constitutions regulate the wearing of religious symbols takes us primarily to situations in which a governmental body stands as what the Canadian courts have come to call a 'singular antagonist' relative to an individual (or group) who (or which) contends that either the government body is invoking a presumptively Charter-compliant statutory provision in a Charter non-complaint fashion or that the statutory provision is per se in breach of Charter rights.[1] Such scenarios have been contrasted (by the Canadian Supreme Court) with circumstances in which the law and/or the government body applying the law is more readily seen as seeking to balance competing private interests: when the law (and the governmental body applying it) stands as a mediator between those interests rather than as a singular antagonist to just one of them.[2] In the Canadian context, the dichotomy is ostensibly significant because the Canadian Supreme Court affords legislatures greater substantive latititude (a notion more readily recognised as 'deference' in the context of British courts' interpretation of the Human Rights Act 1998 (HRA 1998)) in 'balancing' scenarios.

As other contributors to this volume have observed, that dichotomy may often have blurred edges. Perhaps more importantly, it is a dichotomy that shades in analytical terms into the distinction between 'vertical' and 'horizontal' applications of human rights norms; a distinction which prima facies mandates the resolution of vertical disputes according to the requirements of Charter rights and horizontal disputes in conformity with Charter 'values'. Loveland's critique of the way in which Canadian and British law have lent a demonstrably 'public'

---

[1] See the discussion of the point in Loveland's introductory chapter in this volume.

[2] Thus in one of the earliest cases addressing religious freedom, which concerned provincial laws regulating shop opening on Sundays, the Court was ready to countenance quite substantial interferences with owners' religious beliefs if such interferences were designed to protect employees from potential exploitation; *Edwards Books & Art Ltd v R* [1986] 2 SCR 713. And see also the free expression cases discussed in Loveland's chapter at pp 15–17 above.

(or, 'vertical' or 'singular antagonist') nature to defamation law which was previously treated as a 'private (or 'horizontal' or 'mediating') highlights both the overlap between these dichotomies and the sometimes simplistic way in which they have been formulated and applied by the courts in both jurisdictions.[3] Further, as Nicholas Hatzis has suggested in this volume,[4] the doctrinal clarity of the Canadian Supreme Court's jurisprudence on religious freedom has been additionally complicated by the authority which Canadian courts have accorded to the judgment in *Anselem*.[5] *Strictu sensu*, *Anselem* concerns the Quebec Charter, a human rights instrument with horizontal as well as vertical effect, and which was relied upon by the individuals alleging an interference with their religious freedom because the interference came from a private sector rather than governmental body. The Supreme Court nonetheless conflated the analytical approaches taken to the Quebec Charter and the Canadian Charter, even though on the logic of *Dolphin Delivery*[6] the Canadian Charter could provide only 'values' rather than 'rights' as a guide to resolving the dispute between the parties.

This chapter focuses on questions of religious freedom which have an obviously complex character. The complexity arises because it is not immediately apparent if the governmental role is best characterised as 'singular antagonist' or 'mediator' and if the matter before the court is best characterised as 'vertical' or horizontal' in nature.

In both Canada and Britain, tensions between religious belief and the secular state have been played out in similar disputes concerning the family and children's upbringing and education. The religious upbringing of children sits at the intersection of a number of contentious issues: the acceptable limits of religious practice; the respective roles of parents and the state in children's upbringing; and the extent to which the state may legitimately intrude into the 'private' family sphere. The interests of the children themselves are also complex. No upbringing, whether religious or not, can be neutral as to the values by which life is lived. A religious upbringing can be important not only in the shaping the child's beliefs but also in securing their place within the community and developing relationships within and outside of the family. Religious affiliation, closely tied as it often is to culture and race, may also be significant in the formation of children's identities even if the children later reject the beliefs themselves.

For these reasons the freedom of parents to determine their child's religious upbringing is not necessarily inconsistent with the interests of children. It is, however, clear that an upbringing in which children are brought up with little exposure to alternative ideas will limit their opportunity to develop the capacity to make future rational choices about their own beliefs and to participate fully in a society that requires its citizens to understand and respect diversity of belief

---

[3] See in particular pp 157–64 and pp 169–74 above.
[4] See especially the passages at pp 235–238.
[5] *Syndicat Northcrest v Anselem* [2004] 2 SCR 299.
[6] See the discussion in Bamforth's chapter and the sources cited therein.

and ways of life. There is also a public interest in providing the conditions for a harmonious society, resilient to the tensions that may come from negotiating different ways of life. As both Canada and the UK have become more diverse, so attempts have been made to forge collective identity through a shared vision of the foundational values in each country. Within this framework, the beliefs held by children and their families are potentially risky, threatening community cohesion and even creating an environment conducive to extremism. This chapter will consider the way in which the law has responded to these tensions in two areas: parental disputes over religious upbringing; and religious education.[7] In both areas parental freedom has been increasingly circumscribed by the use of collective values but in each of these areas the legitimacy of the derivation of these values has been questioned, along with their ability to draw the boundaries of religious freedom and public interest.

I. Historical Background(s)

The way in which a country responds to the question of the role of parents and state in children's religious upbringing and education will inevitably reflect the history, constitutional foundations and prevailing social conditions within the state. Whilst there are important differences between the UK and Canada, the two countries have much in common, most importantly: the common law roots of the law on religious upbringing; the role of religious conflict in the formation of the constitution; an increasingly diverse population; and a commitment to broadly similar liberal values and rights.

The language of the law in family disputes is also similar in both jurisdictions,[8] with the resolution of disputes about children's upbringing expressed in tests related to the 'best interests' or 'welfare' of the child and the use of the 'harm' principle. Despite the broad similarities between the jurisdictions, terms such as 'best interests' and 'harm' do not have fixed meanings, instead reflecting the values and norms of the society in which they are determined.

The modern law in both jurisdictions has its roots in the common law right of a father to determine the religious upbringing of his child.[9] The foundations

---

[7] These areas present a rather more nuanced challenge to the courts than such matters as the respect to be given to parents' religious beliefs which would preclude their children being given certain medical treatments when the children would if untreated suffer serious harm or death; see especially *B (R) v Chidren's Metropolitan Aid Society of Toronto* [1995] 1 SCR 315.

[8] Many aspects of family law in Canada are governed by provincial law, although the law on marriage and divorce is a matter of federal law (Constitution Act 1867, s 91(26) and is primarily based on the federal Divorce Act (RSC 1985, c3, 2nd supp).

[9] Until the Guardianship of Infants Act 1925 this was primarily a paternal right, save where the child was illegitimate, in which case the mother possessed such rights. See *Young v Young* [1993] 4 SCR 3, 108 DLR 4th 193 at 209–11 and 268–70 for discussion of the common law roots of Canadian law (the case centred on a dispute arising in British Columbia but primarily concerning divorce under the federal Divorce Act) on parental responsibility for religious upbringing. The law in Quebec is based on the civil

of the modern British constitution were born of the deep religious conflicts of the sixteenth and seventeenth centuries, which gave rise to draconian state interference in religious belief, including parental religious freedom[10] and children's education.[11] As the Protestant faith became firmly established, these restrictions began to be relaxed such that by the early nineteenth century children's religious upbringing was largely treated as a private parental freedom.[12] Whilst this right was not absolute and could be forfeited by the father's conduct,[13] the courts were reluctant to intervene in the father's religious discretion, even in cases that arose after the father's death.[14]

Perhaps the best example of this approach is *Agar-Ellis*,[15] in which the Protestant father barred his children from all contact with their mother who had secretly educated them as Roman Catholics. The court refused to interfere with exercise of the father's rights, despite the fact that there had been an agreement at the time of marriage that the children would be brought up as Roman Catholics and that the children's own wishes were that they would continue to be brought up in that faith. In the view of the court, as the father had not forfeited or abandoned his paternal rights, the court 'could not interfere with him in his honest exercise of the jurisdiction which the law had confided to him'.[16]

Cases such as *Agar-Ellis* demonstrate that the prevailing law in both Canada and Britain in the 1860s reflected a primary state response to religious diversity in parenting as one of non-intervention in the private rights of the parent, or, more accurately, the father. This reflected a wider dismantling of religious disabilities and an increase in non-conformist religious observance as religious pluralism became more firmly established.

Julian Rivers, in his survey of religious constitutional change, concludes that by 1870 a new constitutional settlement had been reached, meaning that religious equality and liberty were firmly established with private conscience being given particular protection.[17] 1870 was also the year that saw the introduction of the

---

law system rather than the common law, but the Supreme Court of Canada has noted that the evolution of the law in Quebec is parallel to that in the common law: *P(D) v S(C)* [1993] 4 SCR 141.

[10] For example, *Shaftsbury v Hannam Finch* 323 (1677); *Preston v Ferrard*, 4 Bro P C. 298 (1720); *Teynham v Lennard*, 4 Bro P C 302 (1724), 9 Mod 40, 2 Eq Cas abr 486; *Edwards v Wise*, Barnard, ch.x39 (1740).

[11] See, for example, Act of 1699, 11 & 12 Wm. III c.4 by which it became a crime punishable by life imprisonment for a Catholic to keep a school or educate youth and which compelled Catholic parents to continue to support their children who converted to Protestantism. See Friedman (1916) 'The parental right to control the religious education of the child' 29 *Harvard LR* 485.

[12] Friedman fn 11 supra noting that, de facto if not de jure, this approach appears to be established in judicial practice by the mid-18th century.

[13] Most famously, the poet Shelley was deprived of the custody of his children on the grounds that he professed and acted upon irreligious and immoral principles (*Shelley v Westbrooke* (1817) Jac 266), although other undesirable aspects of Shelley's parenting may have influenced the court; see Todd (2007) *Death and the maidens*. See also *Wellesley's Case* (1827) 38 ER 236, (1828) 4 ER 1078.

[14] *Hawksworth v Hawksworth* (1871) LR 6 Ch App 539.

[15] *Re Agar-Ellis* (1878–79) LR 10 Ch D 49; (1883) LR 24 Ch D 317.

[16] *Re Agar-Ellis* (1878–79) LR 10 Ch D 49, 75.

[17] Rivers (2010) *The law of organised religions: between establishment and secularism* ch 1.

systematic involvement of the state in education in Britain through the creation of board schools. Until this point religious upbringing and education were largely synonymous, with religious groups dominating the provision of education. This together with the introduction of compulsory education in 1880 gave the British state a greater interest and role in the provision of education – the most powerful route to state intervention in the otherwise private sphere of religious upbringing.

Given the historic role of the Christian churches in providing education,[18] state provision was built around the existing religious provision rather than by creating a new secular, state system. This basic approach to partnership between the state and religious groups in the provision of education has continued to the present day. As British society has become more diverse, the state has responded by increasing the number and variety of 'schools with a religious character' based on a deliberate policy of pluralism[19] and respect for parents' rights to choose a faith-based education.[20] As discussed further below, this policy forms the backdrop to many of the most difficult questions of accommodation of religious upbringing in the modern law.

The crucible of religious tension was also a formative influence on the emerging Canadian state and, again, the upbringing and education of children was an important part of the resulting settlement. The origins of this settlement can be traced back to the British acquisition of French Canada, with its largely Catholic population. The resulting Treaty of Paris (1763) and subsequent Quebec Act (1774) granted its Roman Catholic inhabitants freedom of worship and access to public office as yet unavailable to their co-religionists in Britain and its other territories. This relatively early approach of toleration of religious difference found further expression,[21] most importantly, at the creation of Canadian Federation in 1867, when specific protection was given to Catholic and Protestant education in those areas in which they were respectively minorities.[22] This was, however, a limited vision of toleration and did not did not extend to protection for the education rights of other religious minorities.[23] Further, the use of education has a dark side to its history through its use as a tool for assimilation and control, particularly in relation to Canada's indigenous people who suffered great harm through its use.[24]

---

[18] ibid ch 8.

[19] Department for Education and Skills (2001) 'Schools: achieving success' (Cm 5230) and Department for Education (2016) 'Schools that work for everyone'.

[20] See Estelle Morris, Secretary of State for Education, speaking to the General Synod on 14 November 2001, at news.bbc.co.uk/1/hi/education/1655994.stm and www.theguardian.com/politics/2001/nov/14/uk.schools.

[21] Notably the recognition of equality for Jewish subjects in Lower Canada: 1 Will. IV, ch. 57 (1831) and protection from restrictions on the free exercise of religion contained in the Freedom of Worship Act (1851): 14 & 15 Vict., ch. 175.

[22] Constitution Act 1867 (British North America Act 1867), s 93.

[23] An omission which survived later challenge in the Supreme Court of Canada: *Reference re Bill 30, An Act to Amend the Education Act (Ontario)* [1987] 1 SCR 1148. See also the sources cited in Ian Loveland's chapter relating to the persecution of Jehovah's Witnesses in Quebec in the 1950s.

[24] White and Peters (2009) 'A short history of aboriginal education in Canada' in White, Beavon and Peters (eds) *Aboriginal education: current crisis and future alternatives*.

Just as is the case in Britain, this historic approach to education continues to cast a shadow over current debates concerning the reach of the state and the religious upbringing of children.

II. Multiculturalism and Collective Values

Both Canada and the UK have become increasingly diverse in terms of culture, language and religion, and a growing proportion of the population which has no religious affiliation. These trends can be seen by comparing census data.[25] In both countries[26] the 2011 figures record that a majority of the population reported themselves to belong to a Christian denomination,[27] but these numbers represent a steep decline from a decade earlier.[28] In both countries around a quarter of respondents stated that they had no religious affiliation, a considerable rise from 2001.[29] At the same time, whilst other religious groups remained a relatively small proportion of the population, in both countries there was a sharp rise in the numbers affiliating to minority religions.[30] In both countries Islam has the greatest number of adherents after Christianity and in both countries the number of Muslims has shown a considerable increase over the past decade.[31] Whilst there are significant national and regions differences in the stories behind these figures, both countries show a similar picture of declining affiliation to Christianity and a rise in the proportion of people with minority or no religion. In consequence, in both countries, any attempt to achieve a sense of collective identity must look beyond religious tradition and unite those who have very different religious, or non-religious, affiliation.

The primary response to such a dilemma in Canada has been found in the contested concept of multiculturalism. This value is written into s 27 of the Charter: 'This Charter shall be interpreted in a manner consistent with the preservation and enhancement of the multicultural heritage of Canadians'. Section 27 has been regularly resorted to by the courts since the outset of the Charter era as

---

[25] The Canadian Census of 2011 did not ask for religious affiliation, but a subset of households were sent the voluntary National Household Survey, and data from 2011 reflects answers to that survey.

[26] The figures given here relate to England and Wales rather than the whole of the UK. The Census for Scotland shows a similar picture. In Northern Ireland the question on religion were closely related to its history of religious tension, a complexity beyond the scope of this chapter.

[27] In Canada in 2011 67.3% of people reported themselves to be Christian. In England and Wales the equivalent figure was just under 60%.

[28] In Canada in the 2001 Census 77% of the population self-described as Christian. In England and Wales the figure was just over 70%.

[29] In 2001 16.2% of Canadians had no religious affiliation; in England and Wales the figure was 14.8%.

[30] In Canada minority religions, such as Judaism and Buddhism, have remained relatively stable as a proportion of the population between 2001 and 2011, but there has been a 50% rise in the proportion stating themselves to be Sikh, Muslim or Hindu.

[31] In England and Wales the proportion of Muslims rose from 3% of the population in 2001 to 4.8% in 2011. In Canada the equivalent figures show a rise from 2% to 3.2%.

an important factor both in assessing if Charter rights (or in the horizontal context Charter 'values') have been infringed, and in assessing if such infringements can be justified under s 1.[32] However, the meaning of this provision, like multicultural-ism itself, has remained somewhat ambiguous. In 2007, in *Bruker v Marcovitz*,[33] Abella J described multiculturalism in terms of respect for difference:

> Canada rightly prides itself on its evolutionary tolerance for diversity and pluralism. This journey has included a growing appreciation for multiculturalism, including the recognition that ethnic, religious or cultural differences will be acknowledged and respected ... the right to integrate into Canada's mainstream based on and notwith-standing these differences has become a defining part of our national character.[34]

For Deschamps J (dissenting) the respect for difference that underlay multicul-turalism required the court to adopt a stance of neutrality with regard to religious belief:

> Canada's adoption of multiculturalism and attachment to the fundamental values of freedom of conscience and religion and of the right to equality guarantee to all Canadians that the courts will remain neutral where religious precepts are concerned. This neutrality gives the courts the legitimacy they need to play their role as arbiters in relation to the cohabitation of different religions and enables them to decide how to reconcile conflicting rights. In thus protecting freedom of conscience and religion, the courts perform a task that is difficult and complex. It would be inappropriate to impose on them an additional burden of sanctioning religious precepts and undertakings.[35]

To the extent that neutrality merely means that no automatic preference is given to one religion over another this is uncontroversial, but as Abella J explains in the same case, difficulties arise where that religion's adherents espouse beliefs that are potentially in conflict with fundamental values that the Court is also charged with protecting:

> The right to have differences protected, however, does not mean that those differences are always hegemonic. Not all differences are compatible with Canada's fundamental values and, accordingly, not all barriers to their expression are arbitrary. Determining when the assertion of a right based on difference must yield to a more pressing public interest is a complex, nuanced, fact-specific exercise that defies bright- line application. It is, at the same time, a delicate necessity for protecting the evolutionary integrity of both multiculturalism and public confidence in its importance.[36]

Bruker itself is a good example of this problem of the tension between religious freedom and fundamental values or rights. The case concerned a Jewish couple

---

[32] See for example *R v Keegstra* [1990] 3 SCR 697 (in respect of criminalising religiously motivated hate speech); *Ross v New Brunswick School District No 15* [1996] 1 SCR 825 (in relation to the dismissal of public school teachers promoting anti-semitic views; *Edwards Books & Art Ltd v R* [1986] 2 SCR 173 (concerning Sunday closing laws) and the discussion in Hatzis' chapter herein.

[33] [2007] 3 SCR 607.

[34] ibid at [1].

[35] ibid at [102].

[36] ibid at [2].

who had obtained a civil divorce and reached agreement on the financial aspects of that divorce. A condition of the agreement was that the husband obtained a *get*, the religious divorce that could only be sought by the husband and without which the wife was not free to remarry under Jewish law. Unable to force compliance through Jewish law, she therefore sought damages in civil law for her husband's failure to comply with the terms of the agreement over a 15-year period. The majority of the Supreme Court found in her favour, considering that the religious nature of the dispute did not render the enforcement of the agreement non-justiciable and that the husband's claim to religious freedom would in any event be outweighed by the harm to the wife and the public interest in fundamental values including equality between the sexes.

The problem that she faced neatly illustrates what Ayelet Shachar has termed the 'paradox of multicultural vulnerability': in seeking to accommodate religious and cultural difference the state may unwittingly reinforce power hierarchies within the group that disadvantage weaker members of the group and conflict with their citizenship rights.[37] This was an animating concern in the decision by Ontario to prohibit binding religious arbitration in family law matters.[38]

In Britain, a similar debate has centred on the role of sharia councils in resolving family disputes and has primarily been framed as a conflict between the right to choose religious values in negotiating intimate disputes and preventing the imposition of principles and practices that may prevent members of those communities, particularly women, from obtaining the protection available in domestic law.[39] Attempts to use Private Members' Bills to impose certain equality principles on such tribunals have so far failed.[40] A controversial report for the Government has recommended a new regulatory scheme to protect the civil rights of women and children, although it is not yet clear whether this will be acted upon.[41]

Concerns about the limits of multicultural accommodation are not limited to the protection of the citizenship rights of members of the group in question. In both Canada and the UK attempts have been made to restrict religious expression on the basis that is said to conflict with national values and thereby pose a form of threat to a cohesive society.

---

[37] Shachar (2000) 'On citizenship and multicultural vulnerability' *Political Theory* 64.

[38] Arbitration Act, 1991, SO 1991, c. 17, as amended by Family Statute Law Amendment Act, SO 2006, c. 19. Discussed by Greckol (2008) 'Religious fundamentalism and freedom: conflict or common cause?' pp 19–20 in Brunelle and Molinari (eds) *Reasonable accommodation and the role of the state: a democratic challenge.*

[39] The issue is complicated by the fact that in many cases marriage in question is only recognised in religious law as the parties to the marriage have not attempted to marry according to civil law. In such cases the civil courts will have no jurisdiction over the divorce or the redistribution of the parties' assets.

[40] The Arbitration and Mediation Services (Equality) Bill sought to prevent the provision of services that discriminated on the grounds of sex including differential treatment of evidence or inheritance. Arguably such restrictions are unnecessary as the Equality Act 2010 would already prohibit such discrimination in the provision of services.

[41] Home Office (2018) 'The independent review into the application of sharia law in England and Wales' (Cm 9560).

In Canada these arguments have had particular resonance in Quebec where a regional identity rooted in its francophone and Catholic heritage has come under pressure from increasing diversity in Canadian society. Most controversially, a proposed Charter of Values[42] attempted to strengthen 'secular' values in Quebec, including a prohibition on public officials wearing religious symbols. Whilst the Bill did not succeed[43] the episode is a good example of the ongoing tensions between religious freedom and secular values.

A similar attempt to articulate a sense of 'Britishness' through shared values has gained particular currency as a response to religious extremism and terrorism. A pivotal point in this policy was then Prime Minister David Cameron's 2011 speech to the Munich Security Conference, rejecting 'state multiculturalism' and instead advocating active promotion of a liberal value system:

> We need a lot less of the passive tolerance of recent years and a much more active, muscular liberalism. A passively tolerant society says to its citizens, as long as you obey the law we will just leave you alone. It stands neutral between different values. But I believe a genuinely liberal country does much more; it believes in certain values and actively promotes them. Freedom of speech, freedom of worship, democracy, the rule of law, equal rights regardless of race, sex or sexuality. It says to its citizens, this is what defines us as a society: to belong here is to believe in these things. Now, each of us in our own countries, I believe, must be unambiguous and hard-nosed about this defence of our liberty.[44]

These 'fundamental British values' have been defined through anti-terrorism policy as 'democracy, the rule of law, individual liberty and mutual respect and tolerance of different faiths and beliefs'.[45] Active opposition to these values is treated as 'extremism' and considered a key driver of radicalisation and terrorism. Within this framework, the beliefs held by children and their families are potentially risky: signalling potential future violence; creating an environment conducive to extremism; and threatening community cohesion. These 'British' values do not impose uniformity, but are increasingly used to construct the outer limits of acceptable upbringing for children. Schools and other education and childcare providers have been given extensive obligations to 'actively promote' 'fundamental British values' to the children within their care.[46] The definitions have also been used by the

---

[42] Bill 60, Charter affirming the values of State secularism and religious neutrality and of equality between women and men, and providing a framework for accommodation requests, 1st Sess, 40th Leg, Quebec, 2013.

[43] Discussed by Jukier and Woehrling, (2016) 'Religion and the secular State in Canada' in Martinez-Torron and Cole Durham (eds) *Religion and the secular State: national reports*. As Hatzis's chapter in this volume suggests, had the Bill been enacted it would likely have faced a successful challenge under s 2 of the Charter; see especially pp 257–9 above.

[44] Cameron (2011) 'Prime Minister's speech at Munich security conference', 5 February 2011, available at www.gov.uk/government/speeches/pms-speech-at-munich-security-conference.

[45] 'Prevent strategy' (June 2011) Cm 8092, Annex A.

[46] Taylor (2015) 'Responsibility for the soul of the child: the role of the State and parents in determining religious upbringing and education' *International Journal of Law Policy and the Family* 15.

courts in child protection proceedings, such that parental non-violent but vocal opposition to these values is characterised as harmful to children and a legitimate basis for compulsory care proceedings by the state,[47] so providing an increasingly firm limit on beliefs that can legitimately be transmitted to children. Whether these really represent a collective vision of national values is more controversial, it has so far proved impossible to embody them in primary legislation, which may have granted greater democratic legitimacy.[48] Further, their basis in anti-terrorism policy risks, at the very least, a perception that the government agenda is targeted in a way that discriminates against certain forms of Islamic belief and upbringing.[49]

In both Canada and the UK there is a live issue as to how far multiculturalism can be circumscribed by collective values and how any such values are to be derived. The legal disputes around children's religious upbringing considered in the remainder of this chapter are connected to a wider thesis that many states are moving towards a post-multiculturalist form of normative secularism that places limits on acceptable religious belief and practice.[50] If this thesis is correct, acceptable religious difference in children's upbringing may increasingly be bounded by a set of normative values which, whilst in harmony with many religious beliefs, will pose particular difficulties for fundamentalist religious beliefs. This contention will be considered in two contexts in which the state becomes directly involved in children's religious upbringing: judicial resolution of parental disputes; and regulation of religious teaching in schools.

III. Parental Disputes and Children's Religious Upbringing

The question of whether it is best for a child to receive a particular religious upbringing or to be brought up in a secular environment is one has long been deeply contested in both Britain and Canada. It is perhaps inevitable that in a pluralistic state the primary location of decision-making as to a child's religious upbringing, at least whilst they are too young to make their own decision, will remain with their parents who know them best and whose own lives will be

---

[47] Taylor (2018) 'Religion as harm? Radicalisation, extremism and child protection' *Child and Family Law Quarterly* 41.

[48] An attempt to do so in the now abandoned Counter-Extremism and Safeguarding Bill was criticised by a Parliamentary scrutiny committee as the definitions were 'couched in such general terms that they would be likely to prove unworkable as a legislative definition': Joint Committee on Human Rights, 'Counter-Extremism' (2nd Report of Session 2016–17) at p 3.

[49] UN Committee on the Rights of the Child, 'Concluding observations on the 5th periodic report of United Kingdom of Great Britain and Northern Ireland' (12 July 2016) CRC/C/GBR/CO/5, [21(b)]. Jivraj (2013) *The religion of law: race, citizenship and children's belonging* suggests that many of the values presented as neutral or secular find their origin in Christian conceptions of truth.

[50] Discussed by Rivers (2012) 'The secularisation of the British constitution' *Ecclesiastical LJ* 371; and McCrudden (2011) 'Multiculturalism, freedom of religion, equality and the British constitution: the JFS case considered' *International Journal of Constitutional Law* 200.

intimately connected to the choices made in the upbringing of their children. As Baroness Hale observed in a seminal British case on parents' religious rights: "'the child is not the child of the state" and it is important in a free society that parents should be allowed a large measure of autonomy in the way in which they discharge their parental responsibilities'.[51]

Parental responsibility includes a broad freedom, perhaps best described as a Hohfeldian 'privilege' or 'liberty', to bring children up within a particular religion (or in none), including freedom to determine matters such as a child's diet, clothing and education in accordance with the parents' religious beliefs. This broad freedom is, of course, not unique to the religious context; parents have considerable freedom of choice in caring for their children whether their motivation is from religious principle, personal ethics or simply practical concern. The justification for respect for religious freedom in parenting goes beyond this to a general respect for parental autonomy. For devout parents, the proper religious upbringing of their children is often a core religious obligation of the parent themselves and might be claimed as a protected manifestation of the parent's own right to religious freedom.

This does not protect parents from all interference with their religiously motivated parenting decisions; as Masson ACJ and Brennan J memorably explained in the High Court of Australia, 'Religious conviction is not a solvent of legal obligation'.[52] Nonetheless, in both Canada and the UK, parents have sought to argue that restrictions on their ability to bring their child up as they wish are an interference with their protected religious freedoms and are only permissible if they meet the relevant domestic tests to justify interference with that right.

A. Central Principles

In some disputes arising from parents' wishes to raise their children in accordance with particular religious beliefs, the parents themselves will present the court with a united front, arrayed against a governmental body which is seeking to constrain the parents' exercise of their religious freedoms in order to safeguard what that body perceives to be the best interests of the child. As suggested above, such scenarios are difficult to characterise as singular antagonist (vertical) or mediatory (horizontal) in nature. This difficulty is compounded in disputes where the parents themselves are divided as to the extent to which religious beliefs should control their children's upbringing.

Both Canada and Britain are parties to a strong international consensus on the principles to be used in children's cases. The United Nations Convention

---

[51] *R (Williamson) v Secretary of State for Education* [2005] UKHL 15, [2005] 2 AC 246 at [72]. The case concerned a challenge by fundamentalist Christian parents to the prohibition on the use of corporal punishment in schools. For a similar statement in the Canadian context see La Forest J in *B(R) v Children's Aid Society of Metropolitan Toronto* [1995] 1 SCR 315 at 372.

[52] *Church of the New Faith v Commissioner of Pay-Roll Tax (Victoria)* (1983) 154 CLR 120.

on the Rights of the Child (UNCRC) has obtained near-universal international commitment[53] and includes the guiding principle and right for children to have their best interests treated as a primary consideration in all decisions concerning them.[54] Although the precise terms vary, this best interests, or welfare,[55] test provides the standard for the resolution of parental disputes concerning children in Canada and the UK. Although the test is firmly established in both international and domestic law, that consensus does not resolve the underlying constitutional debates as to the reach of the state into the sphere of religious upbringing. The best interests test faces three particular difficulties, all of which have been pertinent to disputes in Canada and the UK.

The first problem is that of court neutrality. It is clearly the case that any a priori assumption that being brought up in a particular religion would be against a child's interests would constitute religious discrimination against the believing parent.[56] The courts have instead tended to consider the secular effects of adhering to a religious belief rather than assessing the belief itself,[57] so, for example, rather than assessing a belief that social interaction with non-believers should be rejected, the court would consider the impact of social isolation on the individual child. This approach does not, however, fully resolve the problem. In religious disputes the parents are often arguing about precisely the question of whether it is better for a child that they are brought up with religious discipline or without those constraints. If the court is to adopt the standpoint that all socially acceptable belief systems are of equal worth the best interests test will struggle to resolve such a dispute in the absence of specific evidence of individual impact on the child in question. If, however, the court adopts a value system by which the child's interests should be assessed, that value system risks imposing indirect discrimination of a religious group that is opposed to those values.

The second difficulty in applying the best interests test is whether and how the fundamental rights of parents should be taken into account. If decisions are taken solely on the basis of welfare, without consideration of parental rights, this effectively means that *any* interference with a parent's rights, not matter how serious, can be justified simply by citing the child's welfare, no matter how slight.

The final difficulty is whether the best interests test should include consideration of the child's right to freedom of belief. The UNCRC recognises that children have a right to freedom of thought, conscience and religion, but this right of the child is connected to the rights of parents 'to provide direction to the child in the exercise of his or her right in a manner consistent with the evolving capacities of

---

[53] All countries save for the US have ratified the UNCRC. The US is a signatory to the Convention but has not ratified it.

[54] Article 3 UNCRC.

[55] For the purposes of this chapter the terms 'best interests' and 'welfare' are treated as synonymous.

[56] *Young v Young* [1993] 4 SCR 3, 108 DLR (4th) 193 at 252; and *Hoffman v Austria* (1993) 17 EHRR 293 at 316.

[57] Ahdar and Leigh (2013) *Religious freedom in the Liberal State* ch 7.

the child'.[58] There is therefore an ambiguity as to whether children have the right to freedom from their parents' religious beliefs[59] and whether this freedom can be asserted in assessing those interests. These three problems of neutrality, parental freedom and children's rights underlie many of the cases on parental religious disputes despite the consensus apparently provided by the welfare principle.

B. Foundations of the Canadian Approach

The Supreme Court of Canada was faced with a number of cases concerning children's religious upbringing at an early stage in its experience with the Charter. The foundations of the Court's approach were established in *Young v Young*,[60] which came to the Court at the same time as its sister case, *P(D) v S(C)*.[61]

Both cases concerned separated parents and in both cases the mother, as custodial parent, objected to the father's attempts to involve the children with his Jehovah's Witness faith and to teach the children aspect of that faith. In both cases the trial judge had placed significant constraints on the extent to which the father could involve the children in his religious activities as conditions on his rights of access. In *Young* the father was prevented from discussing his religious beliefs with his children and from involving them in any religious services or meetings without the written consent of the mother,[62] whilst in *P(D)* he was permitted to teach his beliefs to his daughter but not to 'indoctrinate her continually'.

In both cases the fathers considered the conditions to be a serious interference with their Charter rights to religious freedom and their obligation to bring their children up with an understanding of religious teaching. Preventing the father in *Young* from discussing his religious beliefs with his children seemed to be a particularly draconian interference. For many religious parents, religion is not simply an aspect of life but encompasses and informs every part of their life. A prohibition on discussing religious belief would prevent such a parent from discussing any serious matter with their children with any sincerity. In *Young* the British Columbia Court of Appeal removed the restrictions, considering them to be an unjustified interference with the father's Charter right to freedom of religion. In contrast in *P(D)* the Quebec Court of Appeal upheld the restrictions on the basis that the proper test was the best interests of the child. As a result, the Supreme Court was

---

[58] Article 14(2) UNCRC.

[59] The initial draft of Art 14 would have recognised the child's right to reject their parents' beliefs, but the provision proved so controversial that it threatened to derail the entire Convention. The position in international law is summarised in Taylor (2016) 'The child's right to religion in international law' in Strhan, Parker and Ridgely (eds) *Reader in childhood and religion.*

[60] [1993] 4 SCR 3.

[61] [1993] 4 SCR 141.

[62] The conditions also restricted him from preventing any required blood transfusions for the children and from making adverse remarks as to the religious beliefs of their mother: [1993] 4 SCR 3, 108 DLR (4th) 193 at 206.

faced with a conflict between what might be termed a 'parental rights approach' and a 'family law approach' to children's religious upbringing.[63]

In an important decision that has set the tone for future parental disputes in Canada, the Supreme Court rejected the argument that direct consideration of Charter rights was required, instead adopting the family law approach based on best interests. Giving the majority opinion on this point, L'Heureux-Dubé J reasoned that if the statutory best interests test itself was consistent with the underlying concerns and values of the Charter then a judge properly exercising discretion according to that standard would also be acting consistently with the Charter, without the need for explicit reference to it.[64]

This was an important decision in largely removing disputes about children's religious upbringing from direct constitutional oversight – but it does not resolve the underlying debate about the respective weight to be given to parental freedom to discuss their religion and children's interests in being free from that influence. It was this problem that essentially split the court in both *Young* and *P(D)* and resulted in confusing, shifting majority judgments.

For L'Heureux-Dubé J,[65] the only question was the best interests of the child, and as the children in *Young* had expressed discomfort at their father's religious discussions, their best interests supported the restrictions imposed on their father at trial, the parents' constitutional freedoms playing no part in that decision. At the other extreme, for Sopinka J the fact that the best interests test was to be applied did not mean that the parents' religious freedom were irrelevant to its application. The breadth of the best interests test and its potential to be applied in a manner that overrode Charter values meant that it should be interpreted in line with Charter values, in this case protection for religious freedom. On this approach, Sopinka J considered that the best interests test must be read down so that it could only be used to restrict parental religious expression where there was proof of risk of substantial harm to the child, as the best interests test itself was insufficient to justify significant restrictions on parental freedom.

Whilst McLachlin J, giving the majority judgment in *Young*, did not go quite this far, she also stressed that *evidence* of risk of harm would be an important aspect, but not an essential requirement, in applying the best interests test to reconcile its application with Charter freedoms. In this case there was no evidence of such harm, merely discomfort, and the children's interests were better served by them coming to know their father as he was rather than in restricting his ability to speak freely to them.

In setting the foundations of the best interests approach to parental disputes, *Young* limits the direct application of constitutional rights to parental disputes but

---

[63] See Van Praagh (1997) 'Religion, custody and a child's identities' *Osgoode Hall LJ* 309 for detailed consideration of these approaches.

[64] [1993] 4 SCR 3, 108 DLR (4th) 193 at 236–41. Although L'Heureux-Dubé J was dissenting on the outcome of the case, she was speaking for a majority on this point.

[65] In the minority in *Young* but majority in *P(D)*.

also demonstrates the conflicts that remain hidden beneath the surface of best interests. Fundamentally it demonstrates a split between an approach that views religious upbringing as merely another aspect of parental decision-making and one which views it as a protected manifestation of parental religious freedom. On this latter view, as best interests cannot be isolated from the value system by which they are assessed, courts should only restrict parental religious practice on the basis of solid evidence of actual harm to avoid infringing that freedom. The majority's rejection of this view allows greater discretionary limitation on religious upbringing in the name of children's interests but gives little guidance as to the basis on which those interests are assessed.

C. Constitutional Values and Best Interests in English Law

The approach in *Young* means that inter-parental religious disputes about their children's upbringing are rarely framed as requiring resolution by explicit reference to Charter rights; albeit that this situations arises in large part because judicial inquiry is guided by and resolved according to implicit reference to Charter values. Similarly, the courts in England have generally maintained the view that the best interests test should be applied without direct consideration of the human rights of parents. That view was first expressed, shortly after the HRA 1998 came into force, by Thorpe LJ in *Payne v Payne*:[66]

> [T]he advent of the Convention within our domestic law does not necessitate a revision of the fundamental approach to relocation applications formulated by this court and consistently applied over so many years. The reason that I hold this opinion is that, reduced to its fundamentals, the court's approach is and always has been to apply child welfare as the paramount consideration. The court's focus upon supporting the reasonable proposal of the primary carer is seen as no more than an important factor in the assessment of welfare ...'.

The problems that arise can be demonstrated by considering two recent cases, both of which expose the difficulties that remain behind the best interests test.

The first case, *Re G (Children)*,[67] concerned the future education of five children – boys and girls between the ages of three and 11 – whose parents had separated following their mother's decision to leave the ultra-orthodox Jewish Chareidi community in which they had all been brought up. The children were to live with their mother, but the question remained whether she would be permitted to enrol them in to co-educational Modern Orthodox schools to give them the educational opportunities and future career prospects that were not available in their current Chareidi schools.

---

[66] [2001] EWCA Civ 166, [2001] 1 FLR 1052 at [38]–[39].
[67] *Re G (Children)* [2012] EWCA Civ 1233, [2012] 3 FCR 524.

Unlike the matter before the Canadian courts in *Young*, this dispute could not be resolved by recognising each parent's freedom to express their beliefs to their children as the question of education clearly required a choice to be made between the parents' propositions. Importantly, those propositions were deeply connected to the parents' respective religious beliefs, meaning that it was impossible to fully separate the best interests test from their underlying conception of a valuable life. For the father it was a life based on the culture and practices that generations of the family had followed. It was a life centred on the community and family that the children had always known and the religious beliefs and practices that bound them together. For the mother it was a life where religion played an important role but did not restrict the freedom of educational and economic choice available to the children and their opportunity to forge a future of their own making.

Each of these ways of life are, the court considered, deserving of fundamental respect. To choose between them the court adopted the standpoint of the 'generally accepted standards' of the 'reasonable' parent in the society in modern society. If the hypothetical reasonable parent is the embodiment of the views of the majority, this raises the difficulty of whether minorities can be assessed on the values of the majority without improperly discriminating against those groups. Reliance on 'generally accepted standards' effectively created a bias against same-sex parenting in the 1980s and 1990s, by allowing the court to view it as less conducive to the welfare of the child, solely because it deviated from the accepted norm of heterosexual parenting.[68]

The derivation and content of these 'generally acceptable standards' therefore requires careful scrutiny if they are not to impose the tyranny of majority opinion on a minority group. The Court of Appeal in this case stated the values of the hypothetical reasonable parent to be equality of opportunity, aspiration and bringing the child to the cusp of adulthood with the maximum opportunity to pursue their own vision of the good life. Once these values were applied it was clear that the children should move to the schools advocated by their mother. Laudable as many will think these values are, nowhere does the court explain their derivation despite the fact that their use creates a significant disadvantage for those religious minorities, and their individual members, whose value systems are based on ideas and practices which differ fundamentally from mainstream visions of life. In a system without clearly established fundamental constitutional rights that might reasonably form the basis of a normative framework of shared values, there is a risk that such reasoning is merely a veil for the subjective views of the court, however noble those views might appear to be to the majority.

The 'generally accepted standards' idea has obvious parallels with the contentious 'community standards' doctrine developed by the Canadian courts in the context of obscenity law. As Phillipson and Beattie have argued in this volume,[69]

---

[68] Reece (1996) 'The paramountcy principle: consensus or construct?' (1996) 49 *Current Legal Problems* 267.

[69] See pp 185–88 above.

the doctrine is readily open to criticism as providing a vehicle which in effect conceals majoritarian – or, more pejoratively, 'normal' or 'mainstream' – belief systems under a nominally pluralist cloak. The observation has particular resonance in Canada, where the test has been applied to First Nations children in a manner that has presented as neutral and universal but which has been analysed as incorporating racist assumptions and the means by which children have been disproportionately removed from their families and communities.[70]

The second English case which merits close consideration here, *J v B (Ultra-Orthodox Judaism: Transgender)*,[71] also concerned the Chareidi ultra-orthodox community. Like *Young*, it was concerned with the place of fundamental rights of parents in the assessment of best interests and the potential conflict between a 'family law' and a 'parental rights' approach. But, unlike *Young*, the case had an additional complexity arising from the issue of the equality rights of one of the parents. In *J v B* the children's father[72] left the community in order to live as a transgender woman. Both parents agreed that the five children would remain living in the community with their mother; the question for the court was whether they would have direct contact with the trans parent. The mother was strongly opposed to such contact on the basis that it was very likely that the children would be ostracised by the community if contact were to take place.

At first instance, the court adopted a family law approach based solely on the welfare principle and reluctantly decided that there should be no direct contact, primarily because the unanimous professional evidence supported this outcome on the basis that the children would experience significant hostility from the community that outweighed their strong interest in maintaining direct contact with their father.[73] The Court of Appeal overturned this judgment, requiring the best interests test to be applied through the lens of equality and human rights. The mechanism for doing so was again the 'judicially reasonable parent' who would adopt a broadminded and tolerant attitude consistent with 'changing social values'. This, together with the court's obligation to act consistently with the HRA 1998 and to refuse to take account of any action that would amount to unlawful discrimination, meant that the family court's decision could not stand.

The Court of Appeal's approach in *J v B* is similar to that adopted by McLachlin and Sopinka JJ in *Young*, infusing the family law tests with the parental rights approach, in contrast to the pure family law approach that was evident in the decision of the family court. It may, however, be preferable for courts to address the rights involved directly rather than through the veil of welfare, not least because invoking rights directly provides a far more secure normative basis than attributing

---

[70] Kline (1992) 'Child welfare law, "best interests of the child" ideology, and First Nations' (1992) 30 *Osgoode Hall LJ* 375.

[71] [2017] EWCA Civ 2164, [2018] 4 WLR 60.

[72] Under domestic law a transgender parent retains the legal relationship of 'mother' or 'father' to their existing children, meaning that the trans parent is referred to as the 'father' throughout the judgments.

[73] [2017] EWFC 4.

values to the hypothetical reasonable parent. Further, resolving disputes through the language of welfare, rather than explicitly assessing the human rights of all involved, obscures the central conflicts that can arise in such cases. In *J v B* the central problem was that treating the trans parent with equal respect risked very real detriment to the children's security of upbringing and community.[74] The essence of the decision for the court was how far it would allow itself to be complicit with the intolerant stance of the community in order to shield the children from the potentially devastating consequences of that intolerance. The case is another good example of the way in which these dilemmas are not confronted directly but through the use of judicially observed changing social values to constrain the application of the welfare principle.

IV. Religious Upbringing and Education

It is perhaps in the area of education[75] that parental freedom to determine religious upbringing comes under particular pressure, as the private sphere of family life comes into contact with the public interest in training the next generation and instilling civic values of citizenship. Education is one of the primary means by which the community transmits its culture and values to the next generation, so shaping its own future as well as that of the pupils themselves. Both religious communities and wider society have a deep interest in children's education, and it is unsurprising that education has been one of the key arenas in which pluralism and the limits of acceptable religious difference have been played out.

The courts in many jurisdictions, including Canada, the UK and the other signatory States to the ECHR, have been faced with high-profile religious disputes in an education setting on questions such as pupil's clothing,[76] religious symbols and practices in schools[77] and the ability of religious schools to limit access by defining their own admissions policies.[78] Some of those issues have been explored in Hatzis's chapter in this book,[79] and they are not revisited here. In the space available here the focus will be on the conflict that touches most closely on the subject

---

[74] Indeed, proved impossible to facilitate contact between the children and their father without a 'catastrophic' impact on the children's lives within the community. In consequence the father withdrew her application recognising that pursuing it was emotionally harmful to the children: *Re A (Children) (Contact: Ultra-Orthodox Judaism: Transgender Parent)* [2020] EWFC 3.

[75] For a detailed analysis of Canadian law on this issue see Berger (2014) 'Religious diversity, education and the 'crisis' in state neutrality' *Canadian Journal of Law and Society* 103.

[76] *Multani v Commission Scolaire Marguerite Bourgeoys*, [2006] 1 SCR 256; *R (on the application of Begum) v Head Teacher and Governors of Denbigh High School* [2006] UKHL 15, [2007] AC 100. See further Hatzis above at pp 238–40 and the sources cited therein.

[77] *Zylberberg v Sudbury Board of Education* (1988), 65 OR (2d) 641 (CA); *Lautsi v Italy* (2012) 54 EHRR 3.

[78] *R(E) v Governing Body of JFS* [2009] UKSC 15, [2012] 2 AC 728. See further McCrudden op cit fn 50 supra.

[79] See especially pp 240–41 and pp 247–50 above.

of this chapter: the extent to which parents have the right to object to education that conflicts with their religious and philosophical convictions. This issue has become particularly contentious as policies adopted to promote shared values and respect for diversity have come into conflict with truth claims advanced by parents and religious communities.

The foundational human rights treaties, to which both Canada and the UK are signatories, were drafted in the aftermath of the religious and racial persecution of the Nazi regime. In consequence they emphasise the need to avoid educational institutions being used by states to indoctrinate children in ways that undermine their allegiance to their families and their own culture and religion. In consequence, those treaties emphasise parental rights to choice in education[80] and require the state to 'have respect for the liberty of parents and, when applicable, legal guardians to ensure the religious and moral education of their children in conformity with their own convictions'.[81]

As discussed above, both Canada and the Britain have a history of religious pluralism within educational provision, but the focus on parental choice does not adequately respond to the interests of children. Whilst children may well benefit from an education that develops understanding of the background of their 'cultural identity, language and values',[82] education is an important means by which children are equipped to question those parental values and to forge their own future. A focus on parental choice can also neglect the need to forge a cohesive society, particularly in the light of the increasing diversity within many states. States are therefore faced with a difficult balance between providing the conditions in which children can learn to respect others and question their own upbringing without imposing a state-sanctioned world view. Canadian history provides a particularly stark warning of the damage that can be wielded through the use of education as a means of trying to force assimilation through its use in undermining the culture, beliefs and language of indigenous people[83]

These issues have been raised sharply by the litigation surrounding Quebec's introduction in 2008 of a Program on Ethics and Religious Culture (ERC), which seeks to give children a religious and ethical education from a neutral and objective perspective to prepare them for life in a pluralistic society.[84] The first challenge to the ERC came from Catholic parents at a state-run school[85] who objected to the

---

[80] Article 26(3) of the Universal Declaration of Human Rights.

[81] Article 18(4) International Covenant on Civil and Political Rights; see too Art 13(3) International Covenant on Economic and Social Rights.

[82] Article 29(1)(c) United Nations Convention on the Rights of the Child.

[83] White and Peters op cit.

[84] www.education.gouv.qc.ca/en/contenus-communs/parents-and-guardians/ethics-and-religious-culture-program. For the Quebec Government's explanation of the purposes underlying the initiative and the way in which it was brought to fruition see www.education.gouv.qc.ca/en/contenus-communs/parents-and-guardians/ethics-and-religious-culture-program/background-for-the-erc-program. For an unofficial evaluation see Boisvert (2015) 'Quebec's ethics and religious culture school curriculum: a critical perspective' *Journal of Inter-Cultural Studies* 380.

[85] All state schools in Quebec are now non-denominational.

mandatory nature of the course on the basis that to teach Catholicism alongside other religious viewpoints in this manner would be to introduce a form of relativism and interfere with the parents' religious freedom to teach their beliefs as truth.

In *SL v Commission Scolaire des Chenes*, the Supreme Court unanimously rejected this challenge,[86] in part because the claim had been brought before the programme had been implemented meaning that the claim that it would interfere with the parents' religious freedom were speculative in nature. The failure of the claim was not, however, merely due to its prematurity. The majority judgment gives a central place to the concept of state neutrality which, it found, had 'developed alongside a growing sensitivity to the multicultural makeup of Canada and the protection of minorities'.[87] Although briefly acknowledging that absolute neutrality was impossible, the majority judgment was grounded in commitment to this vision of state neutrality as the means of mediating this multicultural reality. For the majority, the parents' claim, that introducing their children to a variety of religious facts was a breach of their religious freedom, was a rejection of this multicultural reality and a failure to understand the obligations on the Quebec Government.[88] Any suggestion that the state was indoctrinating children, the fear that animated the international human rights guarantees for parental choice was, the majority found, mistaken.

The ERC was once more before the Supreme Court in *Loyola High School v Quebec*,[89] this time at the instigation of a private Catholic school. The school had produced an 'equivalent' programme and applied for an exemption from teaching the ERC, as permitted by legislation. The Minister refused to grant an exemption, on the basis that Loyola sought to teach their programme from a religious perspective rather than the neutral means employed in the ERC. It was this decision, rather than the ERC itself, that was challenged in *Loyola*. This difference, together with the fact that Loyola was concerned with the collective religious identity formed by the school community and was a private institution rather than a state-funded school meant that the ERC was approached in a very different way from SL and the Supreme Court unanimously found in Loyola's favour.

The Supreme Court was united in accepting Loyola's contention that to require the school to teach Catholicism from a neutral perspective was a violation of Loyola's right to religious freedom. To tell a private Catholic institution how to teach Catholicism had a serious impact on religious freedom, including the right of parents to transmit their beliefs communally as well as in the home.[90] Loyola could not then be required to adapt a position of neutrality on its own founding purpose of teaching Catholicism.

The Court was, however, split on the question of whether it could be required to teach other religious and ethical positions from a neutral perspective or whether

---

[86] *SL v Commission Scolaire des Chenes* [2012] 1 SCR 235.
[87] ibid at [21] per Deschamps J.
[88] ibid at [40] per Deschamps J.
[89] [2015] 1 SCR 613.
[90] ibid at [61–[68].

it could do so from a Catholic perspective. For McLachlin CJC and Moldaver J, in the minority, such a requirement set an impossible standard and violated the religious freedom of teachers, parents and pupils. Whilst those teachers could be required to teach religious and ethical difference with respect and tolerance, they could not be required to teach all other perspectives as being equally credible and worthy of belief without undermining their own Catholic perspective and religious freedom. The majority rejected both the notion that it was not possible for a religious school to teach other viewpoints from an objective standpoint and the view that this interfered with their religious freedom. Again, the state's commitment to neutrality could be understood through shared core values of equality, human rights and democracy meaning that the state had a legitimate interests in all citizens being able to conduct themselves with mutual respect in a plural society. The state must be neutral between religions, but need not be neutral on the values it pursues. For this reason, the Minister's decision on the teaching of other religious and ethical viewpoints was upheld.

In the UK similar concerns have been raised as to the legitimacy of the process by which values have been used to limit religious expression, although the means by which these are imposed is very different to that in Canada. The European Court of Human Rights has interpreted the rights of parents to have their child educated in a manner that is 'in conformity with their own religious and philosophical convictions'[91] so that it does not prevent the state from requiring the teaching of diverse religious and ethical beliefs, provided that they are taught in an 'objective, critical and pluralistic manner'.[92] Regulation of education in the UK has tended to grant parents far more freedom to influence the religious content of their children's education than that required by the ECHR. In particular, parents have the right to withdraw their children from both collective worship and religious education,[93] and independent schools have been permitted to focus on preparing children for life within the religious community rather than wider society.[94] This settlement has, however, come under pressure from the imposition of British values discussed above. The change has primarily been driven by the integration of values derived from the Government's anti-terrorism strategy into the inspection regimes for schools. Schools of all kinds are now under an obligation to 'actively promote' 'Fundamental British values', namely 'democracy, the rule of law, individual liberty and mutual respect and tolerance of those with different faiths and beliefs'.[95]

---

[91] Article 2 of the First Protocol to the ECHR.
[92] *Kjeldsen, Busk and Pedersen v. Denmark* (1976) 1 EHRR 711. See also *R (Fox) v Secretary of State for Education* [2015] EWHC 3404 (Admin).
[93] School Standards and Framework Act 1998, s 71(1).
[94] *R v Secretary of State for Education and Science, ex p Talmud Torah Machzikei Hadass School Trust* (1985) *Times*, 12 April.
[95] The Education (Independent School Standards) Regulations 2014 (SI 2014 No 3283), Sch 1, Reg 5(a). For maintained schools see Office for Standards in Education (Ofsted) (2018) *School Inspection Handbook* at paras 145 and 148. See too Independent Education Provision in England (Prohibition on Participation in Management) Regulations 2014 (SI 2014 No 1977), para 2(5)(a) and Local Authority (Duty to Secure Early Years Provision Free of Charge) Regulations 2014 (SI 2014 No 2147), Reg 2(2)(b).

Together these values have operated to restrict the ability of schools to seek to educate children in a manner that fails to prepare them for life in a plural society. Whilst there is clearly a legitimate public interest in requiring children to be properly prepared in this way, the way in which British values have entered schools, through the security agenda and the Government's controversial anti-terrorism strategy, rather than through consideration of the educational rights and needs of children undermines confidence in their ability to act as collective, normative values.

V. Conclusion

Several of the contributors to this volume have concluded – and in quite forceful terms – that the solution adopted under Canadian law to particular moral and social issues is 'better' than its British equivalent, both in the substantive sense of the sophistication of the solution's content and in the procedural sense of the rigour of the decision-making process through which that content has been determined.[96] That conclusion would not seem appropriate in respect of the issues addressed in this chapter. Both jurisdictions display a degree of commonality of process and of outcome which betokens a carefully reasoned attempt to reconcile an often complex mélange of competing private and public interests.

The majority decision in *Loyola* might be thought to exemplify a judicial methodology which reaches for the notion of core, shared values as a means of mediating conflict between religious freedom and a plural society. But by way of conclusion, we might alight briefly on a legal problem which thus far has been presented only in the Canadian context.

As the most recent set of religious accommodation decisions in *Trinity Western*[97] demonstrate suggests that the Supreme Court appears to be far from united in subscribing to the majority *Loyola* approach. While the dispute in this set of cases[98] falls outside the immediate remit of this chapter, it provides an important reflection on the *Loyola* shared values debate. The majority, led by Abella J, who also gave the leading judgment in *Loyola*, affirm the legitimacy of decision-makers reaching for these shared core values, not merely in interpreting Charter rights but in all decisions, whether or not the Charter was directly engaged. The remaining four justices expressed serious concerns about this use of under-defined, judicially

---

[96] Draghici's analysis of assisted dying is perhaps the most trenchant in this respect.

[97] *Law Society of British Columbia v Trinity Western University* [2018] SCC 32 and *Trinity Western University and Law Society of Upper Canada* [2018] SCC 33.

[98] The cases concerned the question of whether the respective Law Societies could refuse accreditation to the proposed law school at an evangelical Christian university on the basis that its members were bound by a commitment to refrain from sexual conduct outside of different-sex marriage. The Supreme Court found that they could do so.

imposed values[99] that operated as a 'counterweight to constitutionalized and judicially defined Charter rights'[100] despite having no explicit basis within the Charter. Given the contested nature of concepts such as 'equality' the incantation of 'Charter values' risked operating as a rhetorical device that allowed judicial moral judgments to prevail over protected rights.[101] For the minority, the result was to limit diversity by restricting the action of private actors whose beliefs conflicted with these judicially imposed values. Speculating as to how a British court might argue and resolve such a problem should it ever arise presents us perhaps with a particularly useful vehicle in which to explore the potential and limitations of Canadian public law jurisprudence as a source of inspiration for our own legal system.

---

[99] *Law Society of British Columbia v Trinity Western University* [2018] SCC 32 at [171]–[173] and [309]–[311].
[100] ibid at [307].
[101] ibid at [309].

INDEX

Lightning Source UK Ltd.
Milton Keynes UK
UKHW022153180521
383950UK00003B/139